Musical Truth Volume 2

Mark Devlin

Incorporating an essay on the lyrical themes and symbolism in the music of Prince, by Dan Monroe.

Musical Truth Volume 2
Mark Devlin

Paperback Edition First Published in Great Britain in 2018
Hardback Edition First Published in Great Britain
eBook Edition First Published in Great Britain in 2018

Disclaimer

All reasonable efforts have been made to contact the copyright holders and that anyone who believes their copyright to be infringed is welcome to contact the author.

ISBN: 978-1-910757-96-3

aSys Publishing
http://www.asys-publishing.co.uk

ACKNOWLEDGEMENTS

My wholehearted thanks go out to the following:

Dan Monroe for the comprehensive essay on Prince.

Nicola Mackin for the publishing advice and assistance.

Robbie Allen for another outstanding job on the cover design.

John 'Razoreye' Hamer and Ellen for the proofreading.

Simon Gudgeon for the massive help with my podcast archive.

Nino Teauoneaux, Emily Moyer, Rose Winter, Sara Hollins, Brent Aquasky, Matt Sergiou, Jon Furbee, William Marino and Douglas Gilgallon for valuable research assistance and tip-offs.

Freepik for the vector images on the covers.

MD

ABOUT THE AUTHOR

Mark Devlin is a UK-based club and radio DJ, music journalist and author. As a DJ he has specialised in all forms of black music and has played live in over 40 countries.

In 2010, he underwent what he refers to as a conscious awakening, bringing a new awareness of what's really going on in this world. His special area of interest was how this ties into the mainstream music industry, and the way in which A-list artists have been used to manipulate and mind-control the masses in line with a much larger agenda.

He now presents public talks on these subjects, as well as appearing on radio, hosting two regular podcast series, and curating conscious music DJ sets.

The Author can be contacted on the following e-mail address:

- markdevlinuk@gmail.com

The author's further work can be accessed at:

- www.markdevlin.co.uk
- www.musicaltruthbook.com
- www.youtube.com/markdevlintv
- www.spreaker.com/user/markdevlin
- https://twitter.com/musical_truth_

Join the Musical Truth Facebook group at:

- https://www.facebook.com/groups/MusicalTruth/

MUSICAL TRUTH 2
... THE STORY CONTINUES

CONTENTS

FOREWORD

"I put my music on the web as a method to spread my message,
People be like, 'DISL, why you getting so aggressive?'
I do it 'cause I'm pissed off,
Our whole lives we've been lied to, cheated, mistreated, deceived and ripped off!"

DISL Automatic: 'Here I Stand' (2010)

"I'm at the age, if I can't teach,
I shouldn't even open my mouth to speak."

Chuck D of Public Enemy: 'WTF' (2012)

"I'm sick and tired of hearing things,
from uptight, short-sighted, narrow-minded hypocrites,
All I want is the truth,
Just gimme some truth."

John Lennon: 'Gimme Some Truth' (1971)

Ever since I can remember, I have hated deception and duplicity, and discovering I've been made a mug of has made me angry. My gaining some advanced understanding of the massive degree to which these elements are present in our everyday lives has been the inspiration behind this book being put into the world. Truth wages war against deception wherever it finds it.

Although the information in this book can be meaningfully absorbed in isolation and on its own merits, I highly recommend that it be digested only after reading everything I had to say in the first volume of 'Musical Truth.' This will give an appreciation of the bigger picture, and render everything presented here in its true context. This also saves me having to recap too much on subjects covered in that first book, instead using this one to present new pieces of the puzzle.

The researching and writing of these two books has been as much a learning experience for me as it will be for the readers. On the day you read these words, I (and everyone else) will know so much more than I did on the day I wrote them. But I'll know so much more tomorrow. I learned long ago that it's a serious mistake to assume you know everything there is to know about a subject, and I'm suspicious of anyone who ever makes so bold a claim. The same limited consciousness also leads an individual to the notion that they're too smart to be fooled, and can't possibly have been duped and misled about a certain subject in a way that somebody else might be suggesting they have. I'm sure we're all familiar with this aspect of the human condition through the back-and-forth, concrete-minded arguments that occur every single day on the average Facebook thread or Youtube comments section, reinforcing the old truism that opinions are like assholes – everybody's got one.

This is not to say that the ego is not important; a well-balanced, consciously-evolved individual understands that the key to navigating this challenging reality we refer to as 'life,' involves striking a balance between the informed consciousness that comes from a connection to our higher selves, and keeping one foot firmly planted in the 'real' world, where we have our physical experiences that are unique to the human condition, and through which our souls undergo so much of their essential growth.

It is this process of continual evolution that has brought the necessity for this second volume. In so many ways, the first only just scratched the surface. As I have delved ever further into the complex, often dark, but continually fascinating question of who really controls the world of 'entertainment,' and the agendas for which it's really being used, I've come to realise that it goes so deep, that even an entire human lifetime dedicated exclusively to full-time research still wouldn't provide all of the answers! All that any of us can do, therefore, is take on as much understanding and knowledge of these subjects as our time here allows.

As well as the new subjects detailed on the Contents page, this book briefly revisits a handful of the topics covered in Volume 1, adding new information where it has come to light, as well as some more informed perspectives that only come with the passage of time. As before, I absolutely encourage all readers to not just take my word for anything, but to do their own further research, (with the obvious proviso of avoiding state-controlled and corporate-owned entities and sticking with independent outlets.) As before, a comprehensive list of resources for further study is included at the end of each chapter. (Just typing the subject line of each into an on-line search may be less clunky than manually inputting each of the URLs. Or see the offer of having a list of the web addresses e-mailed for convenience at the end.)

As I've pointed out many times, the manipulations of the music industry – as colossally far-reaching as they are – are still only one small part of the overall scenario of human slavery; of the few manipulating the thoughts, emotions and actions of the many; of the battle between good and evil which, ultimately, provides the reason why any of us chose – in higher consciousness – to incarnate here in human form. I realise that the reason I myself took on a fascination with pop music from the age of five, and why I pursued a career as a music man, is because it was always my job to expose this one small fragment of the story. I therefore leave insights into other aspects of conspiracy – whether it's banking scams, the birth certificate fraud, geo-engineering, false-flag terror hoaxes, cancer, or whatever else – to skilful and talented researchers who can do a much better job in those areas than I can. The subject matter contained in these two books is where I've needed to focus my own individual contributions. And each and every one of us has a part to play in this overall process – more of that in the final chapter.

So, here's where the story continues. If 'Musical Truth 1' took you on a journey, Volume 2 is about to rip up your return ticket.

As the Beatles once proclaimed, "the Magical Mystery Tour is waiting to take you away."

'Musical Truth Volume 1' is available in paperback, hardback and Kindle versions at www.amazon.co.uk/ www.amazon.com. Signed copies may also be obtained direct from the author. Please e-mail markdevlinuk@gmail.com with requests.

Any reader who would like a list of the Resources web addresses e-mailed to them, to avoid having to input all the clunky URLs, is welcome to e-mail a request to markdevlinuk@gmail.com

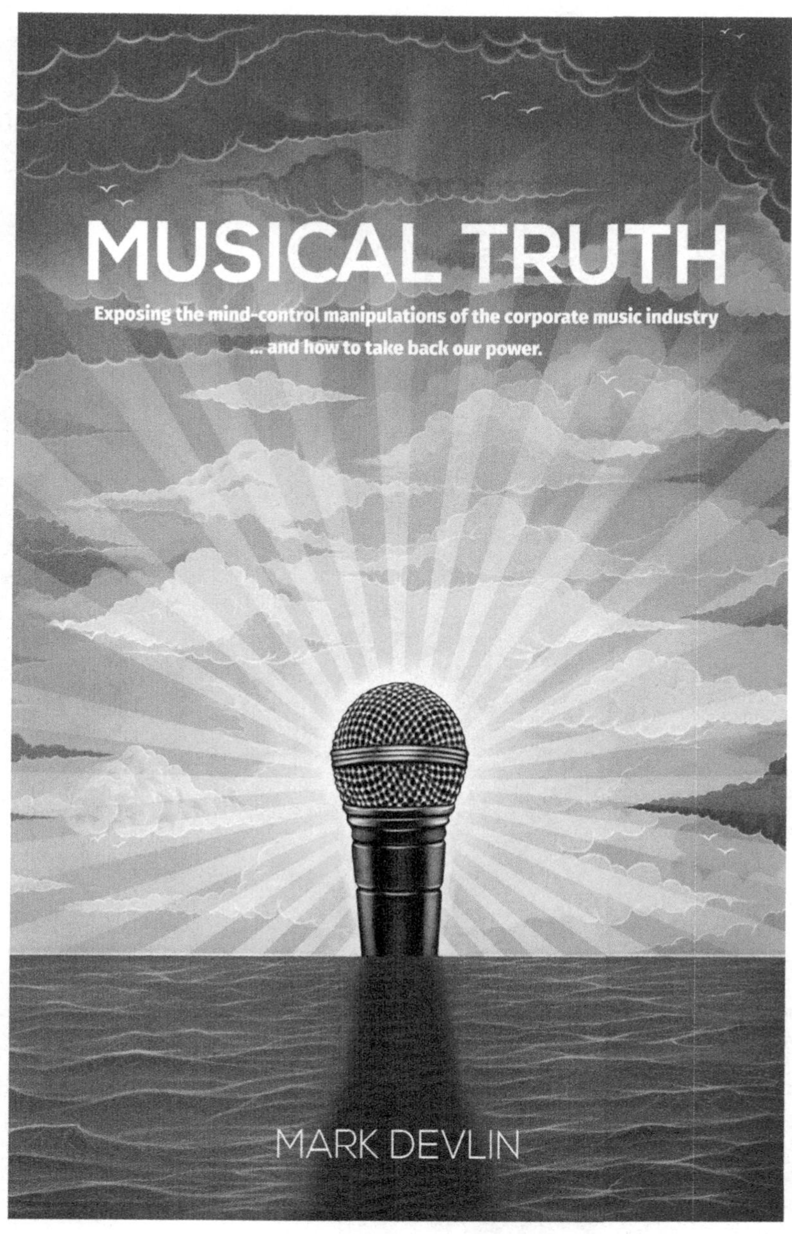

Musical Truth Volume 1
Credit: Robbie Allen Art

CHAPTER 1

ACID REIGN

How Acid House culture paved the way for the worldwide spiritual psy-op of electronic dance music, (and parallels to the manipulations of other, earlier genres.)

> *"Acid, the musical phenomenon,*
> *Only for the headstrong,*
> *Makes you want to dance, move to the beat,*
> *Puts you in a trance, keeps you on your feet,*
> *We call it Acid."*
>
> *D-Mob: 'We Call It Acieed' (1988)*

> *"Es are good, Es are good . . . "*
>
> *The Shamen: 'Ebeneezer Goode' (1992)*

> *"Well, what goes up must come down. And down. And down. Everyone looks ill at the end of the night. All lost the power of speech, desperately avoiding eye contact. Your new soulmate that you've been talking codshit to for the past five hours about the story of Creation or the fourth 'Star Wars' film, is now a complete stranger. You can't even look him in the eye. The only thing you've got in common now is your paranoia. It's coming through the walls, man. The children of ecstasy aren't safe any more. They're no longer 'all together as one,' but separate mental patients that yearn to be ejected out of this poisoned atmosphere to a warm bed and a friendly therapist. Reality's on her way. Where am I? What have I done? Was it worth it?"*
>
> *Dialogue from the movie 'Human Traffic' (1999)*

Through the research I've thrown myself into since the publication of 'Musical Truth 1,' it has become clear that anyone in the public eye who has gained any degree of familiarity, to the point that the average member of the public has heard of them, has had their career facilitated for them. This goes for all manner of celebrities in just the same way it does for world leaders and politicians, regardless of the type of celebrity role. Sports stars, supermodels, television presenters, actors or musicians – it's all the same. The control system that currently presides over this world would not leave to chance which individuals would rise to prominence under their own steam. They don't do 'random.' The network of dark occultists who run every institution in human society have long had the entertainment industry in their grasp. In fact, many would maintain that the very reason for the film and popular music industries being established in the first place, was down to the tremendous opportunities to mind-control massive amounts of people that they present, and to subliminally implant certain thoughts, emotional responses and value systems into the consciousness of the masses.

The ingenious thing about achieving this through entertainment is that an individual's guard is completely down. No-one is expecting to be brainwashed when they simply want some light relief from the drudgery of their everyday life, through listening to a favourite pop artist or engaging in some mindless escapism at the cinema, or through their TV. Suggest to the average person that this is exactly what's going on, and they'll likely dismiss the notion with a derisive scoff, and write off anyone making the claim as 'crazy,' (all the while doing precisely zero research of their own to verify whether there's any foundation to these claims, naturally!) Not only does the entertainment industry provide a unique way to reach the mentality of entire societies, but the cherry on the cake for those doing the manipulating, is that the subjects *pay* quite willingly for their own mind-control!

In the same way that anyone you've heard of will have been shuffled into their position of prominence as a Chosen One – over and above any candidate who might have got there through their own efforts if things had been left to evolve in that way – so it is with *any* fad, movement or trend. Anything with an 'ism' at the end, from fascism to feminism to Buddhism to veganism, (something I recognise despite choosing to be a vegan myself,) displays the hallmarks of having been manufactured. Any social movement which dictates or coerces the value systems or behaviours of entire groups of people, will have been engineered into place by an organisation such as The Tavistock Institute of Human Relations, The Frankfurt School, The Fabian Society, The Rockefeller Foundation, Stanford Research Institute, The Esalen Institute, Cambridge, Oxford, Yale, Harvard, Berkeley or Princeton Universities, or some other 'think-tank' organisation which specialises in shaping and moulding culture. It is through systematic social engineering that terms like 'homophobe,' 'conspiracy theorist,' 'metrosexual' and 'LGBT' come into play.

Occasionally, these organisations test the water with experiments to see how far they still have culture under their psychological grip. This is when we get 'trends' such as the Kony 2012 'viral' video, the placing of a French flag over a Facebook profile picture to 'show solidarity' following the Paris 'terror attacks,' or the Ice Bucket Challenge, No Make-up Selfie, or Wear Pink for Breast Cancer 'fads.' The satisfaction that the controllers must experience in seeing people in their millions responding to these manufactured trends in *exactly* the way they had predicted, must be a source of great satisfaction.

If this is the case with *all* celebrities, *all* social and political movements, and *any* kind of fad, trend or 'scene,' therefore . . . why would anyone expect things to be different with *any* kind of musical movement which emerges very rapidly to unite and give a cultural identity to massive amounts of people – particularly if it ends up having marketable appeal in pretty much every country in the world?

Culture beats

As a 2014 article on the Thump website put it:

> *"Acid House was Britain's biggest youth revolution since the 60s, and its legacy has changed the country's cultural landscape forever. A quarter of a century on, its impact can be felt in everything from fashion to film, to interior design. It redefined our notion of a night out. It even changed the law of the land."*

And from Matthew Collin's book 'Altered State':

> *"Ecstasy culture had become the primary leisure activity for British youth, seamlessly integrated into the fabric of the weekend ritual. From 1990 onwards, as the fall-out from Acid House germinated across the country, its sounds, signs, symbols and slang had become all-pervasive, part of the everyday landscape."*

That, presumably, would have been the plan. And the article's later observation that "every generation is desperate for something to call their own – something their parents don't understand" comes straight out of the social-conditioning 101 textbook. Fomenting discord between the generations is a tactic that's been employed by manipulators of culture for centuries.

This overview of Acid House culture, and how it paved the way for the massive worldwide dance music scene, makes no claims to be an all-embracing account of the story. To do that would require an entire book in itself, and there have already been plenty, (the best of which remains Matthew Collin's aforementioned 'Altered State.') This book's revisiting of the scene takes an approach which has never been employed before, however – to assemble key pieces of information, and to ask whether these provide evidence of a Hidden Hand's intervention in ensuring the movement went off in a pre-planned direction, rather than randomly evolving on its own.

It's very difficult to obtain direct proof that this was the case – as any other researcher setting off on such a mission will surely find – since whistle-blowers and insiders admitting they were employed by some aspect of the intelligence services are in short supply. And to my knowledge, no declassified documents have so far emerged revealing such an agenda. It took the best part of 50 years for the full story of the 60s counter-culture and its co-opting by the CIA to be adequately told. It's my hope that whatever truth remains to be revealed about the scene that came along two decades later on the other side of the Atlantic, however, won't take quite as long. It often takes the next generation to figure out what really happened with a social movement from before its time, since those that lived it have too much personal attachment and nostalgic investment to be able to view things objectively. And such uncoverings can only occur with the availability of new proofs and evidence – a process which was almost impossible before the advent of the internet.

Whereas the 60s hippie scene espoused the overthrowing of the social systems of the day and their replacing with new peace-and-love ideals, (at least on the surface,) its 80s British equivalent lacked any political aspect. Rather than seeking to change the status-quo of the time, the Acid House spirit was simply about escaping from it by way of one long party. Whether he realised it or not, Matthew Collin himself dropped a hint as to a potential connection between the two 'Summers of Love' when he wrote in 'Altered State':

> *"There were so few people involved that friendships became all-consuming. Suddenly, all they could talk about was love, togetherness, sharing, the sheer joy of life. In Ibiza they had discovered something they hardly knew how to comprehend, and so they looked for the nearest comparison they could find – the mythology of the hippie era – adopting a simulacrum of what they believed the sixties were like, a hand-me-down, pick-and-mix bag of fashions and slogans – minus the radical politics of the era – all viewed through a prism of suburban working-class aspirations.*
>
> *"Yet they sincerely believed that the fabric of their minds was changing. Were they turning into hippies, they asked themselves, was this the beginning of a New Age?"*

Further possible clues came from the ethno-botanist-turned counter-culture icon Terence McKenna in comments following his 'Evolution' lecture in London in 1992:

> *"With electronic culture you can create shamans for the global planetary village. And this, to my mind, is the function that Rock 'n' Roll played in the 60s, and House music should play in the 90s."*

And later:

"Through emphasis in House music and Rave culture on physiologically compatible rhythms, that sound, properly understood, can actually change neurological states in large groups of people getting together, creating a telepathic community of bonding that hopefully would be strong enough that it would carry the vision out into the mainstream of society."

Unfortunately, however, it would appear that McKenna's status as a consciousness guru – like that of his contemporary Timothy Leary – may have been sponsored by a familiar type of agency, according to comments he himself made while lecturing at California's Esalen Institute, (itself heavily connected to mind-control research,) in 1994:

"Certainly, when I reached La Chorrera in 1971 I had a price on my head by the FBI. I was running out of money, I was at the end of my rope and they recruited me and said, you know, with a mouth like yours there's a place for you in our organisation and, you know, I've worked in deep background positions, about which the less said the better, and then about 15 years ago they shifted me into public relations, and I've been there to the present."

The author Graham Hancock, on whom McKenna has been a major influence, has tried to argue that by 'they,' McKenna was actually referring to 'alien intelligences' to which he was able to connect when altering his consciousness with psychedelics. It seems pretty clear to me what was implied by the above statement, however, with 'they' directly following his reference to the FBI. Yet another counter-culture 'hero' would appear to have been on the payroll of one of the alphabet agencies, at least for a time.

The Trip

By 1988, House music records from Chicago, New York and New Jersey had come to be a staple part of black music DJs sets in the UK, played alongside more soul and funk-based tunes, and New York Hip-Hop output. The change in attitude towards a more all-embracing approach to music was kick-started by the brief flourish of a scene that came to be known as 'Balearic Beat.' The story behind its inception has long since passed into legend.

Four young London DJs – Paul Oakenfold, Danny Rampling, Nicky Holloway and Johnny Walker, (not to be confused with veteran Radio 1 DJ Johnnie Walker) – had gone on holiday to Ibiza in late August 1987 for Oakenfold's birthday, and were captivated by the eclectic sets being played at Amnesia nightclub by veteran Argentinian DJ Alfredo Fiorito. Alongside the latest US House tunes sat obscure European dance records, Indie Rock, Ambient, Electronica and World Music. Wikipedia's account of the story adds that: "The friends also discovered the music's powerful synergy with the drug MDMA that reduced inhibitions and created a sense of one-ness on the dancefloor." In a nostalgic interview with the UK's 'Guardian' newspaper in 2007, meanwhile, Nicky Holloway recalled:

> *"We all tried ecstasy for the first time together, and then the whole thing made sense. Alfredo was playing (Chicago house label imprints) Trax and DJ International next to Kate Bush and Queen – all the white English acts we'd turn our noses up at. But on E, it all made sense. Half an hour or so after you necked a pill ,you would suddenly feel this euphoric wave go through you, like shooom! – hence the name of Danny's club – and you suddenly felt that everything in the world was alright."*

As the London boys returned to their respective gigs back home, they felt inspired to introduce this more open-minded approach to their sets, and began dropping a variety of different styles on their crowds as they had seen Alfredo doing. The timing was fortuitous, as this period coincided with the increasing availability of US House, prompting British producers to create their own productions, and the Balearic converts to launch new club nights to embrace these styles. In Rampling's case, this led to the inception of his legendary Shoom nights, originally staged at a gym known as The Fitness Centre in Southwark before going on to other homes around London. The name is said to have been inspired by the euphoric rush a raver feels when 3,4-Methylenedioxymethamphetamine

(MDMA, or ecstasy,) first starts to kick in and stimulate chemicals in the brain. Richard West, better known as Mr. C of the rave act The Shamen, alluded to the sensation from necking his first pill in a 2014 interview with the Thump/ Vice website:

> *"At first I felt nothing. Then my hands started to become sweaty and my mouth kind of dry. All of a sudden, I felt these tingles down my spine and the hair on the back of my neck stood on end. Before I knew it I had these big overwhelming rushes passing though my body. The bass in the music felt like it was inside me and all of a sudden, everything made sense, like I knew why I was there. Something cleared deep in my subconscious and I was filled with empathy. I loved everyone, wanted to hug everyone, and not just for the sake of it, but because I really did love them."*

Oakenfold, meanwhile, established the Spectrum event at Heaven nightclub in London's Charing Cross, owned by Establishment asset 'Sir' Richard Branson. This initially ran on Monday nights in late 1987, where the party was dubbed 'The Theatre Of Madness.' You can get a feel for the Balearic vibe of 1988 by listening to one of Oakenfold's live Spectrum sets here – https://soundcloud.com/rave_on/paul-oakenfold-live-spectrum-london-uk-061988

His Friday night promotion, Future, fused House sounds with Indie Rock, and paved the way for him to later remix the likes of the Happy Mondays, The Cure and the Stone Roses, and to become the tour DJ for U2. There's an original recording from a Future session, with DJ Nancy Noise guesting alongside Oakenfold in June '88, here –

- https://www.mixcloud.com/martyn-booers-bower/paul-oakenfold-nancy-noise-livethe-future-london-june-88/

Nicky Holloway's project was the revealingly-titled The Trip, (later re-named Sin,) at the nearby Astoria Theatre. Among other London DJs to embrace the new spirit of House music were Colin Faver, (who died of multiple organ failure in September 2015) and 'Evil' Eddie Richards at Camden Palace, Maurice and Noel Watson at Delirium, Jay Strongman and Mark Moore, (of the act S-Express) at Heaven, and Dave Dorrell at RAW. There was also Judge Jules, (a London School of Economics graduate whose uncle, as a matter of curiosity, is the celebrity chef Rick Stein OBE, and whose dad was an TV producer who worked on the ITV sci-fi series 'Sapphire And Steel,') and Carl Cox, who had installed the sound system at Rampling's very first Shoom party. A great many of this scene's tastemakers had previously been active on the soul, funk and disco scenes. Acid's very loose anchoring in 'black dance music' justified its appeal. As its fashionability became apparent, most of the new converts allowed themselves to be swept along by the electronic wave, rather than returning to their more soulful roots.

Many of the key DJs made use of the new phenomenon of sampling snippets of older records, over newly-created, dancefloor-friendly beats. Several of the resulting cut-and-paste-style records became crossover hits, among them Bomb The Bass's 'Beat Dis,' Coldcut's 'Doctorin' The House,' S-Express's 'Theme From S-Express,' and the earlier 'Pump Up The Volume' by M.A.R.R.S. Jeff Young, a DJ who had come out of the soul scene, (and not to be confused with the former Megadeth guitarist of the same name!) began his 'Big Beat' show on Radio 1 in October 1987, which was ideal timing to harness the new-found spirit of the times and expose the emerging dance scene to listeners across the UK.

The spirit of these clubs, and the convenient convergence with an influx of ecstasy pills on the scene, led to it quickly picking up the moniker of 'Acid House.' This was the catalyst for a new type of electronic dance record to be created. London's 'Acid' sound saw a rush of instrumental tracks produced on synthesisers and drum machines, the trademark sound being bubbling, undulating basslines, heavy on effects such as Flange and Auto Pan, and manipulated to give a 'squelching' sound. Many contained short stabs of vocal samples, often featuring orgasmic moans or wails. The inspiration for so many of these creations had come out of Chicago in 1987 in the form of the epic 'Acid Tracks' by Phuture, often credited as 'the first Acid House record'. Former Phuture member DJ Pierre went on to curate many more of the defining sounds of this sub-genre. The term 'Acid House' is said to have been first coined by Chicago producers in direct reference to the distinctive sounds of the Roland TB-303 electronic synthesiser-sequencer.

The smiley yellow face; icon of the UK Acid House scene, but with some more sinister overtones over the decades.

Credit: The Author

Early Acid House records are very dated by today's standards. But 30 years of hindsight can also remind us of how menacing and unsettling they now sound. Acid tunes weren't happy records; the hands-in-the air euphoric rave anthems with their blissful breakdowns came slightly later as the 90s dawned. Factoring in the drug of choice which permeated the scene, the burbling synth arrangements could be considered an audio mimicking of the chemicals sweeping through the brains of the listeners.

The chosen act name of Phuture certainly turned out to be prophetic given that, knowingly or otherwise, this group was laying the foundations in the 1980s for a style of music that would come to transform societies all over the world in the coming decades.

The Second Summer of Love

It was the middle months of 1988 that came to be conveniently dubbed 'The Second Summer of Love' by the media of the time. It's also of great interest that the term 'Acid House' came to be coined as a moniker for the whole movement in question, as it provides one of many direct throwbacks to the earlier, manipulated social movement of the 60s when 'Acid' meant LSD. (Tragically, the UK's 'Sun' "newspaper" in its naivety, took the term literally when it started documenting the 'evils' of Acid House in Summer 1988, assuming the 'Acid' part to mean this scene was fuelled by LSD!) The Scottish group Danny Wilson paid tribute to this scenario in their 1989 song of that name, whose lyrics include: "Ah, the second Summer of Love is here, so tell your angry friends, to throw away their Gaultier and grow their hair again." And later: "Acid on the radio, Acid on the brain, Acid everywhere you go, Acid in the rain."

This moniker alone may raise the curiosity of anyone who has researched how the original Summer of Love in 1967 was very much the result of culture-creation at the hands of agencies like the CIA. Many books, articles and videos are now available to show how this was done – particularly the work of Jan Irvin at Gnostic Media, his interviews with musicologist Dr. Hans Utter and 'Unspun' podcasts with Joseph Atwill, and the book 'Weird Scenes Inside The Canyon' by the late Dave McGowan. Was this naming of the newly-emerged UK scene a sly and subtle clue towards it also being the product of behind-the-scenes manipulations?

Considering the notion that the truth of a matter is always placed in plain sight, there is certainly no shortage of indicators that this 'new' UK scene was in fact a cynical upgrading of a well-worn blueprint, merely rebooted and tweaked for a new generation on a different continent. So many of these clues can be found in British Acid House records themselves. Arguably the best known of all is the crossover hit 'We Call It Acieed' by D-Mob, an act fronted by 'Dancin' Danny Poku, who had previously been a soul and funk DJ and producer. The song, which reached No. 3 in the UK singles chart, includes the lyric "you turn on, you tune in, you drop out. Acid has that effect" in homage to the popular phrase of the 60s scene. The song's video features dancers sporting a single eye in place of their heads. The track also states that Acid "puts you in a trance."The main intention of it all, perhaps? The 60s LSD apologist Timothy Leary, meanwhile, (who *just happened* to have been a self-admitted asset of the CIA, and had the "turn on, tune in, drop out" phrase gifted to him by the philosopher and intellectual Marshall McLuhan,) is sampled on many a late-80s outing, including Psychic TV's 'Tune In (Turn On The Acid House,') and the phrase is uttered by a Prince Charles impersonator on the same year's 'Don't Believe The Hype' credited to the none-too-subtly-named Mista E.

A further track, simply titled 'E' by an 'artist' of the same name, contains vocal samples of the phrase 'LSD,' along with dialogue lifted from the cult TV show 'The Prisoner' in another 1960s throwback. 'Acid Man' by Jolly Roger, a pseudonym of the producer 'Evil' Eddie Richards, contains the hippie-era phrase 'far out, man!' Coming slightly later, Primal Scream's 'Loaded' contains a sample of Peter Fonda from the 60s biker movie 'The Wild Angels.' E-Zee Posse, meanwhile, were about as subtle as a flying mallet in the titling of their 'Everything Starts With an E.' Vocalist MC Kinky draws frequent parallels between the new drug scene and its earlier American cousin with lines like: "L and an S and a D coming in like love sex and danger. Drop a tab of E and make we rub with a stranger." And: "ETC and Acid is a stoned unwind, trip out to Hendrix solos, 'Scuse me while I kiss the sky."

Visual nods can also be found in some of the accompanying artwork, meanwhile. The flyer for a night called Listen See Destroy (LSD) advertises a session with Divine Styler, 'the Timothy Leary of Hip-Hop'. And promotion for Spectrum's first all-day event in London included the question 'can you pass the Acid test?' in a throwback to CIA asset Ken Kesey and his Merry Pranksters, who distributed free LSD to the attendees of hippie communes and psychedelic festivals back in the California heyday. Paul Oakenfold selected a single bloodshot eye as the promotional motif for his 'Theatre of Madness' nights at Spectrum. The eye had originally appeared on a poster for the Grateful Dead, a group which is known to have been a direct creation of the CIA, with two of its number having also been members of the Bohemian Club secret-society. It got a further airing on the sleeve design to 'Jibaro,' the 'Balearic Beat' single that Oakenfold put out with fellow producer Steve Osborne in the wake of that fateful trip – no pun intended – to Ibiza.

Intriguingly, a 2017 article in the UK's 'Guardian' suggested that things were starting to go full-circle in Ibiza, with a return to the 1960s hippie ideals that once characterised the island – the 'Boho' scene – becoming fashionable to a new generation overfed on electronic dance beats and debaucherous lifestyles. Referencing the newly-established Aniwa Gathering, it stated:

> *"While the Tech House superclubs prepare for another night of narcotics and vest-clad fist pumping, this is an event singing to a different tune. If you've ever wondered what happens when a former Brazilian model and an ex-director of a tech startup discover Ayahuasca, then you've found your answer: they launch a foundation dedicated to the promotion of indigenous culture, start a festival and fly in 40 spiritual leaders from around the world to lead a series of talks, performances and ceremonies, including the ritualistic sharing of cacao, the consumption of "plant medicine" and sweat lodges."*

Where have I come across a scenario like that before?

Harmonic sonics

The timing of the 'Second Summer of Love,' coming as it did when the 1980s gave way to the 90s, is of great personal interest to me. The elite controllers are impeccable planners who play the long game and plot their moves decades in advance. They also time these in line with numerology, astrology, and other esoteric factors. The manipulations of the counter-culture scene of two decades previous seemed, in part, to be all about experimentation on the generation known as the 'baby boomers' – those born immediately post World War 2, and who were coming of age in the mid to late-1960s. There was also much talk, among the occult groups of those times, of tapping into the spirit of the astrological Age of Aquarius, and a shifting away from the previous epoch of Pisces, (even though no scholars or researchers seem able to pinpoint with any accuracy when this Age will actually be upon us, with estimates ranging from 1447 to 3597 AD!)

Could this paradigm shift have been echoed at the time of the British dance music revolution? Or did these events signify some other highly meaningful events occurring? Acid pioneer Danny Rampling has always been one of dance music's more interesting DJs to listen to in interviews. While others are limited in conversation matter to 'the scene' or to their latest career move, I recall Rampling being asked in a video interview with 'DMC' magazine in 2014 where he came from, and replying, 'London . . . and somewhere out in the stars originally.' I also recall him speaking on the radio of driving back from his gigs in 1997 to the sight of the Hale-Bopp comet burning brightly in the night skies, something which no other DJs felt significant enough to reference. His propensity towards cosmic phenomena led to a revealing comment in an interview with the UK's 'Guardian' in 2007. Reflecting on what led he and his mates to embrace the spirit of the dance scene twenty years earlier, Rampling commented:

> *"I'll bring something different to the table here. I felt there was something deeper, spiritually, running through the whole experience. I discovered something recently, through my own research. In August 1987, there was an event called the Harmonic Convergence, a global shift in unity consciousness through dance rituals, which is part of the Maya calendar teachings."*

Wikipedia's account of this event is as follows:

> *"The timing of the Harmonic Convergence was allegedly significant in the Maya calendar, with some consideration also given to European and Asian astrological traditions. The chosen dates have the distinction of allegedly marking a planetary alignment with the Sun, Moon and six out of eight planets being "part of the grand trine."*

Though questions remain among genuine seekers about the true cosmology of the place in which we live, the grand trine is said to reflect a rare alignment of eight planets which, according to astrologer Neil Michelsen's 'The American Ephemeris,' occurred on 24th August 1987, placing it even closer to the four London DJs' fabled visit to Ibiza. Was this all purely coincidental, and ultimately meaningless? Or were Rampling and his friends unwittingly tapping into a consciousness shift that was occurring at the time? According to researchers, '87's Harmonic Convergence marked a 25-year lead-in to December 2012 and the end of the yuga cycle measured by the famous Mayan calendar system.

1990 to Infinity

I might be inclined to opt for the less exciting explanation were it not for other factors which seem to hint at something spiritual happening at the turn of the decade. A number of prominent speakers have pinpointed the years 1989 and '90 as the time when they 'woke up' to great truths. Certainly, many world-changing events were occurring at this time, including the break-up of the Soviet Union and its stronghold over many Communist states symbolised by the end of the Berlin Wall, plus the public revolutions in Communist China, all hinting at changing times, or even 'a New Age.' Most famously, David Icke has claimed to have sensed a presence communicating with him in empty rooms in 1989, leading to his March 1990 encounter with a psychic. Author Andy Thomas, who wrote 'The Truth Agenda' and 'Conspiracies,' also pinpoints 1990 as a time of great revealing. Andy became an organiser and co-host of the Glastonbury Symposium, the UK's leading metaphysical and consciousness conference, which itself held its first event in 1990. There was much talk of environmental and ecological issues in these times, too, even in the mainstream.

I seem to have had some personal experience of this shift myself, too. As 1989 turned into '90, my perceptions of life started to feel different in a way that's still very difficult to pinpoint. It felt as if I was tapping into *something*. In my youthful naivety, I had no idea what was happening, I just knew that I felt 'different.' Had I had access to the internet at this time, and the ability to connect with like-minded individuals, it might have changed the outcome radically. At the time, the only thing I could think of in trying to get some answers was to consult an aunt who was a devout Christian, and who seemed to have a set of answers to life's Big Questions that others didn't. Inevitably, she interpreted this as a calling from 'the Lord' and zealously inducted me into her Evangelical church.

I ended up attending for the next four years, believing I had become 'born again.' But things didn't feel quite right throughout. The church seemed to be like a branch of Freemasonry, with different generations of the same families ushered into positions of authority. I also saw hypocrisy in what certain members preached, versus how they seemed to be living their own lives, and found it difficult to reconcile these factors with people who were supposed to be 'better' and more moral than everyone else. By the time I left, disillusioned, I'd become a bitter atheist, lapping up the work of Richard Dawkins and the like. It wasn't until many years later, around 2008, that I'd started to understand that there was, after all, a divine creative power, and that each of us is an individuated expression of it. This was when I came to a humble acknowledgement of how misguided I'd been for so many years. It's been said that the phrase "I was wrong – this changes everything" is one of the most empowering of all, as it represents a letting-go of ego consciousness. It's one which, it seems, many in this life remain highly reluctant to embrace.

Many times as I've reflected on those years of spiritual wilderness, it's felt to me like wasted time. But I always come back to the knowledge that everything we undergo happens for a reason, and our experiences here give our souls the opportunity for growth and to learn certain lessons. (See this book's final chapter for more on this theme.) Free Will is always present – it's always up to us whether we choose a certain path that's made available to us or not. (And many spiritual scholars will state that Free Will was even present before our higher selves consented to incarnate into our bodies and undergo our life experiences.) Nothing is forced. Everything is consensual. So ultimately, apparent 'mistakes' needn't be viewed as that. Things happen when their time has come, and not a moment before. It seems I wasn't ready to walk the path I'm now on all those years ago. If I *had* 'woken up' back then, it seems unlikely that I would have pursued the journey as a travelling DJ, radio host and writer that I did for the next 20 years, and that would very likely mean that these books wouldn't have come to be written, since I would have lacked the experiences and the insight that has gone into them. Either way, it remains greatly intriguing for me to now realise that I seemed to be picking up on what others were also experiencing at the dawn of the 1990s.

By this point, the British scene was on the cusp of fully embracing the House music trends that were coming over from the US. From '91 onwards, most music heard in dance clubs was relatively energetic tracks of 120 beats-per-minute-plus, getting more uptempo as the decade progressed. But 1990 itself saw a plethora of tunes still steeped in lower tempos, many inspired by the chugging rhythms of Soul II Soul's output of the previous year. Additionally, some dealt lyrically – and in their overall mood and feel – with spiritual, ecological and nature-related messages, creating a fascinating melting pot of sounds. Were these producers also tapping into the consciousness changes of the time? Did these phenomena play a part in how dance and club music evolved at that point in the timeline? British-made tracks which spring to mind in this regard include 808 State's 'Pacific State,' Q-Tee's 'History,' Voices Of Africa's 'Hoomba Hoomba,' Tribal House's 'Motherland,' The Grid's 'Floatation,' Frazier Chorus' 'Cloud Nine,' Plus One's 'It's Happenin,' Innocence's 'Natural Thing,' MC Wildski's 'Wonderful World,' Bocca Juniors' 'Raise,' (featuring lyrics inspired by Aleister Crowley, reportedly,) and Nomad's 'Devotion.' This was also the time of Guru Josh's 'Infinity,' with the tagline '1990's Time for the Guru.' (Josh was Jersey-born musician Paul Walden who sadly died aged 51 on 28th December 2015, the same day as Motorhead's Lemmy, in what is said to have been a suicide.) Bassomatic's 'Fascinating Rhythm' talked of the hypnotic power of the groove and was the public's introduction to the interestingly-named producer William Orbit who went on to work with Madonna.

Let's go back at this point to Wikipedia's account of the Harmonic Convergence:

"The convergence is purported to have corresponded with a great shift in the earth's energy from warlike to peaceful. Believers of this esoteric prophecy maintain that the Harmonic Convergence ushered in a five-year period of Earth's "cleansing," where many of the planet's "false structures of separation" would collapse.

"According to (author and artist) Jose Argüelles, the event came at the end of these "hell" cycles and the beginning of a new age of universal peace. Adherents believed that signs indicated a "major energy shift" was about to occur, a turning point in Earth's collective karma and dharma, and that this energy was powerful enough to change the global perspective of man from one of conflict to one of co-operation. Actress and author Shirley MacLaine called it a "window of light," allowing access to higher realms of awareness."

Is it plausible that the elite controllers – obsessed as they are with metaphysical phenomena – were aware in advance of this incoming energetic shift and, rather than taking the chance of allowing humanity to respond in its own natural way, saw an opportunity to steer the change off into their own direction, where it could be monitored, surveilled, and ultimately controlled? Given that it's so often young people that the social engineers have in their crosshairs, on the grounds that they're far easier to mind-control than their more experienced and cynical elders, could they have moulded the worldwide phenomenon that the party scene became in their own desired fashion, introducing their symbolism, themes, and sound frequencies at every turn, giving the impression that – like so many scenes before it – it had evolved organically, but with the truth of the matter telling a different story?

Interestingly, the generation that was key to getting this movement established, has been directly referred to in three ways by some of dance music's key players. The Prodigy titled their second studio album 'Music for the Jilted Generation,' Judge Jules for many years described his Saturday evening Radio 1 show as "the noticeboard for the deranged generation," while more recently, Paul Van Dyk's VONYC Sessions podcast announces itself as being for "the electrified generation." Was this also, unwittingly, a generation of lab-rats under the watchful eye of the omniscient cultural manipulators?

Have a nice trip

In an interview on the 'Lift The Veil' podcast, IT specialist-turned-researcher Steve Outtrim pinpointed 1986 – the year prior to the Acid House scene's acknowledged beginnings – as having some potentially connected significance:

> *"One thing I've found very useful in my research is when you look at a timeline for these events, and you see that Burning Man was launched in 1986, the Worldwide Web, the internet, was launched in 1986, MAPS, the association for psychedelic studies, was launched in 1986. The Cacophony Society, which is closely linked to both Burning Man and Project Mayhem, that was launched in 1986. So you have all these cult-like groups and the internet coming out, and then you have some of the military guys behind the internet saying, what we need is to draw people together in communities electronically."*

Many will put the timing down to serendipity, or random chance. But there are factors which suggest behind-the-scenes collusion. These include the fact that Acid records were starting to appear out of the US at exactly the same time as the British scene is said to have evolved by pure chance out of the legendary London DJs' jaunt in Ibiza. This observation was in fact addressed by Paul Oakenfold and Pete Tong in an article titled 'The Balearic Beat Story' that they wrote together for 'Mixmag' in 1988:

> *"The emergence of this 'movement' in London has coincided, quite conveniently, with the ever-increasing popularity of Acid House. Indeed, House music does provide a large proportion of the soundtrack at new London clubs considered to be the pioneers of the new 'scene.' It was something that a year later would be massive, thanks to what's been called The Second Summer of Love."*

Taken in isolation, many of the Acid scene's motifs could be considered random, innocent, and devoid of any deeper meaning. Viewed in tandem with other episodes in popular culture, however, several take on added meaning. UK club flyers from the late 80s and early 90s have become collectors' items, providing a snapshot of a seminal, but long-gone era in British nightlife.

Among these are frequent showings of the three-pronged 'peace' sign often favoured by anarchists, (when inverted from its original design,) and derived from the sigil for the Tree Of Life. Besides the ever-present smiley yellow face, (of which, more shortly,) and a smattering of pyramids, there are several renderings of a single eye. Some are altogether more disturbing. A 'Rage' event from Heaven in February 1989, presented by Fabio and Grooverider, features what appears to be a demonic entity presiding over a planetary conjunction, a December 1988 event titled 'Apocalyse Now' shows a figure, looking like a cross between an evil clown and Tom Baker's 'Doctor Who,' grinning maniacally while sporting a smiley face badge. 'Holocaust '89' leaves little to the imagination, showing the world going up in a mushroom cloud. Rush (gettit?) Productions' 'Satisfaction' from November 1989 depicts the kind of hedonistic debauchery that would have been at home in one of Aleister Crowley's sex magick parties. One, at least 20 years ahead of its time, simply shows the Freemasonic all-seeing-eye inside the capstone which appears on the back of the US dollar bill, with illuminated rays all around. A rave entitled 'Vertigo' shows black-and-white chequerboard duality of the type found on the floors of Masonic temples, (also used as an MK-Ultra mind-control trigger design.) Some leave nothing to the imagination in showing actual demonic entities with event names like Omen. (And a pertinent question, I feel, would be why New Atlantic chose to name the B-side to their 'I Know' rave anthem, 'Yes to Satan' (?!) There was clearly a dark side to the scene in contrast to the free-spirited fun which it originally espoused. Was this reflecting some of the bad MDMA trips that some were experiencing?

As the 1990s dawned, however, flyers started to take on far more spiritual themes, also reflected in the naming of this second breed of events, such as Tribal Gathering, Raindance, Biology, Peacefest, Sunrise, Perception and Universe. Themes of UFOs, aliens, ancient gods, cosmology, astrology, celestial alignments and Transhumanist future landscapes were frequently represented. An event called 'Genesis' had a depiction of the pagan god Pan as its main logo. Promoter of the Dreamscape events, the late Murray Beetson, admitted: "On the main stage, we've gone for a pyramid theme with a flashing eye that keeps blinking, just like on the American dollar," when revealing the decor for his 'Dreamscape 20' gathering.

By 1989, the focus had shifted from nightclub and warehouse parties, to large-scale open-air gatherings known as 'raves,' with many of the DJs who played at them, such as Judge Jules and Carl Cox, going on to enjoy international careers that have lasted to this day. (These two have had long-running syndicated radio shows entitled 'The Global Warm-Up' and 'Global' respectively.) Many took place on land around the M25, the orbital motorway that surrounds London, (and the inspiration for the naming of brothers Phil and Paul Hartnoll's act Orbital.) In order to throw the authorities off the track, raves would be advertised on flyers which neglected to reveal the location, but featured a phone number to be called on the day itself, when directions to the site would be revealed at the last minute. These parties occurred in the very early days of mobile phones when handsets were still the size of bricks, and long before the advent of sat-nav. Small cars crammed with clubbers meeting at motorway services to compare directions and travel together in convoys, was a frequent nocturnal sight. A pirate radio ad of the time for the popular Biology brand of raves went:

> *"This is a Party Political Dance Broadcast on behalf of the Biology Party. Here are the following requirements for this Saturday's DJ Convention and gathering of young minds. Firstly, you must have a Great Britain road atlas. Yes, that's a Great Britain road atlas. Secondly, a reliable motor with a full tank of gas. Lastly, you must have a ticket and you must be a member."*

It would become clear when they had arrived at the location – often a farmer's field equipped with ranks of strobe lights, bowel-shaking speaker systems, and circus-style attractions such as fire-eaters, stilt walkers, and exotic dancers performing on illuminated podiums. By this stage many events had become corporatised, profit-hungry promoters seduced by the new financial potential, presenting ever more elaborate productions at ever-soaring ticket prices. The drugs remained in generous supply. Ravers from the original days began to complain about how the scene was already starting to lose its original, grass-roots vibe as everything became mass-market-orientated. It was far from the first time an exciting new culture had gone that way, and it certainly wasn't to be the last.

Enter the Toffs

On the surface of it, a subversive, dynamic party scene ought to have no connections whatsoever with the Establishment old-guard, and should stand as the very antithesis of a Conservative government. Curiosity, therefore, comes from the fact that Acid House's move out of the clubs and warehouses to large-scale raves, was spearheaded by a small group of public schoolboys who would have looked more at home on the floors of London's Stock Exchange, than flitting between a sea of strobe lights in a field at four in the morning, mobile phones clutched to ears.

Tony Colston-Hayter, born in 1965, was the son of a university lecturer and solicitor, and a gambling addict. He used much of the fortune he had accrued from casino wins to finance his moves into the party scene. His first events appeared at Wembley Studios in August 1988 under the brand of 'Apocalypse Now.' Colston-Hayter invited reporters from ITV's 'News At Ten' along to film the action. This sparked a series of 'exposés' into Acid culture from a mainstream media who had previously ignored the movement altogether. The 'Sun' "newspaper" at first appeared to be down with the kids, its Bizarre page in October offering a 'groovy and cool' Acid House T-shirt, and a fun guide to Acid House lingo to help readers "raise your street cred."

Within a few weeks, however, the headlines were grabbing attention for different reasons. Exactly 100 years after tabloids were writing shock stories about the murders of Jack The Ripper, 'The Sun' was now running articles titled 'Shoot These Evil Acid Barons,' 'Ban This Killer Music,' 'Acid House Horror,' and 'Drug Crazed Acid House Fans.' It was a modern rendering of the 1930s American propaganda movie 'Reefer

Madness,' which sought to demonise cannabis by erroneously linking it with hallucinations, violent behaviour and death. In an incident reminiscent of Radio 1 breakfast show DJ Mike Read banning Frankie Goes To Hollywood's 'Relax,' I can recall DJ Jeff Young playing D-Mob's 'We Call It Acieed' on his 'Big Beat' show on the same station, but prefacing it with the disclaimer that "the BBC does not endorse drug-taking of any kind." (Despite this feigned moral stance, the same station had no problem with veteran DJ Annie Nightingale using the none-too-subtle slogan 'Annie on one' for her electronically-fuelled dance show for some years.)

Colston-Hayter was now being singled out as the Mr. Big of this scene, and was the latest to suffer a seemingly orchestrated smear campaign. By 1989 he had renamed his company Sunrise, and was staging ever-more elaborate and large-scale events. He hired a publicist by the name of Paul Staines, who he had met at a video games tournament, and who described himself as 'an anarcho-capitalist,' to be his right-hand man. (Staines went on to reinvent himself as the well-known political blogger Guido Fawkes.)

In response to the scene's rapid evolution, the police formed a new group whose remit it was to clamp down on illegal organised parties, referred to as The Pay Party Unit. As a UK 'Guardian' article on Colston-Hayter put it:

> *"Some members of the government were dismayed that their opponents weren't pierced-and-dreadlocked outsiders, but well-spoken right-wing entrepreneurs who stashed their profits in an offshore tax haven. A baffled Home Office official once screamed at Staines: "You're a right-wing Tory, why are you doing this?"*

From the point of view of this book and its themes, it's a good question!

In response to police obstacles, Colston-Hayter and Staines were seen to launch their Freedom To Party campaign at the Conservative government's 1989 conference in Blackpool. In the spirit of entrepreneurialism, they presented themselves as offering innovative solutions to public demand, implying that events such as theirs were better kept under well-organised and surveilled conditions, than allowing them to go off haphazardly and unchecked. Eventually, the authorities were forced to react. Licenced clubs were granted later closing times, while police continued to crack down on illegally-organised gatherings.

This herding of clubbers into designated indoor spaces, where everything could be more closely monitored, led to the birth of what were known as the UK 'superclubs' of the early 1990s – venues which catered specifically for this scene. One of the first was London's Ministry Of Sound, (of which, more shortly.) Already of iconic status by then was Manchester's Hacienda, operated by the Factory Records empire under its charismatic frontman, the late journalist-turned party maverick Tony Wilson. The Hacienda was a rare venue outside London to have embraced the culture early on, and Factory spawned its own Northern twist on the scene by fusing the indie-rock styles of bands such as the Happy Mondays and Stone Roses with Acid themes, resulting in some distinctive sounds and fashions absolutely representative of that point in time. Not far behind Ministry, meanwhile, were brands such as Liverpool's 'Cream,' Sheffield's 'Gatecrasher,' 'Renaissance,' 'Golden,' 'Progress,' 'God's Kitchen,' 'Miss Moneypenny's,' 'Karanga,' 'Shindig,' 'Fandango,' 'Inside Out,' 'Time Flies' and so many others. Gatecrasher marketed its prolific New Year's Eve 1999 event at Sheffield's Don Valley Stadium with the tagline "It will always be with you." Maybe there was more truth to this than the 'Crasher Kids (as the brand's ravers were known) could have realised?

The prospects of promoters still seeking to organise large-scale open-air raves were no longer so good. In 1994, the Conservative government, now under the leadership of the completely forgettable John Major, introduced its draconian Criminal Justice and Public Order Act, known more regularly as The Criminal Justice Bill. Its Section 5 included measures that appeared to take action against squatters, gypsies, travellers and trespassers, (also criminalising acts such as the disruption of fox hunts in a move that would have been rather convenient for the Bill's creators,) but also encompassed noise-nuisance, in a direct targeting of the free-party/ rave scene.

Demonstrating how out-of-touch the Bill's dusty old architects were with youth culture, the wording of the section aimed at shutting down raves was much mocked by the dance music press of the time, and has now passed into legend: "Music includes sounds wholly or predominantly characterised by the emission of a succession of repetitive beats." An event which had assisted in the Bill's acceptance was a free rave known as the Castlemorton Common Festival in May 1992. The thousands of ravers and New Age travellers descending on the tranquil Worcestershire village, spurred calls for the authorities to take action against such unwanted incursions. Castlemorton and similar gatherings were a contemporary reboot of the first wave of free festivals in the UK, spearheaded by the Isle of Wight Festival beginning in 1968, the Glastonbury Festival two years later, and the Windsor and Stonehenge festivals that followed. These events were based on the counter-culture ethos of togetherness and free expression, and drew hippies, squatters, travellers and anarchists . . . though how long they remained genuinely benevolent in their aims can be questioned, when infiltration by provocateurs inevitably occurs at such large gatherings.

A user known as 'Separ,' who posted on a forum on these subjects on the David Icke website back in 2009, astutely observed:

> *"The way I see it, it had to come across as a genuine grass-roots youth movement for the trick to work. The police and local authorities and the populist party politics talk at the time, were instrumental in creating this illusion of a totally fake 'rebellion' movement that was out of their hands. The incremental steps to implementation of the New World Order agenda, is executed by people who don't have complete knowledge of the bigger picture, so the backlash against raves was a quite genuine thing among the ordinary people, (including those like the police who think they're in control, but they're not.) By being very public in cracking down on raves, they gave the impression a mini-Woodstock was happening at night all over the country.*
>
> *"The sum effect of all this was that electronic beat-based music became widely perceived as the new youth music, (it wasn't so mainstream before,) and the face of pop music was changed so that we have the situation we have today. The Powers That Be succeeded 100%. They achieved the creation of a completely corporation- and Illuminati-controlled type of sound that the masses can vomit their lager out to*

on weekends, and the youth become totally conditioned/ brainwashed thanks to amphetamine-like drugs. It's a fake pressure-valve release that's been engineered to diminish the human experience and destroy the spark of divinity/ spirituality in Man. It's a Saturday happy hour to keep people's minds off the serious business, (globalisation and the NWO), that The Powers That Be think we shouldn't think about. It's like a Che Guevara or Haile Selassie T-shirt: de-fanged rebellion."

James Palumbo, now the Baron of Southwark, a most unlikely candidate for boss of the Ministry of Sound nightclub empire.

https://en.wikipedia.org/wiki/File:Jamespalumbocropped.jpg

Credit: Maxitech03

Colston-Hayter wasn't the only public schoolboy to muscle in on the party scene. Another was Jeremy Taylor, who staged the Gatecrasher Balls, known informally as 'the teenage toff's balls.' Several of these were put on in the late 1980s, some at country estates like Longleat and Weston Park, and others in Central London, with the express intention of allowing public school boarders to party alongside members of the opposite sex. Taylor's co-organiser was 'Fast' Eddie Davenport, better known within aristocratic realms as 'Lord' Edward Davenport, a socialite and property developer. He was also a convicted fraudster, receiving a seven-year jail sentence in 2011 for his part in a series of schemes that had conned millions of pounds out of his victims.

This wasn't the last that the newspaper-reading general public heard of Colston-Hayter, either. In 2014, he pleaded guilty to being the leader of a group which had hacked into the main computer system of Barclays Bank and embezzled £1.3 million from its funds. Still with a taste for high living, he is also reported to have stolen the bank cards of 24,000 customers, which he used to purchase luxury goods at Harrods and Selfridges.

The man from the Ministry

The public schoolboy network cropped up to play another highly prominent part in UK clubland when the era of the UK superclubs dawned. Ministry Of Sound opened in September 1991 in a former warehouse complex in a grim corner of South London, modelling itself on New York City's legendary Paradise Garage, where resident DJ Larry Levan had transformed that city's nightlife scene in the 1970s and 80s. The individual behind MoS came from an unlikely background for a clubland boss. This was James Palumbo, the grandson of an Italian immigrant who had made his fortune in property development, and the eldest son of Baron Peter Palumbo. James himself has since taken the title of Baron Palumbo of Southwark, and is reckoned to be among the 400 richest people in Britain with an estimated £130 million fortune. (I find it bleakly amusing that narcotics kingpins who operate in clubland are referred to as 'drug barons,' given Palumbo's forays into the world of nightlife!) After an education at Eton and Oxford, he became a City of London merchant banker. Palumbo Senior and Junior fell out over the alleged withholding of a trust fund, which saw the two communicate only through lawyers for many years.

Palumbo co-founded Ministry with Justin Berkmann, the son of wine aficionado Joseph Berkmann, who acted as its artistic director and resident DJ, and was apparently the influence behind Ministry's modelling itself on the Paradise Garage. Also involved was a fellow Etonian, Humphrey Waterhouse. In a newspaper interview, Palumbo stated: "I wasn't so interested in the dance music scene, but it was beginning to take off in Britain and the project seemed a sound commercial proposition."

Ministry was an instant hit with clubbers, to the point that soon after opening, reports emerged of how its door staff had been infiltrated by gangland drug dealers. In a 2009 interview with the 'Daily Mail,' Palumbo told how he had taken to wearing a bulletproof jacket to work and carrying a stun gun for protection. On the club's early reputation as a drug den, he stated:

> *"At the height of its popularity, ecstasy sold for £15 a pop and some clubbers took two, three or even four pills in one session. With more than 2,000 people in the club on a Saturday night, the drug profits were astronomical – I estimated they totalled about £50,000 a weekend. And there wasn't anything club owners could do about it. Why? Because security would kill you."*

Palumbo eventually fired the door staff involved and says he lived in fear of retaliatory drive-by shootings. The club took to bussing in door staff from Birmingham each weekend, because no crews from London would take the job.

Working with police, Palumbo claimed to have eventually driven the dealers out, and boasted that Ministry was the only drug-free club in Britain. In keeping with its cleaned-up image, he struck up an alliance with Tom Sackville, the Home Office minister responsible for club licensing. Palumbo recalls that: "The resulting legislation gave the police summary powers to close drug-infested venues. Ministry of Sound was cited in the parliamentary debate as the example of best practice."

From the start, the brand's logo was a distinctive coat-of-arms featuring what appears to be a disco ball fashioned from a portcullis, and topped by a crown. From a standalone nightclub venue, the brand expanded to encompass record and CD compilations, a long-running magazine, and merchandise such as bomber jackets, hats, T-shirts and record bags. The Ministry of Sound Recordings spin-off is said to be the largest independent music company in the world, and was sold in 2016 to the Sony Music Group for $104 million. Clubs have also been opened under the Ministry franchise worldwide. The London spot itself has survived a handful of attempts to have it either closed down in the wake of violent events, or to be demolished to make way for urban development.

Palumbo was a close associate of Tony Blair's Labour Party kingpin 'Lord' Peter Mandelson, (known to holiday at the Corfu home of banking tycoon Baron Jacob Rothschild,) and is reported to have given Mandelson the use of a chauffeur-driven car for the 1997 General Election campaign. (Incidentally, Labour's official theme for this was itself a clubbing anthem in the form of 'Things Can Only Get Better' by the group D:Ream, the early keyboardist for which was one Brian Cox, who went on to become the BBC's go-to man for all matters connected with Astrophysics – even though most of what he spouts on such matters are provable lies. He's a professor, you know. I'll leave readers to look up the meaning of 'ream' in urban slang for themselves, meanwhile.)

Palumbo earned himself the nickname 'Prince of Darkness' in his university days, a title he shares with Mandelson. A 1997 profile in 'The Independent' newspaper referred to him as "a man who is reported to have the ear of the Blair administration on matters concerning young people." Palumbo's political leanings seem complicated; having also fraternised with various Tory MPs, he is now a Liberal Democrat life peer. He ceased running Ministry several years ago, but retained a majority stake in the business.

Given Palumbo's unconventional nightlife credentials, his background, and some of the individuals with whom he is known to fraternise, a suspicious onlooker might conclude that there's more to his establishment of London's most prolific club than meets the eye. Could the naming of the Ministry brand, with its connotations of government, have been a clue as to what it was really all about?

Everything starts with an E

My first book, 2007's 'Tales From The Flipside,' is not what could be called a conscious read, written as it was when I was still in the fog of a mind-controlled trance. It did, however, include some observations which remain relevant to this day – and particularly to this story:

> *"A big clue as to how far drug and dance culture had merged, could be seen in nothing more complex than the opening times of the big dance superclubs. As early as 1990, like the Northern soul clubs before them, most were staying open until 6 or 7 in the morning where licences allowed, and were still rammed at closing time. That much stamina from natural energy and dance-induced adrenaline? (The same suspicions may well arise from 'marathon' DJ sets that are frequently advertised. Junior Vasquez began one at New York's Tunnel club in 1995, for example, where he played non-stop from 11pm Saturday night to 2pm Sunday afternoon every week!)*
>
> *"E-culture became an accepted part of clubbing through the 90s, and nowhere was this more apparent than in the pages of the UK's most consistently popular dance music publication, 'Mixmag,' which aims at an average readership age of 18. Regular cover features with titles like . . . 'Are Drugs Driving You Mad?,' 'Jellies: The Mong-out Menace,' 'Ecstasy: Scared?,' 'Paranoid? You Should Be,' '1993: Year Of The Trip,' 'The Good Comedown Guide,' and 'Taking The Piss: Drug Testing At Work,' summed up the kind of lifestyle the magazine knew its readers were into, and through which it was able to connect meaningfully with them."*

And later . . .

> *"In November 1995 the party came to an abrupt stop. Teenager Leah Betts from Essex collapsed and died after necking a single ecstasy tablet at her 18th birthday party . . . The DJ world has had its occasional victim, too. Liverpool's Mark Johnson collapsed in January 1995, for instance, following a gig at the city's Voodoo club, and died shortly*

afterwards in hospital aged just 22. He had apparently taken an E. Incredibly, in 1996 came the news that clubbers could now take out £100,000 worth of insurance against the risk of dying or being permanently disabled from taking ecstasy and other drugs, courtesy of a London firm, offering the deal for £15 a year – the price of an E!"

One of many renderings of the pre-Acid House Smiley; as an emblem of the Watchmen graphic comic series.

https://www.flickr.com/photos/dannybirchall/6391786127

Credit: Danny Birchall

The dark side of the Smileys

A smiley yellow face has come to be regarded as the iconic emblem of the late 80s scene, and synonymous with the widespread necking of ecstasy pills that accompanied it. The face was etched into certain batches of the actual pills themselves, and it adorned countless flyers from that period. It was weaved into the second 'o' of Danny Rampling's Shoom night on its flyers and membership cards, being made to look like an ecstasy pill with the slogan 'Happy, happy, happy . . .' Commenting on his use of the emblem, Rampling explained:

> *"I picked up on the smiley face logo from a fashion designer called Barnsley. I ran into him one night when he was covered in these smiley face badges and I thought, 'Wow! That's it!' The smiley face completely signifies what this movement is all about – big smiles and positivity."*

An entire fashion industry grew up out of the scene, with T-shirts and hoodies all sporting the same motif. Its history and continued usage, however, casts a very dark and unsettling shadow on the story.

The symbol gained widespread usage in the American advertising industry in the early 1970s, as society attempted to shake off the doom and depression of the ongoing Vietnam War with more optimistic outlooks on life. By the mid-80s, however, some more sinister overtones were present, as it had become a central motif in the 'Watchmen' graphic novel series created by British animator Alan Moore. The stories feature a psychopathic killer known as The Comedian, along the lines of The Joker of the Batman stories. In the 2009 Hollywood film version, The Comedian sports the smiley yellow face on a badge. Just as he's about to get murdered he exclaims that life is just a big sadistic joke that only he understands. It's a satanic and nihilistic mindset – the idea that in the cosmic scheme of things, human life is ultimately pointless – and it's one that appears to lie within the doctrines of Chaos Magick. Indeed, in the opening lines of 'Onion Peelings' from Aleister Crowley's 'Book of Lies,' we find: "The Universe is the practical joke of the general at the expense of the particular, quoth Frater Perdurabo, and laughed." Moore himself has admitted to being an occultist with a fascination for the works of both Crowley and Dennis Wheatley. He has stated that he incorporated references to Crowley's teachings in his 'V for Vendetta' story, and the first date given in 'The Watchmen,' 12th October, is Crowley's birthdate.

Here, we get some links back into the music industry as the spin-offs and connections start to get out of hand, so bear with me as I dart around from place to place, as is necessary sometimes. Alongside the likes of William Burroughs, Timothy Leary and Kenneth Grant, another artistic type who openly espoused Chaos Magick teachings, (which involves the use of occult sigils,) was the musician, artist and video director Peter Christopherson, known by the nickname 'Sleazy.' Christopherson directed videos for artists ranging from Rage Against The Machine to Soft Cell, (whose frontman Marc Almond was a member of Anton La Vey's Church Of Satan.) He was also a part of the experimental/ avant-garde groups Throbbing Gristle and Psychic TV alongside Genesis P-Orridge, (real name Neil Andrew Megson) and Geoff Rushton, known as John Balance.

Psychic TV became active on the Acid House scene in its formative years. A side project was Thee Temple ov Psychick Youth (sic) (known as. T.O.P.Y.,) intended to be a magic(k)al order and a vehicle for the members' occult ideas, and with smiley face emblems never far from the surface. Megson was accused of sexually abusing children in a 1992 British TV documentary, but cleared by the subsequent police investigation, at which point he relocated to New York and began espousing transgender teachings. Christopherson was also part of a design agency called Hipgnosis, which worked on cover art for acts such as Pink Floyd and Led Zeppelin, and formed the band Coil, heavily influenced by the teachings of Crowley. Christopherson is reported to have died in his sleep in Thailand at the age of 55 in 2010. Six years earlier, his partner Balance, (ironically, considering his name,) is said to have accidentally fallen to his death from the balcony of the home he shared with Christopherson.

Anyway, back to the smiley. A couple of years after the first 'Watchmen' comics, the emblem – complete with the trademark bloodstain from the series – appeared on the sleeve design to Bomb The Bass's cut-and-paste track 'Beat Dis.' Bomb The Bass was the alias of DJ/ producer Tim Simenon who was born in South London on the Summer Solstice of 1967. A more relevant date for the original 'Summer of Love' would be difficult to find. A few years later, the smiley had become heavily associated with the DJ/ producer Norman Cook, aka Fatboy Slim. Many of his promotional photos show him interacting with the image in some way; in one he has a yellow smiley bingo ball in his mouth. Cook was married for many years to BBC Radio 1 presenter Zoe Ball, the daughter of BBC TV children's entertainer Johnny Ball. In more recent times, celebrities such as Miley Cyrus and Selena Gomez have been pictured sporting the smiley on their clothing. The emblem also makes a cameo at the very start of the video to David Bowie's swansong 'Black Star,' appearing on the spacesuit of the dead astronaut assumed to be Major Tom.

'The Watchmen' was not the only fictional rendering of the smiley in disturbing circumstances, meanwhile. The US police drama 'The Mentalist,' which ran from 2008 to 2015, had a plotline involving a serial killer named Red John, whose calling card was to leave a smiley face design at the scene of each of his murders. It also gets a rendering in the British TV series 'Sherlock' starring Benedict Cumberbatch. In the first episode, Holmes gets a can of yellow paint found at a crime scene, and uses it to spray a smiley face on his living-room wall. It appears in every subsequent episode.

The smiley face's association with violent death in fiction, seemed to foreshadow and mimic reality in even more unsettling circumstances, meanwhile.

Over the past twenty years, more than 50 young men have been abducted and murdered in more than 25 of the US states. The crimes have come to be labelled as the Smiley Face Killings. Their geographical spread suggests they are the work of a co-ordinated group, rather than one crazed individual. The victims have all been adult males of college age, usually athletic and high academic achievers. They are usually last seen on their way home from drinking at bars or parties. Their bodies turn up, sometimes weeks or months after they disappear, immersed in water – primarily rivers, creeks or lakes. Smiley face emblems appear in the vicinity of the bodies, usually daubed on to trees or walls in paint. In the case of one victim, a smiley face appeared out of nowhere on his tombstone.

There are signs that the co-ordination of these killings could extend beyond the US, meanwhile. Throughout 2016 and 2017, a series of disappearances of young men occurred across Britain in very similar circumstances, the bodies always turning up in water. The murders have attained very little by way of mainstream media coverage, and seem to have been treated by police as a series of random crimes, rather than a connected series. The American author and investigator William Ramsey has done much research into the strange aspects of these murders. A full-length documentary is forthcoming at the time of writing; in the meantime, short videos examining the cases can be viewed on his William Ramsey Investigates YouTube channel at: https://www.youtube.com/channel/UCHbi5KDNq7OMaptZ_JnQmlw

Is there far more to the smiley face than an apparent symbol of 'happiness?' While it may have been adopted naively at certain points along the way, is it also a deep-rooted expression of dark sigil magick at the hands of a network of occultists, who take regular opportunities to place it in the public eye, often in morbid, mocking fashion? And could its adoption by Acid House be just one of many such outings?

Our man at the BBC

Of all the DJs who were present in the British dance music breakthrough, none has experienced such phenomenal levels of success as Pete Tong. From humble beginnings as a mobile DJ, cutting his teeth on the soul and funk scene of the South East, Tong advanced his broadcasting career through Kent's Invicta Radio, through three years at Capital FM, to become a favourite of the BBC. His earliest appearances on Radio 1 involved delivering a dance music report on Peter Powell's daytime show from 1981, followed by some occasional shows on BBC Radio London. In January 1991, Tong was hired as the host of Radio 1's Friday night 'Essential Selection,' and he has remained at the station ever since, now its longest-serving presenter after Annie Nightingale. Tong was never a key instigator of the Acid House sound, and was absent from the big transformative raves. But he was in the right place at the right time to become the most recognisable figurehead for the emerging dance music culture generally.

In tandem with his DJing career, Tong has also worked as an industry executive, running the FFRR imprint of London Records, and with many other interests, investments and consultancies. As far back as the late 90s he was reported to be a millionaire. A leading dance magazine in 1999 proclaimed: "Dance music is bigger than ever, Pete Tong is bigger than God." These days, he's frequently referred to as a 'gatekeeper' for the dance music scene, the status of 'Essential New Tune' on his Radio 1 show having the power to shape an artist's entire career, and with the word 'legendary' rarely being absent from his biographies. As a long-running radio jingle voiced by the rappers Salt 'N' Pepa always proclaimed: "Pete Tong got power." But just how did he come to get so much of it? The writer of this blog has some ideas of his own: http://anonymous-ibiza.blogspot.co.uk/2014/04/pete-tong-illuminati.html

Tong has stood alone in surviving every single cull of specialist DJs at Radio 1; as the likes of Danny Rampling, Judge Jules, Dave Pearce, Fabio & Grooverider, Seb Fontaine, Fergie, Lottie, Tim Westwood, Gilles Peterson and Trevor Nelson have come and gone, Tong has remained immovable. He has spoken of how he was commissioned as a consultant by panicking Radio 1 bosses when the station was losing street-cred in the 1990s, and it was his advice that caused the aforementioned names to be brought on board. But Eddie Gordon, a DJ, club manager and music journalist from Tong's old stomping ground of Kent, who went on to become his manager and agent, speaks in his on-line biography of how Tong has claimed credit for many of the achievements for which he, Gordon, was in fact responsible. As he states:

> *"On Wikipedia, though, he keeps deleting 'his' history, embellishing it with lies. For example, Steve Wolfe came up with the now infamous phrase "It's all gone Pete Tong" one Sunday night at Invicta Radio during Tong's weekly soul show when the studio phones all rang at the same time for tickets to a weekender competition. But on Tong's history, it was Mark & Lard on Radio 1. Total rubbish!*
>
> *"... My very important chat with my main client Jeff Young, the departing BBC Radio 1 DJ, about passing the baton on to Pete to protect the ground-breaking work he had established on the national*

> *radio station, was indeed an essential bit of work for Mr. Tong's career!"*

In 2014, Tong attended a ceremony at Buckingham Palace to receive an MBE from Prince William. These 'accolades' are given to recognise contributions to British culture and ways of life. Curious then, that it was given at a time when Tong had departed Britain to base himself in Los Angeles, (more on this in the following chapter.)

By the time of Tong's MBE, the extent to which the dance scene that had apparently evolved out of that small Acid House community in 1987 had changed British youth culture, had been reflected in the opening ceremony of the London 2012 Olympics, where ravers brandishing glowsticks and adorned with luminous smiley faces had been beamed into living rooms throughout the land.

Superstar DJs

As the early scene gave way to the open-air festivals – then to the massive, purpose-built club nights – the role of the DJ morphed from that of a straight record-spinner and tastemaker, to an evangelist for a new movement that was as much a ritual for Saturday night clubbers as church the following morning would be for their parents' generation. Prior to 1987, scraping together enough of a living to pay the rent was challenge enough for the majority of DJs. Those who specialised in a genre, such as Soul, Hip-Hop or Reggae, were restricted to playing small clubs, pubs or community centres for pocket money. By a decade later, many had become millionaires, living a jet-set lifestyle previously only reserved for rock stars, supermodels or socialites. Although a few seem to have got lucky by jumping on the gravy train, the majority were key players who had been active during the scene's breakthrough years and had ridden the crest of dance music's wave. Judge Jules joined Radio 1 from Kiss FM bringing a rapidly ascending career trajectory. Norman Cook, formerly a member of the student indie band The Housemartins, re-invented himself as a dance music producer under many different aliases including Pizzaman, Beats International, Freak Power and The Mighty Dub Cats. By far the best known, however, was the Fatboy Slim persona mentioned earlier, a guise under which he released a handful of successful chart hits, and is now considered by many as the ultimate British superstar DJ.

Of the four young Ibiza adventurers, meanwhile, Danny Rampling's heroic reputation off the back of Shoom saw him much in demand as a DJ and beatmaker, and after some years at Kiss FM, he moved over to Radio 1 in 1994 to begin his celebrated 'Love Groove Dance Party' show. Apparently burned out, he announced his retirement from DJing in 2005, but a couple of years later seemed to have regretted his hasty decision, and was right back on the circuit again.

Paul Oakenfold enjoyed a secondary career as an in-demand remixer and producer, establishing his own Perfecto Records label, (whose early motif was, interestingly, a hand displaying the 'OK' sign, which, as discussed in Volume 1, has a secondary meaning as a rendering of the number '666.') Following a period as a much-hyped resident at Liverpool superclub Cream, and having played a DJ gig on the Great Wall Of China, he relocated to the US, where he began working on Hollywood film scores and took a residency in Las Vegas, paving the way for that city to become a new epicentre for electronic dance music. Where Siegfried & Roy and Elvis Presley had drawn crowds before, now dance music's titans were doing the same. Another feather in Oakenfold's cap was producing the theme music for the surveillance-normalising 'Big Brother' TV show back in Britain.

Nicky Holloway followed The Trip with a new club venture, The Milk Bar in London's Soho. He later went bankrupt and battled with alcoholism to the point that he was forced to attend rehab clinics. Of the four, Johnny Walker's subsequent career is the most subdued. He opted to leave the fast life of the DJ game to set up his own garden design business in Spain.

Besides DJs and producers, the dance music explosion saw the formation of groups capable of playing live shows and festivals – previously the domain only of fully-fledged bands with instruments. In place of guitars, the new wave of acts had keyboards, synths and samplers. Names like The Prodigy, Orbital, The Chemical Brothers, Underworld, Left Field, KLF and Faithless went on to fill stadiums and sell out tours, and countries throughout Europe – then the rest of the world – followed the UK's example, spawning their own electronic communities. The sonic landscape for the youthful generation had been changed forever.

And that, presumably, was the plan.

Resources:

Thump article: What Really Happened To Acid House?:

- https://thump.vice.com/en_us/article/luke-bainsbridge-Acid-house

The Guardian: The Birth Of Rave: An Interview with the founders of British Acid House culture

- https://www.theguardian.com/music/2007/aug/12/electronicmusic

The Guardian 2008: A Second Summer of Love:

- https://www.theguardian.com/music/2008/apr/20/electronicmusic.culture

Wikipedia: The Harmonic Convergence:

- https://en.wikipedia.org/wiki/Harmonic_Convergence

Danny Rampling DMC Magazine interview 2014

- https://www.youtube.com/watch?v=GzTnrfv9nRs

The Independent: Passed/Failed: An education in the life of Paul Oakenfold, DJ and producer:

- http://www.independent.co.uk/news/people/profiles/passedfailed-an-education-in-the-life-of-paul-oakenfold-dj-and-producer-319036.html

Some classic Acid House flyers:

- https://uk.pinterest.com/pin/112590059411334107/

- https://uk.pinterest.com/Rduzzi/classic-rave-flyers-and-parties-Acid-house-to-ware/
- Vice.com: Thatcher's War on Acid House:
- https://www.vice.com/en_uk/article/8gvp5x/margaret-thatcher-war-on-rave-acid-house-boys-own

The Guardian: 'The hippie dream is still alive': how Ibiza went from techno to boho:

- https://www.theguardian.com/music/2017/sep/08/how-ibiza-went-from-techno-to-boho-aniwa-gathering

Sunrise/ Back to the Future on Wikipedia:

- https://en.wikipedia.org/wiki/Sunrise/Back_to_the_Future

Tony Colston-Hayter: the Acid House fraudster :

- https://www.theguardian.com/uk-news/2014/jan/15/tony-colston-hayter-Acid-house-fraud-barclays

Daily Mail: How I risked my life kicking the drug gangs out of my club, by Ministry of Sound boss James Palumbo:

- http://www.dailymail.co.uk/news/article-1195900/Bouncers-turned-club-Ministry-DRUGS--I-risked-life-drive-out.html

The Independent: James Palumbo/ The Man From The Ministry:

- http://www.independent.co.uk/arts-entertainment/the-man-from-the-ministry-1291579.html

Thump: The Shamen's Mr C Talks Disco Biscuits With His Old Mate Ebeneezer Goode:

- https://thump.vice.com/en_uk/article/4xmxz3/mr-c-interviews-alter-ego-ebeneezer-goode

Alan Moore, Freemasonry, and Aleister Crowley on Pop Culture:

- https://www.veteranstoday.com/2013/06/21/alan-moore-freemasonry-and-aleister-crowley-on-pop-culture/

A Design For Life: The History of The Smiley Yellow Face:

- https://www.theguardian.com/artanddesign/2009/feb/21/smiley-face-design-history

William Ramsey Investigates: Smiley Face Symbolism in Film and Culture:

- https://www.youtube.com/watch?v=rHPcCwTIt9Y

New Dawn Films: The Smiley Face Killers – The Award Winning & Horrifying Documentary Feature Film:

- https://www.youtube.com/watch?v=rD3c1RSLeFo

CHAPTER 2

ELECTRONIC EVANGELISM

Mind control and social engineering through Electronic Dance Music.

"This is where I heal my hurt, for tonight, God is a DJ . . .
This is my church."
Faithless: 'God Is A DJ' (1998)

"Take me into insanity,
Yeah, dream tripping, yeah,
That's where I wanna be,
That's where I wanna be."
Oceanic: 'Insanity' (1991)

"There's a rainbow inside my mind,
There's a rainbow inside my mind.
. . . Injected with a poison,
Are you listening to me?"
Praga Khan: 'Injected With A Poison' (1991)

Tried and tested

Since the massive explosion of electronic dance music in the US – which I would pinpoint as happening around 2007/ 08 – all the same signs and symbols that had previously cropped up in the videos, promotional pictures and stage shows of pop puppets such as Lady Gaga, Katy Perry, Ke$ha, Rihanna and Beyonce – and so-called "Hip-Hop" stooges like Kanye West, Lil' Wayne, Jay-Z, Nicki Minaj, Drake and the like – were getting seen in the output of the prominent dance DJs and producers. They were all there – pyramids, all-seeing-eyes, the covering of one eye on the face, the '666' sign, the 'Baphomet' horned hand, black-and-white Freemasonic duality, dolls, teddy bears and broken mirrors, (all covered at length in 'Musical Truth 1'.) All are indicators as to which names are now part of the club. And it's a safe bet that, in the majority of cases, the artists have been instructed to flash up the signs by the director of the video or their record company handler, rather than doing so through personal choice. In the case of graphics inserted into videos, the artists would most likely be oblivious to their presence until they get to see the final cut along with the rest of the public.

Just as with acts such as the aforementioned – and more recently, the likes of Robin Thicke, Bruno Mars and Justin Bieber – there are clues as to the point in the careers of many successful dance music names where they were given a helping hand up the ladder of success by those that can make these things happen. From that point on, their careers went stratospheric.

Many commentators have found it intriguing how French DJ-turned-producer David Guetta grafted away on the Paris club scene for many, many years, until – very quickly – he started working with artists such as Akon, Kelly Rowland, Rihanna, Chris Brown, Lil' Wayne, Snoop Dogg, Nicki Minaj and Usher, scoring international smash hits with every one. Guetta became arguably the most prominent DJ/ producer in the EDM field at the time the corporations were beginning to combine House music productions with vocalists from the R&B/ Hip-Hop scene, creating a homogenised sound for the commercial market as a result. ('EDM' is recognised as a genre in its own right, its boombastic, 'big room' sound characterised by the likes of Guetta, Calvin Harris, Swedish House Mafia, Steve Aoki and Afrojack, and is distinct from 'electronic dance music' – an umbrella term that encompasses everything from Hard House and Techno, through Trance, Drum & Bass, Dubstep and Garage. In short, any music made with a club dancefloor in mind. Other key players in the EDM transition have included Avicii, Tiesto, Armin Van Buuren, Chucky and Will.i.am.)

The video for Guetta's 'Who's That Chick,' featuring Rihanna, is an A-to-Z of Illuminati symbolism, featuring everything from Monarch butterflies to pentagrams to Transhumanist overtones, (with the vocals all drenched in the abominable Auto-Tune to complete the effect.) Few videos manage to cram as much occult imagery into four minutes.

Guetta took to pushing a highly Messianic image at the time of his career blast-off. Sporting long hair and a beard, he would frequently appear on stage illuminated, and holding out his hands in a Christ-like pose. DJs had gone from straight record-spinners to quasi-religious leaders, controlling the spiritual and conscious state of the assembled throng from their vantage point of DJ booth-turned altar. The group Faithless seemed to have pre-ordained this phenomenon back in 1998 with their track 'God Is a DJ.'

Talking when he guested on my 'Good Vibrations' podcast in 2015, Irish DJ/ producer and host of Alchemy Radio, John Gibbons, observed:

> *"It is a form of control in a sense, in that you are – through your actions or through the music that you play or make – able to manipulate a crowd or a mass body of people, according to what you want them to do or how you want them to feel. So if you have nefarious aims – or if you have good aims – you can transfer that to a large, large body of people."*

And on the sudden success of certain key players:

> *"Now, the big stars are starting to appear overnight in dance music, which never happened. You could always chart a DJ's or a producer's career, and they started off at a smaller level, and they'd work their way up the ladder. And it was almost like the last bastion in popular music that had remained organic. You're seeing huge numbers of really, really young DJs and producers just appearing overnight."*

Dutch producer / DJ Martin Garrix, (real name Martijn Gerard Garritsen,) is a great example of this process. Apparently mentored by Dutch EDM titan Tiesto, Garrix's single 'Animals' appeared in 2013, immediately shooting to the top of the charts in several countries, becoming a worldwide dancefloor smash, and making him the youngest person to ever reach the number one spot on Beatport . . . all at the tender age of 17. In 2016, Garrix topped the 'DJ Magazine' Top 100 DJs poll, (widely considered the ultimate arbiter of a DJ's success,) beating many long-established veterans old enough to be his grandfather. The same year, he changed his logo from one simply rendering his name in a scrawl, to one featuring a Greek cross and a saltire. Honestly... how many teenagers make it that big that quickly just through working really hard and keeping their fingers crossed for good luck?

It was a similar scenario with another Martin. As his accompanying promotional blurb admitted:

> *"Martin Jensen has become one of Danish music's greatest viral success stories, with more than 3 million likes on his Facebook page, and a staggering 600 million views on his videos so far! He appeared out of nowhere in the beginning of 2015... His next massive single, 'Solo Dance,' has already entered UK Shazam's Top 200 within minutes!"*

As John Gibbons adds:

> *"... It comes down to contacts in a lot of cases, and if you can be introduced to the right person at an early age, well then, you're far more likely to succeed. And within music, that's much, much easier, because there's no raw talent needed within the music industry any more. Absolutely none! It doesn't matter if you don't have a singing voice, if you can't produce a track, if you don't know how to DJ. All of that can be done for you. You can be put on stage and you can "rock that crowd," no problem. Paris Hilton is a DJ! And that says everything you need to know about how easy it is to become a DJ now in the technological age. There are hugely talented and skilful DJs out there – loads and loads of them. However, for the guys who are in that final one per-cent, whether they have talent or not is actually irrelevant.*
>
> *"Why are we seeing so many Swedes and so many Dutch emerging in dance music? Yes, there's a work ethic that doesn't exist elsewhere in the world, and we see that throughout business with regard to the Swedes and the Dutch. However, there are also well-connected schools of people... I mean, everybody at the higher level of dance music from Holland seems to now be based in LA... Everyone is starting to reside over there, and it's not just because it's a good base for gigs or*

whatever, it's because that's where the strings are being pulled from. And of course, it's beneficial to have your artists close at hand – much easier to control."

(Paris Hilton, incidentally, fits the model of Monarch Programming mind-control subject down to a tee. See Vigilant Citizen's many articles on this sub-division of MK-Ultra and its connections to the world of celebrity at www.vigilantcitizen.com)

Signs of the times

Besides the videos, with some dance music producer and DJ icons, clues as to the set they may now belong to can be found in the vector logos which they use to promote themselves; whenever they appear on an event poster or festival line-up, their name is rendered in this way. Carl Cox, for example, now employs a logo which looks similar to two winged sun disks of Egyptian mythology, usually in black and white with red edges. (From his beginnings in Soul and Funk, moving through the Rave scene, it was through his embracing of Techno that Cox made an international name for himself. This is a genre which has contained more than a few subliminal hints at Transhumanism. Cox's landmark album, 'F.A.C.T,' stands for Future Alliance of Communication and Technology.) The capital 'A' of Afrojack's logo appears very similar to a pyramid, as do the two capital 'A's in both Paul Oakenfold and Calvin Harris' official branding. (A separate frequent rendering of Harris sees him wearing mirrored sunglasses – another motif associated with mind-control programming.) The three blobs of Swedish House Mafia's motif look like a combination of fingerprints and bullet holes.

Armin Van Buuren's personal logo seems straightforward enough. But the two versions used for his A State of Trance brand have strong Saturn overtones. ('A State Of Trance' has two meanings, of course – as well as implying a trance-like condition, it can also be taken to mean a nation state placed under the influence of a trance. Is this a subtle clue as to the music's true purpose? And wasn't 'Trance' an interesting name to be adopted for that genre in the first place, given its power to affect the consciousness of large numbers of people?) Armin's artist pseudonym, under which he has released tracks with collaborator Benno De Goeij, is Gaia, the name of the Mother Goddess of Greek mythology.

Swedish producer Axwell's image bears more than a passing resemblance to an inversion of the United Nations logo, featuring a capital A (pyramid?) inside an upside-down heart surrounded by two olive branches, while Tiesto's is a phoenix-like bird rising in flight, with three notches carved into the top part of the 'e'.

One of the graphics used by French duo Daft Punk, shows two cyborg heads connected by a chaotic tangle of wires. Transhumanism 101. From the start, Guy-Manuel de Homem-Christo and Thomas Bangalter have dressed in robotic garb with inhuman-sounding vocals to match, (very much in the style of German synth pioneers Kraftwerk before them,) and frequently perform inside a giant pyramid.

More of the same now occurs with dance music's big brands in the events field. Few can top the designs for Electric Daisy Carnival which now runs several events around the world, including a UK one in MK, (Milton Keynes, not Ultra.) This has an owl as its central motif – a bird that has many associations with the occult, mysticism, the underworld and the keeping of secrets, and one popular among musicians. Drake, Justin Bieber and Skylar Grey all sport owl tattoos. The logo for Mexico City's Orus Fest shows a giant pyramid hovering like a UFO over the Bermuda Triangle, complete with engraved sigils and a Masonic all-seeing eye, (nothing to see here, please move along.) Other events with artwork which raises more questions than answers include the Australian Babylon, with its dystopian future designs and 'A New World Is Coming' subheading, Alfa Future People, merging mysticism with Transhumanism and a couple of globes, and Denver's annual Brainwash With Beats event, which pretty much speaks for itself. (Denver Airport, incidentally, is an interesting place to research in itself while we're talking about Illuminati and New World Order symbolism, as this Vigilant Citizen article reveals – http://vigilantcitizen.com/sinistersites/sinister-sites-the-denver-international-airport.

Fingerprints of the spooks

Like Guetta, Paul Van Dyk is another interesting DJ/ producer to examine. From his early years carving out a name for himself in his home city of Berlin, Van Dyk, (real name Matthias Paul,) gained international prominence off the back of his track 'For An Angel,' which remains a staple club classic to this day. He has always been notable for his apparent abstention from the drug-taking habits of many of his DJ peers, quipping once when asked about the spelling of his name that "there's no E in Paul Van Dyk." Although international gigs and regular album releases followed, towards the end of the 2000s, his career seemed to take another jump of several notches up the ladder of success. He topped the 'DJ Magazine' Top 100 DJs poll for two years running, and his solo shows – where he 'creates' tracks live besides playing recordings – now take place in massive arenas, sports halls and live music venues with tens of thousands in attendance. He was absent from the scene for over three months in early 2016, after apparently falling from rigging at an A State Of Trance gig in the Netherlands, and suffering concussion and broken ribs. After a long period of hospitalisation, Van Dyk returned to touring in June of that year. A few months later, he wed his Colombian girlfriend in what was his second marriage. He is well-known for his apparent interest in political issues, having named one of his albums 'The Politics Of Dancing.'

Van Dyk has been pictured throwing up the 'horned hand' sign at many gigs – a gesture which is innocently written off as meaning 'I love you,' but which holds a different meaning among dark occultists, where it represents the entity known as Baphomet, (see 'Musical Truth 1' and many of the articles at www.vigilantcitizen.com.) For several years, Van Dyk has employed a very striking sigil in his promotional artwork, and colossally-sized projections of it are shown above him at events. This appears as an inverted triangle, apex pointing downwards, with two smaller triangles – or pyramids – fashioned into the upper corners. To promote his 'Evolution' album, the sigil appeared as a crop circle design in a large field. I puzzled for months over the meaning of this emblem, always drawing a blank. I then stumbled across the official logo which the British Military Intelligence organisation MI5 used from the 1950s to the 1970s. When Van Dyk's triangle is turned upwards so the apex is pointing to the sky, it takes on a striking similarity to the MI5 sigil, complete with the cut-out corners. (The MI5 logo adds a capstone with an all-seeing eye inside for good measure.)

From humble beginnings in warehouses and fields, to a colossal worldwide phenomenon in youth culture. Can such a movement really happen organically and under its own steam?

https://upload.wikimedia.org/wikipedia/commons/c/c7/Colombian_Party_Cartel._Photo_by_Ellen_Ord%C3%B3%C3%B1ez_for_Colombian_Party_Cartel.jpg

Credit: Ellen Ordonez

But it doesn't end there! The artwork advertising Japanese DJ/ producer Steve Aoki's '3oki' project in 2014 – which saw him releasing three recordings over three weeks, (a Masonic 33?) – featured his profile inside the exact same pyramid employed by MI5 decades earlier, complete with the capstone and eye, and giving off rays of illumination. What possible connection should there be between an antiquated emblem for British Intelligence, and those used to promote a German and a Japanese dance music producer, unless all three components are somehow tied to the same agenda, and we profane ones are being given subtle clues so it's not as if we weren't, in some way, told?

Although they at first appear to be widely unrelated, the worlds of military-intelligence and the rituals of the dark occult are often interlinked, and where you find one you find the other. Intel agencies are not just about keeping secrets on matters of spying and surveillance, but also sequestering information on an occult basis, which those controlling things wish to keep accessible to only a chosen few. Ceremonial magic(k)ian Aleister Crowley worked for British intelligence services during both world wars, and many researchers claim his main contact for a period was James Bond author Ian Fleming, who was a naval commander. Lt. Colonel Michael Aquino, meanwhile, held key positions in the US military at the same time as establishing his own Church of Satan spin-off, the Temple of Set. And a common factor binding these two worlds is mind-altering drugs. These have been used by the intel community for social experimentation on countless occasions, and are a staple part of many occult rituals, bringing about desired energetic shifts through having the participants reach chemically-fuelled altered states of consciousness.

Reflecting on the weaponisation of compounds that *could* be used for spiritual upliftment if taken in the right circumstances – but which bring more nefarious results when their consumption is on the terms of malevolent experimenters – author and researcher John Vibes commented:

> *"Psychedelics are tools that can be used for good or bad, depending on the direction and intent. The negative aspects of psychedelic use and psychedelic culture come from a lack of education. And I think people who do get positive experiences from these substances have somewhat of a responsibility to educate newcomers. That definitely didn't happen in the 60s, and it's sadly not happening in rave culture today."*

The titles of the dance events and festivals at which Van Dyk has been a headliner in recent years are interesting in themselves. The likes of

Dreamstate in California, Trance Nation and Luminosity in the Netherlands, Velvet Hypnotized in Bali, Atlantis in Australia, Spring Awakening in Chicago, Awake in Dresden, Awakening Fridays in LA, Dream Beach in Spain and Delirium Eternity in Argentina, all have spiritual and esoteric overtones. Electronic Family, Digital Society and Toronto's Digital Dreams all hint at electronic ways of doing things being the new norm for humanity, while Tomorrow World in Atlanta, Tomorrowland in Belgium, Future Music Festival in Australia and New Horizons in Jakarta all evoke the Futurist society which is known to be in the plans of the United Nations Agenda 2030 architects. The wording of the events Global Dance and Global Clubbing Nation speak for themselves.

Let's not forget Miami's Ultra Festival (as in MK?) And could Van Dyk's own event brand, We Are One, be taken as a subliminal reference to a one-world government? In 2017, Van Dyk began dropping references to ETs and aliens into his Tweets, a picture from one of his events featuring an inflatable Roswell-style 'grey' among the gathered throng. Additionally, phrases such as "welcome to the future" and "this is the future" began appearing in the promotional blurb for his upcoming gigs. Why has the song lyric "and I see your true colours shining through" just popped into my head?

The strange appeal of La La Land

The Disco music which gave birth to Soulful House emerged largely out of New York and San Francisco. Much credit for the ushering-in of the former's scene has been given to the invitation-only parties hosted by David Mancuso in his Broadway apartment, known as the Loft. The first of these was on Valentine's Day 1970, and was titled Love Saves the Day, (where have I come across those initials before??) Mancuso's Loft sessions also seem to have operated as some kind of communal living experiment, and he turns out to have had an association with the omnipresent Dr. Timothy Leary. As Tim Lawrence, author of the book 'Love Saves the Day: A History of American Dance Music Culture, 1970–1979' writes:

"The psychedelic guru Timothy Leary, who invited David to his house parties and popularised a philosophy around the psychedelic experience that would inform the way records were selected at the Loft, was another echo that resonated at the Broadway Loft. Co-existing with Leary, the civil rights, the gay liberation, feminist and the anti-war movements of the 1960s were manifest in the egalitarian, rainbow coalition, come-as-you-are ethos of the Loft."

As the years progressed, House music styles began emerging from Chicago, with Techno from Detroit, and Go-Go Funk from Washington DC. The genre which has come to be known as EDM, meanwhile, migrated from Europe directly to Los Angeles. As John Gibbons pointed out, many dance music artists, producers and DJs have moved there to be at the heart of the action. We're back to veteran BBC asset Pete Tong, who now pre-records his weekly show for Radio 1 remotely. As noted previously, Tong's career as a radio and club DJ went stratospheric following his LA relocation, well into his fifties. He scored a new show on the iHeart Radio network syndicated all over the US, along with headline slots at the world's major dance music festivals. As the biography on his official website puts it:

"Having spent the majority of his life in England, Pete has recently resettled in Los Angeles to begin a new chapter in his life: 'The electronic dance music scene in the USA has reached a critical mass, and the opportunities for our world are taking us into uncharted territory. I feel now it's essential to be in the middle of all that.' Tong has wasted little time in establishing himself in the US, having helped inaugurate Clear Channel Entertainment's Evolution dance brand in 2013, and recently expanding the programming to the extended two-hour segment, 'The Evolution Beatport Show with Pete Tong,' broadcasting on 90 different Top 40 stations in the US."

Tong is frequently cited as an "ambassador" to dance music, and few individuals have wielded such influence and corporate control over the genre. His co-founding of the William Morris Electronic booking agency sees him presiding over, in his biography's words, "one of the most powerful booking agencies in the world."

(In a bizarre, but probably entirely unrelated story, meanwhile, in 2011 Tong had to take out a restraining order against Shara Nelson, the vocalist on Massive Attack's evergreen 'Unfinished Sympathy,' after he demonstrated to a court that she had been systematically stalking him, telling his colleagues that she was his wife, his manager and the mother of his child!)

For a time in the late 2000s, Tong staged a number of events under the brand Wonderland, (Wonderland Avenue is one of the key routes through LA's fabled Laurel Canyon district.) A handful of recent gig photos show him sporting a Mickey Mouse T-shirt. As detailed in the previous book, the Mickey Mouse emblem is used as a symbol for the presence of mind-control. Pictures also exist of him wearing shirts in the black-and-white checker designs detailed elsewhere. Tong's Twitter page describes him as 'the Pied Piper of Dance,' which is an interesting choice of phrase given that the Pied Piper of the famous folk tale led a community's children away from their parents by placing them in a trance through music. As the late author Dave McGowan pointed out, Laurel Canyon had been a key location for the characters who shaped the music and mindsets of the counter-culture in the late 1960s. A couple of generations on, the same city's districts have become the setting for another big social shift.

Emily Moyer is a researcher, and co-host of the 'Off Planet' TV and radio shows in California, as well as a veteran raver and club dancer. The Pied Piper-like lure of her hometown, she says, comes as no great surprise. There are aspects to the city which get missed in the dazzle of its glossy sheen and perfect toothpaste smiles.

> *"There is something very different about Los Angeles . . . It became clear that what had been going on in Laurel Canyon specifically, was being mirrored in these underground dance parties that I would go to in Downtown Los Angeles, and then being amplified at these larger clubs and festivals, in the same way they were being amplified at Woodstock and the festivals they were having in the 70s.*

"One of the things about Los Angeles is there's a massive, massive underground structure complex. I personally think there is a complete other world underneath Los Angeles county. There are lots of canyons in LA that all have very strange sub-cultures – not bad necessarily, but their own unique sub-cultures living in them. There's Laurel Canyon, there's Topanga Canyon, there's Coldwater Canyon, several of them. I think these provide particularly unique opportunities to experiment within an enclosed location, a little private community.

"But also, I think there's something going on with frequencies in these places, because when you're in any of them, there's no cell phone reception. And when you think, Los Angeles is a huge city with lots of people living there, they would have figured something out about that by now. But they're trying to use other kinds of frequencies to affect people's minds, and they wouldn't want them to be interfered with by anything.

"And then theres what's going on with some of these warehouse parties. I go to these, and some of them are very high-quality events. And I've noticed over the years that we're being observed. These are smaller events with everyone in one room. It's the perfect environment to go and see how people respond to certain frequencies, to experiment with the use of psychotronic weaponry. Some of these events are geared around having really amazing sound systems and really amazing visual shows. These affect people in a particular way. And if people are interested in how to use these to accomplish a goal, they can just go and observe these events and watch how people behave when certain stimulants are introduced.

"So you have 100 people in a room all being pounded by a bath of sound and light. Which can be pleasurable, but it can also be dangerous. The difference between dance music and all other forms, is that it is completely based in different layers of frequency.

"There's a reason why they're so interested in this music. We know that sound and light can be used for healing, but it can also be used for control . . . You can have a transformative experience from this sort of

music and scene, but if we don't take ownership of this, then you're going to have the kind of transformative experience that they want you to have. That delivers you into a New World Order of sorts.

"Or are we going to take control of this and become completely aware of what's going on in our scene and in the world, and use our transformative experience to help change the world? Which one is it going to be? It's time to decide."

Burns night

An event with possibly more occult overtones and a more unusual air than any of the others, is the annual Burning Man Festival. This occurs each Labor Day weekend at the specially-constructed Black Rock City in the Nevada desert. This is former, (or is that "former"?) military-owned land with restricted airspace, four hours' drive from the next town. (A number of early British raves also took place on government or military-owned land – you know, because the Establishment care about us and just want us all to have fun.)

Although it's primarily billed as an 'arts' festival, music acts do perform at Burning Man, and names from the dance world in recent years have included Carl Cox, Skrillex, Tiesto and Diplo. Its climax sees the giant effigy of a human set on fire, in a scene which puts me in mind of both 1973's unsettling British horror movie 'The Wicker Man,' and the Cremation of Care ceremony conducted at the annual 'elite' meeting at California's Bohemian Grove.

Steve Outtrim is a New Zealand IT professional who spent some time working in California's Silicon Valley. He is the proprietor of www.burners.me, the largest independent website discussing Burning Man and the shenanigans surrounding it. Steve states that, within the computer and tech industry, it is almost an expectation that its key players will attend.

"The first I heard of it was from the 'Hot Wired' mailing list, and then 'Wired' magazine put it on the cover. I was in a meeting in

Sydney in about 1997, with quite a high-level executive from SUN Micro Systems, a big computer company spun out of the Stanford University Network, just like Google. And back in the day they were a major military and defence contractor, and this guy, the chief science officer, said, hey, do you go to Burning Man? He was a guy in his 60s, highly respected, a guy that's met presidents and prime ministers all over the world, and I'm like, wow, he knows about Burning Man? What's going on with this thing? I have to go!

"I first went in 1998. Once you've been there more than ten times, you start to look at things a little differently as the initial novelty starts to wear off. I started my blog as a huge Burning Man enthusiast, but as I did more and more research about what's really going on there – the organisation behind it, the occult elements, the military/government elements – I became a little bit more cynical."

California's IT industry, in fact, has many throwbacks to the counter-culture scene of the 1960s. Many of that era's hippies went on to found or join tech companies, the idea being that they took some of the maverick free spirit ethos that earlier scene had spawned with them. As ever, there seems to be rather more to the story. 'Cybernetics,' a name for the early computer industry, was a major component in the series of Macy Conferences which took place at various locations in New York from the 1940s, where 'elite' social scientists, psychologists, anthropologists and propagandists gathered to plan the future shaping of culture. The Cybernetics concept was an early forerunner of today's Transhumanist movement, being planned decades in advance.

Steve has guested a handful of times on the Gnostic Media podcasts to give his take on the mind-control significance of Burning Man. You can access them all via this URL – http://www.gnosticmedia.com/?s=steve+outtrim.

Suits you, Sir

As mentioned in 'Musical Truth 1,' DJs have now started getting knighthoods in the UK, which would have been inconceivable 20 years ago.

Pete Tong followed in the wake of fellow Radio 1 broadcaster Annie Nightingale, who had picked up hers back in 2002. Old-guard reggae legend David Rodigan became 'Sir David' two years before. (Rodigan is the son of an Army sergeant-major, in yet another military family connection to the world of music, and was a stage actor before his DJing activities took off.) Tong and Rodigan have both inducted their offspring into the DJ game. Becky Tong is now a spinner and record promoter, while Jamie and Oliver Rodigan now perform as beat-makers, the latter under the name Cadenza. Notting Hill Carnival mainstay Norman Jay got his MBE in 2002, as did BBC Radio 2 and 1Xtra veteran Trevor Nelson. Soul II Soul pioneer Jazzie B picked up his OBE in 2008. Graffiti artist-turned Drum & Bass hero Goldie accepted an MBE in the 2016 New Year's Honours, in an act that appears to fly in the face of the rebellious, edgy image he had always projected, (although he later threatened to melt it down in protest at Islington Council's decision to shut down seminal London nightclub Fabric. But didn't.)

This process is not exclusive to the UK, either; Dutch Trance DJ-turned-producer Tiesto was appointed Officer of the Order of Orange-Nassau, (the formal name for the Netherland's order of chivalry,) by Queen Beatrix of Holland in 2004. Fellow Dutch DJ Chuckie, who originally hails from Suriname, was made a Commander in the Order of the Yellow Star by that nation's president. Another Dutchman, Armin Van Buuren, was hired to perform at the 2013 coronation of Willem-Alexander, the king of the Netherlands, with the royal family appearing on stage to shake hands with him.

Commenting on this phenomenon on 'Good Vibrations,' John Gibbons observed:

> *"There was nobody being handed MBEs and OBEs and honours and Sirs and knighthoods, and this, that and the other back in the early days. Why? Well, because I think these honours are handed out in recognition of a job that has been well done for the control system. I don't think that those who receive the honours – in the vast majority of cases – are in any way cognisant of that being the case. And if you look at the symbolism behind some of these honours . . . A good example are US military honours, the Medal of Valor. The symbolism, if anyone*

> *cares to delve into that – basically, it is the control system occultists mocking those that they are supposedly honouring, and it's their way of saying, 'well, we own you, we control you, you're our dogs in the street and you have done our bidding.' And the people accepting these honours don't know that that's what's going on.*
>
> *"Look at the police. It's the most in-your-face one. Look at what they're wearing. Why do police forces all over the world use the same symbolism? Why do we see the chequerboard floor, which represents base consciousness, if anyone cares to delve into the mystery schools – Freemasonry, Rosicrucianism? The hat which is covering up the crown chakra, or the 'third eye,' that symbol of consciousness – that's a form of occult mockery! It's saying, 'we have you shut down to the base level whereby you do our bidding.' And then look at what it is the police are asked to do on a daily basis. Well, it all suddenly makes sense when you look at that with any kind of rational mindset. It's not because these patterns look pretty. They're there for a reason."*

For an advanced study on the occult mockery of the police, military and other government-employed personnel, a thorough absorbing of Mark Passio's comprehensive video presentation comes highly recommended. You can watch it here – https://www.youtube.com/watch?v=0Jtg2AGu0ow

Harnessing an ethos

The control which the big corporations now exert over every aspect of the dance music scene, is a scenario about as far removed from the original spirit of Acid House as it's possible to get. Whereas those early days spawned cottage industries – with mavericks expressing themselves in activities from flyer designs to T-shirt fashions – the current situation echoes the consolidation now present in all areas of business. A great British example comes from the radio station Kiss FM. Originally appearing as an 'illegal' pirate in South London in 1985, under the helm of its visionary head Gordon MacNamee, the operation assembled a team of DJs passionate about communicating their love of Soul,

Reggae and Hip-Hop, and frustrated at the lack of legal opportunities to do so. Voluntarily coming off air on New Year's Eve 1988, the station beat several others in its bid to obtain a legal licence from the British government's Radio Authority, and began broadcasting as Kiss 100FM on 1st September 1990. For its first few years, Kiss retained its original ethos and generated a large listening base. Inevitably, this attracted the attention of the corporate world, which wants to steer and control anything which achieves success under its own steam.

The publishing conglomerate EMAP took control of Kiss, resulting in its rebranding in 1998, and the departure of MacNamee as its managing director. The output had moved away from authentic black music to more commercially-viable dance styles. Kiss operations were relocated from its Holloway Road home to EMAP's corporate HQ in Central London. Radio stations in other UK regions were subsequently branded with the Kiss name and shared syndicated programming. Kiss's listening app is referred to as the Kiss Kube, which becomes interesting when you factor in that Saturn – a favourite emblem of the satanic control system – is frequently symbolised by a cube.

Further consolidation followed, to the point that the various facets of the Kiss operation are now owned by the collossally-sized Hamburg-based Bauer Media Group. (Bauer was the original name of the Rothschild banking dynasty back in Germany, as a matter of interest, before Mayer Amschel Bauer created the new family name.)

From a free-spirited local labour of love, to an asset on a German corporate balance sheet. Just another day at the office.

Absolute power

As explored in my 'Good Vibrations' episode on the subject, there are parallels between comments made by John Todd in the 1970s, and the contemporary status of electronic dance music. Todd, (also known as John Todd Collins and as Lance,) hailed from a long-running family of witches, and was ushered into prominent positions in the US music industry. Famously – and at great risk to himself – he broke ranks, became a born-again Christian, and recorded a now-legendary monologue in which he detailed some of the dark occult practices routinely employed by the corporations, (covered in Chapter 17 of 'Musical Truth 1.') He stated that Zodiac Productions, of which he was general manager, was then the largest music conglomerate in the world, owning RCA, Columbia, Motown, and almost all the concert-booking agencies in the United States. In turn, Zodiac is said to have had ties to Chase Manhattan, Standard Oil and Lloyds of London.

Canada's Joel Zimmerman, performing as the EDM titan Deadmau5. Anyone who has studied the symbolism associated with mind-control programming will find the choice of headpiece mighty interesting.

https://upload.wikimedia.org/wikipedia/commons/6/61/Deadmau5_d.jpg

Credit: Deadmau5

The speech in question is available here – https://www.youtube.com/watch?v=Otti-82jEAc&t=28s

The transcript of a separate taped interview apparently made by John Todd Collins, meanwhile, is available here – http://www.beyondweird.com/occult/jtc1.html

This absolute control of several aspects of the industry in the hands of just one umbrella corporation, came to be echoed in the dance music realm in the 2010s by SFX Entertainment. This operation emerged out of bankruptcy at the end of 2016 to become Lifestyle Inc., under the leadership of former AEG Live chief executive Randy Phillips. Prior to this, however, SFX described itself on its website as follows:

> *"SFX Entertainment Inc. is the largest global producer of live events and digital entertainment content focused exclusively on electronic music culture (EMC) and other world-class festivals. SFX's mission is to provide electronic music fans with the best possible live experiences, music discovery, media and digital connectivity. SFX was borne out of the technology revolution, and produces and promotes a growing portfolio of live events that includes leading brands such as Tomorrowland, TomorrowWorld, Mysteryland, Sensation, Stereosonic, Electric Zoo, Disco Donnie Presents, Life in Color, Rock in Rio, Nature One, Mayday, Decibel, Q-Dance and React Presents, as well as the innovative ticketing service Flavorus. SFX also operates Beatport, the principal online resource for EMC DJs, and a trusted destination for the growing EMC community to discover and stream music, follow DJs and keep abreast of news, information and events, in addition to offering year-round entertainment to EMC fans around the globe through other digital assets."*

As Emily Moyer observed during SFX's final weeks:

> *"So, here you have control of everything. And the guy who owns SFX Entertainment is Robert Sillerman. And this is what he does. Earlier in the 2000s he went and bought up a load of different concert companies, sold them to Clear Channel, and did the same kind of consolidation. But this is what he had to say about his company – 'I know nothing about EDM,' Sillerman told Billboard in September 2012. 'I really don't. Of course, I listen to it and I understand its appeal. It's borderless, it's free, it's energetic, it's a party in your mind, and I understand that. But I sit in the meetings and I meet the people whose places we're buying. And I haven't a fucking clue what they do or what they're talking about. Not a clue. And I love it. I just love it.'*

"And to me, that is just disgusting. And while he may not be the kind of evil hand we're talking about, he's the kind of tool that the controllers need to get hold of this whole situation.

"So they own all of these festivals which used to be owned by individual promoters, who ostensibly at one point, had control over their events. Sillerman now owns all of that. He owns the ticketing service that you buy all the tickets to the events from. So they're able to monitor and surveil you from the time you start looking into buying the tickets, to the time you go to the festivals.

"This article that I was quoting from was also talking about how they had acquired something called Periscope, which provides merchandise for these kinds of events, and sells at any place that those people who like electronic music culture would buy merchandise. So you have the front end and the back end.

"And the most disturbing thing, I would say, is you have the ownership of Beatport, which is an on-line mp3 record store which almost all DJs buy the bulk of their music from because it has the largest catalogue, it's centralised, and you can store the stuff there. They often have Beatport stages at these events using their own technologies. So you have the centralisation of the music. And this happened when DJs went from playing vinyl records to playing mp3s off their computers."

(The irony of a periscope being a device for covert below-the-radar spying is not lost on me, incidentally!)

"I would suggest that . . . not only is there something happening with the frequencies being changed, but that this provides the perfect avenue to put a 'spell,' or a charge on every single piece of music that comes through there. It would not surprise me if tracks – when they're taken from independent labels to be sold through Beatport – are being run through some kind of technology, similar to what John Todd was taking about regarding putting a hex on the master tapes of recordings. I would suggest that there's technology now where they can do the same thing. I think it's entirely possible that information is being

> *embedded in these frequencies, and maybe even visual images being piggy-backed on the sound frequencies."*

This reverts back to the other part of what Todd talked about regarding his time in the music industry. It was standard practice, he said, for the master tapes of a new recording to be brought to the 'temple room' which each of the major corporations had within their headquarters. A coven of witches would be brought in to place a spell on it, the idea being that each copy then taken from the master and sent out into the general public, would be imbued with the signature dark energy of the original, because everything happens on an unseen, frequency level.

It seems the practice may not have died out with that decade, either. In a 2014 interview with host Popeye on his 'Down The Rabbit Hole' radio show, Frank Castle of the Hip-Hop/ Rock fusion act HeistClick, revealed that he had seen a similar room in a modern corporate HQ. (Incidentally, at her presentation at the 2016 Free Your Mind Conference, author and researcher Jeanice Barcelo claimed the California porn industry has a similar practice of placing hexes on the masters of the movies it creates. You can watch that talk here – https://www.youtube.com/watch?v=3Kt1-GBPcpU. And, along still similar lines, in 2012, the UK's 'Daily Mail' reported that John McAfee, founder of the McAfee anti-virus computer software, had taken to having Wiccan witches perform drumming rituals at his company HQ, as a way of infusing his product with some of the resulting energy.)

If hexes cast on to recording tape is what was happening decades ago – and the same forces are still controlling corporate music output – how much more sophisticated might practices have now become with the advent of digital technology?

Ravers reflect

There were some very incisive comments from those posting to a thread on the David Icke on-line Forum a few years ago. Whatever anyone may or may not think about Icke himself is irrelevant here, as the detached, everyday perspectives that regular punters have are often far more profound than the views of seasoned professionals. With that in mind, a handful of former ravers contributed the following array of comments, and many of them touched on the idea that electronic music – at a frequency level – may have been having an undetected effect on the crowds who were absorbing it – often in a chemically-altered mind-state:

> *"When the music got more and more hardcore, some of it used to make me feel like it was trying to take over my mind. Not sure how to explain the feeling, but I remember being at a rave and not liking what the beat was doing. The whole scene gradually got more and more aggressive."*

> *"Do you think you started feeling 'creeped out' when the beats mapped themselves in your brain for a reason? I do. I think music can be used to amplify the dimensions from which it is created. If you make music with evil thoughts, give it evil rhythms, it will produce evil vibrations. In the case of rave music, there are so many different varieties of ambient, house, and other genres in the electronic scene. It is very hard to put a label on the types of music which may be seeking to crawl inside the listener's brain and give them a hardwire into some alien type of consciousness, but it says a lot that some people can actually feel the music doing this.*

> *"Knowing what I know now, I think that it might have been part of some massive energy extraction, as the love and belonging and the feeling of being something special was almost spiritual."*

> *"In New York when I used to go in the early to mid-90s, there were a lot of UFO and space-themed parties. One famous weekly party was called NASA (Nocturnal Audio-Sensory Awakening) at Shelter. After reading the Laurel Canyon articles, I really wonder who was behind some of these parties."*

> *"Very interesting. I noticed an agenda in Australia in the 90s to get peeps off the streets and other activities, and into clubs and raves, with no shortage in supply of pills. Since I was under-age and not inside on E, that's why I began to notice it. Those outside would get hassled by The Man until they went home, or into a club. It got me thinking."*

The following comment seems to be key in assessing how the experiences of ravers seemed to differ; while some claimed the sound frequencies in conjunction with the drugs caused them to expand their consciousness in ways which improved their life no end, others seem to have had an altogether darker and more destructive experience. There continue to be frequent accounts of paranoid psychosis and schizophrenia being attributed to the regular ingesting of E, like LSD before it.

> *"I think with your first point you're right, and some will have started with the rave scene to open more doors in the mind and grow, without even knowing it at the time. And while that was happening, they just had fun with it.*
>
> *"There's also a lot of people not in that place. I knew a few people who went rapidly downhill and ended up quite poorly in all ways due to raving. I've also known people who have been in the scene, walked away OK, and are so far away from questioning anything around them it's scary. It's all about perception and where people are at on their journey, I guess.? . . . I wonder if, for every person who has walked away from the scene with positive memories, there is another who has really suffered because of it. But hey, the Powers That Be aren't going to be worried about the 'fallout' of a small percentage of people who start to question. Not when they have their 'suffering' or 'distraction lovers' to balance the mix. They have met their overall objective, whatever it may be.*
>
> *"The raves going legal and organised brought a different vibe, and things changed. The organised gangs are the street soldiers for the Masons, if you ask me, and the classic trick with the government is to take out the competition and get their own versions of the drugs in, which is exactly what seemed to be going on here. Regards the overall agenda – yes, ecstasy can you make you feel good. But what goes up must come down. What was it doing to our serotonin and pineal gland long-term? And perhaps some of this music was specifically designed to fuck with our brainwaves and subvert consciousness, as discussed with rock music, for example."*

There were some particularly deep considerations from the poster known as 'Separ.' (The 303 he refers to is the Roland TB-303 synthesizer, the staple component of early Acid House productions, and there's more on many of the points he raises in Chapter 6.)

> *"There is always something or someone leeching energy at these events. However, regarding demonic influence, this is something that can also be present. It's not in the beats but in the tonal qualities of the music. If you have the wrong type of distortion, you can have odd-order harmonics entering into a sound you like and are tuned into, and this can be the diabolical tritone. Whenever you have this, or a discordant rhythmic layer in the sound, it messes up the body's bio-electrical networks. This overloads the sensorium and destroys neurons, hence causing the feeling of a loss of control ('music taking over.')*
>
> *"When it comes to these discordant overtones, Rave music is more guilty than other genres. The 303, for example, is a transistor-based saw-and-square generator, and the filters on that thing generate mostly odd-order harmonics. You can listen to it for only a short time before it becomes painful, (unless your pain receptors are numbed by drugs).*
>
> *"Those people who went to raves in the 90s were undergoing a kind of 'formatting' to transform them into a different form of life: outwardly, the same as everyone else, but inwardly, their synaptic pathways were changed permanently. The reason why they went voluntarily to these raves was because of a combination of future-shock syndrome, and because their vibration level had become fixated at a certain point and they could not move beyond it easily."*

A poster by the name of 'Iztac,' suggested that modern-day raves could be coercing clubbers to tap into primal states that lie at the very heart of the human experience:

> *"In every ancient culture, song, (mostly drums,) and especially dance, were present at every ceremony. Music and dance, (and sometimes certain sacred plants,) would take people into a receptive state of*

mind where they could commune deeply with nature's consciousness and with their people. Aztecs, for example, called that state of being 'centiliztli' – 'becoming one' as an approximate meaning. Ancient religions everywhere in the five continents share strikingly similar common traits, and one of them was their encouragement of collective trance states.

"... What if raves are a way to prevent many potentially highly energy-aware, spiritually-oriented individuals, from getting in touch with actual spirituality? 'They' appeal to our genetic memory and collective subconscious, and provide an analogue experience to those our ancestors had with drums and dance. The difference is that we are given synthetic drugs, (put in the market by intelligence agencies,) and are exposed to (Tavistock?) engineered hypnotic music, with the purpose of locking many of us into addictive trance states that would divert our energy away from rebellion, creativity, reflection and true spirituality, (not New Age crap or 'religion marketing.') And why not offer the energy we produce to a given spiritual entity?"

In the same way that different human bodies seem to have wildly disparate reactions to certain diets – meat is deadly to some, while a vegan diet seems to be devastating to others – it seems biological reactions to chemicals are equally diverse. If the tidal wave of pills were largely launched at the hands of the social engineers, were the positive experiences merely considered to be collateral damage in an agenda devised with nefarious aims? Or did the controllers really have no idea how the big picture would play out, and the rave generation was being used as a community of lab rats in another giant social experiment?

As Matthew Collin writes on page 294 of 'Altered State:'

"But if no-one really knew what ecstasy did to the body, how could they quantify its effects on the mind? This was, after all, a chemical which had been popular among therapists for its ability to break down psychological barriers. What would happen when huge numbers of people took huge amounts of it for years on end? Would those defences crumble for ever? Each successive generation of initiates

developed its own oral history of mental deterioration, of ecstasy casualties 'losing it,' having nervous breakdowns, being institutionalised, even committing suicide. Were these just people who were halfway to insanity already, and the long, sleepless weekends had simply pushed them over the line? Was the drug itself to blame? Or was it just a way to explain away the inexplicable?"

The following thread from Reddit comes recommended for further, similar insights, meanwhile. (Googling 'Reddit strange happenings EDM festivals' saves inputting the whole clunky URL:)

- https://www.reddit.com/r/conspiracy/comments/36xkrd/strange_happenings_regarding_edm_festivals_raves/

The birth of Molly

Wikipedia describes MDMA as follows:

"3,4-Methylenedioxymethamphetamine (MDMA,) commonly known as ecstasy (E,) is a psychoactive drug used primarily as a recreational drug. Desired effects include increased empathy, euphoria, and heightened sensations. When taken by mouth, effects begin after 30-45 minutes and last 3-6 hours. It is also sometimes snorted or smoked."

The US got its influx of ecstasy late compared to the UK, and it seems to have been the Hip-Hop world which first embraced it. This was at odds with that genre's traditional association with cannabis. Key corporate asset Dr. Dre popularised weed with his ground-breaking album 'The Chronic' in 1992, and there were many more odes to the green stuff with Snoop Doggy Dogg's Dre-produced 'Doggy Style' album the following year. By the end of that decade, however, Dre and the artists he directed had started dropping namechecks for MDMA into their recordings. Its title leaving nothing to the imagination, 'Let's Get High,' from Dre's own 1999 album 'The Chronic 2001,' included the line: "Yeah, I just took some ecstasy. Ain't no telling what the side-effects could be." In an interview from earlier the same year with 'Rolling

Stone' magazine, Eminem described the process of assembling his debut album, 'The Slim Shady LP,' with Dr. Dre as:

> *"I wrote two songs for the next album on ecstasy. Shit about bouncing off walls, going straight through 'em, falling down twenty storeys. Crazy. That's what we do when I'm in the studio with Dre. Dr. Dre on E? Ha ha!"*

Commercial Hip-Hop's first reference to ecstasy, however, seems to have come two years earlier when Notorious B.I.G. rapped: "Some say the X makes the sex spec-tacular" on the track 'Fucking You Tonight' with R Kelly from his 'Life After Death' album. ('X' is American slang for ecstasy.)

A Playboy Bunny, one of many themed batches of Ecstasy pills. Where did they all come from?

https://upload.wikimedia.org/wikipedia/commons/thumb/f/f9/Playboy_Bunny.jpg/765px-Playboy_Bunny.jpg

Credit: Psychonaught

In 2001, Missy Elliot put out another provocatively-titled album called 'Miss E: So Addictive,' which included a track called 'X-Stasy.' As the 2000s progressed, MDMA namechecks became as much a staple of Hip-Hop lyricism as bling, booty and bitches. At some point, the pure form of MDMA used to make ecstasy, picked up the nickname of 'Molly', referring to the drug in its powdered or capsule form. Rick Ross boasted of putting Molly in a girl's champagne glass so she would pass out allowing him to rape her, on the Rocko track 'U.O.E.N.O.' Classy.

Where did all this E/ MDMA suddenly come from? How can it just appear so widespread on a scene overnight – and with every major rapper signed to a corporate label namechecking and endorsing it – if not part of a co-ordinated plan, with the full complicity of record labels, the police and the intelligence services? If law enforcement were really interested in stamping out these 'illicit' substances, (the 'War on Drugs,') why would they not introduce legislation to prevent the record companies from including lyrics promoting that lifestyle to kids?

It appears that Hip-Hop's corporate puppets were being used to popularise MDMA under its new 'Molly' guise, ready for it to be moved across to electronic dance music at the point that it exploded in the 2010s. French-born producer Cedric Gervais took things to the next level with his 2012 track 'Molly,' with its repeated refrain: "And I can't seem to find Molly, Molly, Molly, Molly, Molly, Molly, Molly, Molly, (fucked around and fell in love with her.)" Aspects of Gervais' biography become interesting at this point, in terms of how he came to be in such an influential position to release the track. His father owned a nightclub in the South of France. As his entry on the Resident Advisor website states:

> *"Cedric Gervais has had an extraordinary life. As a young teenager, Cedric, who is originally from Marseilles, headed to St Tropez. There he got a summer residency at the famed Papa Gaio club. He was only 14 years old, not even legally old enough to party with the people he played for... Cedric pleaded with his father to take him out of school so he could concentrate on DJing. His father agreed, and, as is customary in France, went to the local courts to put Cedric's case forward. Then at just 15 years old, and not speaking any English, he*

> *decided Paris wasn't challenging him enough musically, so he packed up and moved to Miami. This was at a time when an exciting movement within the club scene was happening... Cedric saw this opportunity and jumped in."*

Gervais, (real name Cedric DePasquale,) is also an actor, having featured in Hollywood productions such as 'Patriot's Day' and 'Deepwater Horizon,' which reinforced the official narratives of the Boston Marathon bombing and the Gulf of Mexico oil spill respectively.

Never missing an opportunity to court controversy and further the programmes of those who tell her what to do, meanwhile, Madonna – by this point well over 50 years of age – used her appearance at 2012's Ultra Music Festival in Miami to ask "how many people in this crowd have seen Molly?" as she introduced the artist Avicii. Although the crowd cheered in knowing unison, her comments brought the apparent scorn of the Canadian EDM artist Deadmau5, (real name Joel Zimmerman,) who feigned disgust by Tweeting: "Very classy there, Madonna . . . such a great message for the young music lovers at Ultra." Given that Zimmerman's gimmick at his performances is DJing with a massive Mickey Mouse-style head fixture, however – as blatant an indication of corporate-sponsored mind-control as you can get – one could be forgiven for concluding that his move was just as contrived and manufactured as Madonna's.

Madonna herself was not finished, however. Around the same time, she announced that she was dropping the vowels from her name, temporarily becoming MDNA in an obvious further reference to the drug she had been commissioned to promote.

Who let the pills out?

Clubbers and social commentators all have their views on who, ultimately, was behind the influx of ecstasy into both the British and American dance scenes. Although the foot soldiers are easy to identify, pinpointing those who may be employing them becomes a much harder task. It's difficult to prove that personnel from military intelligence and social engineering think tanks were flooding the market – it wouldn't be a terribly successful programme on their part if they could be rooted out so easily – but it can certainly be seen that the results emanating from its widespread use are any social experimenter's dream.

One intriguing aspect of E is that pills appeared in branded batches, with their own logos inscribed. An extremely high-profile one in the British clubs of the 1990s was known as the Mitsubishi, adorned as it was with the motif of the car manufacturing giant. 'Doves' were also extremely popular in the early days, (a 1995 'Independent' article claimed that manufacturers were spiking them with everything from LSD, to fish tank cleaning powder, to dog-worming pills.)

These engravings may have been a way for the suppliers to track where pills from specific batches ended up in the market, and of gauging which ones – perhaps each with slightly different chemical constituents – became the most popular. Among other well-received variations were Nokias, Clovers, Red Triangles, Green Triangles and Heaven's Gates. Former pill-poppers differ in their recollections of their chemically-induced experiences. For every raver full of misty-eyed nostalgia for wonderful days, proclaiming the spiritual enlightenment and sense of freedom their drug-taking brought them, it seems there'll be another whose experiences were far less fun. Might the reasons for these differences go beyond simply the different personalities of the individuals involved? Could the quality of a 'trip' be affected not just by the components of the pill, but by the sigil engraved on it? As discussed in the last book, symbols carry energetic signatures and can be charged with the will of those creating them – all happening on an unseen level, but very real nevertheless. Factor in certain parties who may not necessarily have the personal welfare of those necking the pills as their top priority, and suddenly the story takes on new possibilities.

As John Gibbons considers:

> *"This is mass-produced stuff. People can say, well, it was all covert, and they all just got away with it. Who just got away with it? Because I would argue that the government just got away with it, and people who we perceive to be in control . . . they know what's going on, and they allow things to go on based on what serves their agenda. I don't think there's any doubt that there was – at the very least – some form*

of experimentation at play, and it has led to what we see now with EDM, and with another strand being pulled into the bigger picture of entertainment and mass mind-control.

"That really does go in parallel with that first Summer of Love when people were taking LSD and it was all about freedom and love . . . I think it was almost like a testbed, or laying the foundations or the bedrock for the new form of mind-control as that evolved.

"These drugs, when they become so freely available, when they are mass-marketed – albeit through the underground – that has to be 'allowed' to happen. Because the authorities who have all this control, all of a sudden don't lose control of things when it comes to drugs. And particularly, when they want to carry out some kind of mass experiment . . . And there is a tendency for people to think that, because something happened 50 years ago, it wouldn't happen now. Well, of course it would happen now. So, if governments were capable 50 years ago of flooding the market with drugs in order to test how a population would react . . . well, of course they're willing to do it in the 1980s again, and they're willing to do it now."

The importance of ecstasy to the trajectory of the nascent dance scene in the UK was openly flaunted in its early days with no observable objections from the authorities. Flyers and ads for club nights were flagrant in their knowing use of narcotic lingo, and the naming of acts such as The Chemical Brothers, (earlier known as The Dust Brothers,) Luv Dup, Toxic Two, Smart Es, E-Zee Posse, Ellis Dee, Skin Up and Kicks Like A Mule left little room for ambiguity. Neither did certain song titles. Rozalla's 'Are You Ready To Fly?,' Bump's 'I'm Rushing,' Audio Adrenaline's 'Your Love Has Lifted Me Higher and Higher,' and Hyper Go Go's 'High' with its talk of 'touching the sky,' all came with a knowing wink. Praga Khan's 'Injected With A Poison' and Oceanic's 'Insanity' may have been more veiled portents. The Shamen's calculated inclusion of the line 'Es are good' into their number one hit single 'Ebeneezer Goode' has become a favourite clubber's fable.

For a short phase in 1991-92, UK productions sampled fondly-remembered children's TV programmes. The hook in The Prodigy's frantically-flying 'Charly,' was lifted from a 1970s public service TV ad about child safety, while Urban Hype's 'Trip To Trumpton,' (see what they did there?) and Smart Es' 'Sesame's Treet,' brought similar nostalgic flashbacks for the first generation of ravers. Was it just a novelty marketing gimmick? Or were these produced with the knowing intention of chemically regressing E-heads back to infantile states of mind? Was it a darkly mocking commentary on the loss of childhood innocence brought on by a new world of sin?

As many a raver will testify, the music made little sense to anyone who was not in a chemically-altered mindstate to synch their perceptions with the beats, samples and frequencies they were experiencing. The trump card trick of the Trance genre, which had emerged as the *de facto* 'big room' club sound of the mid-90s, was a strategically-timed breakdown, where the energy of the track faded away, only to build again gradually, eventually crashing into a glorious, intoxicating crescendo, mimicking the euphoria experienced in the brain as the pills do their thing and stimulate the serotonin and endorphins.

In 2016, meanwhile, came the story that an artist by the name of Chemical X – who was reported to have designed the Ministry of Sound's famous portcullis logo, and is said to have worked with Paul Oakenfold and Snoop Dogg – had created a range of artwork made of real ecstasy pills which he himself had cooked up in his laboratory. His website sells prints of each piece. One was a mural said to consist of 10,000 real pills. Although he reportedly moves his mobile lab around to avoid detection, the idea that he would be able to get away with in-your-face displays, if government authorities were *really* as interested in 'stamping out drugs' as they claim to be, is laughable – particularly as images of the works were publicly displayed at an Art Republic exhibition in London in 2013, before the curators axed it citing 'legal implications.' There is also the news that a graffiti artist named Dean Zeus Colman, who attended the Chelsea College of Arts, made a line of plaster sculptures of actual ecstasy pills.

Certainly, the US government seems to have fewer hang-ups about ecstasy than its British counterparts – at least officially – given that the

Food & Drink Administration, after years of lobbying from the Multidisciplinary Association for Psychedelic Studies, decided in 2017 to begin using MDMA in the treatment of medical conditions such as Post-Traumatic Stress Disorder. A study published in the 'Canadian Medical Association Journal,' went further by adding psilocybin mushroom and LSD to the mix, suggesting them as useful in treating addictions, anxiety associated with terminal illness, and depression.

Critics of the chemically-infused dance scene – most of them former ravers and drug-takers themselves – now talk of the false 'one-ness' that Es created. It was false, they say, because many pillheads are all 'loved up' when they're under the influence, but act like complete assholes the rest of the time. It's well-documented that the arrival of E in the late 80s, saw many British clubs full of thugs who would otherwise have been engaged in organised violence at football matches, instead hugging each other in their artificially-altered states. Many clubbers became addicted to the pills and to the scene, and couldn't enjoy themselves properly without them.

There may have been another element at play, too, considers Emily Moyer. Does E emasculate males and blur the lines between gender identification? Could that be part of the controllers' enthusiasm to have it everywhere at dance parties?

> *"One of the things I noticed about ecstasy early on, is that it feminised men. There's definitely been this push. I have no problem with anyone being gay, straight, transgender, whatever . . . if that's what they really are. But if we're being pushed towards something by the media, by the culture . . . I know guys who were always totally straight who, after years of doing ecstasy, were girlier than I am! I've seen people kiss people of the same sex at parties who would never normally do that if they weren't on drugs. I wonder if this is part of the softening-up of society – to blur the lines between masculinity and femininity? I call it the Chaos Confusion Agenda."*

When two worlds collide

A correspondent who e-mailed me in response to some of my public talks, identified herself as being of the generation that was in the sights of the culture-creators behind the 1960s 'hippie' scene. She grudgingly accepted that she and her peers had been used as unwitting guinea-pigs in a massive social experiment when – at the time – they all thought they were so free. As she commented:

> *"I believe that this dark agenda revolved around not only getting the 'best and the brightest' addicted to drugs and drink, loveless sex and of course Rock 'n' Roll, but that it was a carefully-crafted campaign to undermine us at the deepest level of our spiritual core. Complete dis-empowerment from which many of us are still reeling and – thankfully – bouncing back."*

In my last book's analysis of the 60s scene, I quoted a respondent to one of my YouTube videos as follows:

> *"What the 'hippie' movement, did was discredit the voice of the youth by the Establishment that was sending them to die in Vietnam. All their parents saw was a bunch of dropout stoners that didn't 'love' their parents, country or God. They were at worst demonic, at best, freeloading sex-addicted bums. And all the while, their children thought they were 'expanding' their minds, loving their fellow human beings and doing what's right.*
>
> *"They were tricked, lied to and manipulated by a power greater than they were able to understand."*

The above comment bears repeating here, because it's so similar in sentiment to a comment left on a forum recently by a raver from the Acid House scene:

> *"I remember as a young raver thinking I had found total freedom, love and acceptance, while I was hindering my chances of achieving any of those things long-term. I've since researched all of that, and*

> *came up against a lot of stuff that's made me reluctantly re-evaluate. I no longer see it as I did back then . . . 5,000 people on MDMA at a rave who thought they were expanding their consciousness through free expression, didn't realise that they were fully open to psychic attack and subliminal messaging . . . Seems I was not enlightened at all while my thoughts were totally contrary . . . "*

Anyone who didn't know these people were talking about two separate scenes, 21 years apart on opposite sides of the Atlantic, would swear they were addressing the very same event.

When it comes to social engineering and culture creation, it seems there really is nothing new under the sun.

Resources:

Good Vibrations Podcast Episode 098 – Emily Technobrat – The Hidden Side of EDM:

- https://www.spreaker.com/user/markdevlin/gvp-098-emily-technobrat

Good Vibrations Podcast Episode 066 – John Gibbons (Round 2) – The Manipulation of EDM:

- https://www.spreaker.com/user/markdevlin/gvp-066-john-gibbons

Gnostic Media: Steve Outtrim on the occult significance of the Burning Man Festival:

- http://www.gnosticmedia.com/?s=steve+outtrim

Steve Outtrim's comprehensive site on Burning Man Festival and its affiliations:

- https://burners.me/

Tomorrowland – The Demonic Love Festival Alive in America:

- https://www.youtube.com/watch?v=Kq31FC1GeZU

David Icke Forum: Reflections on the imagery on old rave flyers:

- https://forum.davidicke.com/showthread.php?t=69858

Cedric Gervais: From 'Molly' to 'Somebody New' (interview):

- http://www.thenocturnaltimes.com/cedric-gervais-molly-somebody-new-interview/

Urban dictionary: Molly:

- http://www.urbandictionary.com/define.php?term=molly

The Independent: 'Doves' that contain anything from LSD to cleaning powder:

- http://www.independent.co.uk/news/uk/doves-that-contain-anything-from-lsd-to-cleaning-powder-1603496.html

FDA Designates MDMA As 'Breakthrough Therapy' For Post-Traumatic Stress:

- https://www.forbes.com/sites/janetwburns/2017/08/28/fda-designates-mdma-as-breakthrough-therapy-for-post-traumatic-stress/#7c1873047460

Psychedelics Could Trigger A 'Paradigm Shift' In Mental Health Care:

- https://www.huffingtonpost.com/entry/psychedelics-mental-health-care_us_55f2e754e4b077ca094eb4f0

London Evening Standard: Bitter pill: gallery drops Ecstasy art:

- http://www.standard.co.uk/news/london/bitter-pill-gallery-drops-Ecstasy-art-8620421.html

Techno Station: This Art is Made From Real Ecstasy Pills:

- http://www.technostation.tv/Ecstasy-art/

SFX Entertainment corporate profile:

- http://www.insightpartners.com/companies/sfx-entertainment/

Pulse Radio: The Downfall of SFX:

- https://pulseradio.net/articles/2015/08/the-downfall-of-sfx-i-know-nothing-about-edm

Video: David Guetta Featuring Rihanna: 'Who's That Chick'?:

- https://www.youtube.com/watch?time_continue=89&v=EAc4zHEDd7o

Illuminati Watcher: Illuminati & Transhuman symbolism of Daft Punk:

- http://illuminatiwatcher.com/illuminati-transhuman-symbolism-daft-punk/

Popeye interviews HeistClick member Frank Castle on the dark side of the music industry:

- http://www.federaljack.com/down-the-rabbit-hole-w-popeye-09-02-2014-the-dark-side-of-the-music-industry-culture-creation/

Mark Passio: The Occult Mockery of Police & Military Personnel:

- https://www.youtube.com/watch?v=0Jtg2AGu0ow

CHAPTER 3

FOOL ME ONCE . . .

Social engineering, culture creation, and Lifetime Actors.

> *"We are governed, our minds are moulded, our tastes formed, our ideas suggested, largely by men we have never heard of . . . Our invisible governors are, in many cases, unaware of the identity of their fellow members in the inner cabinet . . . Whatever attitude one chooses to take toward this condition, it remains a fact that in almost every act of our daily lives – whether in the sphere of politics or business, in our social conduct or our ethical thinking – we are dominated by the relatively small number of persons . . . who understand the mental processes and social patterns of the masses. It is they who pull the wires which control the public mind, who harness old social forces and contrive new ways to bind and guide the world."*
>
> *Opening page of 'Propaganda' by Edward Bernays (1891-1995,) published in 1928*

> *"There's nothing in the streets, looks any different to me,*
> *And the slogans are replaced, by-the-bye.*
> *And the parting on the left, is now the parting on the right,*
> *And the beards have all grown longer overnight.*
> *I'll tip my hat to the new constitution, take a bow for the new revolution.*
> *Smile and grin at the change all around,*
> *Pick up my guitar and play, just like yesterday.*
> *Then I'll get on my knees and pray,*
> *We don't get fooled again."*
>
> *The Who: 'Won't Get Fooled Again' (1971)*

"Fool me once, shame on you.
Fool me twice, shame on me."
Old English Proverb

In 2017, BBC4 presenter Suzy Klein began her 'Tunes for Tyrants' TV series with the observation:

> *"Many of the political issues of our own day – things like political extremism, social inclusion, identity politics – were all being tested out in the laboratory that was Berlin's cabaret scene."*

The comment speaks to the power that entertainment can have in shaping entire cultural movements . . . though the BBC seems to have forgotten to mention that this dynamic goes a hell of a lot further than just Berlin's cabaret scene of the 1920s!

It was realised some decades ago, that a far more effective method of controlling the behaviours of societies lies not in the type of open, bold-faced tyranny that can be seen, understood, feared and resisted, (think George Orwell's '1984,') but through subtle, hidden means. A key aspect to the controllers' agenda for human domination, therefore, lies in the gradual and systematic changing of culture and human behaviour. If large numbers of people were to realise what's going on, it would be hugely detrimental to the plans.

The only way to steer societies in a desired direction is to be in control of every step of the process, with nothing left to random chance or natural progression. Ensured success in these endeavours, therefore, relies on tried and trusted groups and individuals being commissioned to instigate the changes, masquerading all the time under benign, good-natured public images that completely mask their true intentions.

This dynamic was articulately addressed in a 2017 article on the Mind Unleashed website:

> *"When we look around at people, and they don't resemble unique individuals, but manifestations of cultural templates, we must wonder who is setting the social trends in motion.*

> *"Who pays celebrities and musicians to influence the people around us to act and feel the way they do? We live in a society drowning in social engineering: drowning in behaviours and beliefs that did not rise organically from the people, but from a wealthier class of people who propagate ideas through music, television, and other forms of media.*
>
> *". . . It should be deeply fulfilling to recognise exactly who is trying to programme us. What could matter more than identifying exactly who is creating our culture, how, and why? These people are affecting the lives of us and everyone around us."*

Documentation has shown that a tenet of the subversion ideology espoused by the Soviet Union during the Cold War years, involved the creation of what it called 'False Heroes and Role Models.'

Welcome to the realm of Lifetime Actors, culture creation and Facilitated Careers.

Getting the job done

The over-riding aim of all modern social engineering agendas, has been to employ culture towards the debasement of morals, and the break-up of the traditional family unit. Societies split by discord between the generations – and between social groupings with perceived differences – are much easier to manipulate by malevolent controllers than a population united in solidarity. The lack of unity is exploited to play different groups off against each other. This process becomes yet more effective when society has become so fractured and divided, that most of its members are too distracted to even realise that all, in fact, share the same common enemy.

There are few better ways of understanding these principles, than by studying the minutiae of the LSD and 'free love'-laden counter-culture scene of the 1960s – a movement which so many researchers have now shown to have occurred under the direction of the CIA and its associates, that there can no longer be any legitimate claim that it was in any way 'grass-roots' or organic. A comment in Eddi Fiegel's biography of 'Mama' Cass Elliot, attributed to Cass's songwriting associate John Bettis, speaks to the net effect of that whole engineered movement:

> *"People forget now how dark it was from '69 to '76. America was not a happy place. Far from it. No matter where you turned, whether it was the gas crisis, whether it was the rampant drug problems everybody had, whether it was the fact that we had opened up a Pandora's Box with free love and relationships . . . By the time we got to 1969, everybody between the ages of twenty and twenty-eight was a drug addict. Everybody had been through two or three failed relationships of living with somebody, because we were all kids who didn't know what the fuck we were doing. And by the time you got to 1970, you were exhausted and you were sure that if you could just find another drug you'd be OK!"*

Right on script.

And the YouTube user known as Dayz of Noah, whose work comes highly recommended, summed it all up in the opening lines of his video 'How Media Shaped The Generations: The Chaos Era':

> *"By 1966, a strong black and white trauma bonding psychological operation was at work, and losing one's mind to make sense of it all, presented itself as the only option for a great majority . . . pushing the popular worldview further into satanic perspectives, undergoing spiritual possession and mind-control on encompassing scales."*

The mass mind-control agendas invariably serve to keep people away from understanding the dynamics of Natural Law, also; of appreciating the spiritual aspect of our existence here, and the fact that the actions we choose to take have repercussions throughout Creation that extend way beyond this physical realm. We're conditioned to think otherwise – that life is only about temporary physical fulfilment and personal material gain. But more of that in this book's final chapter.

The entertainment industries play ingeniously into this dynamic. Most people consider music, movies and television as merely fun, light relief from the drudgery of everyday life, and it would never occur to them – until it's pointed out – that these could be used for the shaping of values and perceptions. People are most off their guard against mind-control after a hard day at the slave job, when all they want to do to is unwind from the stress before it begins all over again. The 'think-tank' institutions referred to in the previous chapter specialise in these types of culture creation. Beneath the benign-sounding rhetoric, lies the truth of what certain sectors of these organisations were really set up to do.

The 1960s counter-culture, sponsored by those nice folks at Langley.

https://pixabay.com/en/psychedelic-peace-tie-die-hippie-1503541/

Credit: No attribution required

'Philanthropy,' hiding behind 'foundations' and 'institutes,' has long been used as a smokescreen for societal control, and even eugenics. David Rockefeller, who was reported to have finally died in March 2017 at the age of 101, was described officially as a 'philanthropist,' when he was almost certainly one of the architects of the deadly events of 9/11, and has been responsible for the death, suffering and ignorance of untold millions through the pharmaceutical, vaccination and dumbed-down 'education' systems that have been installed by the Rockefeller Foundation. 'Philanthropy'; it's the new Genocide.

Similarly, a visit to the Rothschilds' country pile of Waddesdon Manor in Buckinghamshire, will proudly display the family's collection of art, with plaques declaring them to be collectors and 'philanthropists' ... but will forget to mention their role in the human slavery brought about by that family's complete domination of the worldwide financial system. As with 'philanthropy,' so many actors hide behind a veil of 'doing good work for charity.' 'Sir' Jimmy Savile earned his status as a 'national treasure' through years of what *seemed* to be selfless deeds for assorted charities. In truth, these were simply to secure his image as an all-round great guy to divert attention from his real nature, and in part to gain him access to many of the children that he would sexually abuse – including those paralysed in the spinal injuries unit at Stoke Mandeville Hospital at which he was a 'patron' with his own living quarters. 'Jim'll Fix It' indeed.

Another 'national treasure' was Rolf Harris, who hid behind the image of a lovely man, good with children and caring about small, fluffy animals. When he, too, was unmasked as a paedophile, the British public could scarcely believe it, so convincing had his cover story been. These people are capable of duplicity and deception at levels that most cannot comprehend, and the fact that so many don't – even when the obvious is pointed out to them – is what allows the evil in which we live to continue unabated.

It's all an act

In one of his final interviews in 2015, for the freemantv.com podcast, author and researcher Dave McGowan commented:

> *"I guess if there's one thing I would say to people, it would be to just be very careful about who you choose as your icons and leaders, because these people may not be who you think they are. Be very sceptical of anyone in Hollywood who has a political agenda."*

Different generations of the same Establishment-serving families are put to use in designated roles. Some go into the world of politics, some into big business, some into science or the military, some into films, some into television, some into music – all to play their influential roles in these different fields. There will even be bloodline descendants who pose as 'truth' researchers and public speakers, but who mislead while pretending to inform.

This is the realm of the Lifetime Actor. It's a term coined by author, researcher and scholar Joe Atwill to address individuals who have become household names through their public personas; Bill Gates as the founder of Microsoft, for example. Their backgrounds tell a different story, however, usually revealing family links to military-intelligence or other aspects of social control. In Gates' case, his father, William H. Gates Sr., had been head of the Planned Parenthood organisation which had evolved out of the American Eugenics Society. An insight into the mindset of these people comes from comments made by Margaret Sanger, Planned Parenthood's founder; "the most merciful thing that a large family does to one of its infant members is to kill it," and "... human weeds, reckless breeders, spawning... human beings who never should have been born," in describing immigrants and the working class.

Now, it becomes far more likely that Gates Jr's *real* role in society is to covertly push eugenics and population-control, something borne out by his close association with the United Nations and its mass-vaccination programmes in Africa, and his ties to genetically modified food monolith Monsanto.

Readers wanting to delve fully into the world of Lifetime Actors and culture creation, are encouraged to absorb the 'Unspun' series of podcasts hosted by Joe Atwill and Jan Irvin which all reside at www.gnosticmedia.com. Episode 8 gives a useful overview of the whole concept. On it, Atwill states:

> *"What a Lifetime Actor is, is simply a personality that is in the media that is completely fake, and the representation that the individual makes about themselves as a person, is false. The term has really developed to try and help people understand individuals historically*

that have lived a lie. Their life has been something that was given to the public, basically, to fool them. So we could mention Terence McKenna, Gordon Wasson, Timothy Leary, Gregory Bateson, Ken Kesey.

"So you have these images of these individuals. Whatever the media has given you about them, that's what's in your head... And then they influence culture, and the next thing you know, you've got a degenerated population. The Lifetime Actor is the correct way to identify these individuals. They were trained to create their persona. And the persona is really necessary in order for their propaganda to be effective.

"So you might think of Leary at a Be-In where he's in his Indian garb and he's kind of acting all spaced-out. This seems like it's the sincere behaviour of a strange individual, but actually, it's a weapon. What he's doing, is he's trying to make this kind of behaviour seem hip, to have people who are influenced by him, adopt these attributes."

Timothy Leary has been shown by documentary evidence to have been a long-term asset of the CIA. The question then becomes; why would the CIA have had any interest in LSD, psychedelics and 'free love' being enthusiastically adopted into the lifestyles of an entire generation? Jan Irvin refers to the CIA more accurately as the Central Entertainment Agency, and it's also been described as the Cultural Infiltration Agency. Either way, it's in direct violation of its charter to only operate outside of the United States. Leary himself admitted to the agency's extensive homegrown activity in an interview:

"I give the CIA total credit for sponsoring and initiating the entire consciousness movement and counter-culture events of the 1960s. The CIA funded, supported and encouraged hundreds of young psychiatrists to experiment with this drug."

The evidence now available certainly suggests that the Agency expends more time and energy on societal shaping and moulding, than it does on matters of spying, surveillance and 'national security.' Britain's intel organisations have had a similar hand in the manipulation of the entertainment industry too – some would argue even more so.

The same dynamic is at play with any kind of social movement which influences large numbers of people and changes societal behaviour. The feminist movement which came out of the 1960s, contemporaneous to LSD and the 'counter-culture,' is no exception, as Atwill continues:

> *"The women who were reading 'Ms.' magazine trusted Gloria Steinem. They trusted 'Ms.' because they thought these magazines were really out to protect them. But then, it turned out that... wait a second. Gloria Steinem is a Lifetime Actor! She's a CIA agent! She's a CIA agent from the time she's at High School! And now, when you look at her that way, then you can see, wait a second... This isn't necessarily being given to us as a way to protect women. This could be a tool to destroy the family."*

As previously noted, the music industry has long had its own Lifetime Actors to ensure this particular mode of entertainment is steered down certain desired paths, usually in synchronised tandem with other changes. A new way of scrutinising 'cultural icons' that are served up to us by the media is required if we are to take back our power in shaping our own societal culture, rather than having it crafted for us.

As Joe Atwill adds:

> *"The media's been weaponised. So when you get someone who is a star in the media, they're not there accidentally.... When you see these elements fitting into the process of the weaponisation – like the Beatles leading to the Stones, leading to the sex, drugs and Rock 'n' Roll culture – you know they're somehow dirty, they're somehow in on the operation.*
>
> *"Jim Morrison and The Doors. Now you've got the son of the Admiral who led the false-flag fake attack in the Gulf of Tonkin that starts the Vietnam War. Who is this guy? He comes out of nowhere, he's very attractive, and he has this appetite for LSD. And because he's a music idol, he influences people. But imagine if he'd come out and said, 'you*

> *know, I'm just a son of military intelligence, and they've told me that they want to have people take drugs . . . so please take drugs.'*
>
> *"I mean, if he came out that way, the culture wouldn't move very far. His persona was developed, all the attributes of his character in the media were developed, so that he would have the most power in terms of influencing people.*
>
> *"So, if these Lifetime Actors are* <u>*considered*</u> *by people as possibly fake, possibly anthropologic weapons, if they're scrutinised and serious questions are asked about them . . . then the damage that they will do is going to be almost nothing."*

Though celebrities and public figures are often presented as being 'just like us,' and can seem to be 'really nice,' it's worth remembering that millions get spent on public relations spin, and that none of us *really* knows the true character and background of the individual behind the surface gloss. The safest way to avoid being duped, therefore, is to consider nobody worth your trust unless you know them personally, and have had direct interactions with them.

Blame it on the bloodlines

Family backgrounds, and the long-running generational bloodlines from which certain household names emanate, are key to understanding their given roles in society. Prince Charles, with some apparent pride, revealed that the maternal side of his family is descended from Vlad Dracul, the vicious Transylvanian nobleman and warrior who earned the nickname Vlad The Impaler through his preferred method of mass-execution. With similar open-ness, former British Prime Minister David Cameron made the apparent throwaway comment to the UK's 'Daily Mail' that he *just happened* to be a distant cousin of Kim Kardashian.

The dysfunctional Kardashian family have been used to debase morality and deplete intelligence through their 'reality' TV show, with Kim's step-father/mother Bruce/ Caityln Jenner utilised as a tool in the Transgender agenda. And Kim herself is rarely out of the gossip columns and celebrity magazines – not least as the wife of Kanye West. This in spite of her displaying little personal talent in any field, but still influencing the lives of millions of impressionable people who have fallen for the hype that she's some kind of 'role model.' Could an ordinary family from regular walks of life achieve this level of prominence on such little talent? Absolutely not. But that's because they're not Lifetime Actors. So, one spawn of this bloodline, Cameron, was ushered into the world of politics, while the other was given the role of being a pointless, vacuous celebrity-for-celebrity's-sake.

Different generations are given designated roles in this way through the centuries. In all cases, the intention is to have a desired influence and effect on human culture. This is why so many crop up, generation after generation, as Hollywood actors, TV personalities, or musicians and singers. They become the most prominent names in their respective fields. In most cases, (the Kardashians being an exception,) these positions appear to be wholly deserved, as they're clearly very, very good at their given crafts. Logic suggests, therefore, that academies or training schools must exist where these individuals hone their skills under the best tutelage, and with money no object. Lifetime Actors get the best training.

Mainstream newspapers have also reported that Cherie Booth, the wife of another former British Prime Minister, Tony Blair, is related to John Wilkes Booth, the theatrical actor said to have been the assassin of 19th-century US president Abraham Lincoln. Booth's uncle, Algernon Sydney Booth, was Cherie's great-great-great-grandfather. Cherie's father, Anthony Booth, was himself an actor, best known for his role in the TV sitcom 'Til Death Do Us Part.' The mainstream media reports such connections as if they're simply amazing coincidences, without asking what the odds really are of public figures from different eras being genetically linked in this way by random chance.

It's now well-known that all US presidents to date have been genetic descendants of European nobility through just one character, the emperor Charlemagne, 8th-century King of the Franks, and it's been said that the candidate with the most European genes is the one that ends up winning each election. In many, Americans are given the 'choice' of two candidates who are in fact distant cousins, as was the case in the 2016 'race' between Hillary Clinton and Donald Trump. Although presented as zealous rivals, they have been pictured socialising together at many events, and in fact share 18th great-grandparents.

Similarly, George W. Bush and Barack Obama are related. On the surface, it *appears* as if you couldn't find two more diametrically-opposed individuals, but the extended family trees tell a different story. The rest of Bush's family tree, as revealed in an article by CBS News, and based on research by www.ancestry.com, similarly boggles the mind. It shows him to be related by blood, one way or another, to his 'opponent' John Kerry, his vice-president Dick Cheney, former president Abraham Lincoln, Princess Diana, 'Playboy' founder Hugh Hefner, the aforementioned Vlad The Impaler, and celebrities Marilyn Monroe, (also a US intelligence asset and probable mind-control subject,) Madonna, Celine Dion and Tom Cruise! Wikipedia additionally reports that Pocahontas is an ancestor of two presidential First Ladies, the wives of Ronald Reagan and Woodrow Wilson!

And www.time.com reported the 'surprise,' (it's only a surprise if you're not paying attention,) that – though we still know so little about him, and the 'birth certificate' he has presented is a proven photoshopped forgery – Barack Obama is a tenth cousin of both his political 'opponent' Sarah Palin, and the broadcaster Rush Limbaugh. Obama, Palin and George W. Bush are said to be related through common ancestor Samuel Hinckley. An article by Von A. Weist on the www.rense.com website, asserts that Samuel Hinckley was also an ancestor of John Hinckley Jr., the man accused of the assassination attempt on Ronald Reagan while George Bush Senior was in office as Vice-President. (The Bush and Hinckley families had close social and business ties prior to the 1981 event, just as the Bush and Bin Laden families had prior to the events of 9/11, for which Osama Bin Laden was blamed.)

Given these revelations, readers shouldn't be too surprised if those rumours about George Bush Sr.'s wife Barbara, (*nee* Pierce,) being the illegitimate daughter of Aleister Crowley turn out to be true. There's certainly a family resemblance.

Anyone still believe that you can rise to high positions in politics, entertainment or big business purely through hard work and a stroke of good luck? When Obama was manipulated into office in early 2009, black people in America made remarks like: "At last! Now *anyone* can be president!" Similarly, schoolkids are often given apparent inspiring advice like: "Work really hard and *you* could be the next Bill Gates or Mark Zuckerberg."

You couldn't.

The UK's BBC1 TV channel launched its 'Who Do You Think You Are' show a few years ago, which was all about tracing the ancestry of various household names. It constantly throws up the 'amazing' revelation that a public figure *just happens* to be descended from royalty or aristocracy, but it's only 'amazing' if you don't know how the game of culture-creation is played. 'Eastenders' actor and 'Cockney diamond geezer' Danny Dyer, for instance, expressed apparent surprise at his blood link to the lawyer and statesman Thomas Cromwell, and further connections to kings William the Conqueror and Edward III. British actor Benedict Cumberbatch, who portrayed the Enigma code-breaking mathematician Alan Turing in the movie 'The Imitation Game,' turns out to be a relative of Turing himself, both of them sharing ancestry from the 14th century Earl of Somerset. According to researcher and claimant to the British throne Greg Hallett, meanwhile, actor and comedian Peter Sellers was an illegitimate son of the royal Lord Louis Mountbatten.

The electronic dance music producer Moby, (born Richard Melville Hall on 11th September 1965,) turns out to be a descendant of Herman Melville, the writer of the 'Moby Dick' novel who hailed from a Freemasonic family.

The Chosen Ones

This is not to say that every single household name has got there through their genetics, however. The ranks of what I call the Chosen Ones are reserved for those who may not come from an all-important bloodline, but who have shown sufficient natural skill to have attracted the attention of the talent spotters. An instinctive tendency towards narcissism – or better yet, psychopathy – is something that will stand an individual in great stead in this regard. It's here that mythical glittering contracts that appear too good to be true get offered, and the success and riches that the industry reps offer, appeal directly to the fame-hungry ego of the individual concerned, ensuring that offers are very rarely refused. This is also the realm, according to insiders, of the 'elite' sex parties of the type knowingly depicted in the Stanley Kubrick film 'Eyes Wide Shut,' which new recruits are required to attend. The prevailing antics – probably best erased from the imagination – are invariably filmed and the recordings carefully stored, should the threat of their 'exposure' ever be required to bring a would-be un-co-operative participant back into line.

Should the rare occasion arise where the conscience of a Chosen One starts to bleed through once they realise the terrible, corrupt nature of what it is they are now a part of, and they start to look for an exit route, at this point the realisation occurs that they are now an owned commodity, and their only two choices consist of continuing to do as they're directed for the rest of their days, or exiting the industry the Prince, Michael Jackson or Whitney Houston way.

The Chosen Ones are beneficiaries of what I call Facilitated Careers. Regular members of the public can struggle and strive for decades to reach the lofty heights at which their idols reside, not realising that these positions, in most cases, have been gifted to these individuals by those organisations who can make careers happen, (because ultimately all facets of society are connected through secret-society networks and fraternities.)

The way this dynamic works was summed up succinctly by the 1970 made-for-TV movie 'The Brotherhood of the Bell' starring Glenn Ford. This film is now extremely difficult to track down, but can be viewed in two parts via the Daily Motion links detailed at the end of this chapter.

Ford plays a businessman and former attendee of a prestigious college, where he had been inducted into a secret society, entirely steeped in oaths of secrecy and obedience, (and obviously a thinly-veiled reference to Harvard's Skull & Bones.) Following the induction of a new member, and after years of inactivity, he is called upon by the Brotherhood to ensure that an old friend of his declines a prominent academic position, so that another member of the Brotherhood can take the role. When his friend commits suicide after discovering the truth, Ford's character is devastated, and vows to expose and bring down the network. The Brotherhood, in turn, make the level of their influence known, as they are able to infiltrate every area of society through the contacts they have placed in key shot-calling positions.

In this insane, satanically-inverted reality in which we find ourselves, our conscious minds are lied to daily by sources that we're conditioned to think of as telling us the truth – such as mainstream news outlets and government ministers. Conversely, it's so often in works of apparent 'fiction,' 'imagination' and 'fantasy' – such as TV shows and movies – where the truth of a matter is communicated to our subconscious minds. Isn't it testament to how great a job has been done on this front when you consider the reaction of the average mind-controlled member of the public, should you suggest that the plotline of a Hollywood movie is *actually* a depiction of cold, harsh truths? You'll very likely be met with a phrase like, "you've been watching too many films, mate. You need to get with reality!"

Disarmament: a military-grade tactic

The mermaids of legend seduced ships to their doom with the sweetest-sounding songs.

The reason many have such a hard time believing that a famous celebrity they admire may in fact be operating to an agenda, is because, on the surface, they *appear* to be well-meaning and sincere in intent. This is where a military-style tactic comes into play. It's an essential tenet of the weaponisation of culture. A disarmed target who would never imagine that any danger is posed by an apparent friend and ally, is far easier to manipulate and conquer than one fully on their guard, and anticipating conflict.

Most people would never *imagine* that such levels of deception could be sunken to, because *they* would not be capable of it themselves. This attitude is what renders so many incapable of accepting the replacement of Paul McCartney, for example, when all the evidence suggests otherwise. Incredulity is a tactical advantage on the part of the controllers. Their all-pervading psychopathic mindset is different to ours. When you have no conscience, no empathy, no moral qualms, any tactic becomes fair game. This dynamic was alluded to in Roman Polanski's

'Rosemary's Baby' movie, where everyone around Mia Farrow's central character turned out to be members of a satanic cult, yet no-one would ever have imagined this to be the case from their genial public personas – friendly neighbours, doting husband, caring doctor.

Famous figures are deliberately given images that make them *appear* to be 'on the side' of those they are affecting, and they're seen to say and do all the right things. This is why so many are seen to undertake 'humanitarian' work. (To be clear, I'm not suggesting that in every single case that a celebrity is seen engaging in good works, that it's cynically contrived – just that in many cases it is, and it's part of a well-worn tactic.) A comment that was heard so frequently when Russell Brand emerged with his 'man of the people' act was: "But so much of what he says makes sense!" The truth of the matter is that Russell Brand is an actor, and a big part of an actor's role involves memorising scripts and reciting them on cue. In 2017, Jim Carrey was packaging the same 'celebrity awakened to truth' act to the American public, reciting all the same sentiments that his fellow actor across the pond had a short while earlier, and far too many were falling for it in exactly the same way.

A variation on this strategy is often used when launching the career of a new musician. An example I've often cited is that of Kanye West. He now stands as one of the key assets in the moral degradation of culture, and has been neutered into obedient subservience. He underwent what appeared to be a total breakdown of his mind-control programming at his concert in Sacramento in late 2016, where he ranted incoherently for around 15 minutes, appearing to call out his 'mentor' Jay-Z as some kind of handler, with phrases like "don't send killers at my head, bro." Kanye ended up being forcibly handcuffed to a gurney and led away for 'psychiatric evaluation.'

But when he first emerged with his debut album, 'The College Dropout,' he showed all the signs of being a conscious and visionary rapper, with some empowering messages to impart. The same was true of Lupe Fiasco who, after a few good messages, has sadly fallen into the same corporate mind-control agendas as his peers.

Robin Thicke, (whose recently-deceased father Alan was a prominent television presenter,) was launched as a credible soul artist . . . before his debauched on-stage pimp act with Miley Cyrus at the 2013 MTV

Awards confirmed him to be just another pawn in the hands of his controllers. Miley Cyrus herself was launched out of her Disney corporation grooming as good old family-friendly Hannah Montana . . . before being transformed into her hedonistic satanic slut persona. Rihanna and Beyonce, before their videos became laden with dark occult imagery, first appeared to be pleasant, wholesome pop acts that no parent could he opposed to . . . before they switched and the true purpose for which they were being used became clear. By this point in the tried-and-tested process, a fanbase is already intact, and is likely to be led down whatever path their idols dictate. This would be far more difficult to achieve if these acts were to make their true nature so blatantly known at the outset.

It's for the same reasons that acts who are clearly playing key roles in steering culture in a desired direction, offer up the odd song here and there to imply that they're among the good guys and just 'one of us.' Somewhere in the canon of most major musicians' work, the odd socially-conscious or apparently 'anti-establishment' song can be found. Bono is now understood to be one of the main celebrity stooges in the United Nations' New World Order plans, and you'd have to be as short-sighted as he is when he places one hand over his eye not to be able to see it. But back in U2's early career, he *appeared* to be making all the right statements on songs like 'Sunday Bloody Sunday,' 'Pride (In The Name Of Love') and 'Seconds.'

As British researcher Carl James outlined in a video linked to at the end, imagery now employed by the group Arcade Fire, hints at them being yet another co-opted Establishment asset. Yet it was a different story with their early music, which drew Carl in and *seemed* to convey inspiring messages. The group Killing Joke have put out many songs that appear to be anti-establishment and consciousness-enhancing. But you somehow have to reconcile that with frontman Jaz Coleman's admitted obsession with – wait for it – the occult teachings of Aleister Crowley, and the band's name evidently being inspired by the passage from Crowley's 'Book of Lies' detailed in the earlier Acid House chapter.

Those who reject the suggestions of Dave McGowan, that the pioneering musicians of the 60s counter-culture were operating to a military-intelligence agenda, will point to the many anti-establishment statements that the likes of Jim Morrison and Frank Zappa made in interviews and in their music. But if these characters really were actors playing a role, it wouldn't be too difficult for part of their convincing cover to involve them *appearing* to say all the things that their fans wanted to hear, would it?

We see another variation on the Disarmament Tactic, when certain artists who are quite obviously controlled assets, make comments or visual statements that *appear* to suggest they have woken up to the true nature of the corporate beast, and are now breaking free and regaining their personal sovereignty. As an example, Lady Gaga – an artist whose complicity in dark occult and mind-controlling ritual has done potential damage to the minds and souls of millions of young people – spoke at a conference in late 2015. Among her proclamations were: 'I feel sad when I'm overworked, and that I just become a money making machine . . . ' and: "That makes me unhappy. It feels shallow. I have a lot more to offer than my image." She even seemed to hint at her own mind-controlled status when she addressed herself by saying: "Okay, Stefani, Gaga, hybrid-person. Why are you unhappy?" And: "Slowly but surely, I remembered who I am."

To an observer with no background knowledge, this *appears* to represent Gaga asserting her independence and making her own decisions. These are options not open to such industry tools, however. A clue was given from the location at which she made these statements . . . Yale University in Connecticut, one of the principle 'elite' breeding grounds steeped in secret-society activity! And however much it may have *appeared* that she was turning a new corner, any doubt was dissipated when she appeared at the 2017 Super Bowl Half Time show adorned in the usual Masonic/ occult regalia in yet another mass-scale ritual, which even some elements of the mainstream media described as 'satanic.' I guess the 'breakaway' didn't go too well then.

A similar scenario ensued when Katy Perry released her song and video 'Chained To The Rhythm' in early 2017. Again, to an untrained observer, this *appeared* to represent her making a statement about the mind-controlling nature of modern society and the vacuous output of the industry, with lyrics like:

> *"Are we crazy? Living our lives through a lens . . . So comfortable, we live in a bubble, a bubble . . . So comfortable, we cannot see the trouble, the trouble . . . Happily numb . . . Turn it up, it's your favourite song, Dance, dance, dance to the distortion . . . Stumbling around like a wasted zombie . . . Yeah, we think we're free . . . We're all chained to the rhythm."*

Naive comments from some quarters like 'she's waking up!' were reminiscent of when British artist Jessie J released her 'Price Tag' song a few years before. On the surface, the song *appeared* to be a scathing critique of modern materialism. But the video imagery and the rest of Jessie's output confirmed that she was anything but a maverick free spirit boldly speaking truth. As for What Katy Did Next, just keep reading.

A far more likely scenario than these artists 'waking up' and showing they're 'on our side,' is that such songs and comments are yet more cynically-concocted tactics from the toolbox of the engineers, intended as mockery of the profane and gullible nature of the public, (as they see it,) just as much as of the helpless situations of the artists themselves. As many have discovered to their peril, their contracts are binding for life.

It is possible, of course, that in certain cases, acts did start out with genuinely good intentions, and that somewhere along the way – having shown great talent and a propensity for influencing the public – they were co-opted into social engineering agendas and remunerated into conformity. This remains a credible alternative to the assertion that bands were formed with such intentions right from the start, as this remains difficult, if not impossible, to prove. But regardless of which scenario is at play, the cultural landscaping gets achieved either way

And so, (best sung to the tune of The Jam's 'That's Entertainment,') . . . that's Engineering.

Extra-curricular activities

Although Lifetime Actors and new recruits are thought of as having a principal public role – a politician, a film actor, a singer – it appears that, occasionally, a temporary stepping-aside into some other useful role is required of them. Being owned commodities who, either through blood or ego are beholden to their controllers, these people have little choice but to fulfil their instructions. This is why we see projects such as the Toilet Strike initiative, helmed by Matt Damon, assembling a ragtag bunch of Lifetime Actors in the form of Sir Richard Branson, Bono and Olivia Wilde, to produce the ad. that you can view here, with all its oh-so-hilarious references to 'the Illuminati,' and taking the piss out of genuine conspiracy researchers: https://www.Youtube.com/watch?v=56PpsudMnC8

This is why Bono, whose public role as a rock singer you might expect to consist of, well, singing, in recent years seems to have spent more time in the close personal company of the likes of Bill Clinton, George W Bush, Dick Cheney, Barack Obama, Tony Blair and the Pope than of other musicians.

This is why one minute, Russell Brand is the world's unfunniest 'comedian,' and the next, is calling for a 'revolution of consciousness' and a more 'egalitarian society,' with primetime slots on BBC programmes like 'Newsnight' and 'Question Time.' Nobody would be allowed on such prominent shows if the message they were putting forward were not, in some way, part of some larger culture-affecting agenda. (Russell's next mission, after a few years of popularising the 'hipster' look of men's skintight jeans, was to help push the Transgenderism agenda forward a few steps by announcing, in late 2016, that he intended to raise his imminent new child as 'gender-neutral.' It was the same year that Bono was named by 'Glamour' magazine as its 'Woman of the Year.')

This is why one minute, Bob Geldof is a scruffy, out-of-tune singer for an Irish New Wave band, and the next is helming the Band Aid and Live Aid projects linked to United Nations agendas in Africa . . . then crops up as the public face of Smart meters, professing how great it would be for everyone to have one in their home. This is why one minute, Jamie Oliver is a celebrity chef who's never off the telly, and appears to be an all-round great 'geezer' with his campaigns to get more healthy food into kids' school dinners . . . but the next is making statements about how he's "super-excited" to be working with the Bill & Melinda Gates Foundation on a "better food system" – almost certainly a reference to human health-damaging genetically modified organisms, if Gates' links with the GMO monolith Monsanto is anything to go by.

This is why actors like Ewan McGregor and Keeley Hawes are wheeled out as the public face of TV charity ads, imploring the general public to part with their cash to find solutions to problems that have been created by governments, all of which could be eradicated overnight if the international banking cartels behind them wished them to be. It's why Lenny Henry has been the face of the BBC's Comic Relief project for years, (earning himself an OBE in the process,) when this charity has been investigated for its investments into tobacco and arms companies. It's why 'Austin Powers' actor Mike Myers was teamed up with Kanye West to plead for public money on a telethon in the wake of the Hurricane Katrina disaster in New Orleans, (before everything went horribly wrong with Kanye going off-script and declaring 'George Bush doesn't care about black people.' But that's a whole different story as covered elsewhere!)

These extra-curricular activities dovetail into another aspect of social engineering too, which is the creation of fads and trends. Any time one of these comes along – involving the coerced participation of the public upon the say-so of some public figure – you can be sure it's the creation of one of the culture-changing think-tanks. Few had heard of ALS, or Lou Gehrig's Disease, before it became the focal point of the Ice Bucket Challenge in the summer of 2014. Upon the example of assorted celebrities, who had filmed themselves dumping a bucket of ice-cold water over their heads, then challenging named associates to do the same, the trend went viral, with millions emulating their idols. I don't profess to know what the attraction was to the social engineers of having large numbers of people dousing themselves in this way, but there would have been one. Quite simply, this fad would not have been so widespread if there weren't.

It was the same scenario when millions of women posed for a 'self' with a bottle of Coke between their breasts in 2015 to apparently "raise awareness of breast cancer," when the faked 'Kony 2012' video went viral in that year, and when the No Make-Up Selfie trend raised millions upon millions for Cancer Research UK, (which, like other cancer charities, purports to be 'researching a cure' in an industry which relies on the constant flow of sufferers to maintain the billions it generates every year, but which never goes anywhere near the many natural and herbal remedies which have been proven to be effective.) Then there was the Pokemon Go 'game' fad of 2016, the main point of which was to further normalise GPS surveillance, virtual reality and the Smart Grid, and which actually saw people walking off cliffs through their total engrossment in their phones and detachment from their physical surroundings.

A job well done all round.

Anyone for pizza?

The extent to which so many celebrities are merely the stooges of those who tell them what to do, appeared to be borne out in the wake of the 'Pizzagate' scandal which emerged in late 2016. This alluded to a child sex-trafficking ring centred around Washington DC, involving some high-ranking names in politics. The scandal gave an insight into the dark underbelly of 'elite' society, and got its name from the food-related phrases apparently used by the pederasts to communicate with each other, 'pizza' being code for a young girl. (Other phrases include 'hot dog' to denote a young boy, and 'chicken' for a young child of either sex. How low can humanity go?) Citizen researchers began to pore over the evidence for such paedophile networks, including many suspect works of 'art' involving images of pizza. A glance back at the output of a handful of corporate music A-listers also threw up some unsettling results.

In 2011, Lady Gaga had released a song titled 'Pizza,' whose toxic cesspit of lyrics included such lines as: "All we want is hot, hot, pizza, pizza, pizza, pizza. Pizza in my fucking shit." A couple of years later, Katy Perry put out the song 'This Is How We Do.' Its accompanying video, directed by New Zealand film-maker Joel Kefali, included items of food dancing around in animated scenes, including slices of pizza. It may or may not be significant that one of the video's brief settings is a ping-pong table, 'ping-pong' having been identified by the FBI as a code-phrase used by paedophiles to denote the passing around of a child for sexual abuse. The name of the restaurant in DC around which the 'Pizzagate' allegations were centred, was Comet Ping-Pong Pizza.

To promote these songs, both singers appeared in multiple publicity shots showing them indulging in the eating of pizza, and wearing dresses fashioned in the form of the food. Gaga's campaign included her declaring a 'pizza party live,' while Perry compered a live event in which she invited children up on stage and spoke for several minutes about how much she loved pizza. Later, Miley Cyrus and Justin Bieber were pictured together biting into slices of pizza. (If nothing else, this at least put paid to the persistent rumours that they are in fact the same person!)

The Ice Bucket Challenge: A masterclass in how to get large numbers of people to adopt a behaviour based on celebrity say-so.

https://en.wikipedia.org/wiki/File:Doing_the_ALS_Ice_Bucket_Challenge_(14927191426).jpg

Credit: slgckgc

Perry was back for more with the video to her song 'Bon Appetit' in Spring 2017. By this point, she had adopted a new look consisting of closely-cropped blonde hair. In the article titled 'What Is Happening To Katy Perry?,' the link to which is in the Resources section at the end, researcher Vigilant Citizen discussed how this look is used to denote newly-programmed mind-controlled slaves.

Right at the same time, Justin Bieber appeared in the DJ Khaled video 'I'm The One' rocking the shaved blonde look, (made famous by Eminem from his initial breakthrough, and interestingly, rocked by Mia Farrow's character in the movie 'Rosemary's Baby' soon after she is ritually abused.) Kanye West had appeared with his hair dyed peroxide-blonde shortly after his infamous 'truth rant' at his show in Sacramento of November 2016.

The 'Bon Appetit' video, directed by the Paris/ Montreal-based film-making collective Dent De Cuir, sank to the very depths of sickness and depravity, as it portrayed Perry assuming the position of the female 'cake' which featured in the 'spirit cooking' dinners hosted by witch Marina Abramović, details of which were closely linked to the 'Pizzagate' allegations. This video stands as a blatant mockery of these events, rubbing the noses of those who have done the research right in it, while going completely over the heads of everybody else. This was evidenced by the hundreds of thousands of 'likes' the video received on YouTube™, along with braindead comments along the lines of: "It's really cool, lol!" The video also hints at cannibalism, as a group of chefs roll Perry in flour, then plunge her into a pot of boiling water along with various vegetables.

Was it pure coincidence – against all the odds – that these artists *just happened* to employ pizza and 'spirit cooking' imagery in their songs and photos? Were they just making independent fashion statements? Or were these appearances all co-ordinated, and intended as a sick mockery of institutionalised paedophilia – in some way foreshadowing the breaking of the 'Pizzagate' scandal in Predictive Programming fashion?

The manufacturing of 'cool'

A textbook example of culture creation came from the movement dubbed 'Cool Britannia' in the mid-1990s, closely tied to the music genre that the mainstream media had dubbed 'Britpop.' The idea was that after years of stagnation, the British music industry was undergoing a creative resurgence led by the two dynamic bands of the time, Blur, (from the South, London) and Oasis, (from the North, Manchester.) The bands were pitted as rivals in much the same way that the Rolling Stones, (from the South, London,) and the Beatles, (from the North, Liverpool) had been in the 1960s. Given the evidence to show that all four bands were highly cherished assets with ties to the Establishment and the world of the occult, it becomes easy to see why they were chosen to herald in the respective societal changes they helped foment.

The campaign that led to Tony Blair's election victory for his New Labour party in May 1997, had much invested in the 'Cool Britannia' concept that Blur and Oasis symbolised. Blair's spin doctors had cultivated an image of him as a dynamic, visionary leader very much in touch with the youth culture of his land. He took care to be seen playing guitar in TV appearances and talked of having been in bands himself – a far cry from the grey, austere image of his opponent, John Major. There were even reports of Blair having smoked cannabis in his younger years. Right on, dude!

Blair threw a reception party at 10 Downing Street in July of 1997, to which a number of 'cool' cultural icons were invited. The most famous image from this event is of Oasis frontman Noel Gallagher sipping champagne and chatting good-naturedly with Blair – a far cry from his own 'rebellious' Rock 'n' Roll image. By 2003, when Blair had co-launched the post-9/11 military incursions into Iraq and Afghanistan, the British public's opinion of him had switched dramatically, the tag of 'war criminal' being frequently applied. In 2011, the Kuala Lumpur War Crimes Commission in Malaysia found Blair and George W. Bush guilty of crimes against humanity. Despite this, in 2013, Noel Gallagher was still voicing his admiration for Blair in an interview for 'The New Statesman,' (which was being edited at the time by his friend

Russell Brand,) and in a 2016 'Daily Mail' interview, recalled Blair's years in office as "amazing."

(By way of some brief background, Blair took leadership of the Labour party in 1994 following the very sudden and unexpected death of its previous leader, John Smith, of reported heart failure. In each of the years he was elected or re-elected, Blair presided over a major public event; in 1997, it was the sudden and unexpected death of Princess Diana; in 2001, it was the events and aftermath of 9/11; in 2005, it was the events and aftermath of the 7/7 attacks in London. When Labour minister and leader of the House of Commons, Robin Cook, resigned in protest at the Blair government's launching of the Iraq War... he died suddenly and unexpectedly of reported heart failure while on a walking holiday in a remote part of Scotland. When Dr. David Kelly, the weapons inspector who had been cited as a source for Blair's claim that Saddam Hussein was in possession of 'Weapons of Mass Destruction,' revealed that this information was in fact false... he died suddenly and unexpectedly while out walking in Oxfordshire woodland, with the official verdict of 'suicide.')

It becomes interesting at this juncture to study some aspects of both Blur and Oasis. Some examination of the imagery on Oasis's key album sleeves yields some curiosities. 1994's 'Definitely Maybe' sports a massive globe floating ominously in a living room. On 1997's 'Be Here Now' a toy globe makes a re-appearance, this time being viewed by a band member through a telescope. Another album shows a landscape encased within a dome, meanwhile. How interesting that it's titled 'Don't Believe The Truth.' 'Standing On The Shoulder Of Giants' shows a New York City skyline obliterated by chemtrails.

Oasis first signed to the Creation Records label in 1993. Creation was founded by Alan McGee, an occultist, and yet another industry figure to have expressed a reverence for the Thelema teachings of Aleister Crowley, (falls back in amazement.) In an interview with the 'Dangerous Minds' website, he stated: "For the last five years, I have been studying Crowley, Osman Spare and the chaos magickians. I got into Crowley because everybody told me not to go there. So of course, I did, and ended up at chaos magick. I 100% love Aleister Crowley. 'The Book of the Law' is my Bible. I love him." McGee produced the movie

'Kubricks,' said to be a tribute to the satanic film-maker and fellow Crowleyite Kenneth Anger. The film's tagline was "Everything Is Synchronicity . . . Even Chaos!"

Noel's brother, Liam Gallagher, appears in a photograph available on-line which he possibly now regrets. He is sat with Jimmy Savile and is flashing the 'devil horns,' which are discussed at length in Chapter 5.

Blur co-founder Damon Albarn subsequently formed the 'virtual' alternative group Gorillaz, (whose titles have included 'Demon Days' and 'Sex Murder Party,') their gimmick being that they appear only as animated avatars living in a 'fictional universe,' and have performed concerts in the form of digitally-generated holograms. The Gorillaz imagery is tied to the slow-drip of Artificial Intelligence into the public consciousness, with things really coming to a head on their 2017 album titled – perhaps ironically – 'Human.' In an interview with the 'NME' at the time of its release, the band spoke of their enthusiasm for virtual characters being able to tour and make music for them with no need for any human input. Albarn stated: "If it works well, then in 20 years' time, there might be a completely holographic Glastonbury."

Despite apparently being an outspoken anti-war activist, Damon Albarn accepted an Order of the British Empire in the Queen's 2016 Honours . . . which could be viewed as a slightly out-of-character thing to do given that the Queen is the figurehead for one of the most murderous colonial empires in human history, responsible for the subjugation by military force of countless foreign lands.

Dystopia awaits

As aspect of the gradual changing of attitudes straight out of the social engineering textbooks, is one that is very often missed. This is the rapid advancement that human society has taken towards the Transhumanist future that has been in the sights of the manipulators for so long. When it comes to the type of society that we're now all able to recognise, it's shocking to reflect that it was depicted as long ago as 1927 in German film-maker Fritz Lang's iconic 'Metropolis.' Equally shocking is that this 'futuristic' storyline was set 100 years into the future, so is now only a few years away. The plot depicts a cityscape greatly reliant on technology, in which the elite class reside in skyscrapers, while the working-class keep the city functioning by toiling in harsh underground facilities. As the workers show signs of being close to revolt, the elites elect to send a robot modelled on Maria, the workers' *de facto* leader, into their ranks to mediate. Societal chaos ensues.

The imagery of 'Metropolis' has been evoked through the decades by artists such as Madonna, Lady Gaga and Beyonce, and notably by Queen in the video to their 'Radio Gaga.' A retouched version of the originally silent film was released in 1984 (of all years,) with a soundtrack by Italian producer Giorgio Moroder. Images of this same 'dystopian' society have been subliminally fed into the public mindset through countless movies in the interim, from 'The Terminator' to 'Robocop' to 'TXH 1138' to 'The Hunger Games' to 'Logan's Run.' There's a good reason why the phone-type is called 'Android'.

It becomes clear – particularly when you factor in the concept of Predictive Programming discussed at length in the last book – that the technological society we now have has been in the plans of the culture creators for a very long time. It was addressed strikingly by rapper Nas, (frequently rumoured to be a Freemason,) on the track 'New World' from his 'Nastradamus' album, released just prior to the new millennium. Among the song's references are: "solar-energized rides, no steering wheel, tell it how to drive," "while the poor people starve, computers taking over they jobs," "new cameras in police cars taking pictures," "covertly starting wars, CIA, Navy Seals," and "your genes and DNA is used to make clones." In some parts of the track, Nas appears to be suspicious of new technology, but elsewhere appears to be embracing it, with lines like: "Say hello to the one world," and "I might be old fashioned, stuck in my ways, but nothing makes me more happier than seeing today."

It's equally clear that the Futurists are far from finished, as every passing week sees new pieces of the picture towards a fusion between humanity and technology, and a complete shift away from natural, organic ways of life. Because these steps are presented to the public as something which is "great," "cool," or which can really benefit their lives, ("who wants the hassle of remembering your wallet when you could just pay for everything with a microchip under your skin?"; "why bother reading old-fashioned paper maps when you can just have your car tell you where to go?",) so much of what's been achieved has been done with little-to-no resistance from the public.

A poster for Fritz Lang's Metropolis from 1927, an alarmingly accurate 'prediction' of the futurist society which is becoming more recognisable with every passing day.

https://c2.staticflickr.com/8/7462/15513625249_0df14c8c6b_b.jpg

Credit: Breve Storia del Cinema

Yet, while we were asleep at the wheel, in the course of no more than two decades, our daily existence is now engulfed in a quagmire of wi-fi and cell phone signals, and micro and radio-waves, all emitting electro-magnetic frequencies that penetrate our brains and bodies 24/7, and whose long-term health implications cannot yet be understood. And the rapid onset of the Smart Grid, through 'smart' meters, TVs, phones, cars, motorways and cities, is only going to take this further. Reliance on technology has been so firmly ingrained into our daily lives that many young people – always the prime targets of such changes – are unable to get from one hour to the next without handling every aspect of their lives on their mobile phones or tablets.

An aspect of how this move in particular has been achieved, involves another factor that is so rarely considered or discussed. This is the dwindling attention-spans – particularly in the under-30s – that has been cultivated in the past few years. Someone unable to hold and develop a thought for more than a few seconds – and who is swamped with things to do and think about at every stage of their day – is someone unlikely to apply critical thought to important life issues, such as scrutinising what the mainstream media tells us about a particular news story, questioning the illusory nature of 'money,' or the very nature of this existence and our place in it. It is into this scenario that the advent of concentration-distracting on-line sites and applications such as Instagram, Snapchat and Twitter play their part.

Instagram's aim is in its name; users are pressurised into documenting every instant of their day, and the minute they post a picture – or record a few seconds of footage – the pressure is there to do it again, as the last one is now old-hat. Then, Twitter's 140-character limit has had its role, since no meaningful message that says anything worthwhile can really be communicated with such restrictions, (though the limit has recently been doubled to 280 characters.)

So users are stifled in their capacity for expression, but still feel compelled to be constantly posting stuff because everybody else is. And all the time the notion that "technology is so cool" is being instilled into the impressionable minds of the young to the point that any other way of getting through the day, like their parents' generation did, is unthinkable without such accessories. A generation groomed in this kind of mindset is going to be a far easier one to sell ideas like brain implants, microchips, Smart Grids and a cashless society to, than one which can remember different ways of doing things. When major societal changes are introduced in increments, a population entrained in shortened attention spans, is unlikely to recall more than two or three increments into the past with any great clarity. And people who can't hold a thought for more than a few seconds are so much easier to control.

That's engineering.

The assault on attention

An alternative aspect of the above harks back to my previous existence as a club DJ, playing gigs every weekend for over 20 years. I highlighted aspects of this rather glibly in my book 'Tales From The Flipside.' But there's a serious element to some of the amusing anecdotes conveyed. A few years in, I'd already started to notice the changing attitudes of clubbers towards what was being played by the DJ. When I started out, it was fairly easy to take a crowd on a musical 'journey,' (to re-use that old chestnut,) and in most cases, people would allow themselves to be led wherever you chose to take them, on the basis that this is your specialist area and you know what you're doing.

As the years went by and the proliferation of mobile phones in clubs increased, however, I noticed a marked difference in how punters were responding to tunes that were played. The initial whoops and cheers that would accompany a track the second its opening bars were recognised were still there. But whereas previously a crowd would have danced enthusiastically to such a song for a good three to four minutes, now it was becoming clear that people would lose interest after 30 seconds to a minute. The energetic dance moves would become more lacklustre, and faces would disappear into phones. DJs use their well-honed instinct to assess a crowd's mood. The only way to re-generate the vibe would be to quickly bring in the next song. Again, whoops and cheers, then the loss of interest within half a minute. (Readers may be familiar with the internet meme that shows a group of young people sat on the sidelines in a club, staring individually at their phone screens with the accompanying caption: "Great party!')

Here, we have a symptom of the instant gratification that the youthful generation has been conditioned to expect. Because everything is now so instantly available at all times and in all places – and because there's such a plethora of options vying for the attention at any given time – attention spans have been reduced to farcical levels. And in the DJ world, this dynamic has not been helped by another expression of the electronic society . . . the almost total move towards DJ sets now being delivered off laptops, through programmes such as Serato and Traktor. Whereas DJs in the vinyl era would exhibit some skill in organising their records and knowing where to find a particular tune, because the next song is now no more than a couple of mouse-clicks away, the temptation to throw on one tune after another in rapid succession, with minimal effort, is generally indulged. And the talent that vinyl DJs used to need to perform a smooth mix by matching the beats of two records by ear, has also been usurped by laptop culture, with many DJs now setting their programmes to beat-match and sequence tracks for them.

Previously, a good DJ would spend much of their free time hunting for elusive tunes – often on overseas imports in record shops – and would impress clubgoers by their knack of playing tracks that other DJs had not been able to acquire. Reputations were built upon it. Now, because anyone can get access to anything, it's rendered the identity of DJs completely irrelevant in the minds of the fickle, socially-engineered youth. Now, a DJ is just some random cunt with a laptop, and I can tell you from experience that anyone not of god-like A-list status like David Guetta or Paul Van Dyk, gets treated with the low level of respect and politeness that such perceptions bring.

This is all part of the long-planned, slow-drip effect of homogenising everything in culture – making everything generic, bland and commodified; of stamping out individual identity and character. Put into its wider context, it's an expression of the cultural-Marxist society and hive mentality the controllers are rapidly working towards, where the populace are instructed in how to think and behave and what to like, and individual expression is made a social crime. I realise I'm going on a rant here, and if I bemoan the state of 'kids today' much more I'll run the risk of sounding like my Dad 30 years ago. But I hope readers will permit this brief blowing-off of steam, and also recognise the relevance of these observations.

That's engineering.

Normalising narcissism

Unsurprisingly, television has played its own vital role in subliminally shaping public attitudes – particularly in the years since the millennium. It was in 2000 that the advent of 'reality TV' hit Britain in the form of 'Big Brother.' (Its name being lifted straight from the pages of Orwell's dystopian '1984' was no accident.) Because it was launched in a fanfare of hype as "the next big thing," it became just that as the public reacted – utterly predictably – *exactly* as the creators knew they would. This show, and others that followed in the same genre, normalised the idea of being constantly surveilled, making it 'cool.' It also played on the contestants' narcissistic tendencies, the one who most pandered to the public and garnered their approval being the winner who walked away with the cash prize. Just the fact that this format has now been rolled out in many other territories outside Britain, is enough to show it's fulfilling a culture-shaping agenda, rather than being simple fodder to fill TV timeslots.

British TV in the new millennium also popularised ruthlessness through the 'The Weakest Link' quiz show, where contestants' psychopathic qualities would be rewarded as they were goaded into doing each other down in order to become the winner. Everyone else was dismissed heartlessly by host Anne Robinson with the phrase "you leave with nothing. Goodbye!", all reinforcing the message that life's winners are the ones who look out for number one, and tread all over everybody else to get to the top. Ideological Satanism by any other name. The same harsh competitiveness – though masquerading as a more friendly type of competition – is now pushed through contests like 'Masterchef' and 'The Great British Bake-Off.'

That's engineering.

Heroes and villains

The public is entrained to think of its military intelligence agencies as benevolent organisations that are out to keep us all safe, when – a recurring factor in this satanically-inverted world – the opposite is actually the case. It has been proven beyond any reasonable doubt, that it is the intel operations of mainly Britain, the US and Israel, who have been behind so many of the attacks on their own citizens blamed on "terrorist" organisations such as ISIS. If this revelation is news to anyone reading this, they are strongly advised to look at the work of Ole

Dammegard at www.lightonconspiracies.com, who demonstrates with great flair how these events are carried off.

The apparent benign nature of operations such as the CIA, MI6 and Mossad, is reinforced in the public mindset through popular culture, and much of these organisations' real activity involves cultivating these very perceptions about themselves! Ian Fleming's James Bond stories have played a huge role in this process. The subject of bloodlines and heraldry is addressed in both the book and film version of the Bond story 'On Her Majesty's Secret Service,' in which arch-villain Blofeld hires a genealogist to authenticate his claim to being a descendant of the aristocratic Bleauchamp dynasty. (Fleming himself was descended from an aristocratic bloodline.)

For his part, Bond is portrayed as a noble and patriotic hero, on 'our' side, and always out to protect us from harm at the hands of dastardly villains. But if we're really honest with ourselves, James Bond is anything *but* a hero and is actually a deeply immoral person. He works for an organisation which, in reality, is involved in covering up institutionalised paedophilia, he is an order-follower – killing others on the say-so of somebody deemed to be more important than him by virtue of their job title – and he carries out such executions without ever stopping to question the morality of the situation, or if one human being ever has the inherent right to kill another outside of self-defence. This is one of the worst places spiritually that an individual can be – in total denial of how Natural Law works, and creating chaos and violence in the world, as a result of failing to take personal responsibility for one's actions and moral behaviour. Accepting the true nature of Bond has been another extremely bitter pill for me to swallow personally, as I loved the books and films as a kid. But letting go of one's heroes is par for the course in the process of genuine acceptance of truth.

No more heroes

My job – and that of the other researchers in this field who try to communicate the truth about manufactured public 'heroes' – is an unpopular one. It's no fun to hear that someone you've looked up to and admired for many years – and who may have inspired you greatly – is not who you thought they were, and probably didn't get to the top the way you've always thought. Often, the individual communicating these uncomfortable truths will get viciously attacked by those their words offend. I speak from experience. I get the objection, because I've been through the process myself of having to re-assess many of the individuals who had previously been role models to me. Besides other DJs and musicians, there have even been a few speakers in the 'truth' arena whose motives and true nature I've had to reconsider upon the emergence of new information.

What becomes clear – having gone through a few such devastating realisations – is that it's a mistake to actually have any heroes at all. None of us *really* know the popular figures we look up to, and because we don't, therein lies the constant possibility that they may at some point disappoint us. Instead, we should be our *own* heroes in recognition of our *own* unlimited potential to change things around us by way of our will, intent and chosen behaviours. We might doubt the motives of others, but we never have to doubt our own.

As Jan Irvin, who has put more work than most into uncovering the true backgrounds of many cultural icons observes, *everyone* has someone about whom they just don't want to hear it. They may accept that every other name is dirty in some way – but not *their* personal holy cow. Surely not *them*? Myself and the others doing this work aren't out to try and piss on peoples' parades and tarnish their perceptions of their personal heroes for shits and giggles. We're simply interested in uncovering, and then communicating the truth wherever we find it. A general rule of thumb with which you'll never go far wrong, is that celebrities are *not* your friends. They're *not* there to enrich or better your life in any way, but rather to influence it in line with covert agendas created by somebody else. People can either accept this, or reject it out of hand, but it continues to be the truth of the matter either way.

On that note, by the way, I certainly don't advocate throwing out all your old albums and never listening to certain artists again. Music can still be enjoyed at face value, once an understanding of how artists are used for certain agendas is understood. When that stuff is all out of the subconscious mind and into the conscious, where it can be properly processed and critically analysed, it loses its controlling power. A great tune is still a great tune, regardless of the circumstances in which it was created, and Beatles, Doors and Rolling Stones albums will always remain classics, in spite of what we now know about how these groups came into their influential positions. One reason why people still hanker nostalgically towards the music of previous decades, is that contemporary output is just so fucking dire – straight satanic at best, and stupefyingly bland and unmemorable at worst. Today's A-list acts will have done well to still be talked about with fondness in five years, let alone 50.

For those actively seeking meaningful message music, however, from artists free of any such corporate shackles, I recommend seeking out some of the uplifting independent material that's still, thankfully, being made by artists with minds to call their own, and the freedom to express it openly. You can always tell these musicians – they're the ones who have a burning spirit of conviction about them and make little to no money as a result! It's my pleasure to put together regular showcases of such artists – both old and new – in my ongoing 'The Sound Of Freedom' conscious music podcasts. See the Resources section at the end for the link to these.

Even those who are thought of first and foremost as activists and freedom-fighters – rather than as any other kind of celebrity – can turn out to be tainted by dubious connections, so far do the tentacles of deception reach. As radio host and independent researcher Randy Maugans commented in discussion of these subjects:

> *"Even the 'anti-war movement' was an invention of intelligence operations. The major groups, like SDS, the Weather Underground, Black Panthers, and later, Symbionese Liberation Front, were funded by the Establishment. The purposes are found in the Communist Manifesto and documents released by government agencies, as well as some former activists like Mark Rudd, Jerry Rubin, and the book 'The Strawberry Statement.' John Lennon and Yoko Ono also played key roles as intelligence operatives in creating the movements. Lennon befriended and funded radical activist Jerry Rubin."*

(On the subject of Yoko Ono, incidentally, isn't it interesting that both she and Linda McCartney, (*nee* Eastman,) happened to live for a time in the town of Scarsdale in Westchester County, New York? Linda attended Scarsdale High School, while Yoko's family moved over from Japan in the early 1950s, and she later joined them there. What are the odds of two future Beatles wives – of all the places they could have been in the world – both setting up home in the same small town? This raises some interesting questions about what's so special about Scarsdale, of course, which has also been home to a number of other musicians, actors, writers and directors.)

*

When you learn about how Lifetime Actors and culture creation work, the question becomes – are you happy you were duped and taken into confidence by these people, and would you like more of it? Or are you rather hacked off that you were treated as such easy fodder, rife for manipulation, and now that you understand how the game is played, do you resolve to never be fooled in the same way again? There's no shame in admitting that you were bamboozled. All of us are from the earliest age. The dignity comes from acknowledging that it happened and knowing better for next time.

As Jan Irvin observed when guesting on episode 672 of James Corbett's 'The Corbett Report' podcast:

> *"Ten years ago, I released 70 hours of Terence McKenna audio to the internet. And now, in hindsight, I'm looking at all of his research and everything, going 'my god, look what he was into!'*
>
> *"So it's my duty – having discovered that I was mind-controlled myself – to put this information out there to help others. And they may hate me for it in the interim. But I think that the people who take the time to actually read the information and look at it closely will find it very liberating, because it's much easier to spend a few hours or days or weeks researching facts, than it is to spend a lifetime believing lies."*

Resources:

'65 to '69: The Soundtrack to a Masterclass in Culture-Creation':

On the basis that music speaks louder than words, a while ago I put together the following story of five era-defining years as told by the music, with a few audio snippets from some key events along the way. The two parts can be streamed and/ or downloaded from the following links:

Part 1:

- https://www.spreaker.com/user/markdevlin/65-to-69-the-soundtrack-to-a-masterclass

Part 2:

- https://www.spreaker.com/user/markdevlin/65-to-69-the-soundtrack-to-a-masterclass_1

There's also this:

Destiny 105: Mark Devlin & Danny Prince run the music soundtrack to 1967's Summer of Love:

Part 1:

- https://www.spreaker.com/user/markdevlin/67-summer-of-love-revival-with-mark-devl

Part 2:

- https://www.spreaker.com/user/markdevlin/67-summer-of-love-revival-with-mark-devl_1

Part 3:

- https://www.spreaker.com/user/markdevlin/67-summer-of-love-revival-with-mark-devl_2

Mark Devlin's 'The Sound of Freedom' conscious music podcast archives:

- https://www.spreaker.com/show/the-sound-of-freedom

Good Vibrations Podcast Episode 111 – Jan Irvin & Steve Outtrim – MK-Ultra & The Counter-Culture:

- https://www.spreaker.com/user/markdevlin/gvp-111-jan-irvin-steve-outtrim-mk-ultra

Good Vibrations Podcast Episode 095 – Joe Atwill – Lifetime Actors & culture creation:

- https://www.spreaker.com/user/markdevlin/gvp-095-joe-atwill

Good Vibrations Podcast Episode 084 – Jan Irvin – culture creation:

- https://www.spreaker.com/user/markdevlin/gvp-084-jan-irvin

CBS News: Bush's Famous Family Tree:

- http://www.cbsnews.com/news/bushs-famous-family-tree/

Rense.com: Hinckley/ Bush family links:

- http://www.rense.com/general45/hink.htm

Hiding In Plain Sight: The Global Paedophile Ring Exposed:

- http://www.trueactivist.com/hiding-in-plain-sight-the-global-pedophile-ring-exposed/

Watch 'Brotherhood of the Bell' on-line:

Part 1:

- http://www.dailymotion.com/video/x2glrg4

Part 2:

- http://www.dailymotion.com/video/x2glu2f_the-brotherhood-of-the-bell-1970-part-2_shortfilms

Gnostic Media: Jan Irvin's article 'Entheogens – What's in a Name?:

- https://www.gnosticmedia.com/Entheogens_WhatsinaName_PsychedelicSpirituality_SocialControl_CIA

Gnostic Media: Jan Irvin's article on R Gordon Wasson, the 'discoverer' of Magic Mushrooms:

- https://www.gnosticmedia.com/SecretHistoryMagicMushroomsProject#R.%20Gordon%20Wasson

Gnostic Media: Jan Irvin & Joe Atwill's article on the Grateful Dead's CIA links, 'Manufacturing The Deadhead: A Product of Social Engineering':

- https://www.gnosticmedia.com/manufacturing-the-deadhead-a-product-of-social-engineering-by-joe-atwill-and-jan-irvin/

Gnostic Media: Who Are You? Jan Irvin & Joe Atwill expose The Who as military-intelligence assets:

- https://www.gnosticmedia.com/unspun044-TheWho-WhoAreYou/

Youtube user Dayz of Noah's excellent video overviews on how social-engineering gets done:

How media shaped the generations – Radio & the teenager:

- https://www.youtube.com/watch?v=blyd_o9uqn8

How media shaped the generations – The chaos era:

- https://www.youtube.com/watch?v=j55daitrtza

How media shaped the generations- Do what thou wilt (sex, drugs, and aliens):

- https://www.youtube.com/watch?v=suwrg7tysfm

T. Stokes: Tony Blair as 'Miranda':

- http://www.whale.to/c/tony_blair4.html

Alan McGee: Talks Magick, Music and his new Movie 'Kubricks':

- http://dangerousminds.net/comments/alan_mcgee_talks_magick_music_and_his_new_movie_kubricks

NME: Gorillaz looking forward to virtual characters being able to perform and make music without them:

- http://www.nme.com/news/music/gorillaz-virtual-characters-make-music-without-them-2055736

Uhoh: TV Food Activist Jamie Oliver Teaming Up with GMO-Pushing Bill Gates Foundation (with Video):

- http://althealthworks.com/4927/uhoh-famous-tv-food-activist-jamie-oliver-teaming-up-with-notoriously-pro-gmo-bill-gates-foundation-with-video/

Vigilant Citizen: What Is Happening To Katy Perry?:

- https://vigilantcitizen.com/latestnews/happening-katy-perry/

Carl James: Arcade Fire – Chemtrails, 9/11 & Other Oddities:

- https://www.youtube.com/watch?v=uRQMLVUkVHM

CHAPTER 4

EVER GET THE FEELING YOU'VE BEEN CHEATED? GOODNIGHT

How Punk and New Wave kept the counter-culture control grid moving on.

> *"Come, mothers and fathers across the land,*
> *Well, don't criticise what you can't understand,*
> *Your sons and your daughters are beyond your command,*
> *Your old road is rapidly ageing,*
> *Please stay off of the new one if you can't lend a hand,*
> *'Cause the times they are a-changin'."*
>
> *Bob Dylan: 'Times They are A-Changin' (1965)*

> *"New York to East California,*
> *There's a New Wave coming, I warn ya."*
>
> *Kim Wilde: 'Kids In America' (1981)*

> *"No more heroes any more,*
> *No more heroes any more."*
>
> *The Stranglers: 'No More Heroes' (1977)*

The degree to which the counter-culture of the '60s was steered by the military intelligence and social engineering communities is now well-documented. The work of the late author and researcher Dave McGowan, and more recently, that of Jan Irvin on the Gnostic Media broadcasts, has shown how, time and time again, key players turn out to have family links back into these worlds, usually through their fathers.

With regard to the findings of McGowan in his 'Weird Scenes Inside the Canyon' book, if it had just been a handful of musicians' fathers who had high-ranking military connections, it could be reasonably written-off as 'coincidence,' 'synchronicity,' or its more fortuitous cousin, 'serendipity.' It's the same with the migration of artists to the restricted Laurel Canyon neighbourhood. A ragtag bunch of them from here and there could be explained away innocently enough. But the mass influx from all over the US, Canada and beyond – as detailed in McGowan's work – goes way beyond the realms of pure chance. Then, when you factor in the ominous presence of the Lookout Mountain Laboratory presiding over the whole community, and couple that with the military family backgrounds of almost all the players on the scene, it would take a very heavy state of denial not to recognise, in the words of Buffalo Springfield, that "there's something happening here, what it is ain't exactly clear."

And even if the endless examples of Establishment meddling in this particular era could be written off as a series of 'coincidences,' when the very same clues, fingerprints and calling-cards then crop up in the scene which pretty much replaces it a decade or so later, the claim that it's mere happenstance really does start to crumble under the spotlight of scrutiny. The same scene spawning its own Theosophical movement, and having links to occult secret societies, Ivy League academia, former US presidents and even serial killers, only serves to make it yet more intriguing.

Could a reader of my last book have been on the right track when he got in touch to comment?:

> *"My ideas are that they have musical styles and associated cultures ready to reel out at different periods to fit in with the technology, drugs, and social attitudes of the time; psychedelic music for the 60s, Rock and Punk for the 70s, House music for the 80s, Drum & Bass for the 90s, etc, etc."*

Punks jump up to get beat down

Early Punk Rock came largely out of New York City, and specifically, the Greenwich Village area of Manhattan, and was influenced by the Beat poet scene which had flourished there from the 1940s onward, populated by the likes of Allen Ginsberg, Jack Kerouac, Lucien Carr and William Burroughs. Research has shown how these characters were connected back into such dubious walks of life as military intelligence, social engineering think-tanks, dark occult mystery schools, secret society fraternities, MK-Ultra mind control and institutionalised paedophilia in a vast interconnected web, (is there any other kind?) Punk, in turn, birthed the scene known as New Wave which followed.

Over in the UK, meanwhile, the British take on Punk is acknowledged to have morphed out of the pub-rock scene in and around London. A youthful generation alienated both by harsh social conditions, and the pretentious and self-satisfied 'prog-rock' scene of the mid-70s, channelled their angst into angry, energy-charged music with a DIY ethos that eschewed the industry rule book. The scene was spearheaded by the Sex Pistols under the calculated control of their dominant manager Malcolm McLaren, of whom, more later. And, as some delving into the finer detail shows, there seems to be more than just lucky timing at play here.

What's in a name?

On the grounds that etymology can be so revealing, and observing that the truth of a matter is often placed in plain sight, Jan Irvin and Joe Atwill began Episode 54 of their 'Unspun' radio show by defining the word 'punk.' It's reasonable to assume, after all, that any clues as to a genre's true nature may be found in its very name. Various official definitions include: "A young man used as a homosexual partner, especially in prison;" "an aggressive and violent young man;" "an inexperienced young person;" "a cowardly or weak young man;" "an inferior, rotten, worthless person or thing;" "a petty criminal or hoodlum." Hardly flattering terms for a tribe of music fans to identity themselves with. And the serial killer in the 'Dirty Harry' movie, sneeringly derided by Clint Eastwood as a 'punk' in 1971, makes for a similarly dubious role model.

To 'punk' someone, meanwhile, is defined as: "To humiliate, to dupe or deceive, to play a practical joke on." Does this reveal the way the manipulators of this scene really felt, in their mocking arrogance, towards those they had in their sights? The same principle is at play with the words 'hippie' and 'hipster,' incidentally, both of which derive from the days of opium dens when addicts would lie on their hips smoking on a pipe, and with obsessives of the (CIA-created) Grateful Dead being referred to, none-too-flatteringly, as 'deadheads' – a giveaway as to the value their controllers really placed on them.

The front facade of the infamous CBGB punk nightspot in New York City's Bowery district.

https://en.wikipedia.org/wiki/CBGB#/media/File:CBGB_club_facade.jpg

Credit: Adam Di Carlo at English Wikipedia

The kingpins of the Beat movement, who had such an influence on both the counter-culture hippies and the first Punks, have some red flag-raising backgrounds in themselves. Arguably the best-known was Allen Ginsberg, a homosexual, suspected CIA agent, alleged paedophile, and a proud member of NAMBLA, (the North American Man/Boy Love Association,) which advocates for the decriminalisation of male adults having sex with male children, and campaigns for the release of imprisoned paedophiles. Equally influential on the Beat scene was William S Burroughs, whose legend earned him a place as one of the 'heroes' of the Beatles on their 'Sgt. Pepper's Lonely Hearts Club Band' album sleeve. Burroughs was a heroin and morphine addict who shot dead his second wife Joan Vollmer Adams in a stunt gone wrong, but avoided any long-term jail time. Quite the hero.

The way the word came to be associated with the music is considered to involve a journalist by the name of Roderick McNeil, nicknamed 'Legs,' who was one of the founders of the 'Punk' fanzine, first published in New York in 1975. The term 'Punk Rock' had been coined by writers on 'Creem' magazine before, but McNeil and his colleagues, John Holmstrom and Ged Dunn, further popularised its usage. They were influenced by the music of Iggy Pop & The Stooges, The Ramones and The Dictators, and the term became associated with these acts. McNeil commented that the name was chosen because it "seemed to sum up . . . everything . . . obnoxious, smart but not pretentious, absurd, ironic, and things that appealed to the darker side." He claimed to have lifted the word from an episode of the TV detective show 'Kojak,' in which Telly Savalas' character utters the phrase 'you lousy punk!'

In its nascent years, the New York scene was very much centred around a live music venue in Manhattan's East Village known as CBGB, (standing for Country, Blue Grass & Blues.) The club had morphed from a run-down Hell's Angels biker's bar at its 1973 outset, into a hotbed for the movers and shakers of Punk and New Wave, the likes of The Ramones, Television, the Patti Smith Group, Blondie, and Talking Heads regularly playing there. Although the venue closed its doors in 2006, its legacy lived on through a CBGB radio show launched on the iheartradio platform in 2010, with music festivals under the CBGB banner beginning in 2012.

Connections for days

Nino Teuoneaux, (pronounced two-one-oh,) is one of a number of citizen researchers who started out as music fans or musicians, but have more recently become independent investigators into the genres they have always loved. In the majority of cases, everything they pull together has long been in the public domain. It's not until this information is collated and cross-referenced, that clues and patterns start to form. Nino has presented much of his data on the 'Hoax Busters Call' radio show, whose host John Adams has also got into this area of research. Nino guested on my 'Good Vibrations' podcast in 2016 to share his extensive findings into Punk and New Wave's unexpected connections. As he commented:

> *"It's an intertwining network... It's a network of a lot of people coming out of a bloodline distinction, or wealth, and they just keep the ball amongst themselves and don't really share it too often unless there's an extraordinary artist, it seems.*
>
> *"Another pattern I'm recognising in aggregating this information, is the unbalanced proportion of people that went to Harvard – in bands, controlling bands, around bands. There's definitely a Harvard music language as a Liberal link."*

The findings of Nino and fellow researcher Masonic Youth, bring a plethora of dubious links and unsettling alliances. Hold tight as we embark on a dizzying rollercoaster ride of fascinating information.

The deep background of New Wavers Talking Heads stands as a great starting point. Alongside singer David Byrne, (himself an adherent of both the Church of Subgenius and Santeria religions,) and guitarist Jerry Harrison, the Heads consisted of husband-and-wife couple Chris Frantz and Tina Weymouth, (who also fronted the Talking Heads spin-off group Tom Tom Club.)

Tina Weymouth's brother, Yann, (a Harvard graduate, naturally,) turns out to have been Chief of Design for the Chinese-American architect I.M Pei on the Grand Louvre Project in Paris, involving the placement of the iconic glass pyramid. The family's Masonic links seem to be represented here, given the symbolism incorporated into the Louvre and into one of the most Masonic cities on Earth. Yann also designed the Salvador Dali Museum and the National Gallery of Art in Washington DC, and was awarded The National Order of Merit from France.

Yann and Tina's father, Ralph Weymouth, was a Vice Admiral of the US Navy and a Master of the Freemason Grand Lodge of Maine. Their great-grandfather, meanwhile, was Anatole Le Braz, known as the Bard of Brittany, a highly-regarded folklore poet and a lecturer at Harvard and Yale Universities. Anatole married Mabel Davidson, the sister to Henry Pomeroy Davison, which brings a link to the Yale secret society Skull & Bones. Henry was a senior partner of the banking monolith JP Morgan, worked with the Astor Place Bank, and was instrumental in the creation of the Federal Reserve System, attending the notorious 1910 meeting at Jekyll Island, (though Wikipedia describes him as a 'philanthropist!')

Chris' brother Roddy Frantz was also in a band, known as The Urban Verbs. Their father was a teacher at The Judges Advocate General's Legal Centre & School – a military academy. Chris was born at Fort Campbell military base in Kentucky, becoming a Harvard alumni with his tuition paid for by the army. He was also stationed at The Pentagon.

Like Tina Weymouth and Chris Frantz, the two principal members of Blondie – Debbie Harry and Chris Stein- were also a couple, (though they didn't marry.) Prior to her days with the group, Harry worked as a waitress in one of the original Playboy nightclubs. Gloria Steinem, touted as the mother of the feminist movement, went undercover as a Playboy Bunny during her days as a journalist, resulting in her celebrated 'exposé' article of 1963. It has recently emerged that Steinem was an asset of the CIA, (the feminist movement having been manipulated at the hands of Abby Rockefeller,) calling into question the authenticity of the socially-changing movement that she spawned. The rabbit ears worn by the Playboy bunnies are said to indicate the presence of mind-control programming, in much the same way as the wearing of Mickey Mouse ears by many Disney-groomed pop stars does.

Debbie Harry, meanwhile, cropped up as a guest at the 'spirit cooking' dinners of the witch/ 'performance artist' Marina Abramović in late 2016. Harry was pictured plunging a knife into the breast area of a cake that has been fashioned in the shape of a woman's body, in a ritual derived from the sex magick practices of Aleister Crowley. Gwen Stefani and Lady Gaga are among other stars known to associate with Abramović and to attend her 'dinners.' Abramović has also been named as a 'spiritual advisor' to Jay-Z, (who donated money to her 'art institute,') as well as to Usher and Kim Kardashian, among others.

In a loose link between Punk and serial killers, meanwhile, Debbie Harry claimed that she almost became a murder victim of Ted Bundy, having accepted a lift from him in New York in the 1970s and narrowly escaping from his car when he started acting strangely.

In 2017, Harry revealed that she had discovered Scottish ancestry on the part of her birth mother. She was adopted and raised by Richard and Catherine Harry when she was three months old, but had been born Angela Trimble. Her mother's maiden name, she told the 'Scottish Sun' newspaper, was Mackenzie. The Mackenzies are one of the principal clans (bloodlines) of Scotland.

The Punk/ serial killer connections aren't quite over yet. One further one is revealed in Maury Terry's book 'Ultimate Evil,' and involves the murder of New York photographer/ pornographer Ron Sisman and his partner Elizabeth Platzman in their Manhattan apartment on Halloween 1981. The two hitmen involved were found to have been hired by a felon named Jesse Turner, all over a snuff movie which Sisman had allegedly filmed, and Turner had been ordered to retrieve. The snuff film is said to have shown the final murder committed by David Berkowitz, better known as the serial killer Son Of Sam. Terry's book quotes Berkowitz as saying that three people were in a van across the street when he committed his last shooting in Brooklyn, (one was Sisman,) and had captured it on tape. He added: "some famous artist wanted that to sell to a collector for about $50,000."

And the Punk connection comes from the artist in question being named as Robert Mapplethorpe, a homo-erotic photographer and sculptor... who was the one-time partner of influential New York punker Patti Smith! Jesse Turner and David Berkowitz have both been connected to the Process Church of the Final Judgement, a spin-off cult of Scientology, with further links to the music industry as detailed in the last book. The Son of Sam murders are claimed to have been directly commissioned by the Process Church, and carried out by others besides Berkowitz. Robert Mapplethorpe died of AIDS in 1989.

The third serial killer link identified by Nino comes from the hardcore Punk outfit The Cro Mags. Group singer John Joseph, who has spoken of being sexually molested while in foster 'care,' – a shockingly common claim among musicians – noted in an interview that he had known the notorious murderer Joel Rifkin, currently serving a 203-year sentence for the killings of nine women. One of Rifkin's victims was a prostitute named Tiffany Bresciani, who was dating Dave Rubinstein, the singer from another hardcore band called Reagan Youth. Following the murder of Tiffany and the death of his mother in a car accident, Rubinstein overdosed on heroin and died aged 28.

Joseph stated:

> *"As a matter of fact, I knew the whole Reagan Youth crew and that fucking guy, Joel Rifkin. I remember when Dave's girlfriend got murdered. That was the body wrapped up in a tarp that they found when they busted him. He was going to dump it in Long Island. But I know Dave. Me, Dave, and HR from Bad Brains in '81 had an organization called the UFF – United Freedom Fighters. I knew Dave before he started getting high. Great, great guy, but shit happens. God rest his soul."*

Joel Rifkin, when not raping and murdering, *just happened* to become a landscape gardener to Sophia Casey, the widow of the former CIA director William Casey. John Joseph himself went on to embrace the Krishna movement, a look and philosophy which strongly influenced the future direction of the Cro Mags, spawning a Punk spin-off genre known as Krishnacore.

On to Cro Mags bassist Harley Flanagan, then. His mother, Rose Feliu Pettet, seems to have been something of a rock groupie with the likes of the New York Dolls and Velvet Underground, and hung out at Andy Warhol's Factory studio before becoming the 'spiritual wife' to the occultist Harry Everett Smith.

Smith was a member of the Ordo Templi Orientis, which itself seems to have a strange, magnetic-like lure for music-makers and celebrities. Everett Smith was one of the original beatniks, put together a folk music collection for the Smithsonian Institute, and was involved in the Theosophy and Dadaism 'art' movements. New York Dolls member David Johansen, (known by the pseudonym of Buster Poindexter as part of the house band on TV's 'Saturday Night Live,') put together a band called David Johansen and the Harry Smiths in tribute.

It was Harley's aunt, Denise Mercedes, meanwhile, who recruited him to play drums in her band, the Stimulators, when he was just 11 (!) When not doing music, Denise turns out to have been a lover to both Allen Ginsberg, and Ginsberg's homosexual partner Peter Orlovosky! Ginsberg had known Harley since he was one year old and they reportedly lived on a farm together. Ginsberg went on to publish the poetry book 'Stories & Illustrations by Harley.' Harley appears on the cover, aged nine, dressed in a leather robe and sporting a horned helmet. Harley's mother turns out to have been present at Ginsberg's bedside when he died in 1997. Harley became widely acknowledged as the first American skinhead when he imported the look from the UK, very much blending into the Cro Mags' Krishnacore image.

Just before we leave Ginsberg, another relationship outside of his long-term one with Peter Orlovsky, was with visual artist and Andy Warhol associate Bibbe Hansen. She went on to become the mother of the musician known as Beck. All are said to be generational Scientologists.

Nothing to see here. Please move along.

Straight outta DC

Two of the members of the Detroit 1960s proto-punk group MC5, (Motor City 5,) Wayne Kramer and Michael Davis, were inmates at The Federal Medicine Centre in Lexington, Kentucky, known initially as the United States Narcotic Farm. Although it is described as "a federal prison for inmates requiring medical or mental health care," it is also one of the key hospitals involved in the CIA's MK-Ultra drug experimentation programme. William Burroughs attended the same institution. MC5 were managed for a time by fellow poet and political activist John Sinclair, who served two years of a ten-year prison sentence for marijuana possession. MC5 embraced Sinclair's White Panther Party political leanings and were considered a 'Yippie' band, with the word invented by counter-culture activists Abbie Hoffman and Jerry Rubin, and defined as "a radically youth-oriented and counter-cultural revolutionary offshoot of the free speech and anti-war movements of the 1960s."

Beat poet and cultural 'hero' Allen Ginsberg. He was also a member of NAMBLA, an organisation that campaigns for men to be able to legally have sex with underage boys.

https://upload.wikimedia.org/wikipedia/commons/0/0b/Allen_Ginsberg_1979_-_cropped.jpg

Credit: Dijk, Hans van / Anefo - [1] Dutch National Archives, The Hague, Fotocollectie Algemeen Nederlands Persbureau (ANEFO), 1945-1989 bekijk toegang 2.24.01.05 Bestanddeelnummer 930-5558

Nino also reminds us that Washington DC has long been a hotbed of Punk music, with its own distinctive sound and style. It becomes an interesting location for such a scene given the many links back to the government and intelligence worlds.

Dave Grohl of Foo Fighters, by way of a great example, was earlier in a hardcore Punk band out of DC named Scream. His father, James Harper Grohl, worked in politics as an assistant to Robert A. Taft Jr. Robert's father was William Howard Taft, the 27th president of the United States, and his father was Alphonso Taft, a founder of Skull & Bones. During John Kerry's presidential campaign in 2004, Dave Grohl joined the trail and dedicated the album 'In Your Honor' to the former Skull & Bonesman. Yeah, rock 'n' roll!

For a time, Grohl dated Kathleen Hanna, now married to Adam Horovitz of The Beastie Boys. Kathleen Hanna was in the bands Bikini Kill and Le Tigre, part of the underground feminist punk movement known as Riot Grrrl, and has stated that she was greatly influenced by the aforementioned Gloria Steinem. Nino reports that at many of the gigs played by feminist punk bands such as Hanna's, the eugenics organisation Planned Parenthood, (of which Bill Gates' dad was a founder,) are to be seen operating a promotional booth. But I'm sure it's all just a coincidence. Apparently they happen all the time.

Grohl was back in the news in 2017, and reminding us of how well-connected he is, after he broke his leg falling off a stage in Switzerland, and "Paul McCartney" (it says here) organised his resulting surgery. "He knows some good fucking doctors," Grohl remarked. Oh, I'll bet he fucking does. Grohl sports three tattoos which he says were inspired by his musical heroes, the occult-obsessed Led Zeppelin, and he has described the group's John Bonham – who died of apparent alcohol poisoning at the age of 32 – as "the greatest drummer of all time."

And, what do you know, we're straight back round to Ginsberg again through a story told by James Harper Grohl, where he claims the Beat poet once tried to seduce him back in his more Bohemian, pre-politics days.

Prior to Foo Fighters, Dave Grohl was the drummer for Seattle Grunge pioneers Nirvana, whose singer Kurt Cobain became a member of the fabled 27 Club when he was found shot dead in 1994. Many researchers doubt the official and convenient verdict of 'suicide.' Cobain's wife, Courtney Love, has since been blamed as being complicit in his death by none other than her own father, Hank Harrison. He has also claimed that she was sexually abused from the age of three in her childcare facility. In a dark twist of irony, Courtney's mother is Linda Carroll, a therapist and counsellor for victims of abuse. She's also rumoured to be the illegitimate daughter of Marlon Brando.

Harrison himself was an early road manager for the Warlocks, who morphed into The Grateful Dead. This group's members have been shown to have been CIA agents from Masonic families, with further links to Bohemian Grove and MK-Ultra. (There are those who additionally claim that Grohl's success with Foo Fighters was in some way facilitated by Cobain's untimely death, as some kind of ritual sacrifice.) The father of the Grateful Dead's music publisher, Alan Trist, *just happens* to have been Eric Trist, one of the founders of the Tavistock Institute of Human Relations in London. But I'm sure it's all just another coincidence.

Would any reader by this point be surprised to learn that Courtney Love is also a distant cousin of Douglas Fairbanks Jr., the actor and decorated naval officer? Also of interest is the fact that her manager for a brief time was Sam Lutfi, who readers might recall was a one-time manager (handler?) of Britney Spears, and became embroiled in a legal case with her family over her 'conservatorship.' In his book 'Drugs As Weapons Against Us,' investigative journalist John Potash writes of how Courtney Love brought large quantities of heroin and other narcotics over to Ireland and England, distributing them among various music scenes there in the 1990s with apparent impunity from any law enforcement. I wonder if I or the average reader of this book did the same, whether we'd be free of any knocks on the door? She's also rumoured to have given heroin to Ozzy and Sharon Osbourne's daughter Kelly, getting her hooked, although Courtney in turn claims to have 'saved Kelly's life' from her addictions twice.

Strange bedfellows

The links between Punk and the development of social movements go on, as Nino highlights:

"We have a ton of vanguards coming out of Punk Rock. So for (rock musician) Jobriath, he was basically the first openly gay rock star. Openly gay is the key. So there were gay ones doing gay things, but he was open about it. Another digression; we have the first openly gay guy on a reality TV show – or on television – and that was Lance Loud from the punk band The Mumps. So the very first reality TV show came from Punk Rock. It was called 'An American Family,' done on PBS. All from Punk Rock. So this is a vanguard movement of social justice! This whole thing is unbelievable."

A link from the Punk scene back to its earlier counter-culture cousin comes via Dr. Timothy Leary, who interviewed British Punker and former Generation X frontman Billy Idol, (a member of the so-called 'Bromley contingent,) for a 1993 ABC show called 'In Concert.' In a conversation which laps at the fringes of Transhumanism, the pair discuss Idol's 'Cyberpunk' album. According to the promotional blurb:

"Billy Idol discusses a small amount of the technology behind the 'Cyberpunk' album. He notes how it was completely produced on a computer. Timothy Leary sees Billy as 'creating his own reality'."

An earlier Punk link with Leary had come in 1987, when Dead Kennedys singer-turned spoken word artist and political activist, Jello Biafra, had shared a bill with him reading poetry at the River City Reunion event in Kansas. William Burroughs and Allen Ginsberg, (who photographed him,) were also present.

Nino finishes with a couple of intriguing links to the JFK assassination of 1963. Yale attendee Jerry Haynes – once a Japanese language specialist in the US Air Force, and the father of Butthole Surfers (classy name) frontman Gibby Haynes – was better known as the children's entertainer Mr. Peppermint. He became one of the first on American TV to report the killing as he was in the vicinity of the TV station WFAA when the story broke. The father of Ian MacKaye, meanwhile, of the DC Punk bands Fugazi and Minor Threat, was in the press bus as part of the JFK motorcade on the fateful day. Also present in Dallas – and in serendipitous attendance at the press conference where police displayed

Lee Harvey Oswald – was future BBC Radio 1 DJ John Peel, who at the time was working as a radio DJ in Texas.

And just before we leave Ian MacKaye, it's worth noting that his grandmother, Dorothy, worked with eugenics kingpin and Planned Parenthood member Paul Popenoe on marriage advice columns, and fraternised with fellow eugenicists like Abby Rockefeller and Margaret Mead. His grandfather, meanwhile, worked for the United States Office of War Information. You couldn't make it up and you don't need to.

Talking of which – a link between child-star actress Shirley Temple and Punk rock, anyone? The grown-up Temple married Charles Alden Black, who was an executive at the Stanford Research Institute, one of the principal social engineering organisations in the US, from 1952 to 1957, as well as serving as an intelligence officer in the Korean War. The pair's daughter, Laurie Black, went on to join a North-Western Punk band called The Melvins. You know, like you do.

And in a nugget uncovered by Masonic Youth linking a present-day rocker with a prominent politician, Pete Wentz of the group Fall Out Boy, turns out to have a maternal grandfather who served as the US ambassador to Sierra Leone, and was also a cousin of former US Secretary of State Colin Powell!

Nino Teuoneaux and Masonic Youth's blog site, documenting much of the above and many other dubious links, can be found at: http://fourhorsesasses.blogspot.co.uk

The natural assumption when it comes to the Punk genre, would be that its community of musicians was made up of disaffected kids – primarily of working-class backgrounds – playing grimy underground clubs, and channelling their angst and contempt for a system which had left them out to dry into their angry, rebellious music. It might reasonably be assumed that the dads of such musicians – if they weren't on the dole – would have occupied professions such as miners, dockers, factory workers, lorry drivers or labourers. Very few of these are to be found.

As Joe Atwill observed on one of his 'Unspun' podcasts on culture creation:

> *"When you look at the backgrounds, and when you see things like Skull & Bones and all these connections into the halls of power and*

wealth, then the idea that there would suddenly be a generation that would decide to produce Punk . . . I mean, that's just so non sequitur! This wouldn't be what these people with their backgrounds would be doing, unless it was something that was organised."

And reflections on what the over-riding motive may have always been came from Jan Irvin on the same show. Drugs, homosexuality, Transgenderism, feminism, nihilism and discord between the generations and social classes, are all in the toolkits of the social engineers:

"The leader of these movements is the Lifetime Actor. It's the Pied Piper, literally. They're the generals, then they get all the plebs to put on the uniform and follow them along. And they destroy our children and our families in the process because – clearly – they are afraid of any family challenging their power. So if they can destroy the family, the backbone of society, and if they can institute this socialist, mom-on-welfare feminist society, then they have total control and they win ('Brave New World' author Aldous) Huxley's final revolution."

Take that Situation

Another link an observer wouldn't necessarily expect to see, is the British Punk and New Wave scene's connection to an intellectual socialist movement known as Situationist International – particularly through the managers of some of the most pivotal acts. SI is described as "an international organisation of social revolutionaries made up of avant-garde artists, intellectuals, and political theorists . . . The intellectual foundations . . . were derived primarily from anti-authoritarian Marxism and the avant-garde art movements of the early 20th century, particularly Dada and Surrealism." It also has ties to The Frankfurt School.

In an article on the 'Louder Than War' website, writer Amy Britton detailed specific links to this movement from some of Punk's key players:

> *"The influence of Situationism on popular culture, particularly on the Punk music of the mid to late 1970s, is undeniable. Managers such as Bernie Rhodes and Malcolm McLaren were committed, consummate Situationists, (the latter's bands, the Sex Pistols and Bow Wow Wow, were initially based around its principles.)"*

And later . . .

> *"The scene that gathered around (Malcolm McLaren and Vivienne Westwood's Chelsea fashion shop) Sex, was somewhat self-lionizing anyway; with members of what would become known as the 'Bromley Contingent' gathering there. Bromley is a very-middle class, suburban area, but the group could be almost feral in their behaviour. (One particularly notable member, Siouxsie Sioux, put her friend on a lead and would walk into pubs ordering a "bowl of water for her dog'.")*

Siouxsie Sioux, real name Susan Ballion, posed for pictures in swastika-laden Nazi/ SS regalia from the Sex store. Other attention-grabbing promotional photos have her sporting a large Star of David/ Seal of Solomon design on her T-shirt, and with one eye painted in the fashion of the Alex character from Stanley Kubrick's dystopian nightmare movie 'A Clockwork Orange.'

Back to Amy Britton's article:

> *". . . As a believer and supporter of Situationism, McLaren would want to fight against what appalled (key Situationist figure) Guy Debord so much, not go along with it. So the 'star' he found could not possibly 'embody banalism' or a 'possible role.' He had to be exciting, with a real role.*
>
> *"Once he had found him in the form of John Lydon, his concept became unstoppable. Lydon was renamed Johnny Rotten . . . His stage name carried with it a whole persona; the barriers of the real and perceived breaking down . . . Pseudonyms appeared everywhere on outlandish characters such as Siouxsie Sioux and the Damned's Captain*

Sensible. But not everybody felt that this was necessary . . . and with McLaren not the only Situationist manager on the scene, ideas about what reflected the construction of a situation varied from person to person."

McLaren had formed the King Mob with fellow art student Jamie Reid as an expression of Situationism. He had set up solidarity demonstrations in London at the time of the infamous May 1968 student riots in Paris, then spent time in New York briefly managing the New York Dolls, before returning to London with the intention of bringing the Punk aesthetic of nihilism back to Britain. The Sex Pistols morphed from a pub-rock band to the ambassadors of the Punk scene shortly after. Perhaps his vision for the band all along was encapsulated in the 'cash for chaos' statement he makes as 'The Embezzler' in the movie 'The Great Rock N Roll Swindle,' (another clue in the title?)which parodied the Sex Pistols story.

Stewart Copeland, one of CIA overlord Miles Copeland's three sons who went to work in the music business. The Police ... gettit?

https://upload.wikimedia.org/wikipedia/commons/5/58/Stewart_Copeland_Marseille_2008.png

Credit: JosuéJacob

It was Bernard Rhodes who introduced John Lydon to the Pistols, before introducing Mick Jones and Paul Simonon to Joe Strummer to form the nucleus of The Clash. Rhodes, like McLaren, has said he was vastly influenced by Situationism, and he was a designer of T-shirts for Sex. Other Situationists in the music game have included the former TV journalist Tony Wilson, who went on to spearhead Factory Records/ Joy Division/ New Order and Manchester's influential Hacienda club, and the group KLF, led by the deeply eccentric Bill Drummond. The latter's anarchic Situationist 'art statements' have included setting fire to a million pounds in cash, and dumping a dead sheep on stage at a BRIT Awards ceremony.

It's difficult to establish exactly what Situationism was trying to espouse, as all its writings are cloaked in pretentious intellectual jargon. What is clear is that it concerned itself with changing human society, and it's not the first time we've encountered this dynamic at play in the music industry.

Ever feel you've been misled?

Running in the family

One family in particular yielded such influence over the development of the New Wave scene on both sides of the Atlantic, that virtually all of the acts that shaped that scene had some kind of working connection back to them. In many ways, that entire musical community was the fiefdom of the Copeland family. And its patriarch, Miles Axe Copeland Jr., was a career CIA man and something of a legend within intelligence circles. I don't know if readers have noticed, but it's never too long before those nice folk at Langley pop back up in these stories. Why should this be if this is an honourable agency concerned only with keeping Americans safe and secure? According to former CIA asset John R. Stockwell, who has admitted to personally flying heroin out of Vietnam into the US on behalf of the agency, it's anything but. In his book 'The Praetorian Guard' he states:

> *"Now, more clearly than ever, the CIA, with its related institutions, is exposed as an agency of destabilisation and repression."*

And also . . .

> *"The CIA and the big corporations were, in my experience, in step with each other. Later, I realised that they may argue about details of strategy – a small war here or there. However, both are vigorously committed to supporting the system."*

And Stockwell is one of only a multitude of whistle-blowers who have lifted the lid on the real role of the CIA, which – in classic satanic-inversion fashion- is the very opposite of what it's publicly proclaimed to be. Jan Irvin has wryly remarked that it should be renamed the Central Entertainment Agency, since more of its resources seem to have been deployed in weaponising popular culture, than in the spying, surveillance and counter-intelligence work it's supposed to be engaged in. The Copeland family story certainly bears this viewpoint out.

Born in Alabama in 1916 as the son of a doctor, Copeland joined the National Guard as a young man, and became one of the founder members of the Office of Strategic Service in the 1940s, which morphed into the Central Intelligence Agency after World War 2. His CIA career involved overseas postings, and he was on the scene at many political coups and regime changes. These included a role in the 1949 Syrian *coup d'etat*, and the 1953 overthrow of the Prime Minister of Iran. From 1957 to '68, Copeland was based in Beirut, during which time he worked closely with the Dulles brothers of CIA repute.

Outside of his CIA activities, he also became a consultant to General Abdel Nasser of Egypt, who had overthrown that country's king. Copeland was involved in the setting-up of the Mukhabarat, that country's version of the CIA. In his book 'The Game Player,' Copeland admitted that he had been sent to Egypt to assess the feasibility of assassinating Nasser. Copeland reportedly retired from the CIA in 1957, but continued to carry out missions for the agency upon request. He relocated to London in 1970, where he became a frequent television guest defending the virtues of the intelligence community. He also helped devise a board game for the manufacturer Waddingtons entitled 'The Game Of Nations,' and wrote an article titled 'Spooks For Bush.' He had earlier named George HW Bush, (who trauma-based mind-control survivor

Cathy O'Brien has named as a rapist, paedophile and satanist,) as his favourite of all CIA directors.

Biographies of Copeland often list him as an accomplished musician outside of his spying activities. Although this aspect may explain why his sons were encouraged to go to work within the music field, there seems to be some doubt as to whether this was actually the case, or whether this was embellishment added to Copeland's CV at a later stage. According to Wikipedia: "There is nothing in Copeland's CIA files to suggest he was ever a "professional musician," but "several relatives and friends have testified to his musical ability." Copeland's books contain "several impressive statements about his days as a jazz musician," including that "he spent a week playing fourth trumpet in the Glenn Miller orchestra," although this claim has been discredited.

Miles went on to marry Elizabeth Lorraine Adie, the Scottish daughter of a prominent neurosurgeon, and herself an asset of British Intelligence. The marriage spawned three sons, who would each become prominent figures within the 1970s New Wave scene.

Displaying an apparent lack of imagination, Copeland's firstborn was named Miles Copeland III, birthed in London in 1944. From 1966, he studied at the American University of Beirut, an institution which not only groomed many future world leaders, but also 19 of the delegates who signed the United Nations charter in 1945, and future Apple founder Steve Jobs. Prior to this, Miles III and brother Stewart had attended Beirut's American Community School, a location which later turned out actors Keanu Reeves and Greg Kinnear, as well as Bran Ferren, who developed the patents for Apple's pinch-to-zoom technology, and who later collaborated with Miles III on visual effects for many of his acts' concerts.

Miles III's first accomplishment in music is said to have been his formation of the group Wishbone Ash. He went on to found the agency and record label British Talent Management, focusing on Prog Rock bands.

By 1977, he was poised to fully exploit (or direct?) the emerging Punk and New Wave scene through his new Illegal Records operation. Later, he established International Records Syndicate, (IRS for short,) which put out releases by many of the key names in the New Wave market. Part of Miles III's extremely efficient business model saw him scoring a music video show with the then fledgling MTV, on which he only promoted his own artists. He now owns and operates Copeland International Artists (CIA – gettit?!) In interviews, Miles III stated that he came to a point where he had to decide whether his career was going to be spycraft or the music industry. Maybe he chose both?

The second Copeland son, Ian, was born in 1949. After military service – which included a tour of duty in Vietnam – he first joined his brother Miles in his music industry activities. By 1979, Ian had founded his own operation, Frontier Booking International, (FBI!), a talent agency to represent emerging acts, ranging from The B52s to The Cure. For a while, Ian was romantically linked to Rolling Stones associate, (and daughter of a British army officer!) Marianne Faithfull, and to Courtney Cox, (who also happened to be his step-sister.) He penned his memoirs in a book, 'Wild Thing,' published in 1995.

The youngest Copeland brother was Stewart, born in 1952, and best known as the drummer for the most prolific of all the New Wave bands, The Police. That's *The Police*. With lead singer *Sting*, as in 'sting operation'. Ever feel like you're being given a clue?! (Though rock lore has it that he got his name because he often wore a yellow and black striped jersey making him look like a bee!)

As Dave McGowan recounts at the end of his book 'Weird Scenes Inside The Canyon:'

> *"Before actually recruiting any musicians, (Stewart) quickly came up with a band name, and designed the band's logo and album cover. The band that he would then assemble . . . would soon become arguably the most critically-acclaimed and commercially successful of the new bands. The initial success of The Police in the US is what largely opened the floodgates for a new British invasion of Punk and New Wave bands. And that was in spite of the fact that the band was in no way a Punk band, and didn't really even qualify as a New Wave band. As the British press pointed out, band members were much too professional, and a bit too old, to really fit into the new scene."*

The Copelands had connections in Beirut to the British spy Kim Philby, one of the so-called 'Cambridge five.' In a 2013 interview with the UK's 'Telegraph,' Stewart stated:

> *"As it happened, we were friendly out there with Kim Philby and his family. In fact, my dad was just about to expose him when his own cover got busted. I knew Kim's son Harry, and they kind of moved in with us when their dad disappeared."*

Sting picked up a CBE. In a link back to Copeland's espionage world, he is said to have written 'Every Breath You Take,' The Police's biggest hit, at the desk of James Bond author Ian Fleming. The meaning of 'Every Breath You Take' is often misconstrued. Far from a love song, it is the dark taunting of a stalker towards his prey . . . or could equally be applied to a mind-control handler addressing his subject. The single's B-side is just as much an eyebrow-raiser. 'Murder By Numbers' is an ode to killing covertly and getting away with it – security services-style – with lyrics such as:

> *"Now you can join the ranks of the illustrious, in history's great dark hall of fame,*
>
> *All our greatest killers were industrious. At least the ones that we all know by name.*
>
> *But you can reach the top of your profession, if you become the leader of the land.*
>
> *For murder is the sport of the elected, and you don't need to lift a finger of your hand."*

Sorry, did I mention that a hugely unlikely number of musicians have expressed fascination with the teachings of Aleister Crowley? Well, Sting is among them. At the end of the Police song 'Synchronicity II,' he sings: "Many miles away there's a shadow on the door, of a cottage on the shore, of a dark Scottish lake." This is a direct reference to Crowley's infamous Boleskine House on the shores of Loch Ness, (owned by

Led Zeppelin's Jimmy Page from 1971 to '91,) where Crowley is said to have performed many dark rituals and seances and to have summoned up entities. Boleskine House burned to the ground in suspicious circumstances just prior to Christmas 2015.

The third Police member was British-born Andy Summers, who was brought in to replace original guitarist Henri Padovani. Summers had been present on the Laurel Canyon scene in LA during its counter-culture heyday, was one of the regulars at the Log Cabin, the one-time home of Frank Zappa, and was a regular attendee of gigs on the Sunset Strip.

Back at the CIA, Miles Copeland Senior had worked with Sumner Redstone, who went on to become a media baron, controlling many of the largest mainstream outlets including CBS Corporation, Viacom, Paramount Pictures and BET Networks. Sumner Redstone's original name was Murray Sumner Rothstein, before he anglicised it to 'Redstone' to sound less German-Jewish and more American. In a neat turn of synchronicity, Sting's real name is Gordon Sumner.

The Copeland brothers split their time between living in the US and the UK, and are said to have become fluent in Arabic through their time in Lebanon. In 1985, they were issued with a 'Humanitarian Award' by the Cancer industry. (Perhaps rather ironically, Ian died in 2006 aged 57 of melanoma.) The wording of their biography in the accompanying programme, may reveal more as to what their real work had been throughout their music industry years:

> *"Early in each of their individual careers, the Copeland brothers were considered mavericks – the new frontiersmen... While they were bucking the established institution, practices and attitudes of the music industry, they were on the cutting-edge of pioneering 'new music' into the United States. Their methods, once scorned, are now imitated."*

Miles Copeland Senior died in 1991. In 2017, Stewart Copeland announced the formation of a new 'supergroup,' Gizmodrome, consisting of himself, former Zappa and Bowie collaborator Adrian Belew, and former Level 42 frontman Mark King.

More on McLaren

Malcolm McLaren was raised in North London by his maternal grandmother, Rose Corre Isaacs, the formerly wealthy daughter of Portuguese Sephardic Jewish diamond dealers. Ian MacLeay's book 'Malcolm McLaren – The Biography: The Sex Pistols, the Anarchy, the Art . . .' notes that Rose frequently filled the house with "luvvies, Bohemians and homosexuals," that she shared her bed with the teenage Malcolm, and that among the various values she instilled in him was that "to be bad is good, to be good is simply boring." As Nino Teuoneaux observed: "I really don't know what that kind of upbringing would do to a child."

McLaren's experimental forays into other genres included his 1983 album 'Duck Rock,' which fused world music from Africa, South America and the Caribbean, with the electro hip-hop sound coming out of New York. During this time, he struck up a friendship with Hip-Hop culture icon and Universal Zulu Nation founder Afrika Bambaataa, (later accused of being a predatory rapist, and of whom, <u>much</u> more in a later chapter.) McLaren also took Opera into the pop charts with his 1984 interpretation of Puccini's 'Madam Butterfly,' and sought to popularise the art of 'vogueing' prior to Madonna.

Besides the calculated controversy he stirred up through the Sex Pistols, McLaren courted further attention with one of his post-Pistols acts, Bow Wow Wow, when he had the singer Annabella Lwin pose nude for an album cover when she was just 14 years old. A photographer has also spoken of a separate occasion where Malcolm coerced a 12-year-old girl intro stripping naked for a photoshoot.

McLaren, drawing on his Situationist ideals, appears to have revelled in manipulating others' paedophilic tendencies for the sake of controversy, or to make some kind of artistic statement that made sense to very few other than himself. As detailed in this extract from the book 'The Sex Pistols: Inside Story' by Fred Vermorel:

> *"He would illustrate his point with a lurid anecdote of how, one evening, he and a companion visited the legendary CBS executive Maurice Oberstein at home. Here, they found a young boy naked under a blanket on the sofa. Oberstein boasted he had picked the boy up at*

a railway station. For Malcolm, that symbolised the corruption and hypocrisy that underlay 'Top Of The Pops' and all the other music biz rigmarole.

"But rather than denounce Oberstein, he sought to expose his latent industry paedophilia by exacerbating it – a Situationist tactic that could also have been taken from the French philosopher who commented, 'the ecstasy of making things worse.' Malcolm just loved making things worse at the expense of anyone who got in the way . . . "

In an article for the 'Cageside Seats' website, writer David Bixenspan, adds:

"It was clear to Fred Vermorel that the situation was massively screwed up. His theory – seemingly proven true to him in a conversation with McLaren, (where the latter expressed his intentions to flee to South America before 'the shit hits the fan') – was that his old friend wanted to engineer a wide-ranging child pornography scandal that would take down EMI, the BBC, and everyone else involved, including Vermorel. McLaren wanted to prove that pop music was pornography for, and using children, and this was his opportunity."

By this time, McLaren had launched a pop/ fashion magazine with EMI's backing, initially entitled 'Playkids,' but changed soon afterwards to 'Chicken.' He claimed that the new periodical would be about "pleasure technology for the primitive boy and girl." This chapter in McLaren's history becomes concerning in light of the 'Pizzagate' pedophile scandal referenced earlier. Those involved were said to have used food-related codewords in their correspondence, with 'chicken' referring to underage boys.

One of the popular T-shirt designs to have come out of McLaren and Vivienne Westwood's Sex store, (Westwood has since been knighted as a 'Dame,') shows an underage naked boy holding a cigarette. McLaren himself has been pictured proudly sporting one with the words 'Cambridge rapist' across it.

As Nino Teuoneaux observes:

"The Sex Pistols were a manufactured Situationist outcry against modern, manufactured music. One of the over-arching principles of Situationist International is the destruction of art, of music. Abstract art is good, and realism and the classics are bad. These are for the elites. Situationists are exacerbating the divisions in art. So Malcolm is using his knowledge of that philosophy to create a band that fits a desire.

So it seems like both his bands were manufactured vanguards of anti-music for the Situationist philosophy."

It's worth remembering that Johnny Rotten ended the Sex Pistols' final concert in San Francisco in 1978 with the phrase: "ever get the feeling you've been cheated? Goodnight." Had Rotten just figured out the true nature of McLaren's exploitation? Or had he been a knowing participant in the process all along?

Malcolm died in April 2010 aged 64, very quickly after contracting the disease peritoneal mesothelioma. His last words were reportedly "free Leonard Peltier" in reference to the jailed Native American political activist.

The 'J' word

Something which I personally find to be of great interest, is the massive number of Jewish family links to Punk and New Wave, and I feel the question as to why this should be is one worth asking. Inevitably, a small minority will instantly, by default, be triggered to brand me 'anti-Semitic' for even raising the issue. Society has been so systematically programmed by the likes of the Rothschild-controlled Anti Defamation League, that 'the J-word' always has that effect among a few. If these music scenes were as widely populated by, let's say, Swedish, Korean or Brazilian people, as they are by people of Jewish origin, I would be asking exactly the same question. Would I then be demonised as an 'Anti-Swede!,' an 'Anti-Korean!' or an 'Anti-Brazilian!' and shunned by all of polite society as a result?

No. Because Jews, (or at least those that describe themselves as 'Jewish,' since the majority of such people in the world today are actually descended from the Ashkenazi Khazars of the Caucasus mountain region, and have no genetic links to the Middle East at all,) are the only group about whom such politically-correct paranoia exists. The phrase 'Anti-Semite!' is levelled before what is even being said is examined to see whether it might, in fact, have validity, and the discussion is shut down there and then. In reference to this instant response, former Israeli minister Shulamit Aloni admitted in a 2002 interview: "It's a trick. We always use it."

This, then, becomes a question in itself. Why are these measures in place for this one group above all others?

The other big question is: What is it about the music and entertainment industries that attracts such a large number of individuals of Jewish descent, way out of all proportion to their numbers in society generally? I don't claim to have the answer. I just think the question is worth being considered.

As Nino Teuoneaux states:

> *"The whole scene is overwhelmingly weighted towards Jewish influence on every single level. In the original bands coming out of New York in the 70s, there was an inside joke that CBGBs was called 'The Synagogue.' Every band that came out of there had a more than 50 per cent Jewish contingent during that time.*
>
> *"So we're talking Ramones, Blondie, New York Dolls, all the connections going back to Ginsberg. And every single Situationist source I have is Jewish-linked. Every single one. Almost every music producer was of Jewish race or religion, or it went through a Jewish distributor. Nine out of ten club owners in New York, LA, were Jewish. Everything top to bottom.*
>
> *"The thing is, I'm not looking for that. I'm not trying to figure out who's Jewish and who's not. It's just part of the data that's available on-line."*

A handful of the key players on the British scene have Jewish family links, too, (and the information is offered without insinuation, purely for the reader's interest.) Clash manager Bernard Rhodes' mother was a Russian-Jewish evacuee. He claims to have never known his father. Bob Geldof, frontman of Irish New-Wavers The Boomtown Rats, had a Jewish paternal grandmother. Mick Jones of The Clash was born in London, to a Welsh father, Tommy Jones, and a Russian-Jewish mother, Renee Zegansky. (His cousin is Grant Shapps, the Tory MP for Welwyn Hatfield.)

Jones' Clash bandmate Joe Strummer, born John Graham Mellor, was the son of a British foreign service diplomat, who had a German-Jewish paternal grandmother. Strummer died suddenly of a reported congenital heart defect on 22nd December 2002, aged 50.

I don't want to go to Chelsea

Just as with the previously-documented Cedars-Sinai Medical Center in Los Angeles, the Punk scene has its own sinister location littered with tales that makes it the last place I'd ever choose to spend a night. This is the Hotel Chelsea in midtown Manhattan.

Originally a residential apartment block built in the 1880s, (at the same time as the Dakota Building outside which John Lennon was murdered, and in which the movie 'Rosemary's Baby' was set,) this establishment has held a magnetic attraction for writers, poets, musicians, actors and counter-culture icons through the decades, many of whom used it as their home for long periods. Arthur C. Clarke wrote '2001: A Space Odyssey' there, Beat poets Allen Ginsberg and Gregory Corso were residents, Jack Kerouac wrote his novel 'On The Road' in its rooms, and playwright Arthur Miller wrote 'The Chelsea Effect' to document his time there in the early 1960s. The writer Dylan Thomas was staying there when he is said to have died of pneumonia on 9th November (9/11) 1953. Charles R. Jackson, author of 'The Lost Weekend,' committed suicide in his room on 21st September, (the Autumn Equinox,) 1968.

Others to have called the Chelsea home at some point or other, include the aforementioned occultist Harry Everett Smith, (who died in its room 328 in 1991,) Stanley Kubrick, Ethan Hawke, Dennis Hopper, Eddie Izzard, Uma Thurman, Elliott Gould, Jane Fonda and Russell Brand, among many others. Punk's Dee Dee Ramone wrote a book, apparently "fictionalised," where he talks of groups in robes holding occult rituals in the hotel's basement.

The Chelsea entered into music lore long ago by way of other disturbing stories. Dave McGowan documented one of these in his 'Weird Scenes' book concerning the once-socially-conscious folk-singer Phil Ochs:

> *"In the Summer of 1975, Phil Ochs' public persona abruptly changed. Adopting the name John Butler Train, Ochs proclaimed himself a CIA operative and presented himself as a belligerent, right-wing thug. He told an interviewer that 'on the first day of Summer 1975, Phil Ochs was murdered in the Chelsea Hotel by John Train . . . For the good of society, public and secret, he needed to be gotten rid of.' That symbolic assassination, on the Summer solstice, took place at the same hotel that Devon Wilson had flown out of a few years earlier. One of Ochs' biographers would later write that Phil/ John 'actually believed he was a member of the CIA'."*

Could the Chelsea have housed some kind of covert mind-control facility connected to the military, and in turn, the entertainment sectors? Could this explain its strange draw and dubious history? In his 1978 song '(I Don't Want To Go To) Chelsea,' British-Irish New Waver Elvis Costello sang: "Men come screaming, dressed in white coats, shake you very gently by the throat." Could he have been displaying knowledge of what goes on at the infamous New York hotel, rather than protesting against visiting the part of South West London which, synchronistically (?) spawned the UK's own Punk movement?

McGowan also reports that, in 1971, a prostitute-turned rock groupie named Devon Wilson – who had reportedly been with Jimi Hendrix the day before his death, and had been romantically linked to Arthur Lee of the Laurel Canyon band Love – plunged to her death from an eighth-floor window of the Chelsea.

New York's Chelsea Hotel. I'll take the Travelodge down the road, thanks

https://commons.wikimedia.org/wiki/File:NY_chelsea_hotel.jpg

Credit: Velvet

An ode to the hotel, meanwhile, was composed by singer/ songwriter Christa Paffgen, known by the artist name Nico, on her 1967 debut album 'Chelsea Girl.' This followed her role in the similarly-titled Andy Warhol avant-garde/ experimental film 'Chelsea Girls' the year before. The movie was shot, in part, at the hotel, and profiled the lifestyles of many of the young women who were known as 'Warhol's Superstars' at the time. Nico had been a vocalist with Velvet Underground before collaborating with Jackson Browne. She died of a reported cerebral haemorrhage in Ibiza aged 49.

Other musical links include Madonna's residency at the Chelsea in the early 1980s, and her return in 1992 to shoot photographs for her book 'Sex' in Room 822. The same room attracted Taylor Momsen's band The Pretty Reckless for a more recent photoshoot. British dance artist La Roux shot one of their music videos at the hotel, as did Depeche Mode's Dave Gahan for his song 'Saw Something.' The Grateful Dead, Tom Waits, Patti Smith, Iggy Pop, Jeff Beck, Dee Dee Ramone, Phil Lynott, Cher, Joni Mitchell, Bob Dylan, Alice Cooper, Janis Joplin, Bette Midler, Pink Floyd, Jimi Hendrix, Canned Heat and Leonard Cohen all spent time there. Why?

The Chelsea itself has been the subject of many movies, including the sex thriller '9½ Weeks,' the Japanese horror 'Hotel Chelsea,' 2001's 'Chelsea Walls,' and the 2008 documentary 'Chelsea On The Rocks.'

In an even more intriguing link, meanwhile, several survivors of the Titanic are said to have stayed for some time after the 1912 disaster, as the hotel is close to the Pier 54 dock where the liner was supposed to have arrived.

Perhaps the very darkest blot on the Chelsea's history connects right back into the Punk scene, however.

Sid & Nancy

Sid Vicious achieved iconic 'live fast die young' status in a remarkably short space of time, and at a very young age. At the time of his death he'd been in the public eye for no more than two years, and was still only 21. His famous moniker is said to have been inspired by a pet hamster of Johnny Rotten's, named Sid. When it once bit him, he remarked, "Sid's really vicious" and the name stuck. Vicious' real name was John Simon Ritchie, known later as John Beverley when his mother re-married. For a period, he shared a squat with three other 'faces' on the London punk scene, and the group became known as 'the four Johns.' One was John Lydon, who became Johnny Rotten, one was John Wardle, better known by the stage name Jah Wobble, the other was John Grey.

Vicious' parents are said to have met in the Royal Air Force in yet another military link. His absent father worked as a guardsman at Buckingham Palace, and was a semi-professional trombone player on the London Jazz scene. Anne married Sid's step-father, Christopher Beverley, in 1965. Sid, who had been a regular face at the Sex boutique in Chelsea, was recruited to join the Sex Pistols upon the departure of original bassist Glen Matlock in early 1977. Vicious quickly garnered attention as a nihilistically flamboyant icon of the Punk scene, going on to provide vocals for three cover tracks on the soundtrack of the Pistols movie 'The Great Rock N Roll Swindle.'

By late 1978, with the Sex Pistols over, Sid was living in New York with his girlfriend, a Jewish rock groupie/ prostitute/ heroin addict/ dealer named Nancy Spungen. Both had been on a path to self-destruction through all of their young lives, and were hopelessly addicted to heroin and other drugs as they holed themselves up in Room 100 of the Chelsea. On 12th October, Nancy's lifeless body was discovered in the bathroom of their apartment, aged only 20. She had been stabbed in the abdomen. The official story that quickly emerged, (and immortalised in Alex Cox's 1986 movie 'Sid & Nancy, which contained Courtney love in an early bit-part, incidentally,) was that a deranged Sid, in a drug-induced haze, had stabbed her, and she had stumbled off to the bathroom to bleed to death. Sid was charged with her murder but was out on bail soon afterwards, the money, according to later comments by Johnny Rotten, having been put up by a benevolent Mick Jagger. Within weeks, however, he had been charged with assault after an altercation in a club with the brother of singer Patti Smith, and was forcibly placed on a harsh detox programme at Riker's Island prison.

Sid's own life came to an end on 2nd February 1979, from a heroin overdose at a party held at a friend's Manhattan apartment to celebrate him having made bail again the day before. The official explanation is that he voluntarily ODed, apparently keeping up his end of a suicide pact that he and Nancy had made. Vicious had already attempted suicide on a couple of occasions since being released. Some tellings of the story have it that Sid's unconventional mother Anne – who had been already been feeding his heroin habit for months – administered the fatal dose, either with or without Sid's consent, depending on who's telling the story. Sid's voluntary suicide conflicts with the testimony of friends, however, who stated that he had become optimistic about the future with plans for a career resurgence.

It's here that – as in all such cases – the waters get muddied as to what really happened to Nancy. As many close to the Pistols have opined over the decades, the lazy and disinterested police found it convenient to wrap up the case with the notion that an out-of-his mind Sid had simply stabbed her, and later OD'd himself. Two more pointless junkies off the street. A neat result, and far easier than doing any real police work.

Anomalies emerge from differing accounts of the knife said to have been used in the killing, however, as evidenced in the 2010 documentary 'Who Killed Nancy' by journalist Alan G. Parker, a link to which is at the end.

According to the official story, a 007 flip-knife was given to the Dead Boys bassist Stiv Bators by Dee Dee Ramone, and Vicious, impressed by it, went out and bought an identical one. But other accounts claim the knife used was a completely different model. The police report stated that, when the murder weapon was found, it had been wiped clean. Witnesses who saw the drug-induced stupor that Vicious was under all night, insist he wouldn't have had the foresight to have done this.

In an interview with the 'Daily Record,' John Lydon appeared to be of the view that Nancy had stabbed herself, stating:

> *"Nancy Spungen was a hideous, awful person who killed herself because of the lifestyle, and led to the destruction and subsequent death of Sid and the whole fiasco."*

Lydon elaborated in his book 'Anger Is an Energy: My Life Uncensored,' released in 2015, suggesting Nancy was a handler for drug gangs, and her death was the result of debts owed.

> *"Nancy was killed, and that poor foolish boy was left holding the knife... To me, there's no mystery in it at all. You owe money, that's what you're gonna get."*

British writer and researcher Neil Sanders got into this when he guested on episode 92 of my 'Good Vibrations':

> *"I don't think Sid did it. I think basically he was asleep. The rumour that's put about – and I asked Glen Matlock about this when I met him the other week – he was told by someone that knew, that it was from the bass player from the Dead Boys, (Stiv Bators,) who had been around at the time, bought a load of smack off this guy, and bought*

a load of hunting knives as well because they liked that sort of stuff. This guy went away, Sid got completely comatose, he came back and said, 'Nancy, I want some of my drugs back.' She said no, they got into an argument, he stabbed her. Sid was just basically none the wiser.

"The same way the claim is made that Courtney Love brought all the heroin in to the Grunge scene, which destroyed it, ultimately, Nancy – along with Johnny Thunders of the Heartbreakers – certainly brought in heroin. She was the one that got Sid on it. No-one was doing heroin until Nancy and Johnny Thunders came in."

The 'Who Killed Nancy' documentary, meanwhile, suggests that Sid – who was carrying large amounts of cash – may have been the target of a robbery at the Chelsea, and that Nancy had been stabbed trying to stop it. Interviewees in the film make repeated references to a character known only as 'Michael' who lived on the sixth floor of the hotel at the time. Some think this could have been a reference to Michael Morra, better known by the name Rockets Redglare, under which he performed as a comedian. Morra was himself a drug dealer and addict who was known to have been around the Chelsea on the night in question.

Sid's mother, herself an addict, was discovered dead of a suspected heroin overdose in September 1996. She had apparently been left dejected at the lack of success of the Sex Pistols' 'Filthy Lucre' reunion tour, which she called "sad and pathetic."

The Chelsea has reportedly been closed to guests and undergoing renovation since 2011.

Resources:

Good Vibrations Podcast Episode 097 – Nino 210 – Establishment links in Punk & New Wave:

- https://www.spreaker.com/user/markdevlin/gvp-097-nino-210-establishment-links-in-

Nino Teauoneau's blog site, documenting many of his findings into Punk and New Wave's dubious links:

- http://fourhorsesasses.blogspot.co.uk

Gnostic Media's Unspun podcast No. 53: Allen Ginsberg Exposed:

- http://www.gnosticmedia.com/unspun-053-allen-ginsberg-exposed-dr-hans-utter/

Gnostic Media's Unspun podcast No. 57: Ayahuasca and William S. Burroughs:

- http://www.gnosticmedia.com/unspun-057-ayahuasca-william-s-burroughs/

Louder Than War: Situationism explained! And its affect on Punk and pop culture:

- http://louderthanwar.com/situationism-explained-affect-Punk-pop-culture/

'Blowing up bridges so there is no way back': Malcolm McLaren, Situationists & Sex Pistols remembered by Fred Vermorel in new exhibition catalogue:

- http://www.paulgormanis.com/?tag=situationist-international

Situationism and Rock by Paul Fitzpatrick (October 2000):

- http://www.furious.com/PERFECT/situationism.html

Bits of Books, Mostly Biographies: Savile, McLaren, The Great Child Abuse Swindle of 1980 and Beyond:

- https://bitsofbooksblog.wordpress.com/tag/maurice-oberstein/

Cageside Seats: David Bixenspan reflections on Malcolm McLaren, 1946-2010:

- http://www.cagesideseats.com/2010/4/9/1412178/malcolm-mclaren-1946-2010-as-carny

Never mind the swastikas: the secret history of the UK's 'punky Jews':

- https://www.theguardian.com/music/2014/feb/27/never-mind-swastikas-secret-history-punky-jews

John Lydon praises Mick Jagger for paying Sid Vicious's murder charge lawyers:

- http://www.nme.com/news/music/sex-pistols-12-1237951

'Who Killed Nancy' a film by Alan G. Parker:

- https://www.youtube.com/watch?v=T7QBlDAT1oY

MTV News: Sid Vicious' Mom Dead:

- http://www.mtv.com/news/508248/sids-mom-dead/

Blondie's Debbie Harry claims serial killer Ted Bundy lured her into car:

- http://www.telegraph.co.uk/culture/music/music-news/8191211/Blondies-Debbie-Harry-claims-serial-killer-Ted-Bundy-lured-her-into-car.html

John Joseph reveals he knew serial killer Joel Rifkin in interview:

- https://noisey.vice.com/en_us/article/cro-mags-john-joseph-interview

Obituary for Dorothy Mackaye, grandmother of Ian Mackaye of Minor Threat & Fugazi bands:

- http://www.nytimes.com/1992/09/08/nyregion/dorothy-d-mackaye-dies-at-88-ladies-home-journal-columnist.html

Fall Out Boy's Pete Wentz' uncle is Gen. Colin Powell and grandfather is propagandist:

- http://fourhorsesasses.blogspot.co.uk/2017/08/fall-out-boys-pete-wentz-uncle-is-gen.html?m=1

12 Things You Never Knew About KLF:

- http://www.clashmusic.com/features/12-things-you-never-knew-aboutthe-klf

CHAPTER 5

HEAVY VIBES

How justified is Heavy Metal's perceived association with satanism and the dark occult? And why should there be any connection between these elements and the music scene in the first place?!?

> *"I've never met anyone who has been like, man, I love that they're playing Eddie Money's 'Two Tickets To Paradise' on the radio again! Nobody says that!"*
>
> *Chris Drapeau on 'Good Vibrations' podcast, 2017*

> *"It's showmanship. Same as Cannibal Corpse singing gore lyrics. People wouldn't buy it if they sang about puppies and rainbows and put My Little Pony on their album covers."*
>
> *'Dogsmilk', commenter on 2012 David Icke on-line forum thread on Heavy Metal*

> *"I don't know if I'm a medium for some outside source. Whatever it is, frankly, I hope it's not what I think it is…"*
>
> *Ozzy Osbourne*

Mention 'satanism' in music to the average member of the public, and their mind will probably go to the genres of Heavy Rock and Heavy Metal, such have been these scenes' mythical connections to the world of the dark occult. Many will doubtless recall images of rockers flashing the 'devil horns.' Antics such as Ozzy Osbourne biting off the heads of a bat and two white doves may spring to mind, (he'd been well-groomed for bloodshed having spent time working in an abattoir,) as will none-too-subtle group names like Black Sabbath, Judas Priest and the 'Big Four' stadium Metal bands – Slayer, Megadeth, Anthrax and Metallica.

These associations were exacerbated among the American public by the so-called 'satanic panic' of the 1980s, the largely Christian-driven moral revolt against the music, and were fuelled by bands' blatant wallowing in evil themes as a way of shifting records. Metal's reputation was strengthened further by claims that the music of Metallica was used for sleep deprivation and the psychological torture of Iraqi prisoners of war at the hands of the US military, and that continued exposure to Hard Rock – particularly the Van Halen song 'Panama' – led to the eventual surrender of Panamanian dictator Manuel Noriega to US troops in 1990.

But, such obvious examples aside, is this association wholly fair? Are these genres more 'satanic' than any other, given that artists ranging from Cliff Richard to Justin Bieber have been pictured putting up the '666' sign, and subliminal images of demonic entities have been hidden in Robin Thicke and Beyonce videos? Has Metal's reputation for profanity been carefully cultivated by the leading names of the scene to generate profitable shock and controversy?

Or have its pioneers been genuine practitioners of occult rituals, and is there something about the vibratory signatures of these sounds, that allows for a very real connection to dark and disturbing energy realms? Could many musicians be genuinely possessed by entities that are conjured during performances?

The satanic scapegoat?

Heavy Metal musician-turned independent researcher Chris Drapeau, who has played with groups including Metallica, Megadeth and Devildriver, guested on 'Good Vibrations' in 2017 to give his perspectives on these matters. As he reflected:

> *"My biggest underlying question here is: has Heavy Metal always been the 'satanic scapegoat,' so to speak? Was that stigma created to take the focus off of the real harmful aspects of real satanism displayed in popular music and pop culture? As if to say, 'Heavy Metal is the devil's music, but please, by all means listen to this song by Rihanna. It's completely clear of any satanism and is totally acceptable for your child to listen to!"*

Given the overblown aggression of Metal and its associated genres, he adds – loud volume, confrontational themes and garish images – it becomes the perfect vehicle for having accusations of dark occult aspects levelled at it.

> *"I feel like Metal has become the satanic scapegoat, where it does divert a lot of the focus away from the real, true satanism that we're seeing in pop culture, and a lot of the satanism that a lot of people are unknowingly living!"*

Some agreement came from musician Jeff Young, who was the guitarist for Megadeth on their first album. Jeff now hosts his 'Music Without Boundaries' show on-line, showcasing inspiring sounds that never ordinarily get radio play, and also guested on 'Good Vibrations' in 2017:

> *"In my research, I discovered that Metal's got nothing on Country music, because from hee-haw and back-in-the-day, all the way up to our modern-day artists – Keith Urban, Blake Sheldon – you can't make it in Country music if you're not a Freemason! I've done a whole lot on this on my show, and there's a whole photo album on my 'Music Without Boundaries' Facebook. I got sick of posting album covers and stage sets and programmes, and Dolly Parton and Garth Brooks and all these people Freemason hand-signing, and standing in a pyramid form and all this stuff. And then you look at a Ke$ha video, with the pentagrams and some of this stuff, and it's darker than Slayer and any of the Metal stuff that we did!"*

Dutch musician Quinz Oldenhof, who played bass in the thrash metal band Chainsaw, and has written extensively for the Metal music press, concurs:

> *"Someone should actually start a research/ investigation in the US, asking all the murderers, serial killers and rapists who are locked up what kind of music they listen to. I would really like to see the end results. Maybe it'll turn out to be Rihanna who has the worst influence on people!"*

All a big joke?

Lifelong adherents to Metal and its many spin-offs – including Extreme, Speed, Power, Metalcore, Grindcore, Gore, Slam, Doom, Death and Black Metal – insist that the bands' apparent obsession with death, torture, rape, mutilation and witchcraft is entirely tongue-in-cheek; simply gallows-humour delivered with a nod and a wink to those who can spot the joke. These enthusiasts zealously evangelise for their chosen forms of music, and many consider their association with it to define their entire identities, going so far as to have tattoos, piercings and body imprints deifying their Metal heroes. They point to the overblown satanic pomp of groups such as AC/DC, Iron Maiden, Slayer, Anthrax and Megadeth as obvious examples of Metal's extreme-seeming, but ultimately harmless nature. As Quinz Oldenhof has observed:

> *"...For the vast majority of the bands it's all about acting evil – not being evil, or trying to make others become evil. It's been a rat race of who can be the 'evilest' for decades. You simply can't put daisies on your album cover when you sing about guts and corpses. Once again, I think that no band has that intent to promote an evil/ satanic cabal, or force a satanic message on to their audience – neither in your face nor subliminal.*
>
> *"...All in all, I think the bands that operate under the level of the mainstream are just looking for good fun and to try to make it. If it takes acting evil, (instead of being evil,) for shock value and record sales, why not? Bands like Baphomet's Blood, (total Motorhead/ Lemmy worship,) Inferno, Chapel and Gehennah, to name but a few – they're all about tongue-in-cheek, shits and giggles. Good clean fun and rock 'n' roll.*
>
> *"Come to think of it, Metal fans are probably the nicest crowd to control for festival security people. There's never any violence, no weapons, no drugs. Of course, there's a few that smoke pot, but overall it's just a bunch of beer drinking-sweethearts that want to have a good time."*

Glen Benton of Florida Death Metal pioneers Deicide, has commented:

> *"I say, don't blame people like me, and (Marilyn) Manson, because we never said, 'hey, we're going to be role models for all your kids.' That ain't what this is about. It's about entertainment."*

Even the heartwarmingly-named Necrobutcher of the Norwegian Black Metal band Mayhem, (of whom, more later,) observes:

> *"The people we scared are scared, and the people who understood the joke are still there, and just smiling about the whole thing."*

Before adding:

> *"It's not totally a joke, of course. It's something that the government couldn't control, you know? They tried to keep us down, and by doing that, what happened? Cult legends."*

Slayer lead singer/ bassist Tom Araya is cited as a good example of one of Metal's many actors. Despite screaming about death, destruction and nihilism, he alleges to be a devout Catholic who makes a cross when he leaves the stage after every gig. It's hard to know how to reconcile his nice-guy off-stage image with his band's recital of early lyrics such as: "Bleeding on your knees, my satisfaction is what I need. The urge to take my fist and violate every orifice. You're nothing, beaten into submission, raping again and again." Even if, in more recent times, Slayer's lyrical themes have shifted towards 'exposing' the agendas of the New World Order and the Illuminati. Go figure.

What's the intention?

In this regard, Metal's apologists often cite the concept of Intent as being key to whatever effect listening to their music may have. Just as with predictive programming, advertising subliminals and covert symbolism, the net effect on the observer depends on what the Will of the creator of the artform was at its source. This is carried forward in the form of an energetic signature, and receivers of the art make a connection with it on an unseen level. It happens whether or not the receiver recognises it, and whether or not their investment in ego prompts them to call it out as 'bullshit.' It doesn't make a difference. It's how the dynamics of this reality work.

If Metal's death-obsessed imagery really is all about shits and giggles, therefore, no harmful effects are likely to be experienced by the listener in this regard. It may well be that many of the prominent musicians in these genres come with no negative intent towards their listeners, and really do believe in the 'fun' aspect of what they peddle.

This benign scenario only takes place, however, if *all* acts within these genres *really are* out for a bit of good-natured fun. Unfortunately – as we've seen in so many other parts of this story – mega-successful music acts of any genre only get there through compliance with the corporate, and so often, social engineering agendas of their record company overlords. And major record labels – again, borne out by so much evidence presented elsewhere in this book – are so often in bed with the military intelligence community who, despite their well-meaning public images, aren't generally known for their goal of unifying and inspiring humanity for the greater good of all.

We'll continue to decipher this conundrum throughout this chapter. But let's, at this point, look at the most enduring visual calling-card associated for decades with all expressions of the harder side of Rock.

The horn section

The 'devil horns' is a concept that goes all the way back to Ancient India, and had a far more positive and empowering meaning than its use in modern times conveys. The hand sign was intended to ward off evil spirits and remove sickness or negative thoughts. Other cultures adopted it as a motif to dissipate the power of 'the evil eye,' a curse believed to be cast by way of a malevolent stare. It became a part of the Apotropaic magic system practiced in parts of Southern Europe.

The sign is considered to take on an offensive meaning, however, when directed towards someone and swivelled back and forth, and was subsequently used as a method of identification and communication by dark occult groups. It remains very similar to the hand gesture which has come to mean 'I love you' as part of the deaf sign language system introduced by Helen Keller, with much confusion arising between the two. Generally, Keller's version involves the thumb being extended outwards, with the 'magick' variation seeing the thumb tucked around the two lower fingers. (Keller is said to have herself been an occultist who espoused the teachings of Theosophy, so maybe there's more to know about her apparently innocent and well-meaning system?)

The thin line between the two has allowed the horns' malevolent appearances to be written off as the user simply stating 'I love you' to disguise what may have a far more negative connotation – particularly when used by a politician, oligarch or some other expression of the New World Order establishment, who are not generally known for their big-hearted love of all.

A further use of the sign is found in American sports. In its guise as the 'Hook 'Em Horns,' it is the slogan and greeting signal of the University of Texas at Austin, where it is said to symbolise the head and horns of the UT mascot, the Texas Longhorn Bevo. Among occultists, the sign is considered an evocation of the Pagan god Pan in Wiccan culture, and of the androgynous 'sabbatic goat' entity of Baphomet, as depicted by the artist Eliphas Levi – both revered within certain secret societies.

Common use of the 'horns' within Rock, meanwhile, can be traced back to the psychedelic band Coven. From 1968, frontwoman Esther 'Jinx' Dawson would start and finish each of the group's gigs by flashing the sign. The back cover of their 1969 debut album showed band members giving it the horns. Whatever the motives of those later acts influenced by their example, Coven's intentions would appear to be less rooted in sales-generating controversy, than in a genuine adeptness at occult ritual. More of that shortly.

The sign was more widely associated with Ronnie James Dio, who became the lead singer of Black Sabbath in 1979. Dio stated that his Italian grandmother had used it to ward off the 'evil eye.' It became something of a personal trademark for him at Sabbath concerts, replacing Ozzy Osbourne's penchant for flashing up the 'peace' sign. In a 2001 interview for the Metal-Rules.com website, he explained:

> *"...I think you'd have to say that I made it fashionable...It was a symbol that I thought was reflective of what that band was supposed to be all about. It's not the devil's sign, like we're here with the devil...It's just a symbol, but it had magical incantations and attitudes to it, and I felt it worked very well with Sabbath."*

(As an interesting aside, Black Sabbath came to be associated with the CIA-linked Copeland family profiled in the previous chapter, when five of the group's albums from 1989 to '95 were released on Miles Copeland Jr.'s IRS Records label.)

Earlier that decade, the sign had been enthusiastically adopted as part of George Clinton and Bootsy Collins' Parliament and Funkadelic acts, being used as the 'password' to the groups' fabled 'Mothership' motif, and being flashed by members of the audience at their live shows as a token of appreciation. The video to Afrika Bambaataa and the Soul Sonic Force's 'Planet Rock' opens with crowd members flashing up the horn sign at a concert. A painting of Gene Simmons of the group Kiss used the horns on the cover of 1977's 'Love Gun' album, and Simmons went on to use the sign frequently, both on and off stage.

Quinz Oldenhof has commented, somewhat wryly, that Anthrax guitarist Scott Ian seems to have a severe case of arthritis that causes his hand to be twisted into a constant horn sign posture. Poor chap. The gesture is also similar to the one adopted by the Los Angeles street gang known as The Bloods to identify its members, and even to one employed by Paul Hogan in the first 'Crocodile Dundee' movie to tame a wild animal.

Where 'art' and ritual meet

Contemporaneous with both Coven and Black Sabbath were the British group Black Widow, whose song and album titles have included 'Attack of the Demon,' 'Come to the Sabbat,' 'Sacrifice,' 'In Ancient Days' and 'Sleeping With Demons.' Founding member Clive Jones certainly didn't sound as if he was being tongue-in-cheek or ironic when asked if he was still interested in satanism in an interview with the Mourning the Ancient website:

> *"Yes, I am still interested, and I have met the devil twice. Once on my own in the daylight, and once at night with some other band members, from another band. So for certain, I am a believer. We learned a lot about black magic for the first album, 'Sacrifice'."*

One of Black Widow's most talked-about promotional pictures, shows vocalist Kip Trevor about to plunge a sword into the naked body of a woman. The band was reportedly contacted by a male witch named Alex Sanders, who warned them that their 'art' was too close to genuine satanic rituals for comfort. As Clive Jones recounts:

> *"Well, there were many moments in the stage rituals that were correct. Alex Sanders always said that we could make something appear on the stage, even if we could not see it at the time. I think when we first started doing the act live, we played at a club in Derbyshire, and priests turned up to try and stop the show, holding crosses up in front of the stage."*

And so, back to the aforementioned Chicago-based Coven, (its name meaning a collective of witches.) This band remains particularly notable within the whole 'satanism in Rock' debate through – seemingly – committing the recording of an actual black mass to vinyl in the form of their debut album, the charmingly-titled 'Witchcraft Destroys Minds and Reaps Souls.' Although the group's sound was more entrenched in the late 60s psychedelic style, they are considered to have been forerunners to the Heavy Rock scene, particularly through their confrontational style and shocking imagery – both standard hallmarks of what would come later.

The band was discovered by a producer named Bill Traut, who was a student of the horror author and occultist HP Lovecraft, and a fan of the British occult writer Dennis Wheatley. Along with a company called Open Door Management, Traut had a record label named Dunwich Records, named after the fictional town which appeared in one of Lovecraft's celebrated horror novels. Chris Drapeau explains:

"At the time, the band were already doing a lot of satanic ideas in their live show. They were doing a very watered-down, shorter black mass. They would be brought out in coffins. This was in the late 60s, around the same time as the advent of Anton La Vey's Church of Satan. This Bill Traut guy wanted to record a black mass. That was his main focus for this project. So the cover has the three main members of the band with a skull, and they're all wearing rosaries with inverted crosses.

"And when you open up the album... the lead singer, Jinx Dawson, is completely nude, laid out on an altar with a chalice on her chest and a skull over her genitals. The rest of the band and a bunch of other people are around her throwing the horns in the air, and they're having a satanic mass."

The album might be one to leave off the playlist for the next children's birthday party then. Song titles include 'White Witch of Rose Hall,' 'For Unlawful Carnal Knowledge,' (which later became the title of an album by Van Halen,) 'Pact with Lucifer,' 'Choke, Thirst, Die,' 'Dignitaries of Hell,' and 'Satanic Mass' – the latter purporting to be just what it says in its title.

Hearing this may conjure up recollections of what John Todd had to say about his time working in the US music industry, as referenced in a previous chapter. What may be an intriguing variation on it, came from a far more recent album by the Foo Fighters, fronted by Dave Grohl, (whose family links and background connections were also discussed in the previous chapter.) Shunning computer methods for a back-to-the-old-school approach, the group's 2011 album 'Wasting Light,' was mastered on analogue reel-to-reel tape, reportedly in Grohl's garage. A far less conventional gimmick, however, involved small shreds of the original master tape being placed inside the first CD copies of the album. Grohl decided it would be "an extraordinary move to destroy all the masters and give the pieces of the tapes to the fans." A live feed of the tape machine in operation was streamed on the band's website during the record's production.

Reflections inspired by Todd's accounts on what could – conceivably – be getting put into music on an unseen level, leads to some other possibilities. Chris Drapeau has considered some potential implications of home recording methods as yet another by-product of the digital/technological age into which we've been flung at an alarming rate over the past two decades.

> *"Now that everything's digital you can have the most minuscule set-up, and you have the wherewithal to create really great, high-quality music right in your house. And there's countless different programmes – what they call Digital Audio Workstation programmes. I have one that I use to record all my music with, and I started thinking while I was listening to the John Todd lecture… what kind of spells could even have been cast on some of these programmes, or what could be baked into them?*
>
> *"Because now, you've got independent musicians and hobbyists that are recording with all these different programmes and platforms, and could be releasing music where these kinds of ideas – these dark hexes and stuff – could have been placed on these programmes. And a lot of these programmes upload a track directly to Soundcloud as soon as you've mixed and mastered it. And then it's out there in the internet domain for people to check out.*
>
> *"If that's the case, then they've got millions of people in their homes doing the work for them!"*

Still along similar lines, a question which has been raised by a number of researchers – particularly by Jan Irvin and Hans Utter on their excellent 'The Secret History of FM Radio' podcasts – is why certain tracks have always been favoured for airplay over and above all others. Most of us will be familiar with the scenario. It seems as if every time you turn on a certain station, or a particular video TV channel, the same handful of songs are on constant rotation, preventing other music from less-familiar artists from getting valuable exposure. (The Eagles' 'Hotel California' or Toto's 'Africa', anyone?)

The cynical view, is that there are backhanders taking place between the record labels and the broadcasters. Certainly, Payola is as old as the industry itself. But what if there are other motivations behind getting certain songs embedded into the public consciousness? This could be for social engineering in terms of normalising certain lyrical themes, but there could also be manipulation at a sonic level with the frequencies involved in the recordings.

Much consolidation has taken place in the US corporate radio industry – just as in mainstream news outlets – with large numbers of music stations being controlled by ever fewer points of decision-making power. The iHeartMedia empire stands as a great example, at last check owning 47 Rock stations amidst its colossal portfolio. iHeartMedia evolved out of the Clear Channel network in 2014, proudly announcing its "success in becoming a one-of-a-kind multi-platform media company, with unparalleled reach and impact." It's not as if we're not told what's happening every step of the way.

Meet the family

Back to Coven's album anyway, (as digression seems to be an inevitable consequence of trying to piece these vast swathes of connected information together!) 'Witchcraft Destroys Minds…' was pulled by its label, Mercury Records, in the wake of the public outcry it unsurprisingly generated. Band member James Vincent, who wrote many of the songs at Bill Traut's request, went on to become a musician in the Christian Rock genre. I guess he wasn't built for an entire satanic career. Jinx Dawson, meanwhile, who rocked a look reminiscent of that of Debbie Harry, has continued to tour under the name of Coven, and appears to have none of the qualms that Vincent did. Her background certainly makes for some interesting studying. In an interview with the 'Confessions of a Pop Culture Addict' website, she revealed:

> *"I was born into the occult. I came from a background as a child where my great-grandfather and great aunts were part of the Post-Victorian Spiritual Age, where popular interests were anything from Houdini, to ghosts, to seances, to mesmerism, to pendulums and fortune-telling,*

to Hoodoo and casting spells . . . and powerful secret-societies were very much in effect, of which they were head members. They had an extensive library of occult books in their large Italianate mansion, which I eagerly read. They held many rituals in that house . . .

"I am from a very long lineage of occult adepts and practitioners of the ancient arts. Some of them were members of the U.A.O.D., (United Ancient Order of Druids.) Others were members of the Rosicrucian group Ordo Aureæ et Rosæ Crucis, (Order of the Golden and Rosy Cross.)

"I am of the Mayflower Society, a direct descendant of John Howland, 13th signatory to the Mayflower Compact. Members of my family were also active in Freemasonry. My father was a 33rd-degree Scottish Rite Mason, and my grandfather, a former Lt. Governor of Indiana, was High Priest of the Royal Arch Masons. My great-grandfather was in the private circle of US president Teddy Roosevelt. And we are listed in the book 'The First Families of America.' So I am steeped in American Illuminati."

No need for baseless speculation or implied guilt-by-association there, then. Yet more examples of popular music's links with all aspects of the Establishment, and straight from the horse's mouth. And anyone still think Freemasons are all about doing good for the local community and helping each other out in business deals?

A valid question might well be: with a background in occult secret-societies and mystery school teachings such as Dawson's . . . why would she feel compelled to pursue a career in the popular music industry if *not* to knowingly implant the teachings of these institutions into the unwitting public's consciousness? It's the same principle as current-day stage shows such as the US Super Bowl and the Grammys, with the likes of Katy Perry, Madonna and Nicki Minaj, flaunting ritualistic symbology right in front of a largely clueless audience.

And finally, in a bizarre twist relating back to the pioneering group which Coven is said to have greatly inspired, its bass guitarist Greg Osborne was known colloquially as 'Oz Osborne,' while 'Black Sabbath' is the title of one of the songs on their debut album. Ring any bells? (The English group has always claimed its naming was inspired by the 1963 Boris Karloff movie 'Black Sabbath.')

A more contemporary band who seem to have continued Heavy Rock's obsession with the occult into the current age, meanwhile, is Tool. And the family links of member Danny Carey – like Dawson's – do not disappoint. As the band's official website openly proclaims:

> *"Relatively normal, an element of mystery was added to Danny's childhood, when one day he spied his father with a large sword conducting a Masonic ritual. Danny would later notice himself performing similar movements when he began playing drums at the age of thirteen . . .*
>
> *"Despite not becoming a Mason or aligning himself with any other school of religion, Danny has maintained his heritage's interest in occult studies. Endeavours into this realm have manifested periodically, such as the time he achieved insight into a hidden aspect of the unicursal hexagram, utilising an astral journey initiated through meditation and DMT.*
>
> *". . . He then performed a ritual utilising his new-found knowledge of the unicursal hexagram, to generate a pattern of movement in space . . . The resulting rhythm and gateway summoned a daemon he has contained within 'the Lodge', that has been delivering short parables similar to passages within the 'Book of Lies.' Danny recommends as a device of protection and containment, a thorough study and utilisation of the underlying geometry of the Temple of Solomon for anyone purchasing their next record."*

Wait . . . was that just a brazen admission that a form of spellcasting takes place with records put out by the industry?

(Incidentally, a hero of the more underground side of electronic dance music through the 1990s, was Richard D. James, who released records under the name of Aphex Twin. He seemed to enjoy toying with his audience by use of mind games, and in interview, admitted to being a spellcaster, stating that the Aphex Twin logo is what is known in magick as a sigil.)

Tool's other band members also talk of achieving altered states of consciousness, and channeling this through their music.

What on earth possessed you?

The notion of genuine demonic possession and its connection to Rock, entered the public consciousness in an alarming manner in late 2015, when a serial rapist and father-of-two named Donnie Renfrew was sentenced to ten years in prison. Renfrew was convicted of sexually and physically abusing and mentally torturing five women over a 26-year-period. He was in relationships with each of the women at the time, and each stated that his behaviour was triggered by his listening to Heavy Metal music. One, giving evidence, told the court:

> *"He would stick his tongue out, his eyes were bulging and he would jump about and dance to the music. It was heavy, heavy Metal he listened to."*

In response, Renfrew told the prosecutor: "I used to open my eyes like Ozzy Osbourne and stick my tongue out," before demonstrating the facial expression. Another of his victims stated that the walls in his flat were all painted red, (one of the principal colours associated with Saturn, from which the word 'satanism' is derived,) with upside-down crosses hung on them.

The shock generated by this case had similarly been evoked in the US over 30 years previous, in the story of a 17-year-old drug dealer and self-professed Satanist named Ricky Kasso. He was also an enthusiastic fan of Heavy Metal, citing Ozzy Osbourne and Judas Priest as his inspirations. In the Summer of 1984, Kasso murdered his friend Gary Lauwers in the woods of Newport, New York, while high on mescaline. As an article on the 'Heavy Blog Is Heavy' site details:

> *"According to the coroner's report, Kasso allegedly stabbed his friend 36 times and sliced out his eyes, which led to media propagation that*

> *the murder was ritualistic in nature...For months afterwards, the media presented Kasso as a satanist who was part of a cult, further fuelling the hysteria that was engulfing America...A press-release following the incident was released by Suffolk County Police, and claimed that Kasso regularly partook in rituals honouring the devil.*
>
> *"The notion that Kasso was a devil worshipper was further backed up by his own father, who claimed his son was obsessed with reading about witchcraft and wearing apparel featuring satanic symbols. On the day Kasso was arrested, he was wearing an AC/DC shirt, for instance, and this led to the inevitable association between Heavy Metal and his atrocities by the media vultures, religious figures and concerned parents looking for a scapegoat.*
>
> *"He would kill himself in prison under 48 hours later."*

In 2005, the UK's BBC2 TV channel aired a documentary under its 'This World' banner, titled 'The Death Metal Murders.' It included a section examining an Italian Metal group known as The Beasts of Satan. Between 1998 and 2004, they embarked on a series of tortures, sacrifices and murders – including within their own group – and cited their obsession with the dark themes espoused in their music as their inspiration. Michele Tollis, the father of one of their murder victims, attended more than 80 Metal concerts during a six-year search for his son, culminating in the discovery of his body. He commented:

> *"No-one can contradict me when I say that Heavy Metal and satanism are closely linked. They go hand-in-hand, they're inseparable. I say this without the shadow of a doubt."*

Priest Don Aldo Buonaito, called for Death Metal to be banned in light of the Beasts of Satan case, commenting: "If music makes itself an instrument of nefarious deeds and death, it should be stopped."

The 'This World' documentary went on to observe, that the average, well-adjusted youth could not reasonably be expected to respond in such extreme ways to their chosen genre of music. Beasts of Satan murderer Mario Maccione commented:

> *"You can count on the fingers of one hand the number of people who have done what we have done. Of the millions of people who listen to Metal music, no-one – I repeat, no-one – has ever been involved in anything like this. In fact, many more people have done things like this who do not listen to Metal at all."*

And as Quinz Oldenhof adds:

> *"Thousands of people commit suicide every year, and thousands do stupid stuff, often ending with an occasional death. They all listen to music, but no one ever makes a court case out of a Chopin or Ace of Base fan incident."*

The problems we do get, it seems, begin with fans who are *already* blighted by some form of depression, mental issues or angst. It is in these circumstances, according to interviewee Don Roberts of Stanford University, that issues of concern arise:

> *"What the music may well be doing, is simply reinforcing beliefs that they might have started with in the first place, and building on them and justifying their worldview, legitimising the way they feel. The lyrics are violent, the lyrics are misogynist, the lyrics are depressed and depressing, the lyrics are satanic. They talk about suicide, they talk about self-mutilation. The very kinds of things we're worried that these problem kids will get engaged in."*

This ultra-violent playout of events, raises the question of whether such scenarios are made to manifest through the participants revelling in dark, negative energy through their lifestyles. There are stories of woeful misfortune befalling the film crews who made 'The Exorcist' and 'The Omen,' the idea being that a full-time immersion in themes of death and destruction – albeit 'art' – bring a synchronistic connection with expressions of these dense energies.

Were these horrific events an inevitable result of this dynamic? And could more untimely deaths of key players within Rock music be attributed to these same factors, if occult ritual is far more a regular part of music industry practice than most of us would ever consider?

The notion of possession got a topical rendering in the 2009 movie 'Crowley,' meanwhile, which was co-written by Iron Maiden frontman Bruce Dickinson, joining that long line of rockers infatuated by the infamous occultist. (Another was Ozzy Osbourne, who created the song 'Mr. Crowley.') In the narrative, Dickinson and director Julian Doyle imagine "the Great Beast's spirit being reborn into the body of a mild-mannered professor, resulting in all manner of horror and chaos."

What lies beneath

Although there were attempts by moral campaigners to associate other violent acts involving young people with Metal, it was a 1990 case based around the music of the British group Judas Priest which really penetrated the American public mindset.

The court heard how two youths, 18-year-old Raymond Bellknap and 20-year-old James Vance, had spent the night of 23rd December 1985 drinking, smoking weed, and allegedly listening to Heavy Metal music. They then headed to a playground at a church in Sparks, Nevada, with the intention of killing themselves with a 12-gauge shotgun in a pact. Bellknap died instantly. Vance shot himself but survived, succumbing to his injuries three years later.

The prosecution, commissioned by the youths' parents, alleged that the pair had been subliminally influenced by an audio message placed backwards into the song 'Better By You, Better By Me' from Judas Priest's 1978 album 'Stained Class.' The message is said to come out as "do it, do it" when played backwards, and this is alleged to have triggered the pair's suicide attempt against their will.

It became the most famous case in the subject known as 'backmasking,' (covered in-depth in this book's first volume.) The lawsuit was dismissed on 24th August 1990, when the judge ruled that the alleged message was a result of an accidental mix-up of background lyrics. There are far clearer examples of purported backmasked messages than 'do it, do it' – Slayer's 'Hell Awaits,' (another one to leave off the playlist for the next family barbecue, I would suggest,) is said to render the message "join us" when played backwards.

Although on face value this seems like a quite ambiguous message, in 1996, the parents of 15-year-old Elyse Marie Pahler took Slayer to a California court in a failed attempt to ban the sale of their brand of music. Elyse had been raped and murdered by three youths. Although they stated they needed to make a 'sacrifice to the devil' in honour of their favoured band Hatred, it was two songs by the group Slayer – 'Postmortem' and 'Dead Skin Mask' – which Elyse's parents claimed had given detailed instructions to "stalk, rape, torture, murder and commit acts of necrophilia" on their daughter. Thy Infernal have a track titled 'Armageddon' which is said to include the instruction "kill for Satan," and many messages were backmasked deliberately – by their own admission – into the music of the Beatles. Either way, the Judas Priest case only served to further cement the idea of dark and sinister elements to these musical styles.

This case also seems to have acted as a precursor to one the following year involving Ozzy Osbourne, and centred around the track 'Suicide Solution' from his 1980 album 'Blizzard Of Oz.' The parents of John McCollum pressed charges against Osbourne when their depressed son committed suicide after allegedly listening to the song, citing a lyric which was claimed to have said "Why try? Get the gun and shoot!" (forward this time, rather than backwards.) This case was also thrown out.

(Another aside... At the time, the manager of Black Sabbath was Don Arden, born into a Jewish family as Harry Levy, the father of Sharon, who would go on to become Ozzy's wife. Arden said of the case: "To be perfectly honest, I would be doubtful as to whether Mr. Osbourne knew the meaning of the lyrics, if there was any meaning, because his command of the English language is minimal." Arden was a notorious figure in the London criminal underworld with later Mafia links, and was widely feared within the music business. He was the manager of the Small Faces for a time. A pair of legendary anecdotes have him dangling record producer Robert Stigwood upside-down from a first-floor window, and grinding a lit cigar into the face of Fleetwood Mac manager Clifford Davis for apparently trying to cross him. Ozzy was fired by Black Sabbath in 1979, and became signed by Arden to his Jet record label. Ozzy's marriage to Sharon in 1982 caused a bitter 20-year estrangement between Arden and his daughter. Sharon once told journalist Mick Wall: "He's an evil old bastard and I can't wait for him to die." He eventually did, in 2007, after a long battle with Alzheimer's.)

The legacy of the Judas Priest affair was far-reaching, as reported by the 'Heavy Blog Is Heavy' website:

> *"In 1985, a committee known as the Parents Music Resource Center, spearheaded by Tipper Gore, made up a playlist of songs they deemed inappropriate. The list, dubbed 'The Filthy 15,' was used to serve as a template for proposed legislation regarding how albums should be rated, suggesting that they should come with extra warnings if the content pertained to sex, violence, drugs/ alcohol or the occult.*
>
> *"Of the fifteen songs, nine were Metal, including: Judas Priest's 'Eat Me Alive,' Motley Crue's 'Bastard,' AC/DC's 'Let Me Put My Love Into You,' Twisted Sister's 'We're Not Gonna Take It, 'W.A.S.P's 'Animal (Fuck Like a Beast),' Def Leppard's 'High 'n Dry, 'Mercyful Fate's 'Into the Coven,' Black Sabbath's 'Thrashed,' and Venom's 'Possessed.' However, what's interesting, is how much they failed to capitalise on the mass satanic hysteria as much as they could have. For example, they chose an AC/DC song with sexual lyrics, as opposed to say, 'Highway to Hell' or 'Hell's Bells,' which were two of the band's biggest hits, and could be interpreted as occult-themed and connected to Richard 'Nightstalker' Ramirez, the satanic serial killer whose murder spree terrorised Greater Los Angeles until the Summer of the year this hearing was held. The fact Ramirez also showed up to court with a pentagram carved into his own flesh, should have been enough to associate the band with satanism."*

It was this process which led to the iconic Parental Advisory Label being placed on records, tapes and CDs by the American Recording Industry Association from 1985 onwards, denoting explicit lyrical content ranging from overtly sexual, to graphically violent, (and later to become as much a staple part of the 'gangsta rap' genre as of the Metal scene.)

(As another curious aside, many of the prominent British groups, such as Black Sabbath, Judas Priest, Napalm Death and Wolfsbane, originated from Birmingham or the Black Country region of England. Black Widow were from the other side of the Midlands in Leicester.)

It's grim up north

However shocking the prominent acts within Heavy Rock were – and whether this was by calculated design or a reflection of the musicians' true natures – their antics pale compared to one niche expression of the genre. The Black Metal scene coming out of Norway leaves little room for ambiguity, representing an outlet for genuine dark occult activity. Wikipedia describes the scene as follows:

> *"…An extreme sub-genre and sub-culture of Heavy Metal music. Artists often appear in corpse paint and adopt pseudonyms… Initially a synonym for 'Satanic Metal', Black Metal is often met with hostility from mainstream culture, due to the actions and ideologies associated with it. Many artists express extreme anti-Christian and misanthropic views, advocating various forms of satanism or ethnic paganism."*

During the 1990s, affiliates of the scene were found to be responsible for a series of church burnings across Norway. The proposed justification, was that many of Europe's Christian churches were built on the sites of former Pagan monuments. The scene's adherents were seeking to re-awaken the spirits of their Viking ancestors and revive their long-lost culture. According to state prosecutor Bjorn Soknes, who interviewed many of the arsonists:

> *"They were young, 16 to 22. They were lonely people. Many of them told us they were listening over hours to Black Metal music before they burned churches."*

The death-obsessed nature of the genre was expressed shockingly through members of the founding group Mayhem, which contains the member Necrobutcher, and whose image fully embodied its ideologies. In April 1991, the group's vocalist Per Yngve Ohlin, who called himself 'Dead,' committed suicide while alone in a house shared by the band. Fellow musicians had described him as being odd, introverted and depressed, to the point of genuinely believing he was a walking corpse. 'Dead' was found with his wrists slit and a shotgun wound to the head by Mayhem member Øystein 'Euronymous' Aarseth.

Nag of Tsjuder, an act on the Norwegian Black Metal scene; can 'music' get any darker?

https://en.wikipedia.org/wiki/Tsjuder#/media/File:Tsjuder,_Jan-Erik_%E2%80%9ENag%E2%80%9C_Rom%C3%B8ren_at_Party.San_Metal_Open_Air_2013.jpg

Credit: Jonas Rogowski

Getting his personal priorities straight, prior to calling the police, Euronymous grabbed a disposable camera and photographed the body. You know, like you do. One of his photographs was later used as the cover of an album, 'Dawn of the Black Hearts,' which showed a knife that he had carefully positioned to make for a better picture before the police arrived. Euronymous is also said to have made necklaces from parts of Dead's skull, which he had removed from the crime scene, and to have given some pieces to Marduk and other bands.

Euronymous didn't last much longer himself. On the night of 10th August 1993, Varg Vikernes of the group Burzum got into an argument with Euronymous at his apartment, resulting in Vikernes stabbing him to death. Varg had travelled there with Snorre 'Blackthorn' Ruch of Thorns, who had just become Mayhem's second guitarist, and had intended to show Euronymous some new riffs. Snorre reportedly saw the two fighting at the top of the stairs and ran off in terror. Vikernes claimed the killing was in self-defence as Euronymous had plotted to stun him with an electroshock weapon, tie him up and torture him to death while videotaping the event.

Wham! with big hair, toothpaste smiles and 'Choose Life' T-shirts it is not.

Shall we move on to something slightly, (only slightly, mind), happier . . . ?

Resources:

Good Vibrations Podcast Episode 104 – Jeff Young – Music's Dark Side:

- https://www.spreaker.com/user/markdevlin/gvp-104-jeff-young

Good Vibrations Podcast Episode 103 – Chris Drapeau – Satanism and Heavy Rock:

- https://www.spreaker.com/user/markdevlin/gvp-103-chris-drapeau

The Overwhelming (and Overlooked) Darkness of Jinx Dawson and Coven:

- http://people.com/music/jinx-dawson-coven-overlooked-Heavy-Metal-influencers/

Wicked Woman: A Conversation with Jinx Dawson:

- http://popcultureaddict.com/interviews/jinxdawson/

Satanic Panic: America's War On Heavy Metal in the 1980s:

- http://www.HeavyblogisHeavy.com/2016/11/30/Satanic-panic-americas-war-on-Heavy-Metal-in-the-1980s/

Kids Interview Bands – Tom Araya of Slayer:

- https://www.youtube.com/watch?v=EjdaW5ufzbg&t=227s

Scottish Daily Record: Tattooed serial rapist who turned into sex monster when he listened to Heavy Metal music is jailed for 10 years:

- http://www.dailyrecord.co.uk/news/crime/tattooed-serial-rapist-who-turned-7015992

Revealed: The dark secrets of Sharon Osbourne's dad, the Al Capone of pop:

- http://www.dailymail.co.uk/femail/article-471446/Revealed-dark-secrets-Sharon-Osbournes-dad-Al-Capone-pop.html

BBC2's 'This World' documentary on Death Metal murders:

- http://www.bbc.co.uk/suffolk/content/articles/2005/11/23/cradle_of_filth_this_world_feature.shtml

Evidence of Conspiracy: Marranos masquerading as Christians:

- https://web.archive.org/web/20140419215337/http://www.pseudoreality.org/westside.html

CHAPTER 6

THE SCIENCE OF SOUND

How frequencies – the building blocks of this 'physical' reality – lie at the root of music and mind-control.

> *"If one should desire to know whether a kingdom is well governed, if its morals are good or bad, the quality of its music will furnish the answer."*
>
> *Confucius, 551 BC-479 BC*

> *"Atmospheres are going to come through music, because music is in a spiritual thing of its own. It's like the waves of the ocean. You can't just cut out the perfect wave and take it home with you. It's constantly moving all the time. It is the biggest thing electrifying the earth. Music and motion are all part of the race of man."*
>
> *Jimi Hendrix, 'Life' Magazine interview, July 1969*

> *"We were working secretly for the military,*
> *Our experiment in sound was nearly ready to begin,*
> *We only know in theory what we are doing,*
> *Music made for pleasure, music made to thrill."*
>
> *Kate Bush: 'Experiment IV' (1986)*

Though I place little credibility on anything put out by the BBC, presenter Suzy Klein was on-point when she began her BBC4 TV series 'Tunes for Tyrants,' analysing how world leaders of the 20th century had harnessed music for political means, with the observation:

> *"What fascinates me is music's uncanny ability to stir us up, to calm us down, to express every possible human emotion. It bypasses language and reason, and aims instead directly for our souls. And that's what makes music so incredibly powerful, and also potentially, incredibly*

dangerous... Music can console us and it can corrupt us; inspire resistance, or collusion."

According to alternative and mainstream sources alike, the very reality in which we find ourselves having our human experience, is founded on sound frequencies. This apparent 'physical' existence only appears that way because of the way we perceive it into 'solidity' through our applied and shared consciousness. This is the origin of the often-quoted phrase "if a tree falls in the woods and there's no-one there to hear it, does it make a sound?," implying that sound only exists audibly when it's decoded into that form. Otherwise, it exists as waveform frequency only.

With sound literally lying at the very core of everything we perceive, therefore, it becomes rife for manipulation by would-be controllers of malevolent intent.

432 vs. 440

Since I started speaking publicly about music conspiracy issues, the question I've had more than any other doesn't concern the untimely death of a beloved rock idol, or which celebrities have sold their souls for fame and fortune. The one that has grabbed people's attention more than any other, concerns the truth about 440 vs. 432 hertz, (hz meaning in this case, 'vibrational cycles per second.') It's a reference to the standard pitch which has been used for the tuning of musical instruments in the Western world – plus the frequency at which recorded music has been mastered – for the past several decades.

For many years, the standard tuning pitch was set at A=432hz, where the musical note A vibrates at that frequency, and all subsequent notes come in proportional accordance. Musicians and audiophiles alike agreed that this was a natural, harmonic frequency, and an obvious choice.

In 1917, however, attempts were made by America's Rockefeller Foundation to change the pitch to A=440hz. This failed to gain any ground at the time, so a second attempt was made towards its instigation at the start of World War II. An international conference held in London in 1939 recommended that A=440 be adopted. This suggestion was apparently supported by the BBC's orchestra of the time, who preferred 440 to the previous 439, as that corresponding frequency was hard to generate using standard electronic clocks.

In 1955, A=440hz was adopted by the International Organization for Standardization (ISO,) under the name ISO16. Wikipedia reports that the US time and frequency station WWV, broadcasts a 440hz signal at two minutes past every hour, with WWVH broadcasting the same tone at the first minute past every hour, and that this was added in 1936 to aid orchestras in tuning their instruments. (The Hebrew letter of 'vav,' incidentally, is interchangeable between V and W in the English alphabet, and carries a numerical value of 6, so WWV in this regard, equates to the number 666. Is it just me, or have we come across that one before somewhere?)

This decision perplexed musicologists, who maintained that 440, (described as 'equal temperament' or 'concert tuning,') was anything but the sensible choice that 432, (known as 'just intonation,') was. 432 is said to synchronise with the rhythms of human brainwaves, the rest of nature and with the frequency of the earth itself, and music performed to that pitch is thought to therefore have healing, or at the very least, soothing and calming properties.

440, in contrast, was thought disturbing and dissonant on an unseen level, with music performed at that pitch having unsettling effects on those exposed to it. It's frequently claimed, (though difficult to prove,) that the Nazis experimented by performing military music pitched at 440, and observed the anxious and stressful states that it would bring about in the soldiers marching to it. Propaganda Minister Joseph Goebbels, so the story goes, added his voice to those campaigning for this to become the standard.

Applications now exist on-line where users can convert recordings made at 440 into a 432 version. It's interesting that a Google search of "432 vs 440hz" mainly throws up results denouncing the idea that the change could have been any kind of malevolent move as "claptrap" or "a ridiculous conspiracy theory," when there are thousands of articles and videos giving the other side of the argument whose results do not get shown, as any intrepid researcher will find.

According to an article on the 'Why Don't You Try This?' website, titled '440hz Music – Conspiracy to Detune us From Natural 432hz Harmonics?:'

> *"Music has a hidden power to affect our minds, our bodies, our thoughts, and our society. When that music is based upon a tuning standard purposely removed from the natural harmonics found in nature, the end result may be the psychic poisoning of the mass mind of humanity."*

Audio producer Long Lastin' expanded upon this idea when guesting on episode 99 of 'Good Vibrations':

> *"432 is about mathematics and sacred geometry, and 432 sits within the harmonies of music. It's the absolutely perfect pitch, and it's a healing pitch. When you come out of 432 and 528 and go to normal tuning like 440, it doesn't sit nicely within the mathematics of the geometry, because sound is actually a shape.*
>
> *"There are certain notes on a keyboard that represent a circle, a triangle, a square, a hexagon. And within those shapes is hidden the degrees – like a circle has 360, a triangle is 180 . . . When it's in 432, it stretches right across the keyboard in perfect harmony. But when it's in 440, certain notes are just out in frequency and don't vibrate well."*

All in the numbers

It seems there's far more to 432 than just some randomly-allotted figure when it gets factored into a particular cosmic sequence. This plays itself out in a number of prominent ways, providing confirmation that numbers are inherently woven into the fabric of creation. All components in the sequence are multiples of 9, and in every case, reducing the figures back down to a single number will always bring you back to 9. It's the only sequence in existence that will bring you back to the same single number in this way.

The sequence starts with 27, a number which has earned its place in music lore through the fabled 27 Club, referring to the large number of musicians who *just happen* to have died at the age of 27 in some suspicious circumstance or other. The number then gets doubled each time, so we get 54, 108, 216, 432, 864, etc. Allotting neutral zeros to these key numbers, we see them cropping up in all kinds of places. Yogic schools apparently teach that all living beings exhale and inhale 21,600 times a day. The Kali Yuga is said to last 432,000 years, being part of the Great Cycle which itself lasts 4,320,000 years. There are 864,000 seconds in a day – 432,000 for day, and 432,000 for night.

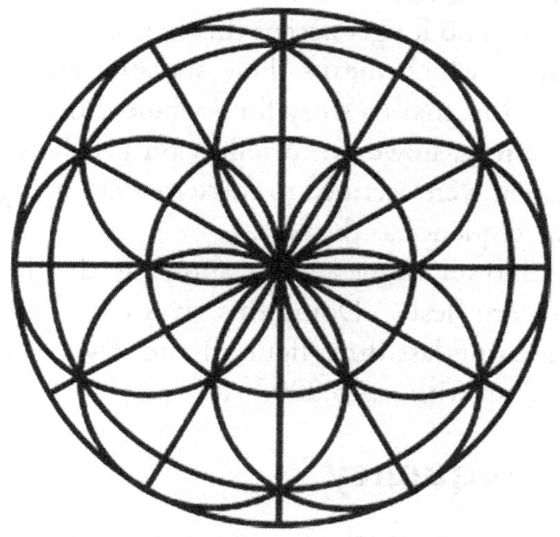

The geometric Flower of Life, associated with harmony of sound.

https://pixabay.com/en/flower-of-life-sacred-geometry-1601163/

Credit: No attribution required

The Pyramid of the Sun monument at Mexico's Teotihuacan has an overall base of 864STU (Standard Teotihuacan Units.) An equilateral triangle whose area and perimeter are equal, gives the square root of 432. The number of times that a healthy human male's heart beats in 12 hours is stated to be 432,000. In Babylonian/ Sumerian folklore, there were ten kings who lived from creation to the time of the Great Flood, a period given as 432,000 years.

Another dizzying array of 432 expressions comes from the article by Joseph E. Mason (of all names,) which resides here: http://www.great-dreams.com/432.htm

The number and its derivatives crop up many times in the traditional heliocentric model of the Earth, Sun and Moon. 864,000 miles is said to be the diameter of the sun. The moon is claimed to have a diameter of 2,160 miles. One Astrological age in a Precessional cycle is said to be 2,160 years. According to Graham Hancock's book 'Fingerprints Of The Gods,' the Great Pyramid of Giza is a representation of the northern hemisphere of the Earth on a scale of 43,200. The polar diameter of Saturn is given as 108,000km, and its orbital period is said to be 10,800 days. I no longer accept this notional model of our Earth and its luminaries, which means these statistics are rendered invalid to me personally. But that's a story for a whole different kind of book! It remains interesting, however, to reflect on just how and why these figures in particular were ascribed to these models, being expressions of the same cosmic sequence as they are.

A real mindblower comes from applying the Jewish Gematria method to the word 'Jesus.' Doing this gives it a numerical rendering of 45666, (interesting last three figures,) and if you multiply all these together you end up with... 43,200.

The Love Frequency

There is another vibration which is cited as being beautiful and harmonic, and it's related to 432. This is what is known as 'the Love Frequency' of 528hz, connected to the original Solfeggio musical scale. As Long Lastin' observes:

> *"You've also got 528hz, which is the heart frequency, which is the frequency of love... You can also tune your music up to 528. You can find that it actually heals people. There's talk of tuning and frequencies being used in the pyramids of Egypt for healing. Also, back in the days when churches used to have choirs, they had Gregorian music and chants, which went on to be banned by the Catholic Church... one of the main reasons is because these chants and these singers were*

> *found to be causing spontaneous healing, and they couldn't have that because the Church wanted to be the only healers."*

One of the most high-profile advocates of 528hz, has been the American natural health activist and musicologist Dr. Len Horowitz. Explaining in a 2013 interview on American 'Coast to Coast' radio just why 528 has such a vital connection to the human condition, Horowitz stated:

> *"There are actually nine core creative frequencies to the universe. We now know that there's a perfect circle of sound. We now know that the sun is beaming 528hz as part of a central frequency within it, and that among those nine core creative frequencies, we find the original musical scale.*
>
> *"The way the entire universe is constructed – including we the people – is through a musical, mathematical matrix composed of nine simple core creative frequencies… The original musical scale was six notes. And the third note – the miracle note of the original scale, as well as the entire universe – is 528.*
>
> *"There's good and evil in the universe… evil is part of nature. It's part of what God created, and it's actually the frequency 741, which in fact is resonating in the A=440hz standard tuning of the Western world's music. So we're actually listening to a frequency in all of the Western world's music today, that vibrates to the tone that vibrates in <u>dissonance</u> to 528 – love, miracles.*
>
> *"If you study the A=440hz standard tuning in music that we're all listening to… then what we realise is that it's suppressing the 528, it's suppressing the heart chakra. Everything from the throat chakra down is suppressed, and everything from the throat chakra up is stimulated, including the left-brain egoic mind – the reasonable, rational mind that science plays on…*
>
> *"This is at least a major factor in science becoming like the new God."*

As with 432, derivatives of 528 also crop up in other walks of life; there are 5,280 feet in a mile, for instance.

Goosebumps abound

Musicologist Dr. Hans Utter guested on my podcast series in 2017. On the subject of how sound affects mood, he observed:

> *"Auditory frequencies are affecting your body. So, even though you're hearing them through your ears, they're also resonating with different portions of your body. Our sense of hearing is mediated. We're constructing the sound that we experience in our own minds. That's why when you hear a song and you get goosebumps, it's connecting with your emotional centres. It may also be connecting with your past. There is an effect that can happen from the frequencies themselves.*
>
> *"Music mirrors the way that we see the world, and the way that we can construct the past. So when you get chills from hearing something, that means the sound itself, and whatever it's evoking, is travelling through your whole nervous system, through your whole being."*

This goes some way to explaining why music – more than any other medium – is so powerful in evoking memories and nostalgia, and hearing a pop song from decades previous can make us feel like we're right back in the times and circumstances that we were when we first heard it. As my friend RW Sanders once remarked:

> *"I can remember all the lyrics to lots of songs from fifty years ago, but I cannot remember why I came into the kitchen. It is true that music touches us in ways nothing else can. Considering all the music ever written uses the same twelve notes, that is amazing."*

Everyone loves some kind of music, whether it's military brass bands, hardcore Drum & Bass, or anything in between. Can the same be said for any other aspect of human culture? A medium that can have this much power over the emotional states of billions of people, is a gift to a malevolent manipulator. Kate Bush's song 'Experiment IV' talked of a secret military plan to create a sound that was horrific enough to kill people. Even Hergé's Tintin comic book stories addressed the concept; 1956's 'The Calculus Affair' is about the military of two nations grappling over a device that can destroy entire cities through the use of sonics. In many ways – psychological and spiritual, as well as militarily – sound could be considered the greatest potential weapon of all.

Weaponised musicology

Music puts people into a heightened state of suggestibility, and when this factor is coupled with the influence of mind-altering drugs, it leaves participants at music events wide open to neurological moulding. With this in mind, it's interesting to note that every popular music genre from the 1950s onwards has come with its own narcotic of choice, from the cannabis of reggae, to the heroin of punk, to the LSD of psychedelia, to the ecstasy of dance music...

Daniel Estulin, who has written books on the Bilderberg Group and the Tavistock Institute, had much to say on these matters in a 2016 radio interview:

> *"So what happens with the hallucinogenic drugs... they mimic certain aspects of our psychosis... one can literally induce temporary symptoms of psychosis and schizophrenia.*
>
> *"The Tavistock Institute had extensively studied the relationship between the brain and behaviour caused by these drugs, and later on, the knowledge gleaned from the research was channelled into marketing and TV and radio stations through classic oldies – songs from 15 to 25 years ago – which are targeted at the adult population.*
>
> *"And so, what several Tavistock studies showed, was that a song or a piece of music associated with one's childhood, when heard later in life, would call forth memories and associations with that earlier period. And so you had, literally, these encoded memories of popular music in the listener, recalled when he or she heard the same piece of music, from 25 years ago.*

"So imagine if you were on drugs. That whole experience would be reproduced again and again. These memories trigger an emotional drug flashback that sets off an infantile emotional state, bringing the listener back to that time in which he or she literally experienced either an identity crisis, or some kind of situation where it was mirroring the drug reaction itself."

This is a process of behavioural entrainment through music. As Hans Utter commented on the subject:

"When you're listening to a type of music, maybe an extremely dark type of music – some type of industrial or death metal or something like that – it's kind of like the first time you ever had a drink of alcohol, the first time you ever tasted coffee, you had a cigarette, it made you feel sick. And you're like, 'man, this is horrible, how can anyone do this?' The next thing you know you're addicted, right?

"So, that's how these negative frequencies, if you keep getting exposed to them, it will start to become part of your environment."

Talking shop

An institution which specialised in experimenting with the science of sound from its inception in 1958 to its reported closure 40 years later, was the BBC's Radiophonic Workshop, located within its Maida Vale studios in London. It was reportedly set up to create unusual sound effects for radio programmes which couldn't be attained through traditional instruments.

Given that the BBC is a propaganda arm of the British Establishment – and factoring in many elements of its true nature as highlighted in the previous book – perhaps we shouldn't be too surprised to find it has an entire department steeped in this type of activity. Arguably, the Workshop's most notable output was the theme tune to 'Dr. Who,' with its eerie use of test-tone oscillator notes.

Its first commercially-released record, meanwhile, was a 1962 reworking of a time signal created by Italian scientist Maddalena Fagandini, credited to an artist by the name of Ray Cathode. This was a pseudonym of George Martin, who trained in methods of sound manipulation before going on to become the prominent producer for the Beatles. (He was also taught music by the mother of Jane Asher, the 1960s girlfriend of "Paul McCartney.") One of the Beatles' early experimental records as they began their transition from boy-band love songs to psychedelia, was 'Tomorrow Never Knows' from the 'Revolver' album. Its Lennon-composed lyrics, based around 'The Tibetan Book of the Dead,' were coupled with Martin's use of the Leslie speaker cabinet, giving the filtered vocals their other-worldly feel.

Beneath the waves

There are various different types of soundwaves which are measured by an instrument known as an oscilloscope. This renders the sound in the form of wave patterns on a screen. Besides sine and square waves, there is also what is known as a sawtooth wave, so named because its form appears similar to the jagged teeth of a saw. In a fascinating interview entitled 'Ex Illuminati Druid on the Occult Power Of Music,' (available on YouTube,) a former practicing witch by the name of William Schnoebelen addressed the application of the sawtooth wave in popular music settings:

> *"It's a very disagreeable sound. It's almost like the sound of fingernails on a chalkboard. And what I find extremely interesting is that, with the advent of the electric guitar – some of the fuzz effect and all these weird sounds that people like The Who and Hendrix and all these early pioneers of rock music would do – a lot of that involves sawtooth waves. And I think that's why so many people would go to these concerts – not that the drugs didn't help along too – but their souls were being destroyed by the workings of these kinds of sounds, especially at these high levels of amplitude and volume."*

On the subject of Hendrix, the very intro to his 'Purple Haze' is cited as using what has become known as 'the Tritone,' or 'the devil's interval.' It's an interval between notes that is three whole tones apart. The result is thought to sound dissonant, as it is out of synch with the human mind's natural rhythm patterns.

The Tritone is reputed to have been banned by the Catholic church, when its use in the classical music of the 18th century was deemed to be disharmonious, and has been generally frowned upon by scholars and musicologists since. It speaks volumes, (excuse the pun,) that it has been greatly favoured by some of Rock's more raucous performers from the 1960s onwards, therefore. Black Sabbath's eponymous song is said to offer another prominent showcase of the Tritone, along with much of the output of Slayer. The theme tune to 'The Simpsons' has been cited as an unlikely example, too.

Len Horowitz reflected further on 'the devil's interval' in his 2013 'Coast to Coast' radio interview:

> *"It causes, if you play those two notes together, such tremendous stress, that you don't want to listen to it. It's really dissonant. And it's strange, because 528 Love harmonises with virtually everything except that.*
>
> *"So what you're left with realising, is that 741 is part of nature and part of the original musical scale, but it's in dissonance to Love. Which leaves us, as readers of the book of 528, realising that evil is part of the matrix of universal design, and we the people have to choose. It's our choice. And of course, freedom of Will and free choice is one of the greatest blessings that the Creator has given us, and that's why we're in this mess right now in the world today."*

Slave to the algorithm

Another symptom of this technological age sits alongside sound frequencies in the manipulators' toolkit. This is the use of mathematical algorithms to determine what will – or will not – make a music recording popular with the masses. Record companies have been employing scientists in this area for decades, working in conjunction with teams of song-writers, and this factor has been increasingly prevalent in recent years, as pop music has become more and more homogenised, and 'artists' have become little more than cloned automatons, performing whatever material is given to them by their corporate paymasters.

Technology has been over-riding human input for some time, and the incoming Transhumanist society is only going to see this dynamic increase unless it's stopped in its tracks. A passionate music-head can immediately tell the difference between a song that was composed because its creator had something genuinely heartfelt to impart, versus one cynically concocted by a computer programme and churned out on a factory conveyor-belt. Unfortunately, the ratio of passionate music-heads, to those for whom music is just generic background noise to their busy lives, is woefully small, which is how the increased dumbing-down of pop music has been able to fly under the radar unchallenged. Discernment has become a lost art.

Though I certainly don't agree with everything he has to say, UK broadcaster Paul Joseph Watson nailed it in his short YouTube video titled 'The Truth About Popular Music' when he opined:

> *"Researchers in Spain using a huge archive known as the Million Song Dataset, found that pop music has become blander. Based on studies of pop songs from 1955 to 2010, the team found that the diversity of transitions between notes, chords, melodies and other sounds, has diminished over the last 50 years. The Spanish study also found that producers are baking volume into songs at the production stage, making them artificially louder. This over-compression has the effect of sucking all the dynamics out of a song.*
>
> *"... Of course, artists used to have to be talented to get a recording deal in the first place. Now, any stupid fucking bimbo or brain-dead twat can be dragged off a reality show, chucked into a recording studio, and have their shrill, warbling auto-tuned for mass consumption. But when it comes to recording live, there's no Auto-Tune to hide the fact that you have zero talent.*

"Songs are also sounding dumber and more repetitive, because the dwindling attention span of the listener demands more hooks. So, whereas decades ago, you only had to write in one hook to get a hit, now there has to be a hook in the intro, the verse, the bridge and the chorus, because a radio listener will change the station on average every seven seconds, unless they get this continual brain stimulation from a recurring hook.

"... The music industry is now largely controlled by a handful of mercenaries who have strangled originality and replaced it with predictive algorithms. Virtually everyone you see is little more than a programmed robot, spewing out noises that a computer has decided upon beforehand. That's why everything is so fucking sterile. That's why there's nothing subversive about music any more. Because whereas musicians used to be interesting people and have actual personalities – and that's where the authenticity of the music came from – now, they're more akin to handpicked Stepford Wives."

Lost in translation

A variation on predictive algorithms comes from the way so many of us now receive our music. There exists a generation of young fans who have only ever known downloadable mp3s appearing as icons on their laptop or iPhone screen, and to whom even a CD is an alien concept, let alone vinyl.

Audiophiles were critical of digital formats when they first emerged, and many pour scorn on the idea of mp3s. The objection is to the way computers decide for themselves, in compressing a much larger audio file into one of more manageable size, which parts of the original recording to leave out. It will strip away certain frequencies and background detail deemed indiscernible to the human ear, with the brain relied upon to fill in the blanks. What remains is a re-synthesised and distorted version of what was there before.

The problem, for those who take the science of audio seriously, is that today's young generation have got used to listening to mp3s of very low bit-rates, (128 or 192kbps,) compressed for space-saving convenience, and because, as one of my audiophile friends put it, "we can't be bothered to wait four times as long for the file to download, because we're lazy humans." The re-encoding process "removes bits that we *would* be able to hear simply in order to get the file size low enough."

How much of the spirit and energy of a musician's original creation gets lost through contemporary listening methods, therefore, is anybody's guess.

Cymatics

The effect that sound frequencies have on physical objects, (or apparently physical,) is measured through the science of cymatics. It's frequently demonstrated by spreading sand across a drum, then applying sound. The sand arranges itself into patterns which vary from harmonious to dissonant according to the frequencies involved. As Long Lastin' illustrates, it serves as a reminder that certain notes and tones are in synch with the beauty of nature, whereas others are clearly not.

> *"You look at the good frequencies, and they actually produce sacred geometry patterns that have been used since the beginning of time, since Man's been drawing on caves and various ancient architecture. There are the images of the Flower of Life, for instance, which come up. And when you watch the pattern, you can actually see when a bad note hits because the shape is all distorted, and when a good note hits you get these beautiful sacred patterns. Especially if you look at the Seed of Life, which is the five circles that fit together to produce the flower. Well, each circle represents a note. And when you put those notes together you get a perfect harmony of F sharp major."*

Another medium through which cymatics can be measured is water. Many researchers have posited that water has its own consciousness and memory. Either way, it makes up the vast majority of both the earth's surface and the human body, so if there are effects to be experienced according to what frequencies it's exposed to, it really ought to be of concern to all.

This area of research was the specialisation of a Japanese scientist named Masuro Emoto. His work involved him exposing water crystals to certain words and phrases, then freezing them very quickly and analysing the results. While crystals exposed to phrases such as "I love you," "wisdom" and "compassion" arranged themselves into geometric patterns, those exposed to phrases such as "I hate you" and "I will kill you," appeared ugly and chaotic. Interestingly, this occurred when the words were both spoken and presented in written form, suggesting that the same signature energy is always there. Amusingly, the discordant results are also said to have been experienced when water was exposed to a Heavy Metal song, though frustratingly, Emoto's notes don't identify which one.

Hans Utter expanded on the concept in his 'Good Vibrations' chat:

> *"It makes sense if we look at the fact that our bodies are 90 per cent water. Our bodies are vibrational mediums... the audio frequency is transformed into a type of electricity, an electrical signal which is going to your brain. Our brains themselves are floating in fluid. So in a sense, internally, we are floating in this fluid and this is a medium that will vibrate. And that's also how sound can not only affect our mind, but it can literally resonate with our entire beings.*
>
> *"So, if we see ourselves as fishes floating around in water, well, in a sense, the atmosphere around us is like a medium for the transmission of all different ranges of frequencies – everything from cell phones – and that's another whole range of frequency which is similar to sound, but it's inaudible and it's quite harmful. Like the 4G. You wonder why they chose to use these frequencies for cell phones!"*

Sound, the great healer

Just as sound can be weaponised, the reverse is a possibility, and here's where so much hope lies. Frequencies and vibrations applied with positive intent – and in the hands of an experienced practitioner – can be used for healing and spiritual upliftment. It's said that with memory loss brought on by dementia, the melodies and lyrics of favourite songs are the last to go, and indeed, exposure to fondly-remembered music has been known to bring people out of deeply-entrenched comas when all else has failed. An institution whose activities lie in this field is the Nordoff Robbins Music Therapy Centre in London. Their application of music – as well as the human voice – has been claimed to get autistic children to communicate for the first time.

As Jayadev Richardson, a session drummer interviewed as part of BBC Radio 2's 'Faith in the World' week in October 2014 noted:

> *"Sound vibration is everything, because the whole universe – according to Vedic literature – was created by sound. Sound is the first thing that we experience in the mother's womb, and it's the last thing that shuts down when we die. So to hear the right kind of sounds is vital. And I discovered later on as I progressed in my spiritual life, that the sounds of the divine, of 'God', have a potency of their own which are separate from whatever else is out there."*

Paul Robertson, a violinist and sound scholar, added:

> *"When you're listening to music, we as human mammals, we intrinsically entrain. That means our own innate body rhythms and responses will tend to coincide with the rhythms and stimuli of the music itself. Even within coma, it's been regularly observed that if you play someone music, they will respond."*

Another sound technique used for healing – and with connections right back to the core of the human experience – is the phenomenon of binaural beats. These come from the realisation that the human brain can be entrained through sound repetition, and that consistent rhythms can have extremely powerful healing and spiritual benefits. The modern usage of the science in meditation techniques, is based upon ritualistic drumming going back to ancient cultures. The spiritual teachers within these groups are said to have been able to induce specific brainwave states for transcending consciousness, healing, concentration and spiritual growth.

Free will choice is always present in our existence. Just as sound *can* be used to control and enslave us, so it *could* provide a gateway to the type of positive and uplifting experience we would all prefer to be having.

Resources:

Good Vibrations Podcast Episode 107 – Hans Utter – The Science & Weaponisation of Sound:

- https://www.spreaker.com/user/markdevlin/gvp-107-hans-utter

Good Vibrations Podcast Episode 099 – Long Lastin' – Demonic Sonics in Hip-Hop:

- https://www.spreaker.com/user/markdevlin/gvp-099-long-lastin-demonic-sonics-in-hi

432 Hz vs 440 Hz/ Frequencies:

- https://www.youtube.com/watch?v=P5ILuyaZIO4

The importance of 432 music:

- http://omega432.com/

Converting music to 432hz:

- http://truthconduit.weebly.com/convert-music-to-432-hz.html
- https://itunes.apple.com/us/app/432-player/id633600716?mt=8
- https://www.youtube.com/watch?v=KO1jSeP-e-o

Musical Cult Control: The Rockefeller Foundation's War on Consciousness with the Imposition of A=440Hz Standard Tuning:

- http://noliesradio.org/archives/64255

Why Are There 5,280 Feet in a Mile?

- http://mentalfloss.com/article/25108/why-are-there-5280-feet-mile-making-sense-measurements

Ex-Illuminati druid on the occult power of music with William Schnoebelen and David Carrico:

- https://www.youtube.com/watch?v=Q0FUaHDEXhY

BBC Hi Magazine: The Devil's music:

- http://news.bbc.co.uk/1/hi/magazine/4952646.stm

Wikipedia: Music in psychological operations:

- https://en.wikipedia.org/wiki/Music_in_psychological_operations

Does pop sound louder, dumber, and more and more the same? One study says so:

- http://www.slate.com/blogs/browbeat/2012/07/27/pop_music_is_getting_louder_and_dumber_says_one_study_here_s_what_they_miss_.html

How do Binaural Beats work?

- https://www.binauralbeatsmeditation.com/the-science/

How words, frequency can change water & human behavior – Dr. Masaru Emoto:

- https://www.youtube.com/watch?v=iu9P167HLsw

Cymatics: Amazing Resonance Experiment:

- https://www.youtube.com/watch?time_continue=2&v=wvJAgrUBF4w

Cymatics: The Science of Dance. The Study of the Effects Sound Has on Matter:

- http://whatmusicreallyis.com/research/cymatics/

CHAPTER 7

IS NOTHING SACRED?

Reflections on apparent cult influence from the earliest days of Hip-Hop culture, and the systematic toxification of what remains.

> *"Old white men is running this rap shit,*
> *Corporate force is running this rap shit,*
> *A tall Israeli is running this rap shit,*
> *Quasi-homosexuals is running this rap shit."*
>
> *Yasiin Bey, aka Mos Def: 'The Rape Over'*

> *"A nigga told me, the record company's the pimp,*
> *The artist is the hoe, the stage is the corner,*
> *And the audience is the trick. God damn."*
>
> *Ice Cube: 'Record Company Pimpin' (2000)*

> *"Made in his image, are we worshipping a man or not?*
> *Uncomfortable feeling every time I hear 'Planet Rock', (damn,)*
> *Disappointed in the leadership and the god,*
> *Evidence is more than the images the camera shot."*
>
> *Talib Kweli & Styles P Feat. Sheek Louch, Jadakiss & NIKO IS: Nine Point (2017)*

It will be clear to anyone who has come this far, that nefarious shenanigans can be found behind any genre which has representation within the corporate music industry. My research hasn't yet led me to the Opera scene, but it wouldn't surprise me that, if it had, the same symbolism and ulterior motives as in other styles would be waiting to be found. Each genre seems to have played its own part in the agenda of moral and spiritual debasement. And of all that has come across my radar, it is the part played by rap music, and its wider Hip-Hop culture, which has bothered me the most.

I was first drawn to these scenes in my formative years, the appeal coming from the rebellious, (apparently) anti-establishment nature of many of the artists, and the fascination that came from the music having its own language, dress code and ways of behaviour. This made it a culture in its own right, rather than just another music type.

Tragically, I noticed Hip-Hop – at least at the mainstream level – straying in the wrong direction many years ago now, and it has been a painful process for many a rap fan such as myself to have witnessed its increasing descent into moral degeneration. A once-meaningful art form which gave a creative outlet to so many, has been debased into a cultural weapon against the very groups that elevated it in the first place.

Although real-deal Hip-Hop of the type that stays worthy of the label is still being made – albeit largely by original-generation producers, DJs and rappers in their 50s or above – this is not material that stands any chance of achieving mainstream radio or TV airplay, and is rarely heard out in bars, shops or clubs. The only stuff that makes that grade is output from the hand-picked stooges of the corporate labels, which serves one of their culture-shaping agendas in some way or other, and slavishly peddled by the likes of veteran British DJ Tim Westwood and others. If it didn't, it wouldn't be heard.

'Urban' music's role has been to push self-serving, vacuous, materialistic lifestyles, revelling in vanity and over-consumption, and reinforcing the view that life is short and ultimately pointless, so we may as well just party hard and buy loads of shit that will make us look good to others for the few glory years that we're around. What else could matter in life, right?

It seems the true story of this entire genre, lifestyle and culture may go even deeper, however.

Base: how low can you go?

Audio producer Long Lastin' guested on episode 99 of Good Vibrations, to discuss the systematic degradation of what is now laughingly referred to as 'Hip-Hop,' but in reality bears no resemblance to what went before. The toxification is obvious from the lyrics, but the aspect that will interest other audiophiles is the production methods and sonic soundscapes that are getting baked into the recordings. This is what I refer to as 'demonic sonics.' As Long Lastin' reflected:

> *"From what I can hear, they've stripped out certain frequencies, and they've left you with bass and treble. They're taking the mid out of the music...And it leaves you feeling quite uncomfortable...I've noticed that the latest 'Hip-Hop' that's coming out is really, really sub-based...It definitely unsettles the soul, without a doubt. And the high-pitch frequency, because there's no mid – it batters your ears."*

During our chat, we discussed how, being of the same generation, and with the same nostalgic memories of better days, neither of us can stand to listen to mainstream output of the type that's now peddled by radio and TV networks, and heard in clubs throughout the land. And it goes beyond a couple of grizzled old bastards having a moan about 'kids today.' Because individuals of our age have a reference point for how things used to be, we can chart the degradation in a way that a teenager, who has only ever known the type of output that's around today, cannot. It speaks volumes, (forgive the pun,) that a generation raised on these sonics finds them perfectly acceptable and 'normal,' whereas many of their elders actually have a bad physical reaction. As Long Lastin' recounts:

> *"I can't even think straight. It's like, my brain goes into panic mode. It's like I'm having a panic attack and I just have to, literally leave the area! If you're not awake and aware, then you're not aware of what you're picking up, and certain things are switched off within yourself. So you're not particularly noticing these things. I can't put my finger on it, but it's all to do with the feeling.*
>
> *"The new 'Hip-Hop' is synth-based, where the producers have more control of the frequencies. And let's face it, these people know about sonic frequencies...And a lot of these producers now...they're kind of*

like witches or wizards. They work for the industry, and they're told what sonics to put in.

"And not only that, I think they're hiding other frequencies that aren't picked up by the human ear so much, but may be picked up by the body... It is kind of re-programming the insides of us... And all this music is on constant repeat on the radio stations... when you first hear it you think, 'oh god, this is rubbish.' And then three months later you've heard it on repeat twenty times a day and you start liking it."

The production styles that have been going into 'Hip-Hop' since around 2008, are electronic in nature. Gone are the days of producers sampling old soul and funk records, and in their place is the proliferation of the dehumanising Auto-Tune, a vocal effect which makes artists sound like gibbering robots.

The new breed of tuneage is aimed at a generation raised in a technological era, where digital ways of doing everything is the norm. Having their music delivered in the form of electronic computer files full of manipulated sonics, is one more aspect of an overall lifestyle just a few short steps away from the full Smart Grid society that the architects of the Internet of Things have been working so thoroughly towards.

Any readers unfamiliar with the type of output discussed here, might like to go to YouTube and search for the following four tracks, which Long Lastin' and I used as examples in our chat. These will give a familiarity with what I refer to as 'demonic sonics.' Just thirty seconds or so will be enough; listening for any longer becomes truly painful. And make sure the kids aren't in earshot.

Future Featuring Lil' Wayne: 'Karate Chop' (Remix)
DJ Khaled Featuring Jay-Z & Future: 'I Got The Keys'
Migos: 'Versace'
Kanye West Featuring Big Sean & Jay-Z: 'Clique' (Remix)

The sound production, coupled with the nihilistic, satanic, materialistic and vacuous nature of 'lyrics' in the above songs – and so many more – makes for a deadly assault on the spirituality of the listener. How strange that people will actually *pay* to be debased in this way!

The current-day degeneration of Hip-Hop is easy enough to recognise once the blinkers are off. But what if the story goes much, much deeper than just these contemporary tactics, and there has been far more of concern lurking beneath the surface of this artform right from the start?

The fall from grace of Afrika Bambaataa

It was almost symbolic of the toxified state to which Hip-Hop had regressed, when one of the most respected figures from its inception became embroiled in multiple allegations of sexual impropriety in early 2016. Any group, movement, religion or philosophy has its own inspirational leader, and in Hip-Hop culture, Afrika Bambaataa's is the name that has been spoken of with great reverence for the past four decades or more. In fact, although Keith 'Cowboy' Wiggins of the Furious Five is recognised as having first coined the term 'Hip-Hop,' it is Bambaataa who claims credit for popularising the term "Hip-Hop *culture,*" representing the wider lifestyle that goes hand-in-hand with rap music. Certainly, I was naively chuffed to have DJed on the same bill as Bambaataa and his cohort Jazzy Jay when they guested at The Forum in Cardiff in 1998.

According to on-line profiles, Bambaataa was born Kevin Donovan in the Bronx in April 1957, though there are claims his real name is actually Lance Taylor. His mother and uncle are said to have been political activists. Evidently, he was very much in the midst of the newly-emerging Hip-Hop scene as early as 1973 – at the age of 16 – when the genre's originator, Kool Herc, (real name Clive Campbell,) is acknowledged as having thrown the first nascent block parties.

The Bronx of the 1970s was a hotbed of criminal activity, (as portrayed in the 1980 Paul Newman movie 'Fort Apache: the Bronx,) and the young Taylor/ Donovan became a member of the gang known as the Black Spades. Street lore has it that, rather than engaging in criminal lifestyles themselves, the Spades were all about recruiting young male members of the community into their ranks, to keep them from falling in with more malevolent gangs. The Spades claim to have been all about the self-improvement of their members, with a strong spiritual ethos rooted in the teachings of Islam, and they weren't beyond taking forceful action against members of other gangs encroaching on their territory when the situation called for it.

According to Wikipedia's account of Taylor/ Donovan's time with the Spades:

> *"He quickly rose to the position of Warlord of one of the divisions. As Warlord, it was his job to build ranks and expand the turf of the young Spades. He was not afraid to cross turfs to forge relationships with other gang members, and with other gangs. As a result, the Spades became the biggest gang in the city in terms of both membership and turf."*

Their philosophy appears to have been one of many offshoots of the Islamic faith specifically packaged for African-Americans. (Many researchers accuse the Nation of Islam of being an offshoot of Freemasonry for black people, in the same way that the Boule secret society – thought to be run along similar lines to Yale University's Skull & Bones – reserves its ranks for 'elite' black members.) The Spades' ideologies, symbolism, art and garb was also rooted in Afrocentrism, encouraging adherents to study their African cultural roots.

Taylor/ Donovan is said to have adopted the Bambaataa persona after winning a trip to Africa in an essay-writing contest in 1975. Here, he became inspired by a Zulu chief named Bhambatha. Also impressed by the tribal warriors portrayed in the 1964 movie 'Zulu,' returning to the Bronx, he sought to incorporate elements of these inspirations into the new gang that he had formed as an offshoot of the Black Spades. This was known as the Bronx River Organization, later shortened to just 'The Organization.' It was from this group that the Universal Zulu Nation evolved.

(A question occurs to me at this juncture: how did Taylor/ Donovan, coming from an impoverished background, come to wield so much sway as to be able to establish such a far-reaching group – which went on to influence the lives of many thousands of young men – when he himself was still in his teens... if not with some kind of assistance from outside forces?)

Afrika Bambaataa (left) performs at The Forum nightclub in Cardiff, 1998.

Credit: The Author

An essential component of gang life in the Bronx of the 1970s, seemed to have involved partying as a tactic to bring community cohesion, and it was through this ethos that the early Hip-Hop block parties began to flourish. Here, the four central tenets of the culture got finely honed – turntablism, B-boying (or breakdancing,) graffiti art and MC-ing, (rapping.) The fifth element was always considered to be Knowledge of Self, and in many ways, these components mirror the four classical elements of Earth, Air, Fire and Water, with the fifth being Ether, or Spirit. The key mission statement of the Zulu Nation was "peace, love, unity and having fun."

As the years progressed, Bambaataa came to be acknowledged as one of the founding fathers of the artform, alongside Herc, Grandmaster Flash, Grandmixer DXT and Fab Five Freddy – although how much of this mythical status was created by his own instigated hype, and some jumping on the bandwagon of a culture that had already been created, has come into question in recent years.

Among Bambaataa's reverential nicknames have been 'The Godfather' and 'The Amen Ra of Hip-Hop Kulture.' His status was cemented considerably by the release of the Arthur Baker-produced 'Planet Rock' in 1982, which – although acknowledged universally as a 'Hip-Hop classic' – in reality isn't in the Hip-Hop style at all, being more akin to electro-disco-funk, and heavily influenced by the music of German synth pioneers Kraftwerk.

In the video to the song, Bambaataa and his associates display the kind of Afrocentric ceremonial garb which characterised the group's persona. Much of the symbolism is similar to that rocked by George Clinton in his Parliament and Funkadelic acts. (Incidentally, Clinton himself has ties to a mind-control cult in the form of the Process Church of The Final Judgement, which has counted Charles Manson, 'Son of Sam' killer David Berkowitz, and alleged assassin of Robert Kennedy, Sirhan Sirhan, among its associates. In his 2014 auto-biography, Clinton wrote:

> *"There was a group called the Process Church that had been founded by a British couple as an offshoot of Scientology, and in the late sixties, they started hanging out with the band, mainly in Boston… We ended up excerpting some of their thinking in the 'Maggot Brain' liner notes, which seemed fine at the time – it was a form of self-actualization, not an uncommon or unpopular philosophy at the time. We did the same thing for 'America Eats Its Young,' but with far different results."*

As the years progressed, UFO and extra-terrestrial imagery crept in alongside the Zulu Nation's cultural stuff – just as it had with Clinton's imagery. The Zulu Nation organised itself as a hierarchy, rather like a religious organisation, its senior members describing themselves as 'Moors' as well as Muslims, and espousing many of the teachings of the Moorish Orthodox Church of America.

The Zulu Nation grew its membership to many thousands, establishing operations all across the US and in many other countries, all espousing the same principles and doctrines.

From an outsider's perspective, everything about Bambaataa's world and that of the Universal Zulu Nation appeared to be positive and inspiring.

Secrets and lies

This benevolent worldview was suddenly shattered in the Spring of 2016, when two former Zulu Nation members came forward with allegations that, over a prolonged period dating back decades, Bambaataa had sexually molested them on several occasions while they were still minors.

The most prominent accuser was Ronald Savage, who had been known during his Nation days by the street name Bee Stinger, and had since become a music industry executive, author and politician. Savage claimed that his abuse dated back to 1980 when he was 15 years old, and he broke his story with a self-published memoir titled 'Impulse Urges and Fantasies.' In a subsequent interview with the 'New York Daily News,' he said:

> *"I want him to know how much he damaged me growing up. I was just a child. Why did he take my innocence away? Why did he do this to me?"*

Immediately in the wake of Savage's allegations, another former Nation member named Hassan Campbell – known by the nickname Poppy – emerged with an almost identical story. Campbell claimed he too was sexually molested by Bambaataa for a prolonged period, and that he had come forward before Savage in the form of a video exposé, but that Savage's story had gained prominence over his.

Campbell has since made multiple videos building on his story, and has been interviewed several times by radio host Troi 'Star' Torain on his YouTube-based Shot 97 channel. Campbell states that Bambaataa's penchant for underage boys was well-known within the Zulu Nation hierarchy, but that it was quietly tolerated and no action ever taken.

(Hearing this put me in mind of Jimmy Savile's historic predatory paedophilia when the story broke in late 2012, a year after his death. Many employees of the BBC, including household-name presenters, then commented that Savile's habits were an 'open secret' within the corporation, but employees just learned to keep their mouths shut for fear of losing their careers if they spoke out. Savile was clearly protected through his connections into British military intelligence, and even the Royal Family. Does Bambaataa's getting-away-with-it for so many years also hint at some kind of protection from higher up?)

In an interview with the Doggie Diamonds on-line TV channel, Campbell commented:

> *"You have to keep in mind, with Bambaataa, he comes along, a Hip-Hop pioneer in Bronx River, legendary status. And he's coming along at a time when the black community was plagued with dope and crack. That was a heavy time and a heavy era, so most of the people in the projects was strung out... So it made it easy for Bam to prey over the youth in the projects."*

(Here's another question: who actually decides when someone gets labelled 'legendary' or 'iconic'? We're back to Edward Bernays' 'men we've never heard of' manipulating public perceptions. We might similarly ask: who decides who gets considered a 'genius,' like Stephen Hawking or Albert Einstein? And who exactly decided that Jimmy Savile and Rolf Harris were British 'national treasures?' These are all questions we would do well to ask, I feel, when figures in the public eye come with these ready-made labels attached.)

(And purely by matter of a curious aside, it was Donald Trump's father, Fred, who headed up the building of many of the iconic housing projects in Brooklyn and other parts of New York City, ("the projects",) that have since become immortalised in Hip-Hop legend.)

Campbell continued:

> *"See, what people don't understand, the majority of times when a young boy gets molested, he never comes to the forefront and tells. That is the hardest thing, to actually tell... People sit up there and they say, 'yo, what took you so long to come forward?... Name one dude that ever got raped in jail that came home and told somebody he got raped?"*

Campbell has spoken of how, although the sexual abuse sickened him, Bambaataa was like a father figure in the absence of his own, and a single-parent upbringing seems to have been a common factor among the young alleged victims.

In the wake of Savage's initial comments, Bambaataa issued a denial of the claims through his lawyer, Vivian Kimi Tozaki. At the same time, Zulu Nation 'Minister of Information' Quadeer Shakur, threatened to file a defamation lawsuit against Savage through a cease-and-desist letter.

In a radio interview with Ed Lover and Monie Love, Bambaataa claimed there was an orchestrated conspiracy against him, and denied having ever known Ronald Savage, but was called out as a liar by – among others – Lord Jamar of the group Brand Nubian, who confirmed that Savage had been Bambaataa's sidekick for many years, albeit under the name 'Bee Stinger,' and that this was well-known within New York's Hip-Hop community.

Not too much peace, love, unity and having fun any more, it would seem.

The Blastmaster speaks

A figure who has attained almost the same level of mythical status as Bambaataa, is the rapper 'Blastmaster' KRS One, real name Lawrence 'Kris' Parker. Born in 1965, KRS – like Bambaataa – grew up in the Bronx, and has attained a similar reputation as a spiritual teacher, preaching Hip-Hop as something of a religion. He was a key figure in the Stop The Violence and HEAL (Human Education Against Lies) activist movements, and established May of each year as Hip-Hop Appreciation Month, (with Bambaataa and the Nation marking each November as Hip-Hop History Month.) Appearing on N.O.R.E. and DJ EFN's 'Drink Champs' podcast, KRS was asked to comment on the Bambaataa situation. He stated:

> *"For me, if you keep it Hip-Hop, nothing can be taken away from Afrika Bambaataa. Nothing. Just keep it Hip-Hop. But if you want to dig into dude's personal life and accusations that's being made and so on . . . personally – me personally – I don't give a fuck. Personally.*

> *"Look, if somebody was harmed or whatever, y'all gotta deal with that shit. Deal with it. That don't stop Hip-Hop. That don't stop what you did for Hip-Hop. It don't take away none of it. History is history. But deal with that. That's personal."*

He also stated that: "anyone who has a problem with Afrika Bambaataa should quit Hip-Hop," and insisted that any leadership within Hip-Hop culture has to be "untouchable."

KRS's comments were interpreted by many as him turning a blind eye to the molestation claims. In the wake of the ensuing controversy, he issued a statement on his website, in which he claimed his words had been taken out of context:

> *"I am indeed concerned about the accusations made against Afrika Bambaataa, but I will not become entangled in a controversy that seems to be less about justice, and more about self-promotion and revenge... I said then as I am saying right now, it is not that I don't care at all about the accusations made against Afrika Bambaataa. I am saddened at the whole controversy and how it is being handled. It is not that I don't care, it is more the fact that I don't gossip. I don't take sides in real disputes that don't concern me."*

Some months later, KRS raised much interest in the video to a Q&A session, where he was asked if he was a Freemason. He replied by saying he wasn't, but that he had studied the teachings of Freemasonry for almost 20 years, had known Freemasons all his life, and that he was considered to be a 33rd Degree Master Mason by those within the ranks, who trusted him with "their secrets, symbols and knowledge." He added that you might consider him "an honorary member, because I understand the truth."

I found this confusing as, from my understanding of how Freemasonry works, (admittedly limited as I've never been a Mason myself,) it relies upon oaths of secrecy undertaken by members – particularly those in the upper ranks – which are not to be shared with anyone outside of the fraternity. This is the whole point of all 'secret' societies.

KRS established the Temple of Hip-Hop as a conceptual theme, and has been trading as a 'teacher' of its wisdoms and doctrines for many years. These include 'The Gospel of Hip-Hop,' a book he says he pretty much "channelled" from 1994 to its publication in 2009.

Placed within the framework of the cult-like Zulu Nation, KRS's 'Temple' certainly bears all the hallmarks of a secret-society fraternity... or a cult?

Bambaataa and KRS have both made anti-Illuminati/ New World Order statements over the years, in interviews and on track; KRS's 'It's All Insane To Me,' and Bambaataa's 'Warlocks and Witches, Computer Chips, Microchips and You,' stand as good examples of these. On the surface, then, the pair *appear* to be indicating their disapproval for elite secret societies and their stranglehold on humanity. There is, however, what I call the duplicitous Disarmament Tactic at play in so many situations, and readers who may have missed what this is all about are encouraged to read the section on it back in Chapter 3.

KRS's apparent defence of Bambaataa, seemed to re-ignite the decades-old animosity between him and veteran rapper MC Shan, as portrayed on the classic 1980s 'beef' tracks 'South Bronx, 'The Bridge' and 'The Bridge Is Over.' Commenting in a 2016 interview, Shan suggested KRS's comments indicated that he had secrets of his own to hide when he said:

> "... *When I used to see Bam, he used to embrace me like, 'Shan, Shan Shan.' But you can't even talk to me right now. You can't say nothing to me. I don't care what you did for Hip-Hop. None of that. And I keep saying, KRS One, you got something to hide, my nigga! Because for you to keep standing up for somebody that did what they did, and you still standing up for this man... you got something to hide and you don't want it to come out!*"

A vexed Hassan Campbell/ Poppy said in one of his subsequent interviews, that the only reasonable action for KRS One to take following his apparent defence of Bambaataa, would be to kill himself, as he questioned what kind of father would stand as an apologist for paedophilic behaviour against young boys:

> *"What I have to say to KRS One is like this: everything I thought he was as a person, he's the total opposite. But I'm realising it's about the music industry, period, it's not just him. The fact that everybody in the music industry is so quiet about this topic is crazy to me.*
>
> *"Here it is – you've got the Hip-Hop pioneer, and everybody's so quiet... For me to go through all the pain I've been through, and then for KRS One to be so inconsiderate. Do you know what it's like being molested?... I've never seen a father be so insensitive towards someone that had been molested."*

KRS's lyrics on the Boogie Down Productions track '13 N Good' certainly don't paint him in a very favourable light in this regard. In it, he conveys unwittingly having sex with a 13-year-old girl, but enjoying the experience nevertheless:

> *"We jumped in the ride, rushed to the crib,*
>
> *I ain't gotta explain what we did.*
>
> *Built to last, I simply waxed that.*
>
> *Asked the question, no need for guessin,'*
>
> *Hey baby, how old are you?*
>
> *Twenty-six, twenty-one, maybe twenty-two?*
>
> *I'm twenty five, she shucked and kinda neighed,*
>
> *And said, "hee, hee, hee, I'm only thirteen."*
>
> *Thirteen!? I need a quick escape.*
>
> *That's statutory rape!*
>
> *...But she was good!"*

The plot thickens

By the end of 2016, Ronald Savage had posted the recording of a phone call to YouTube, in which he says two senior members of the Universal Zulu Nation offered him money to retract his statements about Bambaataa. A voice is heard at the start of the conversation asking him to "name your price," and later suggesting a sum of $50,000. Savage repeatedly insisted that he was not interested in money, and that he had only come forward with his allegations in order for the truth to be known, and to provide support for other victims of sexual molestation.

Savage has said he wants to change a bizarre piece of legislation in New York's statute of limitations, which bars child sex abuse victims from pursuing criminal charges or civil penalties after their 23rd birthday. Both he and Campbell have stated that they felt too afraid and intimidated by the Zulu Nation – of which they remained members for many years – to speak out earlier. By the time they had each decided to seek some recourse, their 23rd birthdays had long since passed. Both Savage and Campbell spoke of how their abusive experiences have affected their sex lives with their female partners. Savage has spoken of how he has contemplated and attempted suicide.

The Universal Zulu Nation has since publicly apologised to Savage and others. The group's statement included the line:

> *"To the survivors of apparent sexual molestation by Bambaataa, both those who have come forward and others who may have not, we are sorry for what you endured, and extend our thanks to those who have spoken out for your bravery."*

Shortly afterwards, Bambaataa seemed to have gone on the run, his exact whereabouts unknown. No official police action had been taken against him by the time of this book's completion, despite the highly public nature of the claims made against him.

By May 2016, another voice had been added to the accusations in the form of an ex-Black Spade, Shamsideen Shariyf Ali Bey, known as 'Lord Shariyf.' He appeared on Star's radio show to back up Savage's and Campbell's accusations, and described himself as having been Bambaataa's bodyguard.

Shariyf confirmed that Bambaataa's alleged sexual encounters with underage boys were a "well-known fact in the Zulu Nation," adding that he had interacted in some way with hundreds of boys since the 1970s. Shariyf stated that visitors to Bambaataa's apartment would often find him in compromising positions with young boys, and he would be accompanied by pre-teen males in his hotel room when away on tour. He seemed to make few attempts to hide his behaviour. On one occasion, he is said to have been stabbed by one of his potential victims in self-defence, causing him to seek emergency hospital treatment.

In his Star interview, Shariyf stated:

> *"I can say I've walked in on stuff where I say, 'what the fuck is going on?'… There's always a boy in his house. When he leaves and gets home, there's always a boy there. I've seen them camped, asking him for money. He travels with late-teens. Those are the ones he takes overseas with him. When I went with him on tour in the States, I would stay in one room and he would have boys in the room with him."*

While relating the story of his seeking to convene a council of Zulu Nation elders, Shariyf stated that he first consulted "my Moorish brother Hakim Bey." Some confusion arises here, as Hakim Bey is the pseudonym of an individual named Peter Lamborn Wilson, described as an anarchist author and spiritual leader, but who also has some disturbing links to paedophilia. Before going any further, it bears clarifying that Shariyf appears to have been referencing a different individual who goes by the name of Hakim Bey, and who can be seen in this video – https://www.YouTube.com/watch?v=yWHoutJs5Qc

Hakim Bey seems to be an unfortunate moniker for this younger individual given that he shares it with Wilson, and it's puzzling as to why he would have chosen it, given that Wilson's links to paedophilia have been known about for many years. Wilson also has connections with Moorish/ Islamic teachings, and it's worth looking a little further into his background at this point.

Coming out of Columbia University, Wilson was a founder member of the Moorish Orthodox Church. Early on, this organisation forged a link with the League for Spiritual Discovery, (LSD – nice touch,) the group established by Dr. Timothy Leary, which Wilson is said to have visited for supplies of psychedelic drugs. Wilson is also credited with having invented Temporary Autonomous Zones, a form of cult-like communal living spaces. In an interview on TAZs, he stated:

> *"The real genesis was my connection to the communal movement in America, my experiences in the 1960s in places like Timothy Leary's commune in Millbrook."*

(Millbrook Mansion was a house in New York State gifted to Leary by the wealthy Hitchcock-Mellon banking family, from which he conducted many of his experiments into the effects of LSD, dosing the guests who would come and stay at the house. Many were prominent figures from academia and entertainment. Beat poet Allen Ginsberg was one such guest.)

Wilson's Moorish Orthodox Church subscribes to various doctrines from the Sufi tradition of Islam, one of which is the advocacy of pederasty. According to the tradition's writings, this concerns itself with men gazing lovingly upon the beauty of young boys, rather than any sexual activity taking place. Wilson, however, also turns out to have been a writer and something of a spokesperson for NAMBLA, the North American Man-Boy Love Association that we encountered in an earlier chapter, by way of fellow member Allen Ginsberg. NAMBLA advocates for grown men to be able to have sexual relations with pre-teen boys without penalty, and campaigns for the release of men who have been jailed for sexual offences against male minors.

Wilson/ Hakim Bey's' Wikipedia entry notes that:

> *"Some writers have been troubled by Bey's endorsement of children's sexuality, and its ability to be expressed without the restriction of age.*
>
> *"In his book 'William S. Burroughs vs. The Qur'an,' Michael Muhammad Knight describes his experiences with Peter Lamborn*

Wilson. Knight befriends Wilson, and is invited to stay at his house; he begins writing a biography of Wilson, on which he hopes Wilson might bestow the label "official."

"However, as he learns more about Wilson/ Bey's writings on pederasty, his view of Wilson sours, and with that their friendship. Knight says: "Writing for NAMBLA amounts to activism in real life. As Hakim Bey, Peter creates a child molester's liberation theology, and then publishes it for an audience of potential offenders."

If Lord Shariyf really had gone to this particular Hakim Bey for guidance on how to deal with Bambaataa's alleged pederasty, it would be a bit like wanting to become a vegan and going to a butcher for advice.

Body count

A further voice to have weighed in with yet more accusations against Bambaataa, was the Universal Zulu Nation's former Minister of Information known as Grandmaster TC Izlam. Shortly after making his comments in an interview his body was discovered on a sidewalk in Atlanta, Georgia, on 8th June 2017. He had been shot, with almost no coverage of the incident given in the media.

In fact, the entire Bambaataa episode has been noticeably lacking from mainstream media coverage. If it were, let's say, Rod Stewart or Mick Jagger who was embroiled in such accusations, does anyone think we'd be hearing as little about it? You might think that radio/ TV stations and magazines that pride themselves on supposedly being at the forefront of Hip-Hop and urban culture, would find a story about one of the pioneering historical figures being embroiled in a sordid sex scandal to be worthy of coverage and investigation.

But there has been a blanket veil of silence over the whole affair both in the US and the UK. It seems as if the Bambaataa accusations have, in some way, struck at the very core of Hip-Hop culture's supposed spirituality – particularly among participants of a certain age – and to engage in meaningful conversation about it is considered too painful a prospect. Denial and avoidance have taken over as the default responses.

TC Izlam had given interviews to Chicago journalist Leila Wills, as part of her upcoming documentary into the hidden secrets of Bambaataa and the Zulu Nation, titled 'TRAPped in a CULTure.' In one, he recounts his first discovering Bambaataa's paedophilia, and the difficulty that would have been involved in his trying to raise further awareness of the problem, given the closed ranks of the Zulu Nation leadership:

> *"... We started internal-affairing the Zulu Nation 15 years ago, and the first one we internal-affaired was Afrika Bambaataa. 'Cause, see, If I would have came out in the 90s saying I had suspicions that Bambaataa is fucking with little boys over the Nation, I would have been dead!"*

As Leila Wills recounted in an on-line article for the 'Metropolis' newspaper:

> *"During our interview, TC stated to me that he was in Atlanta because he had been in hiding and on the run for the past year, after resigning as International Spokesman for the Universal Zulu Nation. TC said he had received numerous death threats via phone calls from what he described as 'Bambaataa's fan club.' He said the threats accused him of disloyalty to 'the Father,' and that he would 'end up in a box."*

On 12th June 2017, Atlanta police announced that they had taken into custody a suspect in TC Izlam's murder, a Trelle Deshawn Hough. The murder charge against Hough was later dropped, though he was kept in custody. A second suspect, Taleeb Paige, was arrested on 30th June, and charged with murder and other offences.

Updates on Leila Wills' 'TRAPped in a CULTure' documentary, scheduled for release in 2018, can be obtained from the film's Facebook page: https://www.facebook.com/tRAPped.in.a.CULTure/

Down with the clique?

The above revelations about goings-on within the Zulu Nation, have to beg the question of any truly open-minded researcher, as to whether the organisation was in fact run as some kind of mind-control cult. The question was raised in an excellent article entitled 'Afrika Bambaataa: Inside the Mind of a Cult Leader' by Leila Wills, which is linked to at the end of the chapter. All the warning signs seem to have been present; cult members are kept largely shut-off from the happenings of the outside world; they are encouraged only to fraternise within their own circle; different members of the same family are brought into the group, as was the case with the Nation, (Hassan Campbell has accused Bambaataa of having sex with his own male cousin); there is an organisational hierarchy with appointed leaders who operate without scrutiny, and according to oaths of secrecy. The other element so often present within cult organisations is institutionalised sexual abuse.

By October 2017, Star expressed the view that the Zulu Nation was effectively finished.

There's been division within the ranks of the other pioneers, too; in 2015, the Furious Five's Scorpio denounced Grandmaster Flash, (real name Joseph Sadler,) as "Hip-Hop's Milli Vanilli," complaining of how he took credit for their groundbreaking single 'The Message' and scored an international career off it, despite not actually appearing on the recording. By 2016, Kool Herc had joined in by accusing Flash of altering history, and describing 'The Get Down', the Netflix series on which Flash had collaborated with director Baz Luhrmann, as "the let down,") and Flash had responded in an open letter, maintaining that he was the originator of several Hip-Hop DJing techniques, rather than Herc.

In September 2017, Flash recorded an interview with AllHipHop TV, (link at the end,) in which he lamented all the fall-outs and addressed his earlier comment to Kool Herc of "there's only two of us left," where he had spoken as if Bambaataa were dead. Interestingly, Flash states in the interview that he never really did know Bambaataa's real name.

How deep is deep?

We can now see that what at first appeared to be a personal dispute between three individuals, goes far, far deeper than this type of simplistic affair. The (third?) eye-opening accusations against Bambaataa – and the implications for the Zulu Nation – have caused some researchers to delve deeper into how far these cult/ secret-society-type arrangements may go within the genre. If Ronald Savage and Hassan Campbell had never blown the whistle, these connections may have gone undiscovered for who knows how much longer?

The adopted monikers of pioneers such as Grandmaster Flash, Grand Wizard Theodore and 'the Grand Wizard' Slick Rick, (who frequently wore a patch covering one of his eyes,) have Masonic/ secret-society overtones. Even the individual perennially cited as being Hip-Hop's founder, DJ Kool Herc, was an early adoptee of the teachings of the Nation of Islam/ Gods and Earths. Was this merely artists being creative with their adopted personas… or were we being given subtle hints as to the fraternal nature of this artform all along?

Wild Prodigy

In the midst of the Bambaataa scandal, Hip-Hop fans were saddened to hear of the death of one of the most respected rappers on the underground scene. Albert Johnson – better known as Prodigy, one half of the crew Mobb Deep – passed away 12 days after TC Izlam.

Prodigy, (not to be confused with the British rave group of the same name,) came from a musical family; his grandfather and grand-uncle had been jazz musicians, his father was a member of a doo-wop group, and his mother had been a member of 60s band The Cristals.

Prodigy formed Mobb Deep alongside Havoc, who he had met while attending Manhattan's High School of Art & Design. They achieved breakthrough success with their track 'The Shook Ones' in 1994, which has since become a staple classic of the genre. Still a teenager at the time of its recording, Prodigy states on the track: 'I'm only 19 but my mind is older.' The group's trademark was always its gritty, graphic and unrepentant tales of street life, crime and violence.

As early as 1995, however, Prodigy had entered music lore by becoming the first rapper known to have namechecked 'the Illuminati' on record, uttering the line, "Illuminati want my mind, soul and my body. Secret society trying to keep their eye on me" in his guest verse on the remix of LL Cool J's 'I Shot Ya.'

Further comments indicated that Prodigy had discovered how the corporate Hip-Hop game is ultimately controlled by secret-society groups steeped in symbolism and ritual activity, and that he was expressing his disapproval of the situation. He commented that he had read the book 'Leviathan 666: The Beast as the Antichrist' by Dr. Malachi Z. York, which had moved him to tears and gave him his "moment of clarity."

Dr. York, (whose real name is Dwight York, and who goes by a number of other aliases,) would appear to have had inside working knowledge of how powerful, controlling groups operate. Besides being a writer, he was the founder of a number of religious/ political sects, the best known of which is his Nuwaubian Nation. This group appears to have been run along mind-control cult lines, with ritual sex practices commonplace, and with York granting himself sexual rights to most of the women in the movement – including the wives and daughters of male members. York is currently serving a 135-year jail sentence. He was charged in 2002 with more than 100 counts of sexually molesting dozens of children, some as young as four years old.

Like the Zulu Nation, the Nuwaubian Nation's early spiritual doctrines had their basis in Islamic/ Moorish teachings, and were geared towards black membership. Later, York incorporated aspects of Judaism, Christianity, Kemetism and UFO religion, and changed the group's name to the United Nuwaubian Nation of Moors.

Further reading occurred during Prodigy's three-year period of incarceration on gun charges, and further lyrical hints at his new-found knowledge crept into his lyrics. He was outspoken in his accusations towards other prominent rappers for having sold their souls for fame and fortune, with Jay-Z as his most prominent target. In 2008, Prodigy penned a five-page open letter from jail, in which he accused Jay-Z of being a Freemason, of being a traitor to his fellow black brothers and sisters, and of promoting "the lifestyle of The Beast." Prodigy stated:

"I have so much fire in my heart, that I will relentlessly attack Jay-Z, the Illuminati and any and every other evil that exists until my lights are put out."

Prodigy died on 20th June 2017 in a Las Vegas hospital, aged 42. He had been taken there a few days previous after falling ill while performing on the Art of Rap Tour. A bizarre story began circulating, (which, in retrospect, sounds more like a form of morbid mockery,) that Prodigy had choked to death while eating an egg in his hospital bed. The real cause of death was cited as complications arising from the sickle cell anaemia which Prodigy had battled all his life. Certainly, his condition was a well-known fact within the Hip-Hop world; Tupac had famously taunted Prodigy about it on his vicious diss track 'Hit 'Em Up,' and Prodigy himself had attributed the nihilistic nature of his lyrics to the permanent physical suffering associated with the condition.

While most seemed content to accept Prodigy's passing as an inevitable consequence of his poor health, more suspicious observers found it relevant that he had been so outspoken about the nature of who really controls the industry, as it certainly wasn't the first time that such a straight-talking individual had met their demise at a relatively young age. There's also the curiosity that Prodigy's death just happened to occur the day after 2017's World Sickle Cell Awareness Day, and one day before the Summer Solstice.

Comments that Prodigy made in one of his final interviews sound like a summing-up of the themes in this book, and clearly, these are not the types of views that the entertainment industry takes kindly to its assets openly expressing:

"You got this power that people call God. There's many names for it – Allah, God, the Creator, the Most High. But the power exists. Some people don't like to admit that power exists, or they just don't believe it – they're atheists. But me personally, I know there's a higher power and that power is real. That power is one force... And we are given free will to do what we want with that power. You can use that power for good, but then, you can use that power for evil too...

"That's what these people are playing with. They're playing with that energy that exists out here that we all have access to. Those people in those positions of power, control and manipulate situations to their favour for their own agenda...Mostly their agenda is population control, mind control. You're being manipulated...

"You learn that they infiltrate groups, and keep positions within those groups, so they can control the decision-making to move things towards their agenda, to control the mass population opinion, and to control the world."

Shortly after the announcement of his death, came the news that Prodigy was planning his next project to be a musical about the Illuminati.

Enter the Clan

Where the fingerprints of banksters, secret societies, religious doctrines and cults have already presented themselves, it's never too much of a surprise to find traces of mind-control and organised crime lurking in the same vicinity. Disturbingly, these elements crop up in the back story of one of the most influential and iconic rap collectives of the 1990s onwards.

The Wu Tang Clan was a collective of rappers that emerged out of the Staten Island borough of New York City under the mentorship of Robert Diggs, known as the RZA, (standing for 'Ruler Zig-Zag-Zig Allah.') Diggs acted as the crew's *de facto* leader. Its members were known for the metaphysical nature of their complex lyricism, coupled with RZA's distinctive production style.

The Clan came with their own logo, a large 'W' usually rendered in black-and-white, and their imagery was heavily associated with martial arts, of which RZA was an obsessive fan; in 2004, he produced the musical score for Quentin Tarantino's 'Kill Bill' movies. The violence and organised crime depicted in many of the Wu Tang's stark lyrics, it turns out, may have more of a basis in reality than many fans realise.

Documentation from the FBI relating to Wu Tang Clan extra-curricular activity, was obtained under a Freedom of Information Request in 2011, and has been made public on the internet. One paper, dated 08/04/99, with certain sections redacted, states:

> *"Information was received from the New York Police Department... about criminal activity being conducted by members of the Wu Tang Clan organization on Staten Island, NY. The detectives have documented that the WTC is heavily involved in the sale of drugs, illegal guns, weapons possession, murder, car-jackings and other types of violent crime."*

It goes on to address the murder of Robert Johnson, aka Pooh, on Staten Island in December 1997, claiming that this was ordered by somebody within the Wu Tang Clan. It further states:

> *"Once individuals have proved themselves to be loyal members or associates of the WTC... they are offered record contracts to record rap-type music."*

Infuriatingly, the section of the document which details where the Clan's funding came from, has been obscured.

The police and the FBI reportedly suspected that the murder of two drug dealers was ordered by RZA, with the complicity of WTC rapper Corey Woods, known as Raekwon. RZA had been acquitted of an attempted murder charge in Ohio some years before. A further Staten Island drug lord was later convicted of the New York murders.

Despite these serious accusations and investigations, law enforcement was evidently unable (or unwilling) to make anything stick with Wu Tang, and so the group was able to continue operating in the entertainment and merchandising industries, and does so to this day.

Meet the family

One of the most prominent rappers in the Clan is Clifford Smith, better known as Method Man. His name cropped up in a radio interview I did with private investigator and broadcaster Ed Opperman, when Ed revealed that Meth once came to his telecoms stall in a Staten Island mall early in his career, and that the only ID he could produce was an identification card from having been a patient at South Beach Psychiatric Center. It puts a different twist on the term 'cell' phone.

RZA, frontman of the enigmatic Wu Tang Clan collective

Credit: The Author

This is an interesting revelation when Method Man is considered alongside fellow Clan member Russell Jones, better known by his artist name of Ol' Dirty Bastard, and a cousin of RZA. Jones' trademark was always his erratic, haphazard vocal style – traits associated with mental instability – and indeed, he spent time in a mental institution, prison and 'rehab' facilities, following a 1999 arrest for drug possession. Dirty spoke in interviews and on record of how he believed himself to be under surveillance from government agencies, with the line, "FBI, don't you be watching me" appearing in his track 'Got Your Money.' Following a history of arrests and brushes with law enforcement – and having been shot and robbed twice – Jones was discovered dead in a New York recording studio two days before his 36th birthday, of what is said to have been an "accidental drugs overdose." He had been complaining of chest pains earlier in the day.

RZA himself is said to be a member of the Almighty Vice Lord Nation organised crime gang, and rumoured to be a 33rd-degree Freemason. In 1970, two of the AVLN leaders achieved a grant from those nice people at the Rockefeller Foundation. The group's activities have included murder, robbery, theft, assaults, intimidation, extortion and fraud. It later incorporated Islamic teachings into its doctrines, (haven't we come across that one somewhere before?) Among the signs and emblems said to be adopted by members to indicate their ties to the group, are a hat cocked to the left side, a glove, a top hat, a cane and a Martini glass. Many of these appear in the promotional photos of prominent rap artists.

RZA is also a stated Five Per Center, a faction alternatively known as the Nations of Gods and Earth, and a spin-off of the Nation of Islam. He is far from alone, as a dizzying amount of other prominent rappers are – or have been – Five Per Centers, including Jay-Z, Nas, Busta Rhymes, Erykah Badu, LL Cool J, Big Daddy Kane, Brand Nubian, Planet Asia, A Tribe Called Quest, X Clan, Poor Righteous Teachers, the now-deceased Guru and Big Pun, and Jay Electronica. (The latter's unlikely relationship with heiress Kate Rothschild was detailed in the last book. After the pair split, Kate went on to date another rapper, London's Stephen Manderson, known as Professor Green. The shared experience of their fathers having reportedly committed suicide, is said to have provided a bond. Kate's father, Amschel Rothschild, was discovered hanged at a Paris hotel in 1996.)

An entire book has been written on the faction's massive influence on the Hip-Hop movement in the form of 'Five Percenter Rap: God Hop's Music, Message and Black Muslim Mission,' by Professor Felicia M. Miyakawa.

In the late 1980s, the Hip-Hop scene spawned a movement known as the Native Tongues, an affiliation of many of the prominent acts of the time, whose output was considered to be thought-provoking and meaningful. Among these were De La Soul, A Tribe Called Quest, the Jungle Brothers, Black Sheep, Queen Latifah and Monie Love. The Native Tongues movement was also heavy on Nation of Islam ideology, as well as embracing Afrocentrism, as George Clinton's Parliament/ Funkadelic and Bambaataa's Zulu Nation had before them. The Zulu Nation received respectful shout-outs on many a Native Tongues track, and Londoner Monie Love – who relocated to New York early in her career to become a radio host – recorded her 1989 track 'Grandpa's Party' in homage to Bambaataa and the Nation.

(On the subject of De La Soul – and just as another of our curious asides – the three members all adopted bizarre pseudonyms. Alongside Vincent Lamont Mason Jr. becoming P.A. Pasemaster Mase, and Kelvin Mercer becoming Posdnous, ('soundsop' backwards,) we had David Jude Jolicouer becoming Trugoy the Dove. His story was that the name was simply 'yogurt' spelled backwards as he just happened to like yogurt. But broken down, his name becomes 'true goy.' "Goy" is a derogatory term used by Talmudic Jews to disparage those outside of their group. Does this name represent a form of cynical mockery? Or am I really just reaching a little bit too far with this one? I'll leave readers to decide.)

A tall Israeli enters

As previously noted, the number of executives in the entertainment industry who identify themselves as 'Jewish,' is out of all proportion to their number in the general population. When it comes to top-level control of the US Hip-Hop industry, there have been few individuals to have exerted as much control over the direction the genre has taken as Lyor Cohen.

Born in 1959 to Israeli immigrants in New York, Cohen's career began in Los Angeles in 1984. After promoting live shows, he collaborated with Russell Simmons on the creation of their Rush Productions outfit, (later Rush Associated Labels,) and as a road manager for Run-DMC. Cohen's artist roster included Kurtis Blow, Whodini, LL Cool J, Public Enemy and the Beastie Boys, and he signed the likes of Slick Rick, EPMD, Eric B & Rakim, De La Soul and A Tribe Called Quest to Rush – all major heavyweights. Cohen went on to work as an executive at Def Jam, the outfit reportedly founded by Rick Rubin in his New York college dormitory, and arguably the most profitable and high-profile rap record label of them all.

Cohen became president of Def Jam/ RAL in 1988, at which point Rubin quit the company. His many years at the helm saw him oversee Def Jam's departure from its parent company Sony, and its merger with fellow corporate giants PolyGram, Universal and Island, before moving across to the Warner group. More recently, he founded his own independent label, 300, bringing through present-day names such as Young Thug, Fetty Wap and Migos in the process.

The list of artists over whom Cohen has had corporate control – including negotiating endorsement deals outside of their music output – reads like a who's-who of A-listers, spanning the likes of Jay-Z, Kanye West, Method Man, Redman, Ja Rule, Ludacris, Foxy Brown and so many others. By late 2016, Cohen had taken up a position with Google's YouTube brand as Global (their wording) Head of Music.

Cohen has been the target of harsh words from Damon Dash, who was Jay-Z's original business partner in Roc-A-Fella (nice name) Records, and himself a high-flying executive until his label was acquired by Def Jam in 2004, which saw Jay-Z being appointed as its president, and Dash being effectively ousted. In a 2014 video interview, Dash criticised "the puppet master" for his financial exploitation of black culture:

> *"My beef was with Lyor because I think he's a fake CEO, and I think he's frontin' on my culture… I'm calling him out publicly, and I want him to stop trying to rape my culture. Go make some money with some other people…*
>
> *"…It's the perfect example of what they always do to us. They try to offer some paper bag of money, or whatever it is, whatever selfish agenda which is the test, and then have us divide, so they can benefit and take the fight off of them."*

(Dash was dating the singer Aaliyah at the time she died in a plane crash in 2001 at the age of 22, and had stated that they had planned to marry. More recently, he has linked with entrepreneur Dez White, with whom he is said to have been developing a new fingerprint payment technology – part of the incoming cashless Transhumanist society.)

For his part, in an interview on Hanukkah Radio, in which the host speaks of "a celebration of Judaism in Hip-Hop," Cohen admitted that Jewish executives have always controlled black entertainment:

> *"Jewish people have always been involved in urban cultural arts, all the way back to the early beginnings of Jazz music. It's just something that's always happened."*

Cohen was the subject of a video from the Vigilant Citizen site entitled, 'The Tall Israeli That Runs the Rap Industry.' It included two Twitter posts from Public Enemy frontman Chuck D, which stated:

> *"The music industry is NOT a game, it's a business enveloping a craft..."*

And, in obvious reference to record executives Clive Davis, Jimmy Iovine, Lyor Cohen and LA Reid:

> *"These Clives, Jimmys, Lyors, LAs, etc, look at black people as less than, and don't consider themselves family..."*

VC ends the video with a clip from Ice Cube's song 'Record Company Pimpin,' in which Cube delivers a scathing commentary on the corporate exploitation of artists. VC observes, however, that the cover for the album on which the track is included, somewhat ironically features Ice Cube rendering the tired old one-eye pose. It's not the first, nor the last time that an artist has *appeared* to be making an incisive, independent statement, but where other aspects of their persona appear to be puzzlingly at odds with such a stance.

Interestingly, when rapper N.O.R.E. once described Cohen as "the most important man in the whole music game," and "a mogul," he responded by stating he's not comfortable with the term and prefers to think of himself as "a humble servant." Cohen has been pictured flashing up the '666' and 'Baphomet' hand signs, which casts interesting light on his 'servant' credentials.

Tellingly, the first sentence of a mainstream article on complex.com about Cohen, states:

> *"If there were a shadowy Illuminati controlling the world of rap, Lyor Cohen would be its all-seeing eye, the man behind the scenes, pulling the strings of the most powerful players and reaping the benefits."*

In his formative years, Cohen worked at the Beverly Hills office of Bank Leumi. This turns out to be an influential Zionist institution that was trying to establish a Jewish state in Palestine decades before World War 2.

In its incisive article titled 'The Tall Israeli Who Runs Hip Hop: An Investigation into Engineered Culture and Bankers,' the mindunleashed.com website observes:

> *"When investigating the money trail of social engineers – people who influence social trends, often to the detriment of society and toward the empowerment of the powers-that-be – the road always seems to lead back to bankers. In fact, bankers are often some of the highest-level power players, higher than government and corporate power.*
>
> *"It is inherently in the interest of power to engineer society, and to steer people's culture in a direction that benefits their system. The financial system is obviously propped up by instilling a culture in people that worships money."*

Preach

The corruption of the rap industry at the hands of outside influences, was addressed on a radio interview with DJ Sway on Shade 45 Radio in October 2015, by Louis Farrakhan, long-standing minister of the Nation of Islam. (It's only right to mention that Farrakhan's own reputation is blighted by constant claims that he was instrumental in the murder of Malcolm X in 1965. Indeed, Farrakhan himself has all but admitted to his involvement. But if I'd stuck strictly to individuals whose good names are blemish-free and absent of any nefarious connections, this would be a very short book!)

Farrakhan told Shade 45:

> *"Our rap artists are more powerful than any preacher. One rap song can turn more people's minds than 100 sermons of some of the great, great preachers. That's the influence that our young people have, and it's not limited to America, it's all over the world.*
>
> *"So here's what we have to decide. Do I want to be an agent of the wicked plans of the enemy to be a destructive force against my own people? Do I want to be the producer of raps that only engage in the most filthy and wicked display of vulgarity to our people? Do I want to do that? Do I want to promote on my radio show the most vile songs that pit one brother against another? Do I want to be an agent of that just because there's a few dollars?*
>
> *"I think we need to unite, and we ought to go to the record producers and argue for the sanity of our people, and make them responsible for the deaths that come as a result of what they cause us to do... See, once you become an agent of our destruction, then if we're united, let's put pressure on our record labels, because our people have more talent than they're showing.*
>
> *"Let them rise to the heights that they wish to rise to, and we should be the vanguard to that kind of approach to all record executives, and charge them with the death of our people that they are promoting. Let's see how they respond to that... When people know that their lives are in the balance by destroying our lives, then maybe we'll see some change."*

The homosexualisation of Hip-Hop

A final, more recent agenda that has been systematically unfolded within Hip-Hop, warrants some exposure. It's another elephant in the room – a factor that few seem comfortable talking about due to the politically-correct mindset that has been fomented by the social engineers, and it involves another group who have been rendered beyond scrutiny in society.

By way of another caveat – just to be clear – this is not *any* kind of judgemental attack on people who happen to be gay. A person's sexual orientation and lifestyle choices are their own business, and so long as it doesn't cause harm to others or take away anyone's rights, there's no problem. This shouldn't even need pointing out taken within the overall theme of this book, but there it is for the record.

We're not talking about individual, personal cases here, though, but about a trend that can be seen to have been calculated by how quickly it has taken root, how all-pervasive it has become, and by how many boxes it ticks in the long-term plans of agencies such as Tavistock, the Frankfurt School and SRI.

The glorification of homosexual and LGBT lifestyles, is a tactic in the eugenics and population-reduction plans of these groups. It serves to further break up the traditional family unit, by destroying the stability that dynamic has, and to stir up discord between different groups within society. And a society fractured by perceived differences is far easier to covertly manipulate, than one in which people stand together against any form of invasive tyranny. Additionally, the frequent flaunting of Transgenderism in the media, ties directly into the satanic mindset of society's occult controllers, which is all about taking what's natural in Creation, (discernible male and female principles,) and inverting and merging them into something completely different.

Rapper Wacka Flocka Flame indicated that he had caught on to the agenda, when he commented in a 2017 interview:

> *"They don't market families and husbands and wives no more. They're marketing young girls, transgenders... they're marketing evil, man... I ain't got nothing against nobody's preferences, man, but, putting it on TV, that's crazy, man. You know, kids is the only people watching TV."*

Historically, Hip-Hop as a genre and as a culture, has been fiercely heterosexual – or at least on the surface. Stories of ritual orgies that artists and executives must undergo to become successful are manifold, of course, and this was addressed in Volume 1. Many public heroes who *appear* to be straight, will have partaken in gay sex acts in exchange for their success.

But for the purpose of this chapter, we're talking about the way artists have always been *presented* to the public. Prior to the 2010s, few rappers had ever come out of the closet. When a rumour emerged that there was a prominent 'Gay Rapper' in the industry in the late 1990s, and everyone speculated on who it could be, it was big news, because it went so against the grain of what that genre had always been about. If, during those years, any A-list artist had appeared in public wearing women's clothing, it would have been headline news in the Hip-Hop press.

How things have changed.

Where the dress-style of choice for rappers used to be loose-fitting jeans, T-shirts and hoodies – and the baggier the better – by the early 2000s, artists such as Drake, Kanye West, Andre 3000 and Pharrell Williams had made it their trademark to rock the 'metrosexual' look, consisting of tight-fitting clothing, heavy on the pink. Not long afterwards came the trendy talk of artists being "gender-fluid," "gender-neutral," or "non-binary."

The London grime artist Skepta indicated the international nature of the agenda when he appeared at an awards event sporting women's knitwear, proudly proclaiming that he was now "gender fluid." The fact that this has been achieved with very little backlash – and with those voicing any kind of objection quickly denounced as 'bigoted' or 'intolerant' – in a genre previously so full of alpha-male machismo, is testament to how successful the manipulators have become at their game, and how socially-intimidated people seem to speak out.

Male artists wearing women's clothing has become more blatant as the years have progressed. Gnarls Barkley star Cee-Lo Green appeared in a photoshoot wearing a wedding dress; A$AP Rocky donned a dress during an episode of BET's '106 & Park;' Lil' B wore women's earrings in the video to his 'Got the Mack Loaded;' Lil' Wayne performed at the 2011 VMA Awards topless, and wearing women's leopard-print leggings, (see the last book's section on the true meaning of this motif.)

Will Smith's son Jaden has worn similar leggings; Yung Joc turned up to an industry event wearing a dress; Young Thug appeared in a photoshoot dressed as Little Bo Beep and had previously worn a leopard-print dress; Lil' Uzi Vert, (say the name quickly a couple of times and see what it sounds like,) is keen on rocking the womens' wear too; Lil Yachty, (what is it with all the Lil's and Yung's??!) had a cover design for one of his releases featuring a gay couple kissing. Nothing wrong with it *per se*, but timing and context are the important factors in establishing whether something is part of a far-reaching agenda. Why did the release come at that specific time, and what else was going on in the scene at large? One thing was a number of artists, such as iLoveMakonnen, Big Freedia and Frank Ocean 'coming out' as gay.

The comments of comedian Dave Chappelle regarding the ritualistic requirement for virtually all black males in Hollywood to wear a dress in one of their films, are worth considering in this context, too. You can hear them in this video – https://www.YouTube.com/watch?v=7lbFRYF-bbM

By the time 'up and coming' Florida 'rapper' (it says here) NewAge Jerkboy (!?!!) had emerged with his video 'Married to the Game,' in which he talks of "your bitch giving me neck" ... while fellating machine guns in a wedding dress with colourful bows in his dyed-blond hair ... all hope for the future of humanity had been lost.

A blurring of the genders is taking place, straight out of the Tavistock instruction manual. And working in tandem with the feminisation of male artists, there is a trend towards females becoming more masculine, (see Angel Haze, Azealia Banks, Melange Lavonne, Temper, Dai Burger, God-Des & She, RoxXxan, Kin4Life.)

(While I think of it, here's *another* slow-drip change that's been creeping up with stealth, and about which nobody else seems to be talking. The ridiculous, retarded and impossible-to-remember spelling of artist names, The likes of Will.i.am, Yxng Bane, A$AP Ferg, A$AP Rocky, Cashh, Ty Dolla $ign, The Weeknd, Lotto Boyzz, Desiigner, MadeinTYO, Mnek, iLoveMakonnen, look like someone fell asleep over a computer keyboard, and resemble expressions of the 'Newspeak' concept out of Orwell's '1984,' where citizens are made impotent by a new, meaningless language.

Why is the Hip-Hop scene so unrecognisable from what it was twenty, or even ten years ago? And why has this genre in particular been selected for so much cultural manipulation? These are the questions that anyone who *doesn't* appreciate having their thoughts and values moulded for them by other people would do well to consider.

Resources:

Good Vibrations Podcast Episode 106 – Lenon Honor – Beyond Gangster Blackface:

- https://www.spreaker.com/user/markdevlin/gvp-106-lenon-honor-beyond-gangster-blac

Good Vibrations Podcast Episode 099 – Long Lastin' – Demonic Sonics in Hip-Hop:

- https://www.spreaker.com/user/markdevlin/gvp-099-long-lastin-demonic-sonics-in-hi

Good Vibrations Podcast Episode 064 – Isaac Weishaupt – Illuminati Watcher:

- https://www.spreaker.com/user/markdevlin/gvp-064-isaac-weishaupt

Afrika Bambaataa's bodyguard calls him a paedophile:

- https://www.YouTube.com/watch?v=U-9MIgbhOuY&t=0s

Audio: Zulu Nation tries to pay Ronald Savage to keep quiet about Afrika Bambaataa :

- https://www.YouTube.com/watch?v=rNCjhB8oMtE

Poppy says KRS-One should kill himself after his Afrika Bambaataa comments (full interview):

- https://www.YouTube.com/watch?v=jYrwGW3lJks&t=0s

Metropolis Newspaper: Afrika Bambaataa: Inside the mind of a cult leader:

- http://metropolisnewspaper.com/afrika-bambaataa1/

Metropolis Newspaper: Revisionist Hip-Hop and the over-glorification of Afrika Bambaataa:

- http://metropolisnewspaper.com/revisionist-Hip-Hop-and-the-over-glorification-of-afrika-bambaataa/

Metropolis Newspaper: Grandmaster TC Izlam's murder and documentary footage:

- http://metropolisnewspaper.com/t-c-izlams-murder-and-documentary-footage/

AllHipHop TV: Grandmaster Flash Discusses Kool Herc, Afrika Bambaataa, And Overcoming Drugs & Betrayal:

- https://www.youtube.com/watch?time_continue=921&v=P-CauhfJ5eA

KRS-One admits to being an "honorary" 33rd-degree Master Mason:

- https://www.YouTube.com/watch?v=-bCcxsV_POk

Freemasonry in Hip-Hop:

- http://thedoggstar.com/articles/secret-societies/freemasonry-in-Hip-Hop/

The Gods Of Hip-Hop: A Reflection On The Five Percenter Influence On Rap Music & Culture:

- http://hiphopwired.com/32991/the-gods-of-Hip-Hop-a-reflection-on-the-five-percenter-influence-on-rap-music-culture/

Millbrook Mansion: This magical drug mansion in Upstate New York is where the psychedelic '60s took off:

- https://timeline.com/drug-mansion-psychedelic-60s-5116867d5041

George Clinton/ Funkadelic's links to the Process Church of the Final Judgement:

- http://dangerousminds.net/comments/funkadelic_and_the_process_church

Vigilant Citizen: Havoc doesn't believe Prodigy (Mobb Deep) choked on egg:

- https://www.YouTube.com/watch?v=19cprNNs7xc

Prodigy says Jay-Z sides with evil to be accepted by the corporate world:

- http://uproxx.com/realtalk/prodigy-says-jay-z-sides-with-evil-to-be-accepted-by-the-corporate-world/

Released FBI File of Russell 'Old Dirty Bastard' Jones:

- https://www.scribd.com/doc/77581648/FBI-File-of-Russell-Old-Dirty-Bastard-Jones

Daily Mail: Secret FBI files show the Wu-Tang Clan were investigated over the murder of two New York drug dealers:

- http://www.dailymail.co.uk/news/article-3302894/Secret-FBI-files-Wu-Tang-Clan-investigated-murder-two-New-York-drug-dealers.html

The tall Israeli who runs Hip-Hop: an investigation into engineered culture and bankers:

- http://themindunleashed.com/2017/04/tall-israeli-runs-Hip-Hop-investigation-engineered-culture-bankers.html

Vigilant Citizen: The Tall Israeli That Runs The Rap Industry – Illuminati Satanic Music Industry Exposed:

- https://www.YouTube.com/watch?time_continue=4&v=OO3WF1Ek7RU

Vigilant Citizen: The homosexualisation of Hip-Hop, part 1:

- https://www.YouTube.com/watch?v=qrgPHD2X_Vw

Vigilant Citizen: Gays & homosexual rituals in the Hip-Hop industry:

- https://www.YouTube.com/watch?v=YkG0LcudZDo

Vigilant Citizen: Gay rappers exposed: P Diddy – music industry black-mail/ homosexual culture:

- https://www.YouTube.com/watch?v=sQESdDbolWQ

The Homosexualization of black American males is getting harder to ignore:

- http://www.thecoli.com/threads/the-homosexualization-of-black-american-males-is-getting-harder-to-ignore.306045/

Skepta explaining why he likes to wear women's clothes:

- https://www.YouTube.com/watch?v=-OPUsQiYTeA

Joy of unisex: the rise of gender-neutral clothing :

- https://www.theguardian.com/lifeandstyle/2017/sep/04/joy-unisex-gender-neutral-clothing-john-lewis

Was Jimmy Savile an inspiration for hip-hop fashion?

- https://www.theguardian.com/culture/2004/apr/20/guesteditors2

CHAPTER 8

IS 'PAUL' PAUL?

Further reflections on the replacement of Paul McCartney. Otherwise known as 'The McCartney Mindfuck.'

> *"Them freaks was right when they said you was dead."*
> *John Lennon: 'How Do You Sleep?' (1971)*

> *"Living is easy with eyes closed, misunderstanding all you see."*
> *The Beatles: 'Strawberry Fields' (1966)*

> *"The test of a first-rate intelligence is the ability to hold two opposing ideas in one's mind at the same time, and still retain the ability to function"*
> *F. Scott Fitzgerald, 1896-1940*

A conclusion I reached a while back when trying to navigate the whole arena of truth and conspiracy – and with the many *cul-de-sacs* that any well-meaning researcher can be led down – is that it's often easier to describe a situation by stating what it <u>isn't</u>, rather than trying to quantify what it is. This is stating things in the apophatic, and it comes as great advice when addressing the <u>possible</u> death (but certain replacement) of Paul McCartney.

As many have discovered to their peril, entering the realm of what's known in conspiracy circles as PID, or 'Paul Is Dead,' can easily dominate an unsuspecting researcher's curiosity to the point of obsession, or potential insanity, (trust me, I know,) and the more you delve into the subject, the more you realise just how deep this one really goes. (If the whole discussion of Paul McCartney having been replaced in 1966 is making any readers go, 'wait... what??!,' by the way, they're advised to read the 15,000-word chapter on the subject in 'Musical Truth 1'!)

You might think that researching the McCartney puzzle in-depth for many hundreds of hours would bring some incisive clarity on the subject, as the pieces get put together, and the contradictions get gradually ironed out. Personally, I've found the opposite to be the case, and I'm just being honest when I say that, at the tail end of such a process, I'm now more confused than I ever was. A short while ago, I'd have maintained that the only thing, that anyone can say with any degree of certainty, is that the individual claiming today to be 'Paul McCartney' is <u>not</u> the biological James Paul McCartney born on 18th June 1942. As far as I was concerned, you started from there with a blank sheet of paper.

I'm no longer sure of even that, however, my stance having now changed to: the only thing anyone can say with any certainty, is that there have been at least two 'Paul McCartneys,' and almost certainly more than two. This much, at least, can be gleaned by considering photographs and film footage from over the years with a keen eye and an open mind.

I was encouraged to see this healthy dynamic of changing one's position upon the emergence of new information summed up wonderfully by the researcher Marty Leeds on one of his Youtube videos:

> *"We are all in the process of learning. We are all in the process of self-discovery. We are all researching and questioning the world around us. No one has all the answers, and I certainly do not claim to. In the course of my life, I have changed my opinion and position countless times on things I was once very passionate about. This is growth. This is the evolution of the self. I may say something I may later regret, disagree with, have to clarify in greater detail, or have changed my position on. I am human."*

I used to consider it a given that the real Paul McCartney was the shorter guy with the rounder, chubby face, and that the full-time impostor referred to as 'Faul' was taller and slimmer with a more elongated face and darker eyes. However, the very process of comparing photographs leaves you with several early pictures of a young "Paul' – many from before his Beatles days – who resembles far more the character known as Faul than he does the chubbier-faced Paul!

Paul McCartney ... or is it?, (wink, wink.)

https://commons.wikimedia.org/wiki/File:Paul_McCartney_black_and_white_2010.jpg

Credit: Oli Gill

Of course, in this age of Photoshop, any image on the internet could have been subject to tinkering at the hands of pranksters or those with more sinister motives. But either way, I have to ask myself whether the individual today posing as 'Paul' may actually be the real Paul, and the chubby-faced character was the impostor?! Have we in fact been witnessing two individuals, whoever they may be, (or more than two,) stepping in and out of the 'Paul' role right from the start, and long before the supposed 1966 switch of PID myth? This idea certainly ties into the first of the alternative theories that I will detail in due course. It also turns your brain to scrambled eggs.

There is a common denominator at play whichever of these theories may be the case, though – if either of them are – and that is the element of deception. Once again, the general public has been duped and played for fools. Deception is the enemy of Truth and all that is pure in Creation. When someone sets out to deceive us, they take away our inherent, sovereign right to Truth. That makes any knowing deceiver an enemy.

Whatever the reason for the switch or the interchanging of two or more 'Pauls,' the parties concerned are deliberately deceiving millions. Whoever else may be OK with that, and who may attempt all manner of justifications as to why it had to be done, I'm not. That's why the McCartney deception has swallowed up so many hours of my time, and will doubtless lay claim to many, many more.

Confessions of a charlatan?

At the time of writing the last book's McCartney chapter, I was fairly sold on the narrative that biological Paul had indeed died in 1966, and had been replaced by an impostor who has been taking his place to this day. It was the huge array of symbolic clues that had me convinced, understanding as I did the favoured tenet of placing the truth in plain sight – or Revelation of the Method – that the elite occultists seem to feel duty-bound to observe. Arguably the most comprehensive overview of the clues comes from the thorough 'The Walrus Was Paul' book by R. Gary Patterson, who sadly passed away in 2017 during the writing of this volume.

I didn't, however, buy into the conventional theory that McCartney had died as the result of a freak accident that nobody could have foreseen, and that Brian Epstein and the other Beatles had worked quickly to find a replacement, so that fans could have been spared the trauma of discovering that their beloved Paul was no longer with them. Many PID researchers seem content to accept that it was a genuine tragic event, that the forces that controlled the Beatles were caring like that, and that the individual stepping into the 'Paul' role did so selflessly and with noble intent. Call me suspicious, (I'm called worse,) but I always considered the circumstances to be far more nefarious.

The waters get muddied in this regard, rather than made any clearer, by the book 'The Memoirs of Billy Shears.' Credited to an author/encoder named Thomas E. Uharriet, this tome is written in the first-person, and purports to be the auto-biographical confession of one William Wallace Shepherd. This individual is said to be the full-time replacement for Paul McCartney since 11th September 1966, (9/11 in the US date format) when, the book claims, Paul died in the aforementioned tragic car accident. (Other tellings of the fable put the date at 9th November of '66 – an alternative rendering of the date 9/11 in the European format.) The whole story is bound together by Masonic fraternal links and oaths of secrecy.

'Memoirs' comes with all kinds of creative touches, such as its 66 chapters running to 666 pages, (a number which continually pops up within the occult aspects of the entertainment industry,) and its paragraphs carrying various hidden codes. I'd not read 'Memoirs' at the time of writing 'Musical Truth 1,' but I now have, and I had an incisive two-hour chat about it with Mike Williams, aka Sage of Quay, the YouTube link to which you can find in the Resources section at the end.

The sheer amount of detail put forward regarding the Beatles, their close circle, and their songs, certainly suggests the book was written by someone with intimate working experience of the group. 'Memoirs' claims, for example, that the lyrics to 'Lady Madonna' partly chronicle the week of Paul's replacement process stage-by-stage, ("Tuesday afternoon is never ending" referring to John Lennon's unbearable anguish at being told Paul had been killed, "Wednesday morning papers didn't come" referring to a journalist by the name of Sam being paid off to not publish his planned exposé, and later cropping up in the "Sailor Sam" reference in the Wings song 'Band On the Run,') and that (real) Paul's song 'Michelle' is not in fact an ode to a lover, but refers to a secret daughter he had with a French woman.

There's either deep inside knowledge here, or the writer has a highly vivid imagination and has dedicated years of painstakingly thorough research to get his facts straight.

The book also makes it clear, however, that it is a work of "historical fiction," its author claiming that, though mostly based in fact, due to the sensitive nature of the subject matter, certain parts of the story have been fictionalised. The reader is therefore left to discern which parts can be considered 'fact' – and therefore the true confession of the McCartney replacement – and which parts are indeed fictional embellishments. No easy task. But then nothing in this realm of research is.

Incidentally, the William Wallace Shepherd of the book, (known by the nickname 'Billy Shears', hence the "so may I introduce to you the one and only Billy Shears" line at the start of the 'Sgt. Pepper' album,) claims to be a descendent of the Scottish nobleman-turned-freedom fighter William Wallace, who was portrayed by Mel Gibson in the movie 'Braveheart,' as well as hailing from a long-running line of high-ranking freemasons. Given the earlier chapter's accounts of how different generations of the same bloodline keep popping up in public roles through the centuries – from politicians to assassins to aristocrats to rock stars – this claim is perhaps not as outrageous as it might at first seem.

'Memoirs' never comes right out and states that Paul's supposed death was a planned-for event, but claims that he had been haunted by fateful premonitions that he was to die young, and that another would take his place. His apparent demise was hinted at through the hundreds of symbolic clues and backmasked messages placed into the Beatles' subsequent album sleeves and recordings, and these have strong occult and mystical overtones.

Given what we're now able to understand about the true nature of those who really control the entertainment industries, it always struck me as feasible that Paul could have been taken out in some kind of occult ritual, for who knows what ultimate purpose? This pre-knowledge on the part of the instigators would validate the long period that Faul ('fake' or '*faux* Paul,' as the replacement has come to be known,) would have had to prepare for the role that he would play for the rest of his days, and get the act down to a fine art.

On the matter of the naming of William Shepherd, meanwhile, it's intriguing to factor in a book, published in 1964, titled 'The True Story of the Beatles,' the writing of which just happened to be credited to one Billy Shepherd, about whom very little else seems to be known. In Amazon's on-line reviews of the book, one contributor has observed:

> *"Bill Shepherd was obviously a competent professional writer... He would have had very limited time in which to research and write this book... Clearly, his job was to write a positive book, but also clearly, he became personally interested and liked the lads. I'm not so sure he really liked their music."*

(A 'Billy Shepherd' also crops up on Amazon, meanwhile, as the author of a book titled 'Strange Death in Venice.' This was published in 2017, however, so it seems unlikely that it's the same individual, given that the two books are 53 years apart.)

For a while, this struck me as a fairly clear-cut scenario, and factoring in all the symbolic hints and the forensic evidence available to us – in spite of there still being no mainstream acceptance that a McCartney replacement had taken place – we could consider ourselves close to being able to tie this one up with a neat little bow on it... right?

Oh, how naive I was. Unfortunately, the world of conspiracy research rarely offers such decisive outcomes. And so it has been with this one as, through the months during which this book was being written, a number of alternative scenarios emerged regarding the possible truth of the McCartney conundrum. If you believed everything you read on the internet, you'd have to conclude that Paul never really died and is now posing as John Halliday, the caretaker of his old childhood home; that he died in a car accident; that he was ritually sacrificed; that he just got bored and disappeared from public view; that he was replaced by a single impostor; that he was replaced by several impostors, including many that were around even before 1966; and that the replacement was also Keith Allison of Paul Revere & The Raiders, Vivian Stanshall of the Bonzo Dog Doo-Dah Band, Phil Ackrill of the Diplomats, Spencer Davis of the Spencer Davis Group, and Denny Laine of the Moody Blues. (Insert Facepalm meme here.)

Of the stupefying array of pet theories out there, however, there are two which, in my view, are worth examining in full. Both – at least in part – seem to carry a degree of credibility. Any genuine truthseeker is therefore invited to contemplate each of them with an open mind.

Twin peaks

A writer whose challenging theories on key world events have caused much divisive debate in recent years, (I know the feeling,) is Miles Mathis, a painter and poet who turned to conspiracy research as a sideline through his site www.mileswmathis.com, (from which PDFs of all his articles can be downloaded.) Among Mathis' various contentions – all laid out in comprehensive articles often with photographic back-up – are that the Kennedy and Lincoln assassinations were faked with both presidents complicit in the hoaxes, and that the Tate/ LaBianca 'Manson murders' of 1969 never actually happened.

Similarly, Mathis maintains that virtually every celebrity who is said to have died at an untimely age, was in fact retired out of the public spotlight, having been assets of the intelligence services. Among their number, he says, are Marilyn Monroe, Jim Morrison, Janis Joplin, Jimi Hendrix, River Phoenix, Tupac Shakur, Notorious BIG, Kurt Cobain, James Dean, Paul Walker, Robin Williams, John Belushi, Natalie Wood, William Holden, Chris Kyle, Brittany Murphy, Bruce Lee, Grace Kelly, Princess Diana, Michael Jackson and Heath Ledger. I certainly don't go along with everything that Mathis claims, but by the same token, I don't discard it all out of hand, either. Each case deserves some examination on its own merits.

Mathis' claim, is that his keen artist's eye allows him to spot subtle inconsistencies in pictures from these events that get missed by most others, which is where the giveaways so often lie. He got in on Beatles territory with his much-discussed article alleging that John Lennon's assassination in 1980 was faked and that, in fact, Lennon continues to perform as a musician under the assumed name of Mark Staycer, the subject of a 2009 independent Canadian movie called 'Let Him Be.' Although the film presents itself as a fictional tale of Staycer being suspected of being Lennon, Mathis suggested that its narrative gives the opportunity to understand what has really taken place.

Mathis then went further by publishing a detailed paper concerning the alleged death and replacement of Paul McCartney. Solving this apparent mystery was actually a very simple matter, he proclaimed. He didn't even want to go to the effort of compiling the article, but did so somewhat reluctantly in response to requests from his readers.

The Paul/ Faul enigma can be explained away easily, Mathis stated, by the fact that Paul was one of two fraternal, (non-identical) twins, born together in 1942. The pair have been stepping in and out of the 'Paul' role from the start of the Beatles' career, hence the slight discrepancies and inconsistencies right from the early days. (This would certainly explain both the obvious differences between the many pictures of 'Paul' in existence, and the early pictures of a young, pre-Beatles 'Paul' looking more like the latter-day 'Faul,' who is only supposed to have come on the scene as late as 1966 according to the conventional conspiracy theory.)

'Mike McCartney,' meanwhile, who goes by the stage name of Mike McGear, is an outside actor who was brought in to play the role of Paul's sibling. Whatever anyone's stance on the theory, it's certainly the case that Mike looks nothing like Paul.

So, according to this theory, the one everyone calls 'Faul' is in fact the real Mike McCartney. And neither Faul/ Mike nor Paul died – at least not back in 1966. Both may still be around today. It was Mike, (the one known as Faul,) who married Linda and was in Wings and has done everything since, as Paul retired from public view early on. Mike, Mathis surmises, enjoyed the limelight, and chose to continue basking in it. To enable this, Mike/ Faul underwent some surgery to the eye area of his face, to give his eyes a similar droopy appearance to those of his sibling. As Mathis comments in his article:

> *"You see, the problem for them after about 1990 was that no matter what they did, they couldn't match all the wrinkles. Faces are going to age in different ways, and need touch-ups in different places. It is doubtful they could make them interchangeable into their 70s. Since Mike did most of the public appearances in the 80s, they had to go with him after that."*

And a further musing:

> *"Or...maybe we just have the names reversed. We called the early one Paul just to suit ourselves, and to match the Paul/ Faul split on other websites. But we can just as easily flip that, because we don't really know who was Paul and who was Mike. You will say the early prominent performer was Paul, and he got to use his name on the records. But that is just an assumption. As we have seen, both were involved from the beginning, and maybe they flipped a coin for which name to use. Which means the early one was Mike and the later one was Paul.*
>
> *"That solves all the problems, because that means the guy now appearing as Paul really is Paul. He doesn't have to lie about that. He just has to continue to hide he is a twin. For those of you still connected to the Faul theory, that means Faul really is Paul, and the early guy you love more is Mike. Mike wrote 'Yesterday,' could hit the high notes, and was left-handed."*

Mathis also contends, however, that there was a third 'McCartney' who has appeared in pictures over the years, who is neither Mike/ Faul nor Paul! This is consistent with other researchers who have concluded that there was more than one 'Paul' seen in public even before 1966. Many of those who veer towards the death-and-replacement theory, meanwhile, also maintain that it wasn't just full-time Faul who played the 'Paul' role, but that there were other stand-ins who occasionally appeared in cameos or photo-shoots, as evidenced by the array of inconsistencies in facial features of the various 'McCartneys.' This notion is backed-up by Uharriet in 'Memoirs' and is a viewpoint shared by Tina Foster, proprietor of the highly popular Plastic Macca blog site.

One of Mathis' earlier papers had alleged that Elvis Presley was also one of twins, (Elvis and Aron Presley,) and that the reported death of 'Elvis' in August 1977 was another hoaxed event. The official record states that Elvis had a twin brother named Jesse Garon, who arrived stillborn, but Mathis questions whether this was a cover story, and whether both twins in fact survived and were placed into the public eye as 'Elvis.' Twins are greatly favoured within the military-intelligence communities, where both are often put to work on covert missions to confound and confuse. (Orphans are similarly favoured – a fact mentioned in the narrative of a recent James Bond movie.)

Mathis' assertion that the Beatles, like many other popular music acts, were a product of military-intelligence, is consistent with the viewpoint of several other researchers in this field. The group were an asset of these agencies right from the start, and the role they played in popularising the LSD-laden counter-culture in the second half of the '60s – after first building a massive fanbase through their simplistic love songs – was always on the agenda. If one accepts this, it seems highly feasible that Paul being interchangeable twins, who could be shuffled in and out of that role at will, could also have been part of the long-term plan.

As Mathis further comments in his article:

> *"Why do you think they were both in the Beatles from the beginning? Well, for one thing, I have shown you early pics of both brothers being passed off as Paul. Then we have voice analysis, indicating multiple Pauls. See the Italian forensic work, 'Wired' magazine, 2009. Plus, we now know they had twins available, so why not use them?*
>
> *"I suggest that is the main reason Paul and Mike were chosen: intelligence loves twins. It is the same reason they hire twins in Hollywood, as with Ashley and Mary Kate Olson. You always have a back-up if someone gets sick, gets cranky, breaks an arm, etc. And you can get twice as much PR done with twins. We know they didn't hire the boys because they were great musicians. The early histories admit that. Maybe they became great songwriters later, maybe they didn't, but early on none of them were great on their instruments, or as vocalists. So there must be another reason they hired them."*

The twins theory also helps explain the discrepancies in height between Paul and Faul, as commented on by so many over the years.

> *"...Notice how tall he is in all the early public appearances, just as he would be on the cover of 'Sgt. Pepper's.' This is how they created*

> *confusion from the very beginning. They got you used to accepting both brothers as Paul."*

Furthermore, Mathis has an intriguing take on why the whole 'Paul Is Dead' conspiracy is said to have begun back in 1966, with the following year's 'Sgt. Pepper' offering some of the best clues. It all stems from Paul's reported moped accident of Christmas '65, in which he is said to have cut his lip and chipped his tooth. This became a problem for the twins' handlers, he asserts, since it would now be necessary for the other brother's tooth to appear chipped in the same way, such was the close scrutiny that fans applied to pictures of their idol.

As this realisation dawned in the early part of 1966, it was decided that it was becoming too much hassle to continue using both brothers. One of them would have to be 'retired' out of the spotlight, enabling the other to continue solo. Although Paul might have been considered to have had a better singing voice, it was decided to go with Mike/ Faul, since he was more personable and chatty in interviews. And so from that point, he stepped into the role full-time.

This timeframe would also explain why the Beatles quit touring after their August '66 gig at San Francisco's Candlestick Park; as Mike/ Faul was taller than Paul, the height differential between him and Lennon would now be too obvious with the two of them sharing a mic front-stage.

Mathis' essay contains a highly intriguing photograph which has been the subject of much internet debate. It shows a group of people on a river boat, and was reportedly first published in issue 61 of 'The Beatles Book' fanzine in August 1968. It appears to show two 'Pauls' in the same picture – one, looking more like early-1960s McCartney standing at the side, with the character known as 'Faul' seated in the centre. Some even maintain that the individual on the other side of the boat looks like a third Paul! Naturally, for every on-line commenter who cites the picture as evidence that Paul was still on the scene in 1968, there is one who will claim the picture is a photoshopped fake.

Mathis maintains that many on-line photos of Paul – as was the case with Elvis – have now been digitally retouched to obfuscate some of the more obvious giveaways that we are looking at twins. While the internet has been an invaluable tool for independent research, its digital nature unfortunately renders it susceptible to such technological hoaxes. Many have also complained that certain early film footage of the Beatles has been digitally tampered with in order to make 'Paul' and 'Faul' look more alike – most notably in facial structure.

There also exists in internet circulation, a picture taken during the filming of the 'Magical Mystery Tour' movie in 1967. The one known as 'Faul' appears front centre, but in the background is a character who looks distinctly like 'real' Paul sporting a goatee beard.

It may well be nothing, but it would be remiss of me in the context of this chapter not to mention that 'Paul McCartney' released a collaborative album in 2005 with DJ/ producer Freelance Hellraiser, aka Roy Kerr, titled 'Twin Freaks.'

In direct correspondence with Thomas Uharriet, author/ encoder of 'The Memoirs Of Billy Shears,' I asked him what his reaction was to Mathis' twins theory, given that this contradicts what he had written in his book. Uharriett replied:

> *"... even if Paul did have an identical twin, which would have been a strange thing to keep secret his entire life, it could not be William. William, as the 'Memoirs' points out, has significantly different DNA than Paul's daughter. An identical twin would have lost that paternity suit.*
>
> *"Past the initial honeymoon phase, William's interaction with the McCartney family was not consistent with being one of them. For example, if William really had been Paul's twin, Jim would have attended William's wedding, and William would have attended Jim's funeral.*
>
> *"Some people can't believe that Paul and William can even be separate people, because they are so much alike. However, that is just the mind playing tricks on us. In many ways, (in musical ability, personality, and in physicality,) they are about as different as two men can be. Most people just refuse to see it because it does not match their*

beliefs. The twin idea might just be someone's way to explain how they can be so much alike – even though they aren't."

A voice from the Rooftop

A lone voice with a tantalisingly alternative theory in the whole McCartney mess, has been American citizen researcher Ellen Raine. Like many, she started out accepting the idea that Paul – whatever the circumstances – had died back in '66, and that Faul had been playing the full-time role ever since.

However, some close scrutiny of the bearded 'Paul' who played the famous rooftop gig above London's EMI Studios in 1969 – as documented in the movie 'Let It Be' – led her to deduce that this individual was different to the moustached 'Faul' who had first appeared on a video reel filmed by Beatles roadie Mal Evans on the trip that 'Paul' took to Kenya in November '66, and the one who appeared in interviews throughout '67.

The new theory, therefore, was that 'Rooftop' Paul may have been the real William Shepherd spoken of in the 'Memoirs' book, and that he appeared just for this temporary period before himself being replaced by Faul 2:0. (I do hope you're following... there'll be questions later.) Always observing that closely-held theories should be open to revision upon the emergence of new evidence, however, upon noting the talent and skill, (left-handed, no less,) and studying the mannerisms and facial features of 'Rooftop' further, Ellen noticed how closely these matched those of true, biological Paul. She takes care to point out that these references to a bearded 'Paul,' are strictly to the one who appeared in the 'Let It Be' footage itself; this individual is markedly different from other bearded renderings of 'Paul' from around the same time, including – confusingly – the very publicity stills promoting the movie, as well as the one appearing on the cover of 1970s solo 'McCartney' album.

As she stated to me in private discussion on the subject:

"Rooftop has haunted me from the day I first watched 'Let It Be' recently; when he looked up from the piano in the opening scene, I

felt sure it was Paul. I kept pinching myself all through the movie. It couldn't be him… Too tall, too heavy, too much forehead, different hair part, acting crazy and/ or 'unPaul-like' at times, (dressing slovenly, picking his nose, doing that stupid "wooo" thing.) Besides which, he was supposed to be dead! All reasons I'd been led to believe by PID that it couldn't be Paul.

"But as I found those 'facts' to be false one by one, I realised – it could be him.

"The hair he was constantly pushing back – which I thought was just a nervous habit – could be trying to fall forward, as Paul's did. He could've gained weight in three years, as he was prone to that from an early age. A receding hairline, which he was rumoured to have, could explain the 'larger' exposed forehead and temple area.

"As for his being dead… what proof was there, really, other than clues that had simply been repeated so often that they came to be accepted as fact?"

In one out-take from 'Let It Be,' Paul is describing in great detail a long camera shot which will close in on Ringo's face. His voice, Ellen suggests, is identical to that of real Paul from early interviews, and scousers have confirmed that it sounds like a genuine Liverpool accent, rather than the, at-times questionable one affected by the older Faul.

Ellen also contends it's a myth that Paul was shorter than the other Beatles at around 5'8", and that his actual height was around 5'11", according to printed pre-1966 biographies, which is consistent with the height of the bearded Rooftop performer.

"Look at any photo of the four of them performing on stage together or sharing a mic; Paul, John and George are equal heights, (presumably around 5'11".) All the fan magazines peg him at 5'11". I've heard everything from elevator shoes to falsification of his height. Why? They didn't 'elongate' Ringo, so why would they Paul? The bronze statue in Liverpool has the three being equal height, with Ringo much shorter. Did they get it wrong?"

Finally, Ellen spied a capped tooth on the 'Let It Be' Paul – the exact tooth Paul chipped in that moped accident in 1965.

And so, a new possibility was born. Paul didn't die in 1966. He was merely replaced, and we can only speculate as to the reason. Biological Paul may well be dead now, having passed in the intervening years... but equally, he may still be alive, living his life outside of the spotlight. His 75th birthday would have been on 18th June 2017.

Paul's BBC interview with David Frost in April 1964 deserves a mention here, as Frost asks him about his future ambitions. Paul replies: "I'd like to retire." When Frost asks him when, Paul replies: "The way things are going, about a couple of years or so!"

We might also factor in comments made by George Harrison in an interview for the Beatles 1964 Christmas show with DJ Chris Denning, (later disgraced during his BBC years when he was revealed to have been a serial child sex offender.) George says:

> *"I'd like to send a request to somebody I used to go to school with, and he used to play bass in the group – Paul McCartney. And if you're listening, Paul at work, it was great going to school with you and we had a nice time, and I'd like to play a nice one called 'Love Me Do'."*

The head-scratcher here is that all three of his bandmates were present as he made his comments. George dropped many an apparent 'clue' pertaining to the replacement of Paul in interviews over the years.

Taking a back seat?

If Paul was away from the scene from 1966 to this suggested re-appearance three years later, Ellen wonders if he may well have been involved in the fabled car accident, but that he was temporarily incapacitated – possibly even left with residual brain damage from a head injury – rather than killed. Full-time 'Faul,' (or some combination of Fauls,) would have played the 'Paul' role during this period, before real Paul was brought back for 'Let It Be.' And there could be a very straightforward reason as to why this was done.

> *"The Beatles – that is, John, George, Ringo and Paul – were contractually obligated to make three, (count them, three) movies . . . 'A Hard Day's Night,' 'Help!' and, you guessed it. And I remain 99 per cent sure they did just that. 'Yellow Submarine' wouldn't have counted as it was a cartoon. And it certainly wasn't Paul in 'Magical Mystery Tour.' Besides which, they discussed, (either in clips or an interview,) what the 'plot' of their third and final movie would be: a surprise live performance."*

The following citation comes from: http://www.metafilter.com/99796/The-Beatles-in-film-the-movies-they-never-made-and-then-some

> *"Very early in their career, the group signed a three-movie deal with United Artists as a way to get increased publicity, with A Hard Day's Night (1964) and Help! (1965) being completed in short time. An early contender for their third film was a western comedy."*

Back to the story, and with 'Let It Be' in the bag – which was filmed in the early weeks of 1969 but not released until the group's break-up a year later – Paul was switched again with Faul for an unknown reason. (I do hope you're still following. I find a cup of tea and a brisk walk often helps.)

An observation of my own, which – as far as I'm concerned – proves the use of at least one 'Faul,' is the fact that in the video to 'Hey Jude,' which is on record as having been filmed in September 1968, 'Paul,' (who is seen to have green eyes in contrast to biological Paul's documented brown ones,) is clean-shaven. By 2nd January 1969 when the 'Let It Be' sessions began, 'Paul' is sporting a long and bushy beard. He is supposed to have grown this in less than four months, which seems unlikely for a beard in such advanced stages. There's also the fact that his hair colour is much darker than in 'Hey Jude.' A stick-on beard and hair dye are possibilities, I guess, but they don't seem very likely. It's fairly clear that the individual in 'Let It Be' is a different person to the one in 'Hey Jude.'

It was only after hatching her theory independently, that Ellen discovered the very same idea had earlier been suggested by the blogger and on-line forum poster known as Apollo C. Vermouth. This was a pseudonym officially credited to 'Paul McCartney,' under which he produced the song 'I'm The Urban Spaceman' for the Bonzo Dog Doo-Dah Band in 1968. (The notion that a heavily-disguised Faul, aka William Shepherd, also played the role of Bonzos frontman Vivian Stanshall, is a major part of the narrative of Uharriet's 'Memoirs' book.)

By the time the Vermouth blog had sprung up in the early 2000s, the popular theory was that this was a pseudonym adopted by close Beatles associate Neil Aspinall, who went on to die in 2008. In various posts, 'Vermouth' alleged that Paul had left the Beatles in 1965 or '66, but came back for a later, temporary period, by which point the others had grown accustomed to his absence.

So, was the fabled car accident just a diversion tactic, and all the symbolic clues pertaining to it deliberately planted as red herrings? Did real Paul just want out of the group by 1966, and so the replacement underwent surgery and training ready to provide a seamless transition? As Ellen reflects:

> *"I believe it's possible there was a car accident, (it was initially reported, then silenced, after all,) he did suffer a head injury, (closed-head and likely fronto-temporal, which affects behaviour, since he acts a little loopy at times in 'Let It Be,') and that he was metaphorically 'dead' as far as the band was concerned. This would explain all the clues, lyrics, and legends which speak to a car accident and head injury, as well as what many see as a personality altered. And not for the better; brain injuries are notorious for this. Hence the end of touring and sightings and the replacement(s.)*
>
> *"My working theory is that someone else penned the music in the studio, someone else portrayed him – usually badly – in public and, once he was sufficiently recovered, he attempted a comeback in 'Let It Be,' but both George and John were over it and were ready to move on at that point. What became of him after that, I have no idea.*
>
> *"Nothing else explains – well, his being so Paul-like in 'Let It Be' – as well as his mates' genuine grief at the time, (the band as they knew*

it was 'dead,') in contrast to the relative calm and acceptance of this ruse by Paul's loved ones, (he was injured, but not lost to them forever.) Who else would, or could create Beatles music before our very eyes as he does in that film, exhibit such talent and skill, (left-handed, no less,) irreverently reprise their past obscure hit 'Basame Mucho,' impersonate Elvis as Paul did in the early days, and desperately try to revive the old magic?

"The film has, to me, the air of a bitter-sweet, ill-fated schoolboy reunion."

Ellen recounts that, when she suggested to Thomas Uharriett that what we may be dealing here is a symbolic or metaphorical death, rather than a physical one, he didn't dispute or contradict it, merely remarking that he "likes how her brain works." Adding that she was an English major, and thus both recognised and appreciated literary licence and allegory, Uharriet responded that he, too, was an English major. However, being pressed on the point, he predictably insisted that his narrative was "mostly" true and that William is real.

Calamity Jane

Leaving no stone unturned, Ellen suggests it might also be worth factoring in Paul's old flame, the actress Jane Asher. Jane's father was Dr. Richard Asher, who reportedly worked on psychological research on behalf of British military intelligence, and who turned up dead in his London home in extremely suspicious circumstances in 1969. He is said to have "committed suicide." His Wimpole Street medical practice was only a few yards from that of Dr. Stephen Ward, (portrayed by John Hurt in the movie 'Scandal,') who was implicated in the Profumo political affair of 1963, and who is also said to have "committed suicide."

Dr. Asher was a pioneer in hypnotic techniques, and had written several articles on the subject for the 'Lancet' medical journal. Jane's mother, meanwhile, was a professor of music, and is credited with having taught piano to George Martin, often known as 'the fifth Beatle.' Jane herself, though best known for her role in the Michael Caine film 'Alfie,' had also portrayed Alice in a 1959 album version of 'Alice Through the Looking Glass.' Lewis Carroll's 'Alice' stories are known triggers in mind-control programming techniques.

According to the pictorial evidence available, Jane appears to have dated both biological Paul, (as we think of him,) and his post-1966 replacement. It was in the very house where her father's corpse was discovered, that Paul had reportedly lived on-and-off for two years, and where he is said to have written many of his most famous songs. These include 'Yesterday,' which Paul once claimed was in his head one morning when he woke and he was worried he may have plagiarised it, and 'Eleanor Rigby.'

Given the nature of Dr. Asher's work, a suspicious researcher, (me,) might speculate as to whether Paul could have been some kind of in-house test subject for his mind-control experiments, and whether the whole scenario didn't end happily. Could this be the real reason for Paul's 'loopiness' as observed by Ellen, with the car crash myth invented as diversion?

Jane has remained closed-lipped about the entire PID conspiracy, and indeed, her very relationship with Paul all these decades. She did, however, publish a book in 1998, a novel entitled 'The Question,' which Ellen later discovered, and which seems to lend credence to her theory. In the acknowledgements, Jane thanks the Royal Hospital of Neurodisability for its help. And according to the promotional blurb:

> *"It all starts with a chance remark on the telephone, just a casual conversation, but it leads Eleanor Hamilton to an appalling and deeply disturbing discovery. John, her husband of twenty years, has been leading a double life – a life of unbelievable duplicity. Feelings of jealousy, anger and confusion follow, driving Eleanor to extraordinary limits. Only one thing is clear: she wants revenge for the mockery John has made of her existence, and for the happiness that she has missed.*
>
> *"Then fate intervenes in the shape of a terrible accident…"*

The references to "unbelievable duplicity," (anyone getting echoes of Heather Mills' 2007 TV interviews?) and a "terrible accident," certainly seems consistent with aspects of the PID narrative. The book contains lines such as "is my father a twin?" and "were there two John Hamiltons?", (remember Faul's interview comment of a few years ago that "there are two Paul McCartneys"?,) in addition to references to a car wreck resulting from a disregarded street light after which – according to his daughter – "his mind was sucked out of his head," ("he blew his mind out in a car"?)

Then there's the sub-plot involving an attempt on the part of the scorned wife, to change the illegitimate daughter's identity and "reprogramme" her personality. Could the book have been a form of catharsis for Jane? The fate of this philandering lover who fathered an illegitimate girl child – as Paul was purported to have done – while denying his wife children of her own, is to enter a persistent vegetative state, a kind of 'nowhere land' from which he emerges only slowly over time. He has suffered a small skull fracture, (his looks left intact,) but extensive damage to the white matter of the brain.

As if there weren't enough confounding discrepancies already, Ellen also highlights a particular pair of very distinctive shoes which 'Paul' can be seen wearing in 'Let It Be.' These same shoes can be seen worn by 'Paul' in a collection of intimate, private photographs taken by Linda Eastman (McCartney) the previous year, suggesting that biological Paul – presumably in addition to his replacement – was around in public in 1968.

Bill and Ed's bogus journey

As for who might have been creating the music in the studio during the three missing years, and appearing in public as 'Paul,' Ellen points to 'Beatle Bill' and 'Beatle Ed' as possibles – both of whom are slyly referenced in a key scene from John Lennon's 'Imagine' film from 1971.

In it, Lennon and George Harrison are sitting in John's home kitchen as Yoko Ono prepares tea. In a clip which has been all over YouTube and widely studied for years, the pair make a reference to "the fab three," before Lennon winks to the camera. They are heard talking about "Beatle Bill." Lennon says: "I hear he's not doing too well these days," to which Harrison replies: "He's number five in Sweden."

I always assumed this to be an accurate rendering of the conversation, and that "Beatle Bill" referred to the aforementioned William Shepherd. In 2016, however, a longer, unedited version of that scene came across my radar, in which the pair reference a "Beatle Ed" in the "number five in Sweden" comment. It would appear that two separate men, Bill and Ed – both alluded to as auxiliary Beatles – are being discussed here.

So it turns out that the widely-distributed clip has been edited, the "Beatle Bill" comment spliced out and re-inserted earlier, replacing the reference to "Beatle Ed" so that listeners assume the whole conversation is referring to "Beatle Bill."

The two questions which emerge, therefore, are: Why would someone go to the effort of distorting this narrative, and... who the hell is "Beatle Ed?!"

For some, this adds weight to the notion that full-time Faul may in fact be an illegitimate son of Aleister Crowley. Uharriet's 'Memoirs' asserts that Faul was born in 1937, whereas Crowley died ten years later. This intimation comes from the clues available on the 'Sgt. Pepper' album sleeve, but also from the fact that 'Aleister' was an assumed name, and that Crowley was actually born an Edward, as was his father. Could Faul, (who has been known to project a giant image of Crowley behind him on stage during performances,) actually be an Edward too – or, rather, Edward III? Could 'Ed' have been one of the 'Paul' touring or studio stand-ins? Could Ed, indeed, be today's touring Sir Paul?

Ellen's take on this:

> *"There were doubles posing for pics and making public appearances in Paul's place, and who performed in the studio is anybody's guess! But they needn't have been the same people; Billy Shears may look nothing like Paul. After all, he was making 'Sgt. Pepper' behind the scenes. And these doubles and stand-ins had to be named something! Why not William? Why not Ed?"*

Which is all inclined to leave one wondering… what if 'Paul Is Dead' is the real psy-op, and has come to obfuscate the truth that Paul didn't die in 1966, but was merely replaced for reasons unknown? Suddenly, these possibilities and more become fair game when the traditional PID myth is subjected to the same close scrutiny as Wikipedia-style 'official versions' of everything else.

In 2017, a YouTube poster by the name of Jairo Parra laid claim to the same theory as Ellen's, claiming he had "solved the mystery." The same year, broadcaster Josh Reeves announced he would shortly be presenting "a big reveal" on the subject of McCartney. In preparation for his promised 'The Spellcasters Volume Two' documentary, Reeves posted a couple of intriguing video snippets. In one, a latter-day Faul states: "I joined the Beatles as an already set-up affair," (whereas the real Paul was a founder member of the group.) In the second, George Harrison appears to be referring to Faul as "the new fella" in the band, when history has it that George joined after Paul. The links to these videos are in the Resources section at the end.

Tales of the synchronistic

There was one particular evening during the writing of this chapter which involved some extensive research, including watching the whole of the 'Let It Be' movie, and obsessing over the whole McCartney conundrum. Finally deciding to call it a night on the grounds that any more pondering really wouldn't be healthy, I slinked off to bed. Just as I was about to settle down, I heard my wife scream from outside the bedroom. I asked what was up. She replied: "There's a giant beetle on the landing." I almost asked: "Is it Ringo?"

I was instantly reminded of this story from Carl Jung in his book 'Synchronicity,' where he recounts a counselling session he once had with a woman patient. He writes:

> *"She had an impressive dream the night before, in which someone had given her a golden scarab – a costly piece of jewellery. While she was still telling me this dream, I heard something behind me gently tapping on the window. I turned round and saw that it was a fairly*

large flying insect that was knocking against the window pane from outside in the obvious effort to get into the dark room.

"This seemed to me very strange. I opened the window immediately and caught the insect in the air as it flew in. It was a scarabaeid beetle."

And not forgetting this section from my last book on the naming of the Beatles:

"The alternative consensus, however, appears to be that the group's name is derived from the horned scarab beetle, a religious symbol of Ancient Egyptian culture. These insects were revered as symbols of regeneration and creation, conveying ideas of transformation, renewal, and resurrection... Synchronistically, these particular beetles have wings, with Paul McCartney choosing 'Wings' as the name of his later group. Intriguingly, 'The Winged Beetle' was the title of a collection of poems by Aleister Crowley. Heard of him anywhere?"

And:

"This ties in with many other suggested clues pertaining to three Beatles, rather than four. Among those unearthed have been the family coat-of-arms of key Beatles producer George Martin. This features three beetle insects in the crest. It has been noted that, with six legs each, the three could be taken as a depiction of 6/6/6. The scarab to the left of the crest appears to have a Kabbalah 'Tree of Life' pattern..."

I recounted this tale to Ellen, at which point she told me that she hadn't planned to say anything, but that she too had had an unusual beetle appear in her room, on the other side of Atlantic, shortly after our last on-line conversation. A few days later, she came across the imprint of a scarab beetle painted on the ground on one of her regular walks to work.

I took it as a sign from the universe. Though of what, I'm not entirely sure.

In the shadow of the spooks

It seems to me that there is a lot of compatibility between the two theories detailed above, and embracing one does not necessarily negate the other. Paul returning from obscurity for 'Let It Be,' then disappearing again, is consistent with the notion of twins. Another thing both theories have in common is that, if true, it means the colossal array of 'Paul Is Dead' clues placed into the Beatles' recordings, album sleeves, videos and photos over the years, (plus the entire narrative of the 'Memoirs' book,) were nothing more than cunning and calculated misdirection, creating the myth of the 1966 car crash to send researchers off down the garden path, and down endless rabbit holes too deep to be climbed out of again.

This would have been a high-level project <u>way</u> beyond the capabilities of four young musicians and their immediate management.

Whichever of these theories – if either – is true, it still stacks up to the same thing. The general public has been monumentally hoaxed for the past five decades-plus. And who has the resources and the clout to be able to pull this off and keep it under wraps for all this time, if <u>not</u> military intelligence? Mere record labels could not implement a stunt like this without major backing from agencies much higher up the Establishment pecking order. Remember that 'Paul McCartney' was knighted by the Queen, and one of the key reasons for the existence of MI5 is <u>supposed</u> to be the close vetting of anyone the British Royal Family comes into contact with.

Even <u>if</u> the Beatles had been able to pull off this stunt themselves, it would have been rumbled at the point where military intelligence officials started some in-depth digging. Consider also the incident in January 1980, when 'McCartney' was detained in Japan after arriving for a tour and being found to have marijuana in his luggage. There are claims that McCartney's fingerprints were taken, but did not match those already held on record, which led to some problems. He was jailed for three days before some intervention from higher-up secured his release, and nothing further was heard about it.

The only rational conclusion is that the intel agencies knew about the whole McCartney deception because they were intimately involved in creating it. And where the fingerprints of military intelligence are found, occult ritualistic elements are rarely far from the surface.

As a friend commented to me in private correspondence on the matter:

> *"It's always good to bring things back to the big picture, because there is a huge meaning for the replacement in occult circles. The impostor, the fake. The grand deception. Laughing at the public as they go crazy and hand over their money. While signing on to a culture that a lot of them will defend with energy and emotional outbursts. And yet, that culture was actually designed by men they have never heard of, and who do not have their best interests at heart.*
>
> *"Music and film are designed to affect people's minds, and they are the product of occult ritual, channelled information, and years of gruesome experiment to reduce these dark arts to scientific principles that can be written in manuals, and handed around to elite circles who hire performers, and learn over decades how to place into music (and film), rhythms and tones and sequences of notes that can programme the human consciousness to think in certain ways, and slowly self-destruct."*

The path to truth

I fully understand how baffling all of the above information will be to readers, because I went through these confounding processes myself. I realise also that this book's title, 'Musical Truth,' may suggest that it is offering the indisputable truth behind all matters it discusses. The fact is, no book could ever make so bold a claim. Without being a personal part of the various events under discussion, <u>none</u> of us can say for sure what is the truth in any of these matters.

This is not to say that we shouldn't at least <u>seek</u> the truth and get as far along the path to discovering it as we're able, of course, which is why I feel the possibilities chronicled above at least deserve being thrown into the mental blender of any committed truthseeker. Naturally, many theories will come to be rejected when subjected to the spotlight of discernment. Each reader forming their own conclusions based on what resonates with them personally, is a process which needs to happen.

The 'Truth' part of this book's title, therefore, can be applied to the fact that no aspect of the corporate music industry is really the way it's presented to us with all its glossy packaging, and that there's always truth waiting to be discovered by those who dare to embark upon the mission towards finding it.

Will we ever get to know the real truth about the McCartney switch, and will the subject ever get addressed in mainstream society after Faul (and/ or Paul) has passed, in rather the same way that the full revelations about Jimmy Savile's true nature only emerged after his death? I wonder if the powers-that-be who instigated this whole mess still have a handle on what's what and who's who, or if even they have lost track of it all?

I know I won't be alone in wishing I could get my hands on Heather Mills' "box of evidence" that she claimed to have stashed away safely somewhere. That surely would be the Holy Grail of 'PID' research.

Resources:

Good Vibrations Podcast Episode 109 – Ellen Raine – Did Paul Really Die?:

- https://www.spreaker.com/user/markdevlin/gvp-109-ellen-raine-did-paul-really-die

Good Vibrations Podcast Episode 096 – Mike Williams – William Shepherd is Paul McCartney (Part 1):

- https://www.spreaker.com/user/markdevlin/gvp-096-mike-williams-pid-p1

Good Vibrations Podcast Episode 096 – Mike Williams – William Shepherd is Paul McCartney (Part 2)

- https://www.spreaker.com/user/markdevlin/gvp-096-mike-williams-pid-part-2

Miles Mathis' website, from which PDFs of all his articles on McCartney, Lennon and many other subjects can be downloaded:

- http://mileswmathis.com/writings.html

Beatles Rabbit Hole blog – a source of endless fascinating musings on assorted Beatles mysteries:

- http://beatlesrabbithole.blogspot.co.uk/

Billyshears.com, portal for the book 'The Memoirs of Billy Shears' and its derivatives:

- http://billyshears.com/

Tina Foster's Plastic Macca blog site:

www.plasticmacca.blogspot.com

Watch 'Let It Be' film on-line:

- https://archive.org/details/LetItBe_724

John Lennon's 'Imagine' movie: John Lennon and George Harrison refer to 'Beatle Ed' and 'Beatle Bill':

- https://www.youtube.com/watch?v=QS_Ytpn27XQ

George Harrison accidentally exposes fake Paul – Josh Reeves: The Spellcasters volume two teaser

- https://www.youtube.com/watch?v=kW28mGCWlNw

FauI McCartney – "I joined The Beatles as an already set-up affair."

- https://www.youtube.com/watch?v=J_YlhJMNAN8

Transcript of Paul McCartney interview with David Frost, April 1964:

- http://www.beatlesinterviews.org/db1964.0415.beatles.html

Paul McCartney live Q&A session, April 2017:

- https://www.youtube.com/watch?v=DBdYplVbDMs

CHAPTER 9

SO IT'S GOODNIGHT FROM ME, AND IT'S GOODNIGHT FROM HIM

Navigating the labyrinth of Prince and George Michael death clues.

"Some say a man ain't happy truly until a man truly dies"
Prince & The Revolution: 'Sign O' The Times' (1987)

"And the wounded skies above say it's much, much too late,
Well, maybe we should all be praying for time."
George Michael: 'Praying For Time' (1990)

2016 came to be known colloquially as the year of the Celebrity Death Cull. Book-ended by the reported passings of David Bowie in January and George Michael in December, the year saw the exit of a vast number of celebrities, many of them from the music world. There are too many to list in full, but just a few musical departees included Robert Stigwood, Glen Frey, Maurice White, Vanity, Phife Dawg, Billy Paul, Leon Russell, Holly Dunn, Pete Burns, Leonard Cohen and Rick Parfitt, while Carl Palmer remained the only living member of Emerson, Lake and Palmer when Greg Lake and Keith Emerson both checked out.

Inevitably, this led to speculation that some were being deliberately taken out in a series of ritual sacrifices, (numerologists have noted that 216 – 2016 minus the redundant zero – equals 6 times 6 times 6,) but equally, that it was all down to random chance and bad luck. Experience has taught me that it's unwise to make a blanket statement about all music industry deaths – no matter how suspicious the circumstances might at first appear – but to examine them on a case-by-case basis... though there's no guarantee of coming to a definitive answer even after applying the probing spotlight of scrutiny!

To dissect each of 2016's reported celebrity deaths in detail would take an entire book in itself, probably involving several years of thorough research. David Bowie got covered in 'Musical Truth 1.' For the purposes of this one, therefore, we'll look at some of the anomalies and oddities, (for there's never any shortage,) of the other two most prominent names.

Death of a Prince

So often it's not in life, but only after their reported death that a full appreciation of the complexities of an artist's character becomes apparent. This is especially true in these times of citizen researchers being able to conduct their own investigations through the opportunities afforded by the internet, rather than having to rely on establishment sources to tell them what happened. The litany of quirks, idiosynchrasies, and character traits associated with Prince which emerged following his reported death on 21st April 2016, was matched only by the wealth of discrepancies and contradictions surrounding the nature of the event itself.

The first official reports of Prince's passing, included the detail that he had died alone in an elevator on his sprawling Paisley Park estate in Chanhassen, just outside his home city of Minneapolis. Paisley Park housed living quarters and studio facilities, as well as acting as the main HQ for Prince's business empire. The many symbolic features of its architecture included a rooftop pyramid which would reportedly glow purple to indicate that Prince was present. The elevator detail caused many to recall the lyrics to his 1984 song 'Let's Go Crazy,' where he asks: "are we gonna let the elevator bring us down? Oh, no let's go . . . "

Dissecting the word etymologically, gives us the prefix 'el,' which means 'God' in Hebrew. To rehash a comment from the occult researcher Jordan Maxwell included in the last book: "The god Saturn was referred to as El. If you continue today to worship the planet Saturn, you become known as an elder, you got elected, with elections. Now you're one of the elites, now you've got elevated." A short while after the death announcement, the record producer and industry mogul L.A. Reid, related in an interview how Prince had once asked him, "do you know what the elevator represents?" When Reid said he didn't, Prince replied, "the devil."

As with the demise of so many celebrities, the 'official' cause of Prince's death changed somewhat in the first few days. Some accounts claimed it had been a heart attack, others that he had overdosed on pharmaceutical medication, others that it was heroin. A claim even emerged in the mainstream press that he may have secretly been battling AIDS and that it finally got the better of him, and another that he succumbed to the Zika virus. Eventually, the cause of death was given as an overdose of the painkiller Fentanyl, with the medical examiner's statement insisting there were no indications of foul play or suicide.

Prince had allegedly been discovered dead in the elevator by the son of Dr. Howard Kornfeld, a physician who had been called by the musician's concerned staff requesting medical advice. Prince was 57 years old, a vegan and a Jehovah's Witness, and had apparently been in good physical shape. Attendees of his Piano & A Microphone solo concerts in Australia just a few weeks earlier, had spoken of how fit, healthy and of positive spirit he had seemed.

The waters get somewhat muddied, however, by reports that Prince's private jet, returning him home from a rescheduled show in Atlanta on 15th April, was forced to make an emergency landing, at massive financial cost, at an airport in Illinois when he was suddenly taken ill. It was during his brief hospitalisation before his return to Minneapolis, that reports of influenza and dehydration first emerged.

Despite the incident, Prince went ahead with a small-scale performance at Paisley Park on Saturday 16th, telling the audience at one point to "wait a few days before you waste any prayers." In the days prior to his death, Prince was seen shopping at a record store, riding his bicycle around Paisley Park, and, on the 19th, attended a performance by singer Lizz Wright.

A short while before the announcement, the image on Prince's Twitter page was changed to an animated picture of him with a third eye in the middle of his forehead, symbolising his pineal gland having been opened, providing a portal to higher consciousness. During the same period a message had been posted, (then quickly deleted,) to Prince's Instagram page, which stated: "just when U thought U were safe." It turned out to be his last. The accompanying image had Prince's right eye obscured by darkness.

The concept of predictive programming wasn't far from the surface throughout the death narrative, meanwhile. Among the examples identified by vigilant researchers are the following:

An episode of the US TV show 'Scandal,' titled 'Til Death Do Us Part,' shows a poster of Prince on a wall, right next to another promoting 'Dead Poet's Society.' This particular episode was scheduled for release on 21st April 2016, the very date of Prince's reported death.

An episode of 'Celebrity Death Match' from 1998, shows Prince Charles in a boxing ring competing with Prince, on this occasion represented as a lifesize version of his obscure symbol. This scene ends with Charles defeating and killing Prince with a little assistance from his mother, The Queen, (more on her soon!) who jumps in the ring to help him.

This, in turn, brings to mind the 2008 episode of 'The Simpsons,' (a show which has previous when it comes to foreshadowing,) in which Homer is instructed by music industry executives to kill Prince because he wasn't following orders, and ends up strangling the musician with his own guitar.

The more you know, the more you know you don't know

There are many parallels between Prince's life and career, and that of Michael Jackson. Both were born in 1958, were child stars, and went on to become the biggest black music crossover artists of the 1980s, their respective albums 'Purple Rain' and 'Thriller' now consistently cited as the most iconic of the decade. Both came from poor backgrounds and grew up in homes with abusive and dominant fathers; Prince's story is documented in the semi-autobiographical 'Purple Rain' movie. Both complained towards their latter years, of how world history had been re-written by the manipulative powers-that-be.

A more sinister element linking the two, meanwhile, is the apparent presence of dissociative multiple personalities, hinting at trauma-based mind control. Prince has been equally noted for his eccentric behaviours as Michael was, appearing to take on an entirely different identity when performing, as to when encountered in private. Prince was a master of pseudonyms, recording or songwriting under alter-egos that included Jamie Starr, Alexander Nevermind, Christopher Tracy, Joey Coco, Spooky Electric, Kat and Camille. It's been widely assumed that these are the colourful creations of a wildly creative imagination . . . but have we in fact been witnessing something far more disturbing the whole while?

Prince performs at California's Coachella festival.

https://upload.wikimedia.org/wikipedia/commons/c/c1/Prince_at_Coachella.jpg

Credit: Penner

Another factor shared with Michael Jackson, (besides an untimely death seemingly involving pharmaceutical meds, that is,) involves Prince's high-profile legal battles with the Warner Brothers corporation in the 1990s, over publishing and intellectual rights issues, heavily mirroring Jackson's ongoing spat with Sony. Prince had battled Warner through lawyers to obtain the ownership of his own master tapes, and after much wrangling, had reportedly achieved a victory shortly prior to his demise.

His fall-out with the label that had put him on the map was what had led to him wearing the word 'slave' written on his face, in protest at how the industry treats its artists, and his wish to be known as The Artist Formerly Known As Prince.' Commenting at the time, he said:

> *"Prince is the name that my mother gave me at birth. Warner Brothers took the name, trademarked it, and used it as the main marketing tool to promote all of the music that I wrote. The company owns the name Prince and all related music marketed under Prince. I became merely a pawn used to produce more money for Warner Brothers . . . "*

Taking things further, Prince then opted to change his artist name to an unpronounceable symbol, its components representing a union of the sacred male and female principles inherent in nature. Interestingly, the concept of duality was represented through his star sign of Gemini, representing twins, and he was born in one of the twin cities of St. Paul and Minneapolis. All along, Prince had emphasised both the masculine and feminine elements of his character at different points, swinging from bass-laden deep vocals, to his famous squeaky falsetto – an androgynous blurring of the genders that pre-dated the systematic Transgender Agenda of the 2010s by decades. As writer Isaac Weishaupt observed in an article on his Illuminati Watcher website:

> *"There could be more behind the LGBT movement than just equal rights if you consider the beliefs of the secret history of the occult. They believe that humans were originally androgynous beings, and someday will return to this 'perfected' state.*
>
> *". . . We know that there is an attempt at destroying the male-female paradigm in order to usher in the digital matrix hell through Transhumanism. So maybe this was one form of early predictive programming sent to us from Warner Brothers, under the guise of a staged rebellion from this famous musician."*

The concept of androgyny is embedded in the figure of Baphomet/ the Goat of Mendes, a favoured motif of satanists and black magick practitioners, as we saw last time around.

Motive for a murder?

The inconsistencies in the mainstream's reporting, led to the usual suggestions that Prince had become the subject of another ritual sacrifice at the hands of the music industry's occult priest class. Considering this notion, there is no shortage of possible motives.

In his latter years, Prince appeared to have undergone something of a conscious awakening, (or a breaking-free of his mind-control programming?) He had begun absorbing the outspoken comments of veteran black comedian-turned-activist Dick Gregory. (Gregory, as a matter of interest, is credited with having first presented the famous 'Zapruder film' of the JFK assassination to the American public, when he and Robert Groden arranged its airing on the ABC TV network in March 1975. This prompted Congress to re-open the investigation into the killing.)

In his now-famous interview on Tavis Smiley's 'Late Night Show' in July 2009, Prince spontaneously recalled some of Gregory's comments regarding the phenomenon of Chemtrails. He also referenced the New World Order plans of the United Nations, remarked that humans are all indentured servants and slaves on a plantation, and that the US had eight presidents before George Washington took office in 1789, a fact kept out of the official history books. Discussions of this nature by celebrities are few and far between on mainstream TV. It certainly seemed as if Prince was going 'off-script.' Gregory was subsequently asked about his relationship with Prince, whereupon he snapped defensively that he had never met him, and that he didn't care to be in the company of celebrities.

As a clued-up friend of mine commented to me by private e-mail at the time:

> *"Every now and again, a true, creative, visionary maverick comes along, like Prince or David Bowie. The industry will tolerate them as*

> *long as they feel they're keeping them in line and making billions off them, but when it seems like they're going off-script or are no longer of use in that way... we know the rest."*

And, as Dick Gregory himself hinted in an interview with the Reel Black YouTube channel in 2016, the forces that control the industry are the type that will patiently sit on a grudge for many years before finally acting on it. By the time they do, any earlier motive will have long faded from the public's mindset:

> *"Why did they want him dead now? Because the white folks that killed him, they're not like niggers and ignorant white folk – 'I'll kill you, motherfucker!' They do it ten years later!"*

Dick Gregory died on 19th August 2017, after being admitted to a Washington DC hospital a week earlier with a urinary tract infection. Although he was 84 years of age, he had been a natural health food advocate for many decades, and three days before his death, both Gregory and his son had commented that he was in excellent shape and was looking forward to coming home.

He is said to have died of heart failure. In a dark twist of irony given his life's work, his death occurred on World Humanitarian Day. It was also two days before the total solar eclipse that swept across the United States. The researcher known as Conspiracy Dude, or CDFury, commented in his video 'Why They Killed Dick Gregory' that a hospital or a prison are the worst places for a genuine political activist to find themselves in. Links to CDFury's video, and the e-book on the death of Dick Gregory which he is making available to his Patreon subscribers, are in the Resources section at the end of the chapter.

Hints that Prince may have had access to inside-knowledge of 'elite' plans, meanwhile, had already come in December 1998, when at a concert in Utrecht in the Netherlands, he had ended the show by saying:

> *"We got one more, then we gotta get out. I gotta go home, y'all. I gotta go home to America. I gotta go get ready for the bombs. Osama Bin Laden gettin' ready to bomb, yeah."*

Before adding:

"2001 – hit me!"

Less than three years later, in September 2001, the events of 9/11 were pinned by the Bush Administration on (former CIA undercover operative) Osama Bin Laden.

A ritual take-out . . . ?

Having established many potential motives for a ceremonial slaying, further support for this idea came from the strange circumstances surrounding Prince's passing.

The date given for his death, 21st April, *just happened* to coincide with the 90th birthday of the Queen of England, (Germany really, but you know what I mean.) As the Commonwealth 'celebrated' the birthdate of a Monarch, (insert facepalm meme here,) a Prince died. Poetic symbology. Not only that though, the period around 20th April has spawned many death-laden events over the years, including the Oklahoma City Bombing, the Waco Texas Massacre, the Columbine school shooting and the Virginia Tech Massacre, all of which contained hints of having been ritualistic killings.

This period turns out to be of great importance in occult tradition. The thirteen days leading up to 1st May, 'Walpurgisnacht,' were marked in the ancient world by human sacrifice, often involving fire, to the god known as Ba'al. 1st May itself was also known as the festival of Beltane in the Pagan Gaelic tradition, marking the mid-point between the Spring Equinox and Summer Solstice.

21st April saw a number of monuments illuminated in purple, reportedly to 'celebrate' the Queen's birthday. The story here, was that that purple had long been a colour associated with royalty. Isn't it interesting that it's also long held a connection in the minds of the public to Prince, not least through his song, album and movie 'Purple Rain,' and his nickname of 'the purple one?'

The question has to be considered – as well as referencing the Queen's birthday, could this purple-fest have also been pre-announcing the imminent death of Prince which was known to be coming – possibly as a symbolic sacrifice to the Queen? During this period, Greene King, the UK's largest pub chain, launched a promotional beer brand, ostensibly to mark the royal 'celebrations', which it rolled out to all its venues. By way of some inventive wordplay, it was known as 'Purple Reign.'

One of the key monuments to have received a purple drenching was Niagara Falls on the US/ Canada border. By way of coincidence (?), it was here that the singer Denise Matthews, better known by her stage name of Vanity, was born in 1959. Vanity went on to become a protégée, and reportedly a love interest of Prince, and her public image was closely associated with him.

Vanity died two months before Prince at the age of 57, reportedly of a liver failure resulting from years of drug abuse. The plot thickens when you learn that Vanity's date of death was exactly the same as that of Prince's mother 14 years earlier, 15th February, and that Prince's father died on the exact same day as Aaliyah, on 25th August 2001. This was 17 days before the events of 9/11. '17 Days' was the title of the song which appeared as the B-side to Prince's 'When Doves Cry.'

. . . or cunning hoax?

Every time the suggestion that an artist may have been ritually sacrificed emerges, the counter-claim that their death was in some way a hoax is never far behind.

One clue in particular has been cited for a pre-planned death hoax involving Prince's complicity, (perhaps similar to the apparent 9/11 foreshadowing at the Utrecht concert in 1998.) He had long favoured the use of numbers in place of words in his song titles, ('When 2 R In Love,' 'Nothing Compares 2 U,' etc.) The track of interest here is 'I Would Die 4 U,' one of the singles from the 'Purple Rain' album. Ascribing the numerical value of 21 to the letter U, marking its point in the alphabet, the title becomes 'I Would Die 4 21,' 4/21 being the US-format rendering of the date on which he would apparently die, 32 years into the future, (though it would certainly have been more convincing had the song been titled 'I Will Die 4 U,' and if it had been Masonic 33 years into the future, rather than 32!)

Additionally, a YouTube researcher known as MrE, (among others,) claimed that Prince had 'returned' in the form of his sister, Tyka Nelson, who appeared in interviews and at a Prince memorial event. It was claimed that no public photographs exist of the pair together, and that very little can be found by way of Tyka's background history.

For so much more on Prince's personas, alter-egos and recurring lyrical themes, do not miss Dan Monroe's highly comprehensive essay 'Lovesexy to Spooky Electric,' situated at the back end of this book.

George Michael: strangeness abounds

UK news bulletins on Christmas Day usually consist of regurgitated parts of the Queen's Christmas speech, and not a whole lot else. So it was a jarring shock to the nation when the sudden death of the former Wham! singer-turned successful solo artist, aged 53, was announced on the evening of 25th December 2016.

(In some interesting links to two other deceased artists, this was ten years to the day after the death of the Godfather of Soul, James Brown, on Christmas Day 2006, amid theories that he was another industry sacrifice who had made a 'crossroads' type 'deal with the devil' in exchange for his long and successful career, and ended up being poisoned in hospital. See the video links in the Resources section at the end for some other researchers' theories on this, plus the related untimely deaths of soul singers Otis Redding and Sam Cooke.

(Additionally, George Michael's birthday was 25th June, the date in 2009 on which Michael Jackson was reported to have died. James Brown, Michael Jackson and George Michael, now join the ranks of a large number of musicians who have met sudden deaths on the 25th of the month, others including Aaliyah and Lisa 'Left Eye' Lopes.)

Just as with Jackson himself – and with Prince – there were immediate discrepancies regarding the cause of George Michael's death, accounts ranging from an overdose of heroin, to complications from pharmaceutical meds, to a cardiac arrest. The straightforward account of 'heart failure' was the one first offered by the mainstream media. This seemed to be a dark twist of synchronicity, given that the song with which George was arguably most associated was Wham!'s 'Last

Christmas'. What are the chances of a singer best known for the line "last Christmas I gave you my heart" dying of heart failure on Christmas Day, suspicious researchers asked?

As it is every year, the song had been on constant rotation on radio stations throughout December. But on this occasion, it had also featured prominently in the two most popular British TV soap operas, watched by tens of millions, in the hours leading up to the death announcement.

The BBC's Christmas Eve edition of 'Eastenders' featured the return of a character who had been killed off years previously. Heather Trott had always been an obsessive George Michael fan. Her voice was heard on an old tape recording, on which she states, "we can't have Christmas without a bit of George, can we?," as she proceeds to play 'Last Christmas.' As she's heard asking character Shirley Carter to press play on the tape, Shirley replies, "what did your last slave die of?" Then, on the Christmas Day episode of 'Eastenders,' Wham!'s 'Last Christmas' crops up as the answer to a question contained within a Christmas cracker... before the other characters around the table learn that every one of their crackers contains the same question. Pub landlord Mick Carter then raises a glass "to absent friends." Quite the 'coincidence.'

Over on ITV, meanwhile, 'Eastenders' main competitor, 'Coronation Street,' "unknowingly" (according to the mainstream media accounts,) paid tribute to George, as a choir was heard singing 'Last Christmas' accapella-style, in the episode screened at 8pm on Christmas Day. News bulletins would announce his death very soon afterwards.

'Eastenders' was still pushing the George references long after his reported demise. In May 2017, character Kim Fox is heard singing Wham!'s 'Club Tropicana,' and says, 'love George!', (as opposed to love<u>d</u>?) Years before, meanwhile, the final episode of BBC1's fascinating 'Ashes To Ashes' drama had Daniel Mays' character, (who is implied to be the devil,) listening to 'Club Tropicana' in a car and declaring, "I think we should listen to this all the way back home!' Of all the pop stars who could have been referenced by these shows, why was it always George Michael?

The movie world is laden with George Michael death references, meanwhile, particularly by way of three films released during the year of the Celebrity Death Cull. 'Deadpool' has a storyline involving bets as to which famous people will be the next to die. The film's main character, Wade 'Deadpool' Wilson, is portrayed as a superfan of Wham! Later, George Michael's 'Careless Whisper' plays over the closing credits.

The musical 'La La Land,' which received its theatrical release over the Christmas 2016 period, has a scene where the female lead character yells out George Michael's name for no apparent reason.

The US comedy movie 'Keanu,' co-written by one of its actors, Jordan Peele, is a real puzzler. Its central character, Keegan, is portrayed as another obsessive George Michael fan – a factor at odds with his cool, streetwise persona. Keegan sports a George tattoo, complete with a cross on his arm. At one point, Keegan takes a hit from a crack pipe in a club and enters an altered state, the film implying he has gone to Heaven. There, he encounters a ghostly apparition of George Michael as seen in his 'Faith' video. The character expresses his thrill, declaring "that's my favourite fucking song!"

George's manager, Michael Lippman, had struck a deal with the movie makers for four of George's songs to be featured in 'Keanu's soundtrack. Lippman commented in an interview: "The way it was described to me was that (George Michael) was so cool that even drug lords have got a tattoo of him . . . they turned George into a cool badass!" He added later: "It's great for George and his songs, as people become more curious about his music."

Indeed.

A short while earlier in 2013, meanwhile, the British drama 'Having You,' included a scene in a public toilet, (perhaps in a sly throwback to George's indecency charge of several years earlier,) when a character makes a remark about 'the ghost of George Michael.' The protagonist remarks, "George Michael isn't dead!" To which his friend replies, "really? Are you sure?"

The recent exposure of George's music through film doesn't even end there. He also had placements in 'Zoolander,' and the Martin Scorsese movie 'Bleed For This.' A world-weary cynic could be forgiven for thinking massive interest in his back catalogue was being systematically built up, in the years and months leading to his sudden (announced) death.

George Michael: An exhaustive influx of references to him and his music appeared in popular culture in the months leading up to his death.

https://commons.wikimedia.org/wiki/File:George_Michael_at_Antwerp_(BRAVO).jpg

Credit: Yves Lorson

Wham!'s 'Choose Life' slogan of their 1980s heyday, formed the basis of Ewan McGregor's cutting monologue in the original 'Trainspotting' movie. And there was more of the same with its 'T2' sequel, yet another film to be released in 2016.

And just when you think you've completed the list, another one always comes along. 2017's 'Atomic Blonde' has Charlize Theron's central character prepare for a fight with assailants in her apartment, by playing George Michael's 'Father Figure' on her hi-fi. (Note to movie producers; other singer-songwriters' music is available.)

Something which observers have also found rather strange, was the tribute at the February 2017 Brit Awards (sigilfest) event, which saw George's former partner in Wham!, Andrew Ridgeley, make his first public appearance since the 1980s to deliver a reading. A further part of the tribute involved Chris Martin of Coldplay in live performance, while footage of George played on a large screen in the background. At one point in the recital of the song 'A Different Corner,' a piece of footage of Prince rapidly appears, in which he utters the words 'peace to George Michael.'

The film was clearly taken from the period in which Prince had jettisoned his artist name and had taken to sporting the word 'slave' written on his face, (remember the comment "what did your last slave die of?" in the Eastenders episode?) Some have asked whether this could have been included as a veiled threat to musicians who speak out about the corrupt nature of the record corporations, given that Prince, George Michael and Michael Jackson all fell out very publicly with their labels, the latter two having both been signed to the Sony corporation. It didn't (seemingly) end pretty for any of them.

Alongside his asserting his artistic rights with his record label, George Michael – like Prince before him – also showed signs of having woken up to uncomfortable truths about the world, and took opportunities in interviews to air his views. Most notable was a February 2003 sequence with the BBC's 'Hardtalk,' in which he was highly critical of Tony Blair and the engineered second Iraq "War" which was about to be launched. In the same interview, he described the Britpop movement which helped formulate a favourable public opinion of Blair, as "a load of bollocks to me."

The previous year, George had released the song 'Shoot The Dog,' with its animated video, as a satirical commentary on George W Bush's foreign war policies, (or, more likely, of those that told him what to do.) Blair is depicted as Bush's obedient lapdog, while George's cartoon self is seen seducing Blair's wife Cherie. These moves add fuel to both the hoax and the taking-out ideas; either fake motives were being set up to give his reported death some credibility, or he was genuinely becoming a loose cannon who needed to be stopped.

For F's sake

On to some of the bizarre aspects of George's death as reported by mainstream media, then. His body is said to have been found on Christmas morning by his boyfriend, Fadi Fawaz, in bed at his home in Goring on Thames, Oxfordshire. He was said to have "passed away peacefully," although, if no-one else was present at the time, as per the official story, how could this have been known?

Fawaz's account to the police of the circumstances in which he found the body changed, according to mainstream reports. He first stated that he had spent the entire Christmas weekend with George at his home, but then changed his story to having slept in his car outside the house, and only waking at 11.30am. Who *really* sleeps in their car outside their lover's house on Christmas Eve, only waking halfway through the next day, sceptics asked?

Fawaz's call to emergency services was made around 2pm, despite him claiming to have found the body over two hours earlier. It remains unclear why he has never been treated as a suspect in the death, therefore, since the police are not known for their tolerance of being lied to under official questioning. If I, or the average person reading this book had done the same as Fawaz, it's a fairly safe bet we'd have spent the same night in a police cell at the very minimum. In what seems like a rendering of the 'doublespeak' straight out of Orwell's '1984,' Thames Valley Police announced they were treating the death as "unexplained, but not suspicious."

Fawaz is a celebrity hairdresser and photographer from Australia, and George Michael is not the first of his music industry friendships that has ended in tragic death. Fawaz is described as having been 'good friends' with Boyzone member Stephen Gately who died in October 2009 when his heart stopped beating, said to be a result of 'sudden adult death syndrome.' In 2014, Gately's family announced that they were hiring a private investigator to look afresh into his death, as they still had unanswered questions arising from the official account. (I know how they feel.)

George Michael's cousin Andros Georgiou, told the press that Fawaz was "not really George's boyfriend," that he was not welcome at the funeral, and that the family "hate him." Georgiou expressed further suspicions at the nature of Fawaz's phone call to the emergency services, saying:

> *"It didn't make sense when I read the transcript, and I have listened to the call over and over. Fadi sounded way too calm, when really you'd be hysterical and crying. Also, he said he waited for hours for George to wake up. Really? On Christmas Day you wait for hours?"*

Fawaz is said to have entered into a relationship with George shortly after the singer's break-up with his previous partner of 13 years, Kenny Goss. The ambiguous nature of Fawaz's true relationship to George has inevitably led to claims that he was acting as his mind-control handler, and these suggestions have been fuelled by a disturbing 2012 picture of the pair together, which was published by the 'Daily Mail' on-line. In it, George appears to be in a trance, and is being led by the arm by Fawaz. George's neck appears to show signs of him having been garrotted. There's a link to the picture in the Resources section at the end.

Fawaz told the police his Twitter account had been hacked into, and that messages claiming that George had wanted to kill himself, and had finally succeeded, were not written by him. Fawaz subsequently took up residence in George's £5 million mansion near London's Regent's Park, amid reports of the family looking into legal action to get him removed.

In July 2017, Fawaz posted a series of Tweets beginning with the cryptic message: "The truth is yet to be told... not long now," and going on to hint that he was so broke he couldn't afford water, milk, or to put petrol in his car.

A coroner's cause of death was given on 7th March 2017 as, "natural causes as the result of a dilated cardiomyopathy with a myocarditis and a fatty liver."

Nostalgicide

It could be argued that four of the five very biggest and most successful solo pop stars of the 1980s, were Michael Jackson, Prince, George Michael and Whitney Houston, and that anyone of a certain age who grew up on their sounds, would carry some kind of attachment to their output. All of them exited between the ages of 48 and 57. It dealt a devastating blow to the nostalgic musical memories of a generation, as the reported deaths of Jim Morrison, Jimi Hendrix, Janis Joplin, Brian Jones and others had done a generation earlier.

The fifth and final superstar of the 1980s would be Madonna, (like Prince and Michael Jackson, also born in the midwest region in the Summer of 1958,) who lives on with the nickname 'the Grand Priestess of the Industry.'

POST SCRIPT 1: Chris Cornell

It seems a music conspiracy researcher's job is never done. And so it was that, on the completion of this chapter, news came in of another untimely rock star death, replete with the usual elements to suggest that there may be more to know than was communicated through the official account. This was the reported suicide of former Audioslave and Soundgarden singer Chris Cornell in the early hours of 18th May 2017.

Cornell was born Christopher Boyle to an Irish father and a Jewish mother, and was acclaimed as one of the forerunners of the Seattle Grunge scene, alongside Nirvana's Kurt Cobain. He was found dead in room 1136 of the MGM Grand Hotel in Detroit, shortly after finishing his gig with Soundgarden at the Fox Theatre. (Researchers have noted that 1136 encodes 9/11 when the 3 and 6 are added together, and that 'Fox" equates to 666 in Gematria.) The coroner's verdict was that he had committed suicide by hanging himself with an exercise belt. A variety of prescription medications were found in his system.

Cornell's death shares many parallels with that of INXS frontman Michael Hutchence, who is said to have hung himself in a Sydney hotel room almost 20 years earlier. There are also similarities to the death of Kurt Cobain, who is said to have shot himself at his Seattle home in 1994.

It's certainly the case that Cornell had a history of heavy drug and alcohol abuse, and of battling depression, But according to the entertainment portal TMZ, his widow Vicky had spoken of how he had been in a positive frame of mind in the period leading up to his death. An article on TMZ's website states:

> *"Sources who spoke with Chris' wife Thursday morning tell TMZ, Vicky Cornell spoke with her husband during soundcheck before he took the stage in Detroit, and after Wednesday night's show. According to our sources, Vicky says Chris was not in any way, shape or form in a suicidal state. She doubled down and said there were no signs he was at all depressed."*

Vicky seemed to change tack slightly in a subsequent press statement, however:

> *"Many of us who know Chris well noticed that he wasn't himself during his final hours, and that something was very off. We have learned from this report that several substances were found in his system. After so many years of sobriety, this moment of terrible judgement seems to have completely impaired and altered his state of mind."*

(Hutchence, too, is said to have been in good spirits and planning for the future the day before he supposedly took his own life, incidentally.)

Researchers have pointed to the possible relevance of the video for Cornell's 2015 single 'Nearly Forgot My Broken Heart,' as it depicts him with a noose around his neck about to be hanged. He does, however, survive this scenario in the video's narrative. Inevitably, some of the occult symbolism employed by Soundgarden over the years has also come in for scrutiny – not least in the songs 'Jesus Christ Pose' and 'Black Hole Sun.'

POST SCRIPT 2: Chester Bennington

Just over two months after Cornell's demise, the music world was rocked by another tragedy involving similar circumstances. Linkin Park lead singer Chester Bennington, was also reported to have committed suicide by hanging, aged 41. This is said to have occurred at his home in Palos Verdes Estates in California, on 20th July 2017. The date just happened to be Chris Cornell's birthday.

Bennington and Cornell were close friends, and had collaborated at gigs together. Like his friend, Bennington had also struggled with drink and drug problems, as well as depression. Bennington was named as the godfather to Cornell's son Christopher. Bennington had commented on Cornell's death on Instagram by stating: "I can't imagine a world without you in it."

Internet rumours began circulating that both musicians had been looking into 'elite' pedophile rings connected to the music industry, with the implication that this had led to their deaths. This theory has not been substantiated by any verifiable evidence, however.

In Bennington's case, claims emerged following his death, that he was in fact the illegitimate son of John Podesta, political aide to both Bill and Hillary Clinton, and the central figure in the 'Pizzagate' allegations of a child sex trafficking network operating out of Washington DC. Certainly, there is more than a passing resemblance between the two, but no validation of the claims has emerged. Bennington had revealed that he himself was sexually abused over a six-year period as a child at the hands of an older 'friend.'

Resources:

Good Vibrations Podcast Episode 080 – Esoteric & Occult Aspects of Prince (Part 1):

- https://www.spreaker.com/user/markdevlin/gvp-080-esoteric-occult-aspects-of-princ

Good Vibrations Podcast Episode 081 – Esoteric & Occult Aspects of Prince (Part 2):

- https://www.spreaker.com/user/markdevlin/gvp-081-esoteric-occult-aspects-of-princ

Celebrity deaths in 2016:

- http://fiftiesweb.com/dead/dead-people-2016/

LA Reid says Prince thought elevators "were the devil," finds friend's death 'haunting':

- http://www.etonline.com/news/187280_prince_thought_elevators_were_the_devil_la_reid_says/

Illuminati Watcher: Prince and the Illuminati blood sacrifice conspiracy:

- http://illuminatiwatcher.com/prince-and-the-illuminati-blood-sacrifice-conspiracy/

Vigilant Citizen: The end of April: a time of human sacrifice:

- https://vigilantcitizen.com/latestnews/the-end-of-april-the-most-magickal-time-of-the-year/

BBC: Prince death: Five strange stories about mysterious US musician:

- http://www.bbc.com/news/magazine-36059247

MrE's Youtube videos alleging Prince 'became' his sister, Tyka Nelson:

- https://www.youtube.com/watch?v=dtr1gP1_-n4

- https://www.youtube.com/watch?v=FTptzKMujkU&t=88s
- https://www.youtube.com/watch?v=EEP2Qn_53_8&t=320s
- https://www.youtube.com/watch?v=oWWLTuCXo-k

Prince's July 2009 interview on The Tavis Smiley Show, Part 1:

- http://www.pbs.org/video/1189739252/

Prince's baby son reportedly died of natural causes:

- http://www.eonline.com/news/34703/prince-s-son-died-of-natural-causes

Dick Gregory – "They Killed Prince" (RBTV Exclusive):

- https://www.youtube.com/watch?v=ItJO7VOXe8w

CDFury Youtube video: 'Why They Killed Dick Gregory:'

- http://www.beatsloop.com/video/ZewJrAF6xFc

CDFury e-book on the death of Dick Gregory, available to his Patreon subscribers:

- https://www.patreon.com/conspiracydude

George Michael hoax – British TV show EastEnders 'Last Christmas' predictive programming:

- https://www.youtube.com/watch?v=DYAARDjBEGc

Keanu movie (2016) 'predicts' George Michael's death:

- https://www.youtube.com/watch?v=3iTj4MGNb6U

Picture of George Michael and Fadi Fawaz – mind control-handler?

- http://www.dailymail.co.uk/news/article-4079644/The-thing-George-Michael-wanted-DIE-Lover-Fadi-Fawaz-says-singer-tried-kill-times-insists-24-7-end.html

George Michael's lover Fadi Fawaz reveals the singer died alone after he slept in his car and denies posting tweets saying the star had tried to kill himself many times:

- http://www.dailymail.co.uk/news/article-4079644/The-thing-George-Michael-wanted-DIE-Lover-Fadi-Fawaz-says-singer-tried-kill-times-insists-24-7-end.html

Who is Fadi Fawaz? George Michael's boyfriend who found the singer's body and is living in George's £5million mansion – all you need to know:

- https://www.thesun.co.uk/news/2488299/fadi-fawaz-george-michael-boyfriend-banned-funeral-mansion/

George Michael's heartbroken lover Fadi Fawaz already scarred by death of Boyzone's Stephen Gately:

- https://www.thesun.co.uk/tvandshowbiz/2486497/george-michaels-lover-fadi-fawaz-already-scarred-by-death-of-boyzones-stephen-gately/

BBC Hardtalk with George Michael, February 2003:

- https://www.youtube.com/watch?v=YKYM7NtjQbY

A full transcript of George Michael's February 2003 BBC Hardtalk interview with Tim Sebastian:

- http://news.bbc.co.uk/1/hi/programmes/hardtalk/2808095.stm

George Michael's 'Shoot The Dog' video:

- https://www.youtube.com/watch?v=ABhZQ_VRbsQ

James Brown's son speaks: How James Brown really died & the deaths of Sam Cooke and Otis Redding:

- https://www.youtube.com/watch?v=EBiFUDzl07I&feature=youtu.be

James Brown went to the crossroad for fame & fortune, part 1:

- https://www.youtube.com/watch?v=eMrdgx2ru9c&feature=youtu.be

James Brown went to the crossroad for fame & fortune, part 2:

- https://www.youtube.com/watch?v=vVtIiqz2w-c

Illuminati Watcher: The passing of Chris Cornell: esoteric and Illuminati symbolism:

- http://illuminatiwatcher.com/the-passing-of-chris-cornell-esoteric-and-illuminati-symbolism/

Chester Bennington's wife, family & friends claim mainstream media guilty of murder cover-up:

- http://directoryofus.com/ash/index.php/breaking-update-chester-benningtons-family-friends-claim-media-guilty-of-murder-cover-up/

The Vigilant Citizen forums:

Chris Cornell's death:

- https://vigilantcitizenforums.com/threads/chris-cornell-has-passed-rip.547/

Chester Bennington's death:

- https://vigilantcitizenforums.com/threads/chester-benningtons-death.1119/

CDFury and Dayz of Noah Youtube channels – two excellent resources for incisive videos on culture manipulation:

- https://www.youtube.com/user/ConspiracydudesFury
- https://www.youtube.com/user/metalfingerz

CHAPTER 10

SAME SHIT, DIFFERENT DECADE

Decoding 1980s pop videos through a new set of lens.

"Are we living in a land,
Where sex and horror,
Are the new gods?"
Frankie Goes To Hollywood: 'Two Tribes' (1984)

"It's the terror of knowing what this world is about."
Queen & David Bowie: 'Under Pressure' (1981)

"Don't be fooled by what you see,
Don't be fooled by what you hear."
Howard Jones: 'New Song (1983)

This book's first volume examined the symbolism pertaining to dark occult rituals, secret societies and trauma-based mind-control, that has been appearing with alarming frequency in the mainstream pop videos of the past ten years. Artists whose 'work' has subliminally communicated these elements include the likes of Katy Perry, Lady Gaga, Rihanna, Beyonce, Miley Cyrus, Kanye West, Jay-Z, Ke$ha, Britney Spears, Will.I.Am and Black Eyed Peas. The meaning of the visual motifs contained has been thoroughly documented in the ongoing articles on the Vigilant Citizen website, and any reader as yet unfamiliar with what is being conveyed through visuals such as broken mirrors, mutilated dolls, teddy bears, Mickey Mouse ears, black and white checkerboard floors, animal skin print, single eyes and pyramids, is highly encouraged to head on over to www.vigilantcitizen.com and take a look, or to absorb some appropriate videos on YouTube before proceeding to the following examples.

You can also find a good, concise summary of the main elements contained in videos of this nature on the following link, (or just type '10 secret mind control symbols in music videos and movies' into a search engine for short):

https://indianinthemachine.wordpress.com/2010/04/05/10-secret-mind-control-symbols-in-music-videos-and-movies/

As I delved further into my own research, I came to realise that this type of imagery is far from limited to pop promos of the 2000s, but actually goes back many decades further. For the purpose of this section, I've decided to focus on a handful of pop videos from the 1980s to make the point. I'd always considered the song lyrics and video imagery of the first half of this decade to be highly ambiguous, and had put it down simply to artistic pretensions. With the research opportunities now afforded to us by the internet, however – and with new understandings of both symbology and the telling backgrounds of many A-list artists – I started looking at the output of those years with fresh eyes, wondering what I could have missed in my naivety.

Most of the acts involved are British, (but with a couple of Americans thrown in for good measure,) to further indicate how this agenda of subliminal mind control is truly an international one, with the complicity of a great many record labels and video production companies, and with the same motifs rolled out decade after decade. This will be far from a comprehensive list from the 1980s, and I welcome any further suggestions that readers may themselves identify, by e-mail to the address at the back of the book.

All of the following can be viewed on YouTube. If readers type in the artist name and track title followed by "official video," these should all be easy enough to find.

The name of each video's director, where it is known, is detailed in each case. A few names take on 'usual suspect' status in this regard.

Adam Ant

The videos of Adam Ant, born Stewart Goddard, are a great place at which to start. Could the lyric "a new Royal Family, a wild nobility, we are the family" in the group's 'Kings Of The Wild Frontier,' have been more of a clue as to their status as industry 'chosen ones' than a simple throwaway line? It's commonly acknowledged that Stewart is a sufferer of bi-polar disorder and other mental health issues, which has been used to explain his sometimes erratic behaviour and long absences from the public eye. He's also reported to have suffered anorexia, and to have attempted suicide.

Adam Ant: So much to see, so much to know.
https://upload.wikimedia.org/wikipedia/commons/8/8b/Adam_Ant_at_100_Club.jpg
Credit: Steve Speight

He incurred mockery and derision through the mainstream headlines which followed the January 2002 incident, in which he is said to have pulled out a gun and 'gone beserk' at the Prince of Wales pub in London's Kentish Town. He was forcibly detained at the Royal Free Hospital at this point. Some years before, during his period of living in LA, he was forcibly committed to that city's unsettling Cedars-Sinai Medical Center, an institution long suspected of being a front for the state-sponsored mind-control programming of celebrities. During this period, he was romantically linked to American actress Heather Graham, whose roles included that of Rollergirl in 'Boogie Nights.'

Adam's situation is reminiscent of that of Syd Barrett, the original frontman of Pink Floyd, who was axed from the group after only a couple of years due to his mental state. This has always been put down to his heavy use of LSD and other hallucinogens, with the idea that it destroyed his sanity. Given the widespread prevalence of programming known to be endemic throughout the entertainment industry, however, is it possible that these official accounts are convenient fronts to cover up what happens when mind-control goes wrong? (It's interesting that there are more military/ establishment family links with both singers – Adam's father was in the Royal Air Force, while Syd's worked as a pathologist involved in disease cell research for the University of Cambridge, an institution closely linked to the government, and a breeding ground for military intelligence operatives.)

Syd is said to have become schizophrenic, depressed and socially withdrawn from late 1967, at one point going missing for a long weekend and, according to friends, returning "a completely different person," with a blank, dead stare and unable to recognise old friends. Syd's father died at the early age of 52 of cancer. Syd himself followed suit, aged 60. Was there a hint at what really happened to him from the 'best of' album 'An Introduction To Syd Barrett?' The sleeve features Syd in an Eyes Wide Shut-style face mask looking into a mirror frame with teddy bears scattered around.

In a 2010 interview for The Sun, Adam Ant spoke of his mental condition in terms which could easily be those of a trauma-based mind-control subject:

> *"In the past I've been a robot. It's been an out-of-body experience. Bipolar means up and down, and that's me... Music has always been the best medication. I was on sodium valproate for seven years.... I might as well have been dead."*

Those who knew him in his younger years, have spoken of how Stewart transformed very quickly from a quiet, shy boy, to a shock-generating punk. At one point, he had the word 'fuck' carved into his back with a razor blade.

The historical record leaves Adam's father, Alfred Leslie Goddard, with a less than noble past. He was jailed for two years in 1987 for sexually preying on young runaway boys, and his name cropped up during investigations into an alleged Westminster paedophile/ child murder ring in the wake of the Jimmy Savile scandal, with suggestions that he had been a procurer of child victims. The 'Daily Mail' reported in 2015 that Goddard Sr. had been a member of a network which included Sidney Cooke, who was later convicted of the sadistic gang rape and killing of a teenage boy. Cooke was also an associate of Savile. At the time, Goddard lived in Pimlico, close to the Dolphin Square apartments where the VIP child abuse ring is said to have been based. Alfred Leslie Goddard died in 1997 shortly after release from prison, with Adam later claiming in interview that his father's jail stint was what shortened his life.

Not to leave Adam's mum out of the picture, meanwhile. She was a seamstress, and once worked as a domestic cleaner for Norman Hartnell, (who was a Royal dress designer to the Queen, the Queen Mother and Wallis Simpson,) and to a Wings-era "Paul McCartney."

The manager of the earliest incarnation of Adam & The Ants was the previously-discussed Malcolm McLaren. A key part of Adam's distinctive image was his wearing of a patch covering one eye, while he would appear in frequently-changing personas in his early heyday – a dandy highwayman, a pirate, a King of the Wild Frontier, etc, all hinting at multiple personalities. The unsettling video to his solo hit 'Puss N Boots,' features depictions of dissociative mindstates and alternative realities, human/ animal hybrids, and the wearing of Mickey Mouse ears.

Puss In Boots was directed by Mike Mansfield/ Adam Ant.

Adam & The Ants: 'Prince Charming'

Where to start? It's all there. Mind-control/ duality and Masonic symbolism; a black and white checkerboard floor; androgyny; multiple personalities as Adam morphs into four famous celebrities in succession at the end; a shattered mirror; face masks. The video also features British actress Diana Dors who was a sex symbol in the 50s and 60s in the same 'blonde bombshell' vein as Marilyn Monroe. This very distinctive look ties into Beta sex slave programming, another facet of MK-Ultra-style mind control.

Directed by Mike Mansfield and Adam Ant.

Kim Wilde

A consistent face on the 1980s pop scene, and the most successful British female artist of that decade, was Kim Wilde. Hers is an interesting background to study. Her image has always been fashioned in the same 'blonde bombshell' iconography, and the title of one her 1980s hit singles was 'Love Blonde'.

Born Kim Smith, she hails from a deep music industry family. Her mother, Joyce, was a performer with the Vernons Girls musical ensemble. Her father, Reg Smith, changed his name to Marty Wilde under the mentorship of producer Larry Parnes in the late 1950s, when he was marketed for a stint as something of a British Elvis. Later, Marty inducted Kim into the industry as a singer, along with his son Ricky, who co-wrote many of her hits. Later, Kim's younger sister Roxanne, 19 years her junior, became a backing singer for Kylie Minogue.

Marty is now an MBE. His own father had been a British army officer. Kim suffered a nervous breakdown shortly after her 30th birthday. After a long period out of the public spotlight, she re-appeared as an asset of the BBC, fronting a television gardening show. She co-designed a feature for the Royal Horticultural Society's Tatton Flower Show entitled All About Alice, based on Lewis Carroll's Alice stories, (which are known to be mind-control programming triggers.) She has also been a public supporter of the LGBT agenda, and of gay rights.

There's lots of interest hidden, (and sometimes not-so-hidden,) in many of Kim's videos. 'Chequered Love,' for instance – with a hint in the title – makes prominent use of black and white duality in the form of a checkerboard design. There's more of the same on the wall, for some strange reason, during this 1986 TV interview with Kim:

https://www.youtube.com/watch?v=zuvwYP8BXZw

'Chequered Love' was directed by Brian Grant.

Kim Wilde: 'View From A Bridge'

The gems in this one are not contained in the official music video, but in another promo sequence that was shot specifically for a German TV show called 'Bananas,' which ran from 1981 to '84. You can view it on the following link to ensure you have the correct version:

- https://www.youtube.com/watch?v=diVn05ahKvw&index=2&list=FLrH-occNth-zNbTt2grEVlA

The video begins with characters from a masked 'elite'-type ball, before cutting directly to a Masonic checkerboard floor on which the band perform the rest of the song.

Directed by Brian Grant.

Kim Wilde: 'Born To Be Wilde'

Kim has made something of a music comeback in recent times. In 2017, performing at the age of 56, she released this (poor) re-interpretation of the Steppenwolf classic, whose video features Masonic black and white checkerboard flooring, (is there any other kind?) and a leopard, (see Beta sex-slave programming.)

Directed by Phil Griffin.

Toyah Willcox: 'I Want To Be Free'

Is there a clue in the song title here? Because the video drops more than a few subtle hints about trauma-based mind-control experimentation – a dissociative dreamstate reality; erratic behaviour; screaming inside what appears to be a monitored cell, and desperate attempts to escape. The cell appears to be watched over by a couple of 'elite' aristocrat types.

Toyah Willcox: 'Brave New World'

Its title being taken from MK-Ultra architect Aldous Huxley's portentous 1932 'novel,' (and guidebook for the incoming New World Order society,) raises interest in itself. The video gives us a birthing from primordial waters; multiple personalities; Transhumanism; a dystopian future.

Toyah Willcox: Plenty to see here, don't yet move along.

https://upload.wikimedia.org/wikipedia/commons/a/a8/Toyah.jpg

Credit: Eddie Mallin

Another of Toyah's popular songs was the deeply bizarre 'Ieya,' whose lyrics asked the question, "are lasers interfering?" and referenced "Zion" and "the Necronomicon." The latter is a reference to a compendium of macabre images by the Swiss artist H.R. Giger, which is said to have influenced the visual tone of director Ridley Scott's 'Alien.' Toyah detailed some strange occurrences in the studio at the time of recording the song, writing in her auto-biography:

> *"The atmosphere in the studio became terrifying. Just like when 'The Exorcist' was made, things started going wrong. Technical equipment wouldn't work, arguments would start out of nowhere."*

Toyah's first appearance in the public eye was when she appeared in the BBC Second City Firsts TV production 'Glitter' in 1975, having won the role of Sue in an audition contest in her hometown of Birmingham. In the play, her appearance is very ordinary, and a far cry from the punchy 'Toyah' persona under which she burst forth as a fully-formed pop star a short while later.

Wikipedia reports that she was born "with a twisted spine, clawed feet, a clubbed right foot, one leg two inches shorter than the other, and no hip sockets. Because of this she endured years of painful operations and physiotherapy." (Otherwise known as trauma?)

Toyah has been pictured sporting monster fangs and a Masonic one-eye ring, in animal print, (see section on Kylie Minogue later in this chapter,) as a demonic alien, wearing pseudo-Egyptian goddess Isis-style garb, flashing the 'devil horns' and Masonic triangle hand signs, making a Masonic 'hush' gesture, and with a Monarch butterfly tattooed over her eyes. She was drawn with wings and holding a severed head on her album 'Anthem,' and wearing horns on the cover of the follow-up album, 'Changeling.' Did I miss anything out? Oh yeah, a favoured early look involved her wearing black contact lenses to give her eyes a 'dead,' inhuman look. She went on to marry Robert Fripp of the group King Crimson.

The 'Brave New World' video was directed by David Mallet.

Toyah Willcox: 'It's A Mystery'

Dystopian future landscapes; hints at psychic powers.

Visage: 'Mind Of A Toy'

Ever feel like the truth is getting placed in plain sight? As per the song title, this one is replete with mind-control programming symbolism, with dolls and toys representing a victim's lost innocence. Visage frontman Steve Strange, who was a one-time heroin addict and suffered a nervous breakdown, was the son of a British army paratrooper. He became a prominent promoter in London clubland, and died very suddenly in 2015, aged 55, of a heart attack in Sharm-El-Sheikh, Egypt.

Directed by Kevin Godley and Lol Creme, (formerly of the group 10cc.)

Duran Duran: 'Union Of The Snake'

In retrospect, Duran would appear to have been major assets of the British industry machine in the early 1980s, and it remains open to conjecture how complicit the members may have personally been in the symbolism that often surrounded them. The group named itself after a rogue scientist from the 1968 movie 'Barbarella,' yet another depiction of a dystopian/ Orwellian futurist society.

The video to 'Union Of The Snake' got a thorough analysis in 'Musical Truth 1,' containing as it does a secret underground desert base in the style of Nevada's Area 51, children and human-animal hybrids kept in cages underground, reptilian beings, and mind-control visual triggers. They sure weren't backwards in coming forwards on this one. As a nice added touch, the vinyl record sleeve features an ominous all-seeing eye.

Directed by Simon Milne. Conceived by Russell Mulcahy.

Duran Duran: 'Is There Something I Should Know?'

It's a good question. A recurring pyramid throughout; sigils; a naked toddler; a fractured screen representing a splintered mind-state.

Directed by Russell Mulcahy.

Duran Duran: 'Wild Boys'

Where to begin? A dystopian future landscape, (because there's no future other than a dystopian one, right?); Transhumanism; mutant cross-breeds. It's all there. As Wikipedia's account of the video's filming puts it: "John Taylor was strapped to the roof of a car suffering a psycho-torture with pictures of his childhood and early past."

'The Wild Boys: A Book Of The Dead,' was the title of a 1971 novel by Beat poet and Punk Rock influencer William Burroughs, and director Russell Mulcahy used the overblown Duran video as a teaser and a practice run for a full-length feature film he had hoped to make, but which never came to fruition.

Directed by Russell Mulcahy.

David Bowie: 'Ashes To Ashes'

This will be far from the only Bowie video to justify close analysis, but it serves as a good example of this section's points. Dreamstates; fractured dissociative realities; clowns; a mental institution; androgyny.

Directed by David Bowie and David Mallet.

Bucks Fizz: 'The Land of Make Believe'

Illusory reality; dreamstates, and nods to 'The Wizard Of Oz,' (often used as a mind-control trigger,) 'Cinderella' and 'The Lion, The Witch And The Wardrobe.'

Bucks Fizz: 'My Camera Never Lies'

An all-pervading all-seeing eye right from the start; surveillance; black and white duality.

Ultravox: 'Vienna'

Dreamstates and altered realities; an 'Eyes Wide Shut'-style 'elite' party.

Directed by Russell Mulcahy.

Bonnie Tyler: 'Total Eclipse Of The Heart'

Set in an 'Eyes Wide Shut'-style 'elite' mansion, (and filmed at the Holloway Sanitorium Victorian Gothic hospital in Surrey); hints at possession; a full moon; a child with wings and people flying, representing dissociation; a plethora of doves, (the Babylonian goddess Semiramis, an aspect of the sacred feminine figure also symbolised by Mary/ Diana/ Britannia/ Isis, etc, is represented as a dove,) and a nice Masonic handshake to finish things off.

Directed by Russell Mulcahy.

Queen: 'Radio Gaga'

Replicating scenes from Fritz Lang's 1927 'Metropolis' movie, depicting a futuristic city where slaves serve the elite class, (rather like a letter from 'the elites' to Santa Claus at Christmas.)

Directed by David Mallet.

RAH Band: 'Clouds Across The Moon'

It's more the sleeve to this whimsical futuristic tale created by producer Richard Anthony Hewson, (aka RAH,) which draws the scrutiny here. Certainly, the video ties into the technological space-age theme of the song, with talk of colonies on the moon, (epic fail!) But this 1985 single's cover leaves little doubt as to the credentials of those behind it, showing the moon encased within a pyramid, with a blood-red Saturn hovering ominously overhead.

The System: 'You Are In My System'

This 1982 promo shows that all these interesting signs and symbols are not limited to any one genre, here making an appearance in the black music/ soul/ funk scene. Alongside the band performing against a futurist landscape backdrop, complete with a massive half-globe, and with hints at Transhumanism and split personalities, singer Mic Murphy flashes the industry favourite '666' hand sign at the camera three times, (though sceptics would doubtless say that this is simply to emphasise the word 'oh', which he is singing each time he makes the sign.) The concept of something being "in my system," is generally taken to refer to the singer's love interest... but could equally be interpreted as drugs, or some kind of possessive entity.

'You Are In My System' was later covered by Robert Palmer. On which note...

Robert Palmer: 'Addicted To Love'

One of the most famous videos of the 80s, with Palmer surrounded by a group of identically-dressed, hot-looking girls. Except that their robotic movements and blank stares suggest them be Stepford Wives-style mind-control clones. One of the girls, Mak Gilchrist, revealed in an interview with 'Q' magazine that she and her colleagues were instructed to behave "like showroom mannequins." Looking into Palmer's family background, we find yet another interesting link to military intelligence, his father having been a British naval officer. Palmer himself joined the dubious ranks of rock stars to suffer early, sudden deaths, when his body was found in a Paris hotel room in 2003 at the age of 54. The cause of death was given as a cardiac arrest.

Directed by Terence Donovan.

Billy Idol: 'Eyes Without A Face'

Multiple personalities; one eye; hints at possession; ritual torture; 'Eyes Wide Shut'-style masked and robed beings.

Directed by David Mallet.

Iron Maiden: 'Number Of The Beast'

The video kinda tells its own story!

One video version of Iron Maiden's 'The Trooper,' from 1983, has the group deliver the entire song on the ever-popular Masonic checkerboard floor. That's about it…oh, apart from the grinning demonic entity presiding over the whole performance, that is.

Directed by David Mallet.

Madness: 'Tomorrow's Just Another Day'

The second half of the video features the group with spinning umbrellas. These are known triggers in mind-control programming, (making the group name rather appropriate in this case,) and 'spinning' is a sensation reported as being experienced by victims. The band also appear dressed creepily as animals, (see Stanley Kubrick's 'The Shining,' and accounts of 'elite'-style sex parties.)

It's interesting that Madness were known by the nickname 'the nutty boys,' and that their self-titled song includes the lyrics "Madness, madness, they call it madness, I'm about to explain, that someone is losing their brain," and "I won't be the one who's gonna suffer, you are gonna be the one."

Directed by Dave Robinson.

Madness: 'Bed And Breakfast Man'

Like the majority of Madness videos, directed by Dave Robinson, and featuring more mind-control symbolism as the group perform on a Masonic checkerboard floor, (zzzzzz.)

Directed by Dave Robinson.

Bee Gees: 'You Win Again'

Taken from an album entitled 'E.S.P.,' standing for extra-sensory perception. A sigil-fest from start to finish. And none too subtle, either.

Eurythmics: 'Love Is A Stranger'

Mind-control experimentation. Annie Lennox, (OBE,) was one of the main pushers of androgyny and Transgenderism imagery, (both aspects of intelligence services-controlled social engineering,) throughout the 1980s. She also rocked the closely-cropped blonde hair look mentioned in Chapter 3.

Directed by Mike Brady.

Eurythmics: 'Sweet Dreams'

Mind-control; androgynous gender-bending; Masonic one-eyes; globe/ NASA indoctrination, as footage of a Saturn V rocket launch is shown on a TV screen.

Directed by Chris Ashbrook.

Eurythmics: 'Sexcrime (1984)'

The song and video to accompany the film remake of George Orwell's '1984' novel/ instruction manual, released in the very year it was supposed to be prophesying, and depicting a nightmare totalitarian police and surveillance state. Rather like the one that's being rolled out more with every passing month right now, come to think of it.

Belinda Carlisle: 'Heaven Is A Place On Earth'

Straight from the bat we get a selection of small globes arranged in the form of a pyramid. The globes then re-appear being clutched by a group of characters in creepy face masks. What could be the significance of all these globes in these mind-control videos, I wonder??? A dizzying, spinning sensation, of the type reported to be experienced by dissociative mind-control victims, (see Kylie Minogue section,) is conveyed.

Directed by Hollywood actress Diane Keaton (of 'The Godfather' fame.)

Nena: '99 Red Balloons'

Some analysis of the original promo for this song, from 1984, and its relevance to other events, came from a very incisive video by the researcher Zod 44 which you can view here:

- https://www.youtube.com/watch?v=I3TQOznid8o

Many years later, a technofied version of the video and song appeared, (with the lyrics delivered in French and German,) and – surprise surprise – there it all is. Transhumanism; black and white Masonic duality/ mind-control triggers; Orwellian police state; Nena sitting atop a pyramid with a removed capstone amid apocalyptic destruction. Oh, and a nice Chemtrailed sky to top it all off.

The updated version is here:

- https://www.youtube.com/watch?v=6wMeOSED5W8

Madonna: 'Like A Virgin'

Madonna didn't earn her nickname of 'Grand Priestess of the Industry' for nothing, and entire tomes could be written covering her involvement in occult ritual symbolism... and have been. The video to her

'Like A Prayer,' (also directed by Mary Lambert, whose sister is former US senator Blanche Lincoln of Arkansas, incidentally,) can be endlessly analysed, and even mainstream scholars with no grounding in truth/ conspiracy issues acknowledge that it's loaded with spiritual symbology.

Madonna, Grand Priestess of the Industry.

https://upload.wikimedia.org/wikipedia/commons/4/4f/Madonna_-_Rebel_Heart_Tour_-_Antwerp_5.jpg

Credit: Pascal Mannaerts.

We'll just concern ourselves with the prior 'Like A Virgin,' therefore. It was early days for Madonna, and the video seems to have been part of her industry induction rituals. In it, she is pursued around the waterways of Venice by a lion, (see Beta sex kitten programming,) and by the end, the beau who has been romancing is seen sporting a creepy lion mask himself. It's straight out of 'Eyes Wide Shut' and 'The Shining' with reference to 'elite' ritual abuse and mind control... and doing a Google image search with the phrase 'Rothschild party 1972' will bring up a few interesting results.

By the following year's 'Into The Groove' video, Masonic symbolism had been introduced, in the form of a jacket embroidered with a pyramid, a removed capstone and an all-seeing eye. Was this symbolising Madonna swiftly moving up through the ranks?

Directed by Mary Lambert.

Madonna: 'Borderline'

The video begins with Madonna dancing on the street with her friends, when a sleazy photographer makes her a job offer, (a metaphor for the way the music industry selects its assets?) She is seen posing in his studio, the shots rendered in black and white to indicate the soullessness of it all. The interesting thing about the studio is that it *just happens* to be adorned with two Freemasonic pillars and – you might want to sit down here – a black and white checkerboard floor and walls.

Directed by Mary Lambert.

Kate Bush: 'Babooshka'

Kate Bush has been one of the most endlessly-fascinating and enigmatic artists of all time. Her music and look remain utterly unique. But the question has to be reluctantly asked as to whether she may have been yet another of the industry's mind-control subjects? Her father was a doctor, (very little information can be found on-line about his actual work,) which is a common factor in test subjects, and Kate's painfully shy persona is a far cry from the flamboyant charisma with which she 'comes alive' during performances.

Was the CBE that she received from the Queen in 2013 a symbolic nod for services rendered, of a different type the ones we all think? The video to her early song 'Babooshka,' shows her displaying robotic-like dance moves (programming,) before morphing completely from one personality and look to another, along with the breaking of glass, (symbolising shattered personalities?)

Directed by Keith MacMillan.

Kate Bush: 'The Man With the Child in His Eyes'

This promo does not disappoint either, (and yes, I know this was 1978 rather than into the 80s, before anyone points it out!) and the song title itself is an eyebrow-raiser when considering ritual abuse and mind-control from an early age. The song begins with the ghostly whispering of "he's here, he's here" – as if an alter has been brought the fore? The whole video has a surreal, dream-like feel to it, and at one stage, three versions of Kate appear in the same frame.

Kate wrote the song when she was 13 years old. In a 2010 'Daily Mail' interview, Steve Blacknall, said to be Kate's first boyfriend, claimed that he was the lyrical inspiration. At the time he worked as a toilet cleaner in a local hospital, but went on to land a marketing job at Decca Records, and said he had become Kate's 'first true love' by the Spring of 1975.

Directed by Keith MacMillan.

Kate Bush: 'Cloudbusting'

A video of a whole different kind accompanied this 1985 outing, filmed at the mystical White Horse Hill near Uffington, England. This masterpiece stands as a fully-fledged movie in its own right, and indeed, features Hollywood actor Donald Sutherland portraying the suppressed scientist and psychologist Wilhelm Reich.

The film touches on the relationship between Reich and his son, Peter, played by Kate, and depicts his orgone energy technology being used for cloud-seeding and weather manipulation, much to the chagrin of some dark suits in government. These are not subjects ordinarily addressed in pop promos! Everyone should watch this genius video at least once in their lives.

Directed by Julian Doyle, with input from Monty Python's Terry Gilliam.

Culture Club: 'Victims'

Could the title be hinting at the industry's ever-present MK-Ultra mind-control programme – especially with lyrics like: "The victims we know so well, they shine in your eyes when they kiss and tell. Strange places we never see, but you're always there like a ghost in my dream?" Boy George also makes reference to his "puppet strings." It's probably the case that far more otherwise ambiguous 1980s pop songs than we would ever suspect, are actually revealing veiled secrets, in the same way that so many famous rock songs are said to have been written in 'witch language.'

This video features an androgynous globe sigil at the beginning, along with hints at dissociated dreamstates. The video for the group's breakthrough single, 1982's 'Do You Really Want To Hurt Me,' shows George facing courtroom judgement wearing a Jewish Rabbi's hat, and a long white shirt adorned with Hebrew writing, apparently spelling out 'Culture Club.' In photo shots from the set of the video, a 'Star of David' symbol, (also the sigil adopted by the Rothschild bloodline,) appears on his shirt.

Many years later, an ageing George was pictured with a collage of bizarre images painted on to his bald head. Taking centre stage was the same 'Star of David'/ Seal of Solomon symbol. What am I missing here?

Directed by Kevin Godley and Lol Creme.

Steve Winwood: 'While You See A Chance'

A recurring pyramid. About as subtle as a flying brick. Winwood was a child star, performing in bands from the age of eight.

Directed by Clive Richardson.

Gary Numan: 'Cars'

Technically from 1979, but still in an early 80s style. It could be said to have been ahead of its time, which is what Numan's whole futurist persona was all about.

He started making music in a Punk and New Wave style, but later became seduced by the electronic Synthpop sound, in which genre he found his success. Gary Webb's core image very much promoted Transhumanism, (his debut hit was titled 'Are Friends Electric?), even down to his chosen artist name of 'Numan' = 'new man,' as in one 'augmented' by technology.

This video runs the full gamut – mirror images; duality; multiple personalities, Masonic black and white duality represented by the keyboard. And to top it all off, the song is performed from inside a large pyramid structure!

Directed by Derek Burbidge.

M: 'Pop Muzik'

Back to '79 for this one, too, but worth mentioning in light of its lyrical hook of "New York, London, Paris, Munich . . . " While it could just be coincidence, alert observers have pointed out that this was the order of major "terror" events which would ensue in the years to come – New York with 9/11, London with 7/7, Paris with . . . take your pick, and Munich with the shopping mall shooting of 2016, which ended outside a McDonalds displaying its big 'M' sign.

The lyrics to 'Pop Muzik' include "mix me a Molotov," "wanna be a gunslinger" and make a reference to "infiltration." Readers must make of it what they will. M was the alias of Robin Scott, who was an early associate of Malcolm McLaren and Vivienne Westwood. M was also the name of James Bond's boss, of course, in a tenuous link back to military intelligence. Robin Scott's 1980 album was titled 'Official Secrets Act,' and in the video to 'Pop Muzik,' he appears as a spy of the *film noir* genre.

Directed by Brian Grant.

The Boomtown Rats: 'I Don't Like Mondays'

And just one more from '79. It's more about the lyrical theme than the visuals . . . though we do get creepy schoolkids straight out of the movie 'Village of the Damned,' and Bob Geldof in a black and white chequered jacket for good measure. Geldof has explained that his writing of the song was inspired by the shooting spree of 16-year-old Brenda Ann Spencer at a San Diego school in January of 1979. The line, "the silicon chip inside her head gets switched to overload," becomes intriguing when you factor in the phenomenon of mind-control programming and the brain implants that are said to be used.

The song seemed to foreshadow the spate of school shooting/ "shooting" events that would follow in the intervening years, such as Virginia Tech, Columbine, Dunblane and Sandy Hook.

Directed by David Mallet.

Depeche Mode: 'Enjoy The Silence'

A video which just missed the other end of the 80s, being released at the very start of 1990, came from British Synthpop heroes Depeche Mode. Although this track carried a different official video, an alternative version was recorded for French TV, which featured the group performing the song atop the South Tower of Manhattan's World Trade Center. At one point, Dave Gahan sings the lyric, "come crashing in, into my little world." The towers had a little over eleven and a half years left to stand.

YouTube seems to have banned every copy of this video uploaded to its channel on 'copyright' grounds. I'm sure that's the only reason and that it's nothing to do with the fact that truthseekers are now all over such subjects and starting to ask some pertinent questions. It is, however, available to view via Vimeo on the following link:

- https://vimeo.com/74354252

Thomas Dolby: 'Hyperactive'

Obvious mind-control evocations with lyrics like, 'and they're messing with my mind… ripping me apart." Elements of hypnosis, mind-control triggers and the omnipresent black and white duality are all there, with Dolby also appearing as a creepy ventriloquist's dummy, hinting at dissociation.

Directed by Daniel Kleinman.

Mr. Mister: 'Is It Love?'

This was filmed in what looks to be a Rothschild-style country house, but turns out to be Greystone Mansion and Park in Beverly Hills, and was apparently sponsored by the Vidal Sassoon brand.

It pretty much contains everything you'd expect from a Weekend with the 'Elites.' The band perform amidst Masonic garb and – would you believe it – a black and white checkerboard floor!!! The lead female shows signs of being a Stepford Wives-style mind control slave, and there are hints at dreamstate dissociation, trauma and ritual sacrifice. Just another day at the office.

"Paul McCartney" (it says here) & Stevie Wonder: 'Ebony & Ivory'

Black and white duality; multiple/ shattered personalities.

Directed by Barry Myers.

Michael Jackson: 'Beat It'

A full analysis of this one came from the researcher Lenon Honor in the following video, demonstrating how it depicts group male masturbation. (The song title, seemingly, is no accident.)

- https://vimeo.com/100178568

Directed by Bob Giraldi.

Strawberry Switchblade: 'Since Yesterday'

Contains coloured dots of the type reportedly used as mind-control triggers. (A woman wearing a polka-dot dress is said to have been seen disappearing from the vicinity of Sirhan Sirhan when he is said to have assassinated Senator Robert Kennedy in 1968. BBC children's entertainer Justin Fletcher, in his CBeebies guise as 'Mr. Tumble,' carries a bag with the same design. Fletcher has been pictured flashing the familiar '666' hand sign.)

At some points, the dots appear as Mickey-Mouse-ears behind the girls. In a 2002 interview, the group's Rose McDowall talked about Soft Cell frontman Marc Almond being inducted into Anton La Vey's Church of Satan in the grounds of her house:

> *"... Boyd Rice initiated Marc Almond into the Church of Satan in the little grotto that's just a walk down there... I don't think the landlord would appreciate that!"*

Boyd Rice is an American experimental sound/ noise musician, and proud social Darwinist, (an expression of satanism,) who collects Barbie dolls. These are symbolic of dissociative mind-control programming. Rose stated that her interpretation of his role in the Church of Satan, was that it was merely all about doing whatever you want without concern, and that it's ultimately just harmless and fun.

(If readers will allow another couple of related side notes, meanwhile, in 1989, Dave Ball, who had been in Soft Cell alongside Marc Almond, formed the dance music act The Grid alongside Richard Norris. The following year the pair released the track 'Origins of Dance,' featuring the 1960s 'acid guru' (and CIA asset) Dr. Timothy Leary, just as the UK's own acid culture was in full throttle for a new generation of malleable youths. In 1994. The Grid put out their album 'Evolver,' which contained a track called 'Golden Dawn' in apparent homage to the one-time leader of that occult mystery school, the omnipresent Aleister Crowley. One of The Grid's later singles was 1995's 'Diablo,' the Spanish word for 'devil.)

Directed by Tim Pope.

Dead Or Alive: 'You Spin Me Round'

Androgyny; one-eye imagery; hints of Hindu god Vishnu. See following section on Kylie Minogue for more on the concept of 'spinning.'

Frontman Pete Burns, whose father was an army soldier and his mother Jewish, had embodied Transgenderism for years, and had an early gimmick of covering one eye with a patch. In a similar bizarre 'coincidence' to George Michael singing, "Last Christmas I gave you my heart," and going on to die on Christmas Day of heart failure, on a track on Dead Or Alive's second album, 'Youthquake', Pete Burns sang, "Get me to the doctor, my heart goes bang, bang, bang, bang," and went on to die of a reported cardiac arrest as part of the 2016 celebrity death pandemic, aged 57.

Directed by Vaughan Arnell.

Dead Or Alive: 'In Too Deep'

See above, plus human/ fish hybrids.

Murray Head: 'One Night In Bangkok'

Yet more shenanigans on a black and white checkerboard floor. There's a fairly credible excuse for this one, given that the song is taken from the musical 'Chess,' and the characters are supposed to be on giant chess boards. But either way, it's a continuation of a familiar theme.

Directed by David G. Hillier.

Over to America for a couple.

Toni Basil: 'Over My Head'

Dissociation; multiple personalities; altered reality; dreamstate; black and white duality, (mind-control trigger designs.) Basil has primarily been a dance choreographer, and was an actress in a handful of movies, most notably in the hippie/ counter-culture classic 'Easy Rider.'

Directed by Toni Basil and Michelle Simmons.

Laura Branigan: 'Self Control'

This one deserves an essay all of its own, and got one from Vigilant Citizen, (see link at the end.) It was directed by William Friedkin of 'The Exorcist' fame, and is as blatant an exposé of 'elite' mind control and ritual abuse as it's possible to get, coming some 15 years before 'Eyes Wide Shut' offered many of the same visual motifs.

Branigan died suddenly aged 47 in 2004, from what is said to have been a brain aneurism. It was reported in the media that she had been experiencing headaches for several weeks.

Sinead O' Connor: 'Troy'

This debut video from 1987 is full of subtle hints towards mind control. Sinead has talked openly of her battles with mental illness over the years, and has been outspoken about Establishment corruption. Her exposure of paedophilia within the Catholic church is reminiscent of the likes of Michael Jackson, George Michael and Prince going "off-script" in their latter years. The shaven-head look she has always rocked is also a motif closely associated with programming.

Directed by John Maybury.

Kylie Minogue

An artist who emerged in the late 80s, but whose key videos date from later years, is Kylie. Her most frequently-pushed image ties very much into the 'sex kitten' look prevalent throughout entertainment. This is an aspect of Beta Programming, where sex slaves are symbolised by animal print designs, representing their sexual, animalistic nature being exploited. (This dynamic was alluded to in Robin Thicke's video to his song 'Blurred Lines', and its lyrics "tried to domesticate you, but you're an animal, baby, it's in your nature.") And does this song's title refer to a blurring of the lines between reality and mind-dissociation?

A Google image search under 'Kylie Minogue animal print' brings some rewarding results in this context. So does substituting Madonna's name for Kylie's.

Three of Kylie's song titles evoke aspects of trauma-based mind control. Victims are said to often experience spinning, dizzying sensations when they dissociate from reality, with electro-shock used as an aspect of programming. Were these factors being communicated with dark, morbid irony through Kylie's 'Spinning Around' and 'Shocked' songs?

Brain implants and microchips are also used, (remember fellow 'blonde bombshell' Britney Spears commenting on "getting these things out of my head" during her famous hair-shaving incident?) Kylie's 2000 comeback hit was entitled 'Can't Get You Out Of My Head,' its video showing a futurist cityscape with dancing Stepford Wives-style cyborgs. Kylie becomes dissociated and robot-like herself.

'Can't Get You Out of My Head' was directed by Dawn Shadforth.

Going back to 1988, finally, the Chris Langman-directed video for Kylie's rendering of 'The Locomotion,' sees her and her dance troupe gyrating on – would you believe it – a black and white checker-board floor. (Note to all video directors – other designs of flooring are available.)

It could be argued that it's not as if we haven't been told, all along, what we've really been looking at for all these years.

Howard Jones

Just to end this section on a more inspiring note, however, lest I be accused of wallowing in the dark stuff for too long – perish the though – an artist whose music I lapped up in the '80s, but whose lyrical themes I've only begun to appreciate in recent years, is the English Synthpop soloist Howard Jones.

Although the string of hits he scored from 1983 to '85 appeared, on the surface, to be nothing more than chart-friendly pop songs with catchy hooks, close examination of his lyrics reveals some deeply philosophical messages being sneaked into the listening public's psyche. It turns out that many of the lyrics featured on his breakthrough 'Human's Lib' album were actually penned by a Buddhist practitioner named Bill Bryant, who became something of a mentor to Jones. The pair later became estranged, however, and Jones appears to have given no public recognition to Bryant's influence on him since.

Either way, Jones' debut 'New Song' spoke of the triumphs of individuality – throwing off mental chains and not being led by the crowd. 'Pearl In The Shell' claimed "the fear goes on," hinting at a kind of societal mind control. The album track 'Assault And Battery,' was a sobering commentary on the hypocrisy of carnism.

Howard's real gem, however, was the 1984 single 'Hide And Seek.' Here, he talked of the divine Creator wishing to experience itself through All Possibility, and so creating the earthly realm, then splitting itself into individuated units of consciousness which forget their true nature, (hide) in order to come and learn their life lessons, (seek.)

'Agadoo' it was not.

Resources:

Daily Mail: Adam Ant's father dragged into VIP child abuse probe: Alfred Leslie Goddard was jailed for preying on runaway boys nearly 30 years ago:

- http://www.dailymail.co.uk/news/article-3215608/Adam-Ant-s-father-dragged-VIP-child-abuse-probe.html

The transformation of Stewart Goddard into Adam Ant:

- http://dangerousminds.net/comments/young_adam_ant_looking_like_a_pretty_punk_rock_adonis

The Telegraph: Adam Ant in mental ward after gun scare:

- http://www.telegraph.co.uk/news/1381673/Adam-Ant-in-mental-ward-after-gun-scare.html

Vigilant Citizen analysis of Laura Branigan's 'Self Control' video:

- https://vigilantcitizen.com/musicbusiness/self-control-laura-branigan-creepy-80s-video-mind-control/

Lenon Honor's analysis of Michael Jackson's 'Beat It' video:

- https://vimeo.com/100178568

Illuminati Watcher analysis of Robin Thicke's Blurred Lines video:

- http://illuminatiwatcher.com/illuminati-symbolism-in-robin-thicke-blurred-lines-music-video/

Miles W Mathis analysis of Robin Thicke's Blurred Lines video:

- http://mileswmathis.com/blurred.pdf

Occult aspects of Duran Duran's 'Wild Boys' video analysed:

- http://www.occulomency.co.uk/duran-duran-video-analysis/

Culture Club: Behind the Videos:

- http://www.boygeorgefever.com/behind_the_videos.html

Complete Strawberry Switchblade interview by subject:

- http://www.strawberryswitchblade.net/print.php?section=interviews&item=bysubject

Dazed Digital: The story behind Kate Bush's Cloudbusting video:

- http://www.dazeddigital.com/music/article/27217/1/the-story-behind-kate-bush-s-cloudbusting-video

Daily Mail: I'm The Man With the Child in His Eyes: Kate Bush's first boyfriend reveals he was the secret inspiration for classic hit:

- http://www.dailymail.co.uk/tvshowbiz/article-1314539/The-Man-With-The-Child-In-His-Eyes-Kate-Bush-lover-reveals-classics-secret.html

The mysterious lyrics of Howard Jones (and William Bryant:)

- http://mineforlife.blogspot.co.uk/2009/06/mysterious-lyrics-of-howard-jones.html

Howard Jones' 'Hide and Seek' lyrics:

- http://www.lyricsfreak.com/h/howard+jones/hide+seek_20066159.html

CHAPTER 11

THE FINAL CHAPTER . . . IS WAITING TO BE WRITTEN

The generation reading these words is the one which will decide whether humanity seizes its greatest moment, or suffers its worst nightmare. What will we choose?

"Did you alter the face of the city?
Make any change in the world you found?
Or did you observe all the warnings?
Did you read the trespass notices, did you keep off the grass?
Did you shuffle up the pavements just to let your betters pass?
Did you learn to keep your mouth shut, were you seen but never heard?
Did you learn to be obedient and jump to at a word?
Did you demand any answers?
The who and the what, and the reason why?
Did you ever question the set-up?
Did you stand aside and let 'em choose while you took second best?
Did you let 'em skim the cream off and give to you the rest?
Did you settle for the shoddy and did you think it right,
To let 'em rob you right and left and never make a fight?"

Ewan MacColl & Peggy Seeger: 'The Ballad Of Accounting' (1964)

"It's hard.
Easy?
Is not an option.
It's hard.
Living.
Life is hard.

You will go through things, and while you're going through them you can't understand why it's happening to you.
But after you go through it, you get back and you look at it, and you say, 'Oh, now I understand why I needed that lesson.'
And you look at it and embrace whatever comes to you.
Don't run from it. Step towards it!
Don't try to duck it like most people do.
See, most people want it easy.
See, 'cause easy come, easy what?
Easy go!"

'Soapbox' skit from Apollo Brown & Skyzoo 'The Easy Truth' LP (2016)

"Life is the supreme Game that all must play. There can be no spectators... Life is raw science God realisation. And like all games, there must be rules and regulations, principles and codes... Welcome to the Game."

Gensu Dean & Wise Intelligent Featuring Hakhem U.L Allah: 'Life' (Skit) (2017)

"If I should die this very day,
'Don't cry, 'cause on earth we wasn't meant to stay..."

Whitney Houston: 'Your Love Is My Love' (1998)

Having visited such dark and dangerous topics as mind control, Transhumanism, social engineering, malevolent sound frequencies and subversive occult influences, readers may be surprised at the tone this book will now take – like watching a movie which appears to be of a particular genre, but then switches its nature in the final frames.

I – and any other researcher – could go on for days listing the various problems humanity faces, and exposing the methods by which they came about. While this certainly gives people the opportunity to understand the tactics being used against them – and to make a free-will choice to unplug from their control – the solutions that humanity ultimately needs to tap into lie beyond this physical reality. It's only by addressing things on this basis that long-lasting, wide-reaching change can be affected. And it really can. Like everything in Creation, it's a choice.

I addressed the eternal, universal concepts of Natural Law, (or whatever other name anyone cares to put on it,) in the last book. Humanity remains bound by this immutable dynamic whether any one individual likes it or not, believes it or not, or chooses to look at it or not. It really doesn't make a difference. It goes on being Truth, and we go on being bound by its tenets either way.

A society, ultimately, gets what it deserves, and so the fact that we have a music industry that *should* be all about free-spirited creativity and fun, but is in fact controlled at a corporate level by a dark occult priest class, means that humanity – collectively – has allowed things to get this bad through its lack of spiritual Care.

It's for the same reason that we live in a reality ruled over by a force of evil in which paedophiles in positions of power go unpunished, bankers enslave us with imaginary 'money' that never existed, and animals suffer all manner of unspeakable cruelty daily. If the element of Care had been present in line with deep understandings of the way spiritual laws work, this type of situation could never have taken a hold; only one rooted in morality could have done so.

First division: Attackers

It's becoming clear that there are now three main groups of people in the world when it comes to where the consciousness of humanity is really at.

A central tenet of the aforementioned Five Per Cent Nation, (or Allah's Five Percenters,) is that the worldly population is split into three groups in terms of conscious enlightenment; 85 per cent are in ignorance of all Truth, a controlling ten per cent seek to keep true knowledge to themselves, to gain a tactical advantage over everyone else, and the remaining five per cent are the 'poor righteous teachers,' who know the truth and seek to enlighten the 85 per cent. This dynamic formed the foundation of the Minister Louis Farrakhan-featuring 1992 track 'The Meaning Of The Five Per Cent' by Brand Nubian.

I have my own personal take on this dynamic and the percentages involved.

First off, there are those who like to think of themselves as the 'elite' class. This is the smallest of the three groupings by number. These are individuals with an advanced understanding of the occult – knowledge of the human psyche and how it operates, and how it, in turn, interacts with the rest of Creation. These people have studied the nature of reality, and understand how consciousness – and the applied Will of the individual – can help shape the reality that is experienced both on an individual, and a collective basis, if properly applied.

Unfortunately for everyone else, this group is not out for the upliftment and advancement of all humanity. They do not serve Creation and the force that most would refer to as 'God.' They are steeped in their own ego-consciousness, and see themselves as 'gods,' and therefore superior to those who do not belong to their group.

This is what lies at the root of satanism, which, in its widest sense, is *not* about an entity called 'the devil,' or dancing around a fire in robes and sacrificing chickens in forests at three in the morning, but refers to absolute service-to-self. Satanism took its name from the Hebrew, (and rendered in Arabic as *shatain*,) meaning 'adversary,' or 'opposer.' This infers that it opposes the one true Creator, and the morality of Natural Law. It maintains that the individual gets to decide their own interpretation of right and wrong, that any one individual's take on it is just as valid as the next man's, and that nothing else matters but the appeasement of one's personal wants and desires. Moral relativism by any other name.

The 'elites' belonging to this group, believe that only their own kind are worthy of taking on occulted knowledge, and they go to great lengths to keep or distort truths from those outside of their circle. This group's arrogance is so deeply entrenched, that they even believe they will soon find ways of cheating physical death by making themselves immortal, which is where the insanity of Transhumanism and futurism lies, with its ideas of humans being able to upload their consciousness into a computer for later downloading into an upgraded body. This explains their obsession with these methods, and why depictions of them are so frequently encoded into music videos and movies and the like.

Most in this group are either primary or secondary psychopaths, and have been systematically bred to be that way. Their humanity and empathy towards others has been removed, usually through being subjected to mind-control or Satanic Ritual Abuse from early childhood. They remain mentally ill, spiritually corrupt, and something less than a well-balanced, authentic human being.

Only someone of this condition could perpetrate the activities that this class does – manipulating wars, devising false-flag 'terror' hoaxes, inventing the scams of the cancer industry, establishing the horrors of the meat industry, and so much else – without their conscience troubling them so much that they are incapable of continuing to be a part of it.

Second division: Defenders

The second group are increasing in number by the day, and are the real enemies of the first group. These are individuals who are coming to the same understandings about the nature of self and reality, our true power when our Will is engaged, and our inherent connectedness back to Creation. These truths, deliberately hidden from the masses, are now being widely understood, largely as a result of the internet. The worldwide web was initially developed as a tool for data-gathering and surveillance by the 'elite' class, but I would suggest this was their biggest tactical error ever, and that it has backfired on them majorly in terms of how the public has made it its own to share empowering information widely and quickly.

This book would not have been written had the internet not been in place, as I personally would not have gained access to any of the information within it. The controllers will not be able to shut the internet down, or even place major worldwide restrictions on its usage – much as they might like to – without *massive* resistance from the general public. There aren't many things that I believe would galvanise the masses out of their passivity and into revolution . . . but this is one. The generations populating the world today are privileged to have access to information on a scale never before seen in human history, and the opportunities for the evolution of their souls through taking on these great truths are truly profound.

In each case, it is the individual's free will consciousness that has spurred them on to embrace the truths to which they have been given access; they could just as easily have chosen to ignore it, (see Group 3 below.) As the researcher Crrow777 wrote in his on-line article 'Woke Up, Got Out Of Bed, Heard The Songs Inside My Head':

> *"The truth hurts – at first. Like anything else, once this knowledge is gained, you can accept it and begin to understand reality, or you can ignore it and go on as you always have. It comes down to choosing to accept your cell,' or choosing to change your current situation. After all, the control system can be described as a prison, but it is more accurately viewed as a prison for your mind. If you become aware you can then begin to seek freedom."*

The phrase 'where there's a will there's a way' didn't come about by accident.

This group's people are *not* obsessed with gaining control and power over their fellow humanity, and have the natural states of empathy, compassion and conscience in their rightful place. Although some will choose to sit on the information for their own personal empowerment, most in this number – having taken on these new understandings – will feel compelled to share what they have come to know with everyone they can reach with it. A common criticism of secret society and mystery school groups, is that they seek to sequester their teachings for themselves and to keep them hidden from the 'profane' masses, who they see as unworthy of taking them on. Truth is the gift of Creation to *all* humanity. Understanding it is the *right* of each individual, and *no-one* has the right to keep it deliberately hidden from others.

With Truth comes responsibility, and an individual taking on new understandings about the nature of this reality and our place in it, takes on also an *obligation* to communicate that truth as widely as possible. Never by force, but by using whatever methods they find effective to invite others – through their own free will – to embrace those same understandings.

Many hundreds of thousands are now observing this tenet. This process explains the phenomenal growth in human consciousness which is now taking place, (though happening nowhere near as rapidly as it needs to,) as well as the all-out assault by a desperate control system, now using every method at their disposal to halt it and keep the masses wallowing in ignorance.

Third division: Wanderers

The third group is the largest of all, and is in the crosshairs of each of the other two. This group comprises the vast majority of humanity. It is the masses who are still deeply entrenched in the ignorance of base consciousness. They are 'trapped in the Matrix,' as the popular truth community phrase goes – living in an illusory world which has been systematically made that way by the 'elite' controllers, with no comprehension that anything's amiss.

Unless we happen to be born into the world of the 'elites,' this is the group we all enter this reality being a part of. Through a programme which starts from the moment we leave the womb – through the indoctrination of the 'education' system, (which teaches only the Establishment's version of events,) and through entertainment, popular culture, and a calculatedly deceptive mainstream media – we are conditioned to perceive the insanity of this world and the way it's been made to be over thousands of years, as 'normal'.

We are taught, as a mass herd, that war, death and suffering are necessary and "just the way it goes." We're taught that we need an entity known as 'government,' (which literally means 'mind-control' when you get into the origins of the word,) to tell us what we can and can't do, and to punish us if we disobey their dictates, because we're incapable of organising our societies without them there to instruct us. We're taught that billions upon billions of animals must meet terrifying and brutal deaths in slaughterhouses because eating their corpses is just 'normal' and we can't live without it. (We can.)

We're taught that there's no other way to run a financial system other than having cartels of private bankers create imaginary 'money' out of thin air, then charge everyone else interest for its use.

We're taught that millions dying every year of cancer is just another of "those things," and that savage and harsh radiation and drug treatment, (which actually causes cancer in itself) is the only way to deal with it, because the natural, plant-based remedies provided by Creation are 'pseudo-science.' They *must* be, because a bunch of men in white coats with letters after their name, who studied at prestigious schools and so must be so much cleverer than us, tell us so.

We're taught that working all week and paying taxes for 50 years just to be able to afford to live in the places we call home, (but spend very little time occupying because we're so busy out earning the funds,) and to buy a load of 'stuff' from a bunch of corporations with tax attached – and raising new generations to grow up to do exactly the same – is the ultimate point of life. Then one day we die and go into oblivion, (and our families get taxed just a little bit more,) and that was it. That was your life. Thanks for coming. Close the door on the way out.

Battle of the souls

The first group have nothing but scathing contempt for those that populate the masses. They see them as base and profane, and wholly deserving of the spiritual darkness in which they dwell. As the speaker, researcher and activist Mark Passio, a former member of satanic groups before breaking out and committing himself to conveying liberating truths to the world, has revealed, the dark occultists refer to the general public as "the unbegun," or "the dead." They are seen as nothing more than flesh robots – a walking dead so lost in ignorance and removed from knowledge of their true spiritual nature, that they have not even begun their first baby steps towards true knowledge.

And this is the condition in which the few 'elite' controllers, working through their networks and groups, want to keep humanity rooted. They feed off the physical, mental and spiritual slavery of the masses. They need large numbers of people to keep their industries going, and to generate (illusory) profits and interest for the immoral monetary system which keeps just a few thousand of them in privilege and affluence, and the rest of us as indentured debt slaves.

A Wheel of Dharma, a concept representing the governing spiritual laws of all the universe.

https://commons.wikimedia.org/wiki/File:Wheel_of_Dharma.svg

Credit: DarkEvil

Large numbers of people 'waking up' to their true spiritual nature – as individuated aspects of Creation with infinite power to shape the reality we all wish to experience – is the control system's worse nightmare. As the late comedian George Carlin so astutely observed: "They don't want well-informed, well-educated people capable of critical thinking. They're not interested in that."

The last thing the controllers want, is for people in their millions to come to a deep understanding of Natural Law and the Law of Correspondence – that the thoughts, emotions and actions which humans put out into the world come back to us, and that if a society has been manipulated towards adopting a satanic mindset, putting themselves and their own selfish needs before the greater good of humanity, then the *whole* of society will experience the results of that consciousness reflected back to them in their everyday reality.

Death, suffering, hardship, injustice, immorality. Sound familiar at all? It's unfortunate that individuals who *do* take a personal responsibility towards understanding spiritual truths and applying them in their life, still have to reap the collective consequences of a society in which the vast majority do not, and therefore cause the negative results of their ignorance to be experienced by all. This process serves as a reminder of the old phrase 'no man is an island,' and that all humanity remains ultimately connected.

The flipside, though, is that if the same society *were* to come to a deep understanding of how, if we were to apply our thoughts, emotions and actions towards upholding the inherent spiritual rights of all, the *whole* of that society would experience *these* collective results instead. This really is the last truth that a force of malevolent controllers would ever want their human prey to take deeply within themselves, and it explains why they go to such great lengths to keep people stupid and docile through the many different methods they employ – from brain-eating food and drink additives like Aspartame, to the unseen ocean of unnatural wireless, microwave and electromagnetic frequencies that we now bathe in, to chemtrails, to moronic and spirit-sapping TV, movie and pop music – and all points in between.

I expanded upon this whole dynamic in the final chapter of 'Musical Truth 1,' and feel a comment included there from Mark Passio bears some useful repeating to help illustrate the point:

> *"The solution is so simple. It always has been. Don't treat others the way you yourself wouldn't want to be treated. State it that way and it becomes real unambiguous, and so simple that a child could figure it out.*
>
> *"You don't want to be harmed, defrauded, stolen from, raped, have your rights taken away? Don't do that to other people. Period. The end. It's so simple it's almost stupid, folks. It can't get any simpler than that, and yet humanity has proven we still can't grasp it, we still can't understand it, and we want the associated suffering and death that's going to come with refusing to live by that basic rule."*

My own take on these concepts was further articulated by the researcher and spiritual scholar Marty Leeds, when he guested on Greg Carlwood's 'The Higherside Chats' in January 2017:

> *"The Great Creator, The Great Spirit...didn't create earth to be a hell! Man, in my opinion, is put here, and we were given this gradation of experience to use our free will and our sovereignty to go through this spectrum of reality...*
>
> *"So every single second of every single day, we're given that choice between the extremes of good and evil. And we have to find balance within this scale. So I think, centre-ing the self, (not being self-centred,) is ultimately what the drama of the human experience is all about.*
>
> *"... Throw all the numbers out, throw all the language out, throw all the Bibles out, throw all the Qurans out, throw all that shit out. At the end of the day, when you cross the gates of death, your heart's going to be weighed. How light your heart was is what's going to count. And that, to me, is the true experience of God."*

The last bars in the prison

In the same way that the first group's very survival depends on keeping the third group in this state of spiritual imprisonment, so the only hope for the second group – and therefore humanity as a whole – is in influencing as many as possible to snap out of their mind-controlled trance and get on the battlefield.

As anyone who has ever engaged in this process will understand – and as many a futile chat thread argument has borne out – it ain't easy! The mind control of a lifetime runs very deep, to the point that most of humanity is engaged in a kind of societal Stockholm Syndrome. Things have been the way they are for so long – and it's all people have ever understood as 'normal' – that many will actually fight to ensure its continuation, and will viciously resist anyone who attempts to persuade them to change. Why get angry at the evil psychopaths making this world a living hell when, you can simply write off the person telling you about it as 'crazy?' No personal responsibility or effort required there, then. Phew, that was close!

Most people, it seems, are not of a level of consciousness that allows them to even *envisage* any kind of change. At the same time, the satanic mindset has been so deeply and successfully implanted, that they cannot see beyond their own individual and immediate needs, and the personal sacrifices that may be required to transform human society into a better version of itself, are too much for them to consider. It can often seem pointless, therefore, for those who have resolved to communicate truths. Certainly, it can seem like they are banging their heads against a brick wall with certain individuals who are not having any of it, and have clearly chosen to live out an entire human lifetime in base ignorance.

American writer and broadcaster Sonia Barrett offered some perspectives on this during her 'Good Vibrations' interview with me:

> *"I think that it really boils down to the journey, the experience, that each character or individual or being came into this life for. To play the role of a certain character requires certain kinds of experiences... You either come in as a bit more aware, a bit more awake, or you come in really, what we define as asleep... And then there are those that go completely against the grain.*
>
> *"Some people get triggered by one thing or another, and they get really curious. And then, you have people who will stone you for trying to wake them up! They don't want to hear it. It's 'don't wake me up, this is the dream I'm having, and I don't want to know all of that, because it would take me away from whatever my character is right now. If I wake up I can't play that role I've been playing, so leave me alone'!"*

Just as trying to reach certain individuals is an exercise in futility, therefore, there will be others who *will* be receptive to new information which resonates with them, and a new path awaits should the right trigger give them that initial boost that they need. It's with people of this status that the real work lies. Reaching a critical mass of the population who wilfully embrace and apply spiritual truth is something that has to happen sooner rather than later. The question that remains is whether those on the path will succeed in influencing the rest of humanity while there's still time, and before the increasingly desperate controllers get to put the final bars in place for the New World Order prison they have planned for us... and are getting dangerously close to completing.

Joe Atwill mused on the crucial nature of time being the deciding factor on episode 51 of the 'Unspun' podcast:

> *"Really, history is hinged on this one moment. We have been under mind control, under fake history, for hundreds of years. The oligarchs are unified; they control the media, they control the financial system, they own the government. But they don't own the internet, and the citizen researcher is starting to make inroads into the minds of the population.*
>
> *"And we have a better case to make, because so many people are starting to say, 'well, wait a minute, I'm being poisoned, the democratic elected representatives seem to be working with the banks, not with me. I'm poor every year. My family's shattered. There's pornography everywhere. What the hell is going on? 'The population is sceptical.*
>
> *"So if the internet stays open another couple of years, I honestly don't think they're going to be able to shut it off."*

Getting on the playing field

We need more leaders, not followers. If the information in this book has spoken to you and inspired you, become a teacher yourself. It's the Each One Teach One process. I concur with what Mark Passio has articulated on several occasions – that the most satisfying response a researcher can get from a listener or reader of their work is not: "Thank you for what you do. Your information has helped me understand things so much better now," but: "Thank you for what you do. Your information has made me realise that *I* need to get out in the field myself, and make *my own* personal contribution, and I will now be doing that." For as long as all the work is left to a comparative handful of individuals, the transformation that needs to take place will not happen. We just don't have the numbers.

As Passio himself put it during his provocatively-titled 'Fake Ass Christians' presentation in Philadelphia in June 2017:

> *"If the so-called Christians and so-called truth movement focused their grass roots efforts and resources into a worldwide campaign to teach the truth of universal, cosmic, moral Natural Law to everyone... think how many people could be reached with a message of self-improvement, conscience, and freedom. For everyone to know the truth of Natural Law will truly make us free."*

When I first 'woke up,' I was naive enough to assume that, by pooling my consciousness with other like-minded individuals on the same path, we could actually shake off the chains of this control system within my lifetime. Getting drunk and giddy on well-meaning intent is a common symptom of those first piercing the veil of the Matrix. I've found, however, that as time goes on, it brings with it a spiritual maturity and a sense of sober realism, and I've come to realise that, of course, it will take way, way longer than just the next few decades to see any real, positive change play out. It's far more likely that – if it *does* happen – it will be many, many generations into the future before the results can be truly felt and enjoyed.

For many, therefore, this realisation might make the process of trying to effect change in this lifetime seem futile. Those of us alive today can expect only to spend the rest of our days toiling away with ever-increasing obstacles placed in our path.

The first thing to remember for those of us who have children, however, is that it's our descendants – who will carry our DNA and may look just like us – who will have to live in the nightmare world that's planned, if those of us who are conscious enough to understand the game, don't do whatever we can <u>now</u>. What if our own ancestors had had the opportunities that we now have, but they'd squandered the chance to do what needed to be done, either through laziness, cowardice, or a sense of "it's futile, so why even try?" If we and our children were now living a worldwide concentration camp straight out of

Orwell's '1984,' in absolute servitude to slavemasters, and with no prospect of ever breaking free – how would we feel about the generation that could have helped prevent it, but didn't?

In this regard, a truly thought-provoking movie to take in, is 2012's 'Cloud Atlas' from the Wachowskis, the same team that brought us the 'Matrix' trilogy and 'V For Vendetta.' (By way of a caveat, the Wachowskis are industry insiders who wouldn't have been allowed to make such high-profile movies if they weren't playing the game, and the sex-change operation of Larry to Lara Wachowski, appears to be directly out of the Transgender Agenda 101 handbook. But either way, this film – like their others – conveys great spiritual truths, and presumably the fact that it does, is all part of the 'Revelation of the Method' which the 'elites' seem to feel duty-bound to observe in their various activities.)

'Cloud Atlas,' based on the book by David Mitchell, tells the story of several characters reincarnated through six timelines. The tagline for the movie's promotion was: "An exploration of how the actions of individual lives impact one another in the past, present and future, as one soul is shaped from a killer into a hero, and an act of kindness ripples across centuries to inspire a revolution." The tagline seems to have been inspired by the celebrated "what we do in life ripples through eternity" quote from the Roman Emperor Marcus Aurelius.

The narrative reminds us that the actions we choose to take in one lifetime, can have ramifications affecting others – and the very course of human history itself – in either a positive or negative way. By way of example, the character played by Tom Hanks in the first story, is a morally corrupt doctor who seeks to poison his charge and steal his possessions. A couple of generations on, his soul is already seeking to redeem itself for its past actions, as he has become a whistleblower revealing secrets about a defective nuclear power plant, which may pose grave threats to human life if not heeded. He pays for his good deeds by being assassinated by his enemies.

By the final timeframe, much of humanity has gone to live on off-world colonies, (it's fiction, remember!,) the earth having undergone some unstated disaster, (nuclear, maybe?) which has rendered it largely unfit to live upon. This latest incarnation of Hanks' soul has to overcome superstitious fear to provide a vital role in connecting the remaining human population with the new colonies.

The journey of the Hanks character's soul shows how, through learning from past mistakes and resolving to redeem them, we can spiritually evolve, and have a wide-reaching transformative effect on the shared experience of all. His story is contrasted with that of favourite Wachowski actor Hugo Weaving. Through the six timeframes, we see *his* soul *regress* through the choices that he makes. He starts out as a slave trader, ending up so far devolved, that he's become some kind of demonic entity and isn't even human any more. It could have turned out so differently if his free will choices had been better made. But they weren't, and so it is what it is.

I've not come across any other story which shines light so well on what our souls come to this place we call home for – and the way that consequentialism works – and I recommend at least two or three viewings of 'Cloud Atlas' to get the full impact of its message. I am, however, reminded of the final episode of the BBC's uncharacteristically excellent 'Ashes To Ashes' drama, in which the audience finally discovers that its ragtag mob of troubled cops are in fact dead, and have been living in some kind of purgatory between the physical world and the next. Philip Glenister's Gene Hunt character reveals that their world is "somewhere we go to sort ourselves out" – a cunning metaphor for the human experience, indicating some deep knowledge on the part of the show's creators.

Another great allegory, this one disguised as a mainstream comedy, is the 1993 movie 'Groundhog Day'. A sneering and cynical TV weatherman played by Bill Murray, is made to live out the same tedious day over and over, with no escape from the cycle until he learns how to improve his relationships with others. There's little doubt that what the film's makers were communicating, was how our own lives are like the day in question, and getting the point of *why* we're living them, is the key to escaping the prison. It's what Michael Jackson was referring to in the lyrical sentiments of his 'Man In The Mirror.'

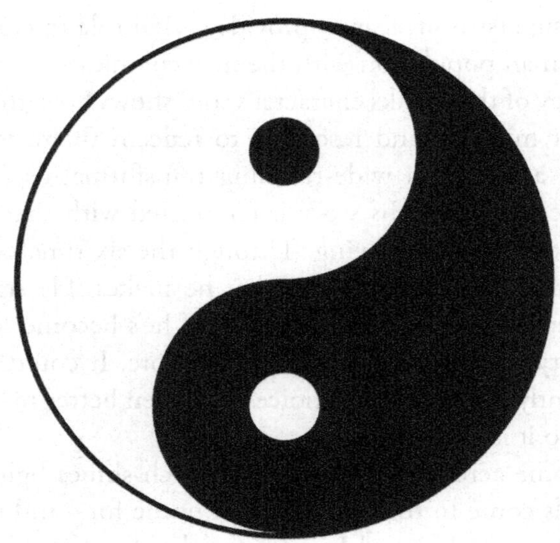

The Ying Yang symbol, reflecting the intertwined duality of all things in nature

https://commons.wikimedia.org/wiki/File:Yin_yang.svg

Credit: Gregory Maxwell

Whether any one individual has children or not, it becomes a moral responsibility to communicate truth to others once they've come to understand it, and to resist evil as far as it's within their capability to do so. Each of us is a spirit-soul – an aspect of Creation – before we make the choice, in our higher selves, to incarnate into this realm of existence and go through these experiences that we call 'life.' We forget this fact when we are born, of course, which is all part of the 'game' that we consented to participate in. If we remembered, we would not go through the situations our individual souls need – usually through several human lifetimes – to evolve and grow.

There are factors at play in this reality which contribute to the experiences we undergo. These include the apparent 'physicality' of matter, the passage of what we think of as 'time' – and the ageing and eventual death of our bodies that it brings – our attachment to ego consciousness, the need to eat, drink and sleep, the light and heat of the sun, the dualities of night and day, cold and hot, the fears and phobias we undergo, pain, emotions and even fetishes. None of these criteria exist in the spirit realm, but they form a vital infrastructure here, in order that we can be bound by their workings, and therefore gain the experiences that we need.

It *is* possible to come to this understanding during our lifetimes, however – particularly in the times in which we are living right now. The truth about all things *can* now be known by any individual with the mental capacity to process the information, and – most importantly – the Will to *want* to know.

This is why, when people first hear that they're not discovering their true spiritual nature for the first time, but they're having this higher-self aspect triggered by *remembering* who they really are, it resonates so much. Suddenly, the path that we're meant to be treading during our time here becomes so much clearer. Those responding to this process find themselves led by intuition, by a higher *knowing* of where they're supposed to be. Intuitive *knowing* trumps intellectual and 'logical' thought every time, because it represents our direct connection back to Creation.

One act, many impacts

The nature of contribution that any one individual can make will differ from person to person, of course. Not everyone is cut out to write books and host radio shows, in the same way that there are so many things that I'm woefully hopeless at doing, (my house won't be featured on any DIY TV specials any time soon, as my wife will wearily confirm, and I won't be winning any sporting trophies.) So I don't waste my time trying to get better at those. I recognise that *my* time and resources are best spent on activities to which *I* feel naturally drawn. Large numbers of others need to respond to the same calling, and, having understood the nature of the problems that humanity faces, to identify ways in which *they* can be an essential cog in the wheel of change.

A meme which I created for my public talks a while back, reads: "One person can't change the world, but they can be an essential component in the process that can."

I often expand upon it by asking people to imagine a dejected, disillusioned individual sitting alone at home, appreciating the world's problems at the hands of a malevolent control system, but lamenting that: "I'm just one soul. What difference can I possibly make?"

Now, picture a million, or ten million, or 100 million other individuals in *exactly* the same situation, all sitting at home saying the same thing. When you now envisage all these people pooling their positive intent in the same direction – and instead of regretting their lack of effectiveness, resolving to do whatever they can do to bring about a better existence, regardless of how little those around them might seem to be doing – now you have an entirely different potential future waiting to be played out.

The Transhumanist/ AI nightmare is the biggest threat facing humanity in these times at the hands of mentally-ill maniacs like Ray Kurzweil and Elon Musk. Those who have pierced the veil and can see this madness for what it truly is, need to extricate themselves from the control system in any way they can. It's small gestures which will lead the way here, such as opting to avoid surveillance-laden smart phones, smart TVs and smart meters, (or anything else with 'smart' in the name for that matter,) and choosing the supermarket checkout still manned by a human being, rather than the robot self-serve machines.

We should use cash rather than electronic currency while we still can. Opting to use old-school paper maps and to keep the skill of navigation alive, over having GPS systems instruct us in where to go, is another great way of asserting our individuality, and of symbolically telling the architects of the would-be AI future where they can stick it.

Microchips and any kind of bodily implants, however seductively they're marketed, are a big 'no' for anyone vaguely awake and aware. The same goes for human health-damaging vaccines. These acts all seem trivial in isolation, but large numbers of people making their individual choice not to take them, would throw a major spanner in the works in terms of getting the desired Transhumanist infrastructure fully in place. We need more spanners.

I find it deeply ironic that these very sentiments were articulated by none other than Mrs. Betty Battenberg, (you know her better as the Queen of England, well, Germany,) during her 2016 Christmas message. You'd struggle to find a better poster child for this system of human enslavement, so you have to wonder whether these words were spoken as a form of mockery, or whether it was another rendering of 'placing the truth in plain sight.' Either way – and I never thought I'd hear myself saying this – the Queen spoke eternal truth when she stated:

> *"Even with the inspiration of others, it's understandable that we sometimes think the world's problems are so big that we can do little to help. On our own, we cannot end wars or wipe out injustice. But the cumulative impact of thousands of small acts of goodness can be bigger than we imagine."*

(It's very tempting for me to make further comments about references to 'wars' and 'injustice' coming from the figurehead of an empire with a personal wealth reckoned to be in the trillions . . . but I'll refrain!)

Many survivors of near-death experiences, along with spiritual mediums, speak of the 'life review' which awaits each of us as we exit our bodies at 'death,' and go back to the spirit-source from which we all came. This is where we relive all the experiences we ever went through during the lifetime that has just passed, all revisited simultaneously, (because there is no passing of 'time' outside of this realm of existence.) It's said that we experience the results of the free will choices we made with regard to our behaviours, from the perspectives of those they affected, (because, ultimately, all living things are connected.) I can't imagine the life review of a despotic dictator, a murderous eugenicist or a slaughterhouse operative will be much of a picnic in that regard.

Keeping this in mind can be very effective in influencing the daily decisions that we make, therefore. It can also be challenging to question; if we were to 'die' unexpectedly this very day and re-experience everything we did with the life that we just went through – would we be proud of what we did with our time here? Or would we be filled with regret that we had squandered opportunities, and had spent too much time catering selfishly to our own egos?

If we're honest with ourselves, I feel most of us would gravitate towards the second option, I certainly would. Bringing this dynamic to mind every now and again can be a powerful tool in navigating you back to the path you know you need to be on, I often find. Though the music style isn't my cup of tea, this process of considering the net worth of your time on earth is summed up strikingly in the lyrics to 'The Ballad of Accounting' by Ewan MacColl, (Kirsty's Dad,) and Peggy Seeger. I highly recommend a look at the lyrics, which can be viewed in full through the link at the end.

The Last Generation

It's very grounding to realise that the generation of adults alive today, is the one which will determine whether humanity gets steered into the nightmare trap that's been prepared for it, or whether it will finally take the reins towards freedom which remain the alternative option, (but only just.) The analogy I always keep in mind is of humankind in a prison cell. The iron door has almost been slammed shut, and once it has, it's game over. There's still a very small gap before it gets locked into place, however – just enough to jam a foot in to prevent it from closing completely.

Will we jam that foot?

We are the last generation to retain some living memory of how things used to be in a time before the digital smart grid and daily Chemtrail bombardments. Once we're gone, that connection back to slightly more sane times goes too, which is why so much effort is being invested in mind-controlling today's young people who will replace the Last Generation. The outstanding YouTube user known as Dayz of Noah, summed up this scenario incisively in the opening lines to his video 'How Media Shaped The Generations: Radio and the Teenager:'

> *"For many years, youth culture creation has been a forerunner in Western civilisation engineering. The younger generation of any given time represents the influential group of the future. Therefore, these generations of youth – in order to ensure civilisation follows the intended direction – must be, and always have been, conditioned and inculcated via culture . . . "*

This is why in the UK, the state broadcasting institution that is the BBC, has been pitching its flagship radio station, Radio 1, at ever younger audiences. Its official remit now states its target audience begins at 15 years of age, and that, "it should also provide some programming for younger teenagers." The station, working in tandem with other broadcasters such as Kiss FM and Capital Xtra – who, ultimately, are all owned and controlled by a shockingly small number of corporations as a result of many years of consolidation – bombards its audience with 'the official version of everything' – re-packaging mainstream news (lies) for a younger listenership, playing music whose lyrics deal with themes of cultural debasement, and pushing the latest technological gadgets as something "great" and aspirational.

Considering things this way enforces the crucial importance of what happens in the next couple of decades. I can't help recalling the lyrics to Tina Turner's 1985 hit 'We Don't Need Another Hero,' (the video to which, appropriately, depicted a nightmare dystopian landscape as if to emphasise the point!)

> *"We are the children, the last generation…*
>
> *"And I wonder when we are ever gonna change?"*

Only those of us alive today can make that decision.

Let's make it a wise one.

Resources:

The Queen's Christmas message 2016: full transcript:

- http://www.mirror.co.uk/tv/tv-news/watch-queens-annual-christmas-message-9512643

Crrow777: Woke up, got out of bed, heard the songs inside my head:

- https://www.crrow777radio.com/woke-up-got-out-of-bed-heard-the-songs-inside-my-head/

Lyrics to 'The Ballad of Accounting' by Ewan MacColl and Peggy Seeger:

- https://genius.com/Ewan-maccoll-and-peggy-seeger-the-ballad-of-accounting-lyrics

APPENDIX 1

LOVESEXY TO SPOOKY ELECTRIC

Sin, redemption and rebirth in the music of Prince. An essay by Dan Monroe.

> *"That's when you find out that you're better off making sure your soul's alright."*
>
> *Prince: 'Money Don't Matter 2 Night' (1991)*

The popular music industry's trend of embracing the signs, symbols and motifs of ancient mystery schools, fraternal orders, or – as dubbed by some – the satanic, has become easy to spot by alternative and mainstream journalists alike. Its proliferation – so intense and noticeable that it is even self-referenced by those same artists who, whether seriously or jokingly, align themselves with these ancient groups and their symbolism – supports the idea that those same groups are the hidden rulers of world or, somewhat less dramatically, the influencers and dictators of society.

Another trend which has emerged in the output of popular music, and coinciding with the rise in occult themes, is the increase in musical, lyrical and visual content that displays lewd and lascivious material, hyper-sexualised imagery, and undertones of violence and corruption. Materialistic ideals are also widely promoted.

It could also be argued that contemporary popular music suffers from a lack of contextual awareness, in which issues of politics, social injustice, war and terror, are not readily addressed in the way they were so vociferously by artists in the 1960s and '70s.

To the untrained eye, it appears that some of these themes are relatively new phenomena. But as some researchers have called attention to occult and sexual imagery in music, they have started to revisit music history only to discover the same themes recurring – though somewhat more discreetly – in the work of some of pop music's greatest icons.

The Beatles, the Rolling Stones and Led Zeppelin have featured prominently in studies of the occult in popular music, and the great icons of the 1980s that were Michael Jackson and Madonna, have been dissected for not only what their output indicated, but also their intimate, complex relationships with the music business itself.

Little or nothing has been written about Jackson's and Madonna's great contemporary rival Prince Rogers Nelson, however.

A dynasty begins

The prodigal virtuoso signed to Warner Brothers aged just 17, and went on to create an incredible catalogue, as well as to become one of the most enigmatic musical personalities of the last thirty years. He is known not only for the content of his music, but for his complex relationship with the industry and the press.

From the peak of his commercial success in the 1980s, when he was arguably one of the biggest music stars in the world, his notoriety and presence in the public consciousness slowly slipped away in the 90s, due to a series of conflicts with the music industry and his place within it.

Notoriously reclusive, there are few of Prince's opinions on public record, and – as stated by Mica Paris in her narration of the BBC radio bio 'Prince: A Purple Reign' – to truly understand his world view, you must study his music.

This essay seeks to study the music, the imagery and the symbolism of Prince, and to look for clues that might lead to interesting revelations about the influence of mystery school teachings on his work. Given Prince's level of fame, if the arguments for occult influence in the music industry are true, we may well see it reflected in his work. If not the occult, then we will discuss what is revealed by Prince's music, focusing primarily on the period that was the peak of his commercial and popular success in the 80s.

Prince was a man who could well be accused of laying the foundations of the sexual revolution in music that we see today. From his hypersexual lyrics and imagery – in songs, on stage and in music videos – he was chief among the artists cited as the catalyst for the first Parental Advisory stickers on album covers. His lyrical content included depictions of oral sex, masturbation, sexually dominant characters both male and female, and even incest, all while maintaining a semi-androgynous visage which hinted at homosexuality in both genders.

Frame that against the backdrop of an increasingly conservative US and Britain, (with both Reagan and Thatcher in charge,) and it's easy to see why Prince would name his 1983 album 'Controversy.' There was a contradiction here, wound up in all of the sexual darkness. Proclamations of love and deep spirituality were resonant in the music, as well as numerous concerns about the state of the world, and the strong notion that society was on the brink of Apocalypse and self-destruction.

Using Prince's own terminology, he was clearly aware of the antagonistic conflicts within his own music. What is revealed by his output, is an inner conflict between spirituality and love, and the forces of darkness.

Like other artists before him, such as George Clinton's Parliament/ Funkadelic, he created his own personal mythology within his music through 1988's 'Lovesexy.' On this album, (which will be discussed in greater detail later), he presents a spiritual battle between the forces of light -= characterised as the eponymous "Lovesexy" – and the forces of darkness, called 'Spooky Electric.' The content serves as the most obvious example of the same battle played out through his musical output, both before and after the album. This essay will argue that the "battle" was not just an internal personal struggle, but one which he projected on his understanding of the wider world around him.

Prince's output began in 1978 with the release of his first album, 'For You,' a collection of short R&B songs which did not make much of an impact, apart from displaying the exceptional range of Prince's mastery of musical instruments.

However, lurking on the inside sleeve, was the start of a recurrent theme in his imagery – nudity. There is an image of Prince naked on the bed, his "modesty" covered by a conveniently-placed acoustic guitar. The nudity would be carried over into his second album, entitled 'Prince,' which would present him naked from the waist up, and straddling a white horse with wings.

This is most clearly a reference to the Greek mythological character and astrological constellation Pegasus, often associated with aspiration to the heights of accomplishment – certainly something reflective of Prince and his goals to ascend to the top of the music industry. It could also be argued, however, that this was merely pretentious imagery chosen by a callow 21-year-old discovering his musical and personal identity.

Of more interest in terms of his musical content, the album 'Prince' would indicate his future trademark direction with more sexually-charged lyrics in songs such as 'I Wanna Be Your Lover' and 'Sexy Dancer.' While these songs seem minor forays into explicit content, the track 'Bambi' reveals a darker edge to Prince's work. Representing the author's desire to engage in sexual relations with a lesbian, he argues that Bambi should renounce her sexuality, because only a man can deliver the sexual satisfaction required.

Semi-homophobic attitudes aside, Prince goes further:

"Bambi – I know what U need, Bambi – maybe U need 2 bleed."

In a lyric that probably disturbs more in a politically sensitive environment, the suggestion that rough penetrative sex is a cure for female homosexuality, still sits uncomfortably today. It represents a step into an even darker moral abyss that Prince would explore in his next LP.

'Dirty Mind' is the album that is generally acknowledged to have announced that Prince was going to be a major musical force. Its unique blend of New Wave and Punk Rock – fused with Prince's R&B and funk heritage – began to establish his reputation as a potential 'next big thing.'

It is also Prince's most controversially-charged album, with lyrics and imagery encompassing a large swathe of taboos. It introduced a political and social consciousness in the artist's work, that would contrast against the darker sexual overtones throughout his first twenty years of recordings.

The album cover is one of the most provocative of the period: Prince, dressed in a flasher-style overcoat with bikini brief underwear and thigh-high stockings, is probably the most unsubtle representation of androgyny in music history. This blending of the male and female – through costume, appearance, songwriting and symbolism – is another major theme. The black-and-white colour scheme and barbed-wire scratching on the front cover, serve to reinforce the punk stylings of this album.

On the inner sleeve, Prince is back on the bed – not naked this time, but equally provocative in the bikini-and-stocking combination. The songs cover a mass of lurid material, from the title track, in which the artist simply wants to take his latest conquest "in his Daddy's Car", to 'When U Were Mine,' in which his lover was so unfaithful that, "she didn't have the decency to change the sheets."

Finally, there is the unambiguous 'Head', in which Prince steals a bride on her wedding day, ejaculates on her dress, then proceeds to give her oral sex "morning, noon and night." Prince addresses his most controversial subject in 'Sister,' however, and suggests the cause of his sexual proclivities:

"My sister never made love to anyone else but me,

She's the reason for my sexuality.

She showed me where it's supposed to go, a blow-job doesn't mean blow,

Incest is everything it's said to be."

While most critics suggest that the material is not auto-biographical, given the political climate of the time, ('Dirty Mind' was released the year Ronald Reagan was elected,) it appears Prince was deliberately positioning himself in a controversial stance that would antagonise a progressively conservative society. Unique to his record deal with Warner Brothers, he had a large amount of control over his output, so the blame for this material seems to sit largely at the artist's own feet.

However, given that Prince was on the third album in a contract, and had yet to deliver a serious commercial reward, the faith shown in him and his extremes on 'Dirty Mind' was remarkable. It seems hard to believe that Warners did not understand this controversial positioning, and were happy to exploit it and see where it would lead.

As mentioned, 'Dirty Mind' would also mark the start of a nascent political/ social commentary in Prince's work. On the final track, 'Partyup,' he argues for a 'revolutionary rock and roll', and seems to be arguing against making young people fight for American foreign policy:

"They got the draft, uh-huh. I just laugh.

Party up. Fightin' war is a such a fucking bore.

Party up."

After all of these lurid encounters, Prince ends the album with the somewhat under-developed, yet earnest, "you're gonna have to fight your own damn war, 'cause we don't wanna fight no more." As simplistic as the lyric is, it would begin to point to another lyrical direction juxtaposed against the more sexual themes. Both would be controversial and – given the title of the next album – it seems that Prince was fully aware of the direction he was taking.

Cultivating controversy

1982's 'Controversy' saw Prince move away from the raw New Wave rock sound that defined 'Dirty Mind,' and towards a more electronically funk-focused album, which would remain influential in dance music for years to come. The title track laid the foundations for a personal creed; as music critic Paul Gambaccini described in a documentary, "a sort of 'pan-sexuality."

"I just can't believe, all the things people say. Controversy.

"Am I black or white? Am I straight, or gay? Controversy."

And later in the track:

"Listen, people call me rude, I wish we all were nude,

I wish there was no black and white, I wish there were no rules."

In the context of occultism, with the last line of this song in mind, it is worth bringing up Aleister Crowley, whose infamy seems intertwined with the fate of late 20th century pop music, and still reverberates to this day. From his inclusion on the Beatles' 'Sgt. Pepper' album cover, to Jimmy Page of Led Zeppelin buying his Scottish house; from David Bowie and Ozzy Osbourne both directly referencing him in song, to the recently (mysteriously) deceased Peaches Geldof, who claimed membership of the Ordo Templi Orientis mystical order which he founded, Crowley has had a strong influence on some of rock music's most famous names.

Clearly, Crowley displayed vast interest in the occult teachings and writings of the mystery schools, tied into a personal philosophy encompassed by the phrase, "Do what thou wilt." This ethos, (most recently brought to public attention by Jay Z,) summarises another area of Crowley's lifestyle – his libertine sexual experimentation of all types, but particularly, sexual ritual or sex magick. Prince's creed of "I wish there were no rules" best describes his view of sex as a liberating force and, like Crowley, a life philosophy.

Indeed, we only have to wait until the next track on 'Controversy,' titled 'Sexuality,' for Prince to clarify this standpoint:

> *"Stand up everybody, this is your life,*
>
> *Let me take you to another world, let me take you tonight.*
>
> *You don't need no money, you don't need no clothes, the second coming, anything goes.*
>
> *Sexuality is all you'll ever need, Sexuality, let your body be free.*
>
> *C'mon everybody, yeah, this is your life, I'm talking about a revolution, we gotta organise.*
>
> *We don't need no segregation, we don't need no race, New Age revelation, I think we got a case."*

In Prince's world, anything goes via letting your body succumb to its sexual instincts. But 'Controversy' points to the other side of his concerns with the inequality of the world.

In 'Sexuality,' it is important to pick up on the "New Age revelation." The New Age and a new breed leader, are important concepts when looking at the mystery schools and the occult, both of which deal with the creation of a new world. Some have argued that this might be a call for a Luciferian worldview – that is, a new world free of religious and social inhibitions – which makes it all the more interesting that Prince would deal with the concept of an Antichrist on the album in the character of Annie Christian. Annie Christian = Antichrist?

Prince certainly does not celebrate it, laying the blame for John Lennon's and Ronald Reagan's shootings, and the deaths of black children in Atlanta in the early 1980s, on this Annie Christian individual, as well as calling her a "whore, looking for fun." We certainly see Prince putting some boundaries on what type of sexual freedoms are to be approved of, and which are not.

Reagan would get a second mention on 'Controversy' in the curious period piece 'Ronnie Talk to Russia,' as Prince begins to expand on the anti-war leanings hinted at on the previous album. He also addresses a subject that would become very important on his next album and resonate through his work for years to come, as he implores Ronnie to talk to Russia "before they blow up the world."

Armageddon dawns

'1999,' Prince's fifth studio album, marks a significant change in the artist's development for a number of reasons. It becomes his first commercial success, marking his first truly impactful singles and video airplay as the age of MTV arrives. Additionally, it is the first to feature the name of his band the Revolution, the first to feature lyrics on the inner sleeve, and the first which sees him choose symbolic imagery for the front cover, rather than a picture of himself. The title track, probably his most sonically-advanced to date, is ostensibly a party song about the end of the millennium, but plays into long-held fears about the date being associated with the Apocalypse, setting the stage for the ultimate party in the face of impending destruction:

"I was dreamin' when I wrote this, forgive me if it goes astray,

But when I woke up this mornin', could've sworn it was Judgement Day.

The sky was all purple, there were people runnin' everywhere,

Tryin' to run from the destruction, you know I didn't even care."

Prince would also warn us that "we can't run from revelation," mixing a biblical worldview with the fears of mutually-assured destruction. This was a period when antagonism was growing between the US and USSR after a period of relative Cold War thawing. This ostensibly Christian worldview was not the first time Prince would introduce a theological perspective to his music. The liner notes from 'Controversy' onward would "thank God" in the first line of his acknowledgements. The artist would openly acknowledge his Christian faith until 2001, when he was baptised as a Jehovah's Witness.

Much has been made in recent times of the symbols used by music artists, especially when linking occult ideas to the industry. When we examine the cover artwork previous to '1999,' we are treated to a feast of telling imagery. Interestingly, there are several symbols which are indicative of themes which Prince would explore in later albums, such as the 'Ban the Bomb' motif, which does have relevance to '1999' with its apocalyptic themes. This is directly referenced in the title track, when a child-like voice wonders "why does everyone have a bomb?" There is the sunrise, (the Dawn of a new day,) a ladder to a house in the clouds, and the traditional symbols for male and female – both separate and combined – which would become synonymous with the artist from this point on, (and an elaborate version of this symbol would represent his name for several years.)

The other symbol which stands out on the cover – and one to which Prince would return frequently – is the Eye of Horus. In Egyptian mythology, this is representative of the solar deity in its new-born state at the Dawn, (the origin of the word 'horizon.')

The Eye is one of the most easily-recognised occult symbols, largely through its placing atop the pyramid on the reverse of the American dollar bill. It has widespread use within secret societies, such as Freemasonry and the Order of the Golden Dawn. It is also the symbol of the Bavarian Illuminati, the origin of modern-day concepts of "the Illuminati" as a loose term to define a group of people practicing occult knowledge, with an agenda to control the world. Furthermore, it is sometimes referred to as "the All-Seeing Eye," denoting enlightenment and knowledge, and has astrological significance in the celebration of the newborn sun within mystery school teachings.

Here, on the '1999' cover, it appears twice in the holes of two of the 9s. It would be easy to dismiss these symbols as mere artistic egotism, had the artist not returned to this motif numerous times later in his career, as well as to the concept of the Dawn imagery.

One of the most oft-cited examples of occult influence on recorded music, is the Law of Reversal, or the use of backwards writing or speech. The phenomenon is well-known to even casual observers; even so, not much credence is given to it and, when it makes an appearance, it is usually written-off as some sort of drug-fuelled foolery.

In the world of magickal rites, however, reverse meanings are important for several reasons. One is the ability to communicate a message subliminally to the subconscious mind. Another is to convey an esoteric meaning within an exoteric one – usually as a sign of notification to other initiates of the hidden knowledge. There are two reversals on the cover of '1999;' in the 'i' of Prince's name is written "and the Revolution" in reverse, marking the first mention of the band name in any of his work to this point.

The second reversal is more telling: when the '1999' album is flipped 180 degrees, the 999 in 1999 becomes 666, and the number 1 is capped with a bulbous head which bears a striking resemblance to the male phallus. As with the Eye of Horus, phallic symbolism is prominent in Egyptian mythology, is representative of the rays of the sun impregnating the Earth, and is used in a symbolic sense to channel male sexual energy.

What does this all mean with regard to Prince's career? Sceptics are quick to proclaim that apparent occult symbolism used by music artists, amounts to nothing more than coincidence, or a desire for controversy. Is every eye on an album cover the Eye of Horus, they ask? Does every hand gesture bely that person's involvement in the occult, and so on?

It may well be a tough argument to lay every errant symbol at the door of deep-rooted occult leanings. But when we start to stack up the motifs and themes repeated throughout a particular artist's work – as compared to that of their contemporaries – important patterns do emerge.

So here we have Prince who, in his previous work, had displayed a tendency to push boundaries of a sexual nature, foreshadowing a move to greater sexual expression throughout the music industry. He also preaches against a certain type of capitalism, and argues for some sort of "revolution" to coincide with the Dawn of a "new breed" or "New Age." Along comes '1999' with its musical styles, themes, and sounds formatted for a mainstream audience, in tandem with the overt display of occult symbols on its cover.

This, his most successful record to date, would set the stage for the following album, one which would make Prince a bona-fide world superstar.

Deep purple

It is easy to forget now, 30 years-plus after the fact, how important an album, (and accompanying feature film,) 1984's 'Purple Rain' truly was. After six years and six albums, Warner Brothers had their faith in the potential of Prince realised with a record that was a multi-million seller worldwide, and yielding numerous number one singles. For a time, Prince was the only artist since the Beatles to hold the number one position for a single, an album and a movie simultaneously. Grammy Awards and Oscars followed, and Prince became the phenomenon he had always suggested he could be.

Though 'Purple Rain' is clearly one of Prince's most commercially-accessible albums, fusing a more palatable mainstream sound with his funk roots and electronic pioneering, it has considerably more lyrical and conceptual depth than '1999.' The opening sermon on 'Let's Go Crazy' set the tone, presenting an argument for a positive, spiritually-charged afterworld that we must bear in mind when the metaphorical "elevator tries 2 bring U down."

'When Doves Cry' would become one of Prince's most famous songs and his first US number one single, addressing the consequences of parental influence, and writing the narrative of the accompanying feature film. However, despite the increasing maturity in some of the lyrical content, Prince continues his reckless abandon when pushing the boundaries of sexual exploration – though in arguably a less gratuitous way than encountered in the earlier albums. 'Darling Nikki's graphic portrayal of an uninhibited "sex fiend," who "masturbates with a magazine," seduces the author, subjecting him to a dark sexual experience:

> *"She took me 2 her castle and I just couldn't believe my eyes,*
>
> *She had so many vices, everything that money could buy.*
>
> *She said 'sign ur name on the dotted line,'*
>
> *The lights went out, and Nikki started 2 grind . . . "*

The song would later achieve infamy at the hands of Tipper Gore, wife of future presidential candidate Al Gore. She founded the Parents Music Resource Center, which led to the use of Parental Advisory stickers on album covers, when she caught her 11-year-old daughter listening to the song. It would later be covered by many other artists, including the Foo Fighters and "Princess of the Illuminati" Rihanna, on her 2011 tour.

There is an interesting post-script to 'Darling Nikki,' however, and one which could indicate a great many concepts, according to Prince's sound engineer Susan Rogers. On the aforementioned BBC radio documentary 'Purple Reign,' she indicates a desire on the part of Prince to balance the dark with the light using the Law of Reversal. The frantic guitar strains at the song's finale fade into eerie wind and rain sounds with a vocal which, it soon becomes clear, is a backwards recording. When reversed, the message reveals itself to be: "Hello, how are you? Fine. Fine, 'cause I know that the Lord is coming soon, coming soon, coming soon."

Rogers, (no relation to Prince,) was convinced that this was a purposeful attempt to offset the darkness inherent in the song. When viewed from an occult perspective, though, it becomes more entrancing. First, it's a piece of recorded music tracked backwards, as (it's argued) Led Zeppelin and the Beatles did with 'Stairway to Heaven' and 'Strawberry Fields Forever' respectively. The idea is that when certain songs are played backwards, they would reveal dark, satanically-inspired messages, and create dissonant and mysterious sounds.

Prince turns each concept on its head; he reverses the music, but maintains an angelic, yet eerie sound, followed by a spiritually positive message as the reversal reveals itself. Could this be a statement purposely damning other artists' negative uses of the occult?

Additionally, the message is concerned with the 'second coming of Jesus Christ,' which, as we have seen from some of Prince's earlier work, is tied to his concept of the New Age. On the face of it, the Second Coming appears to reflect a distinctly straightforward Christian perspective. When combined with his earlier themes of a New Age revolution leader, however – plus the Dawn and other astro-theological hints – perhaps the coming referred to here is the sun born under the New Age.

This 'coming' was also declared as a striking innuendo earlier in 'Let's Go Crazy,' the track closing with the artist breathlessly declaring 'he is coming,' multiple times. If we suspect that Prince himself did not understand the power of the hidden message, he confirmed it in one of his few press interviews during this period. In 'Rolling Stone' magazine, he told Neal Karlen in 1985 that: "I've always had hidden messages, and I always will."

The concept of the new leader, the death of the old world, and the Dawn of the new, would come to a head in the title track of the album, and the one with which he is still most closely associated. 'Purple Rain' is an eight-minute guitar-based epic, full of emotive and melancholic chord progressions, and remains one of the most iconic songs of the 1980s. It is also the track that most directly references events in the accompanying movie. Indeed, when discussing the meaning of the song, the most commonly-held theory is that each of the verses directly addresses the key relationships of Prince's character in the film. The first verse concerns his parents; the second his lover; and the third, his band, with all of whom he struggles throughout the film, and with all of whom he reconciles through the playing of that song.

It is interesting to see another statement making its first appearance on Prince's sleeve liner notes with 'Purple Rain.' At the end of the acknowledgements, he would sign off with the message, 'May U Live 2 the Dawn,' and would continue to do so until the 1990s.

The significance of "the Dawn" is interesting, particularly considering Prince's growing concern with a potential Apocalypse, and earlier calls for "a revolution" and a "new-breed leader." The Dawn is of significance in Masonic and Communist writings – especially when one considers the astro-theological roots of many modern religions, and Christianity in particular.

The Dawn that is referred to in such literature, and quite possibly here by Prince, is the Dawn of a New Age, the precessional passing of the sun from one astrological star sign to another that occurs approximately every 2,160 years. Musicians in the 60s were already suggesting that the 'Age of Aquarius' was upon us, and – however trite we may think this 'New Age' to be – the astro-theological importance to the occult mystery schools is vast. One such fraternity is another Crowley-linked society – the Order of the Golden Dawn.

It is also significant that the Da'wn of a New Age ties into exoteric understandings of this Dawn being associated with the end of the world, and notions of the impending destructive Apocalypse over which Prince seemed to obsess. Indeed, the 'purple skies' of '1999' had already set up the association between that colour and the theme of Armageddeon. It seems that the third verse of 'Purple Rain' may see Prince leading us into some sort of post-death heavenly state. If we remain in doubt as to the meaning, then one of the few public insights from Prince himself, attributed to him by the 'New Musical Express,' should elucidate:

> *"When there's blood in the sky – red and blue = purple. Purple Rain pertains to the end of the world, and being with the one you love, and letting your faith/ God guide you through the Purple Rain."*

Ironically, if 'Purple Rain' the song is transitioning between the death of an old world and the start of a new, the album would mark a significant turnaround in Prince's work. His critics have often remarked that he would 'reject' his success from this album onwards, by abandoning the rock-funk fusion so critical to its success, in favour of alternative styles, including psychedelic, baroque, jazz and R&B.

What is more interesting is the framing of his previous thematic concerns – sexual freedoms, apocalyptic fears, the Dawn of a New Age and a new breed – into a new context: the battle between a darker side, which almost always concerns the descent into sexual temptation, and a lighter side that is yearning for a spiritual awakening.

It is important here to discuss the sigil that has become most associated with Prince. Its earliest incarnation appeared on the '1999' album cover, and it would retain that format up to 1992's 'Love Symbol,' where it would be embellished to the format with which we are familiar now, and which would stand as the artist's legal name for seven years.

It is a combination of the shorthand symbols for the male gender, (a circle with a pointed arrow to the North-East,) and the female, (a circle with an arrow pointing south with a cross at the bottom.) In the Prince version, the arrow points South, with the arrow at the bottom and cross in the middle. In an exoteric understanding, the combination of male and female seems an obvious fit with Prince. His clothes, make-up, singing style and high-heeled boots all embrace the feminine, and some of his most famous songs are about powerful female protagonists, or express curiosity about female perspectives.

Prince also dons the guise of the phallic guitar-playing rock-and-roll Alpha-male protagonist – certainly a role he would play in real life, as a disciplined band leader marshalling his musicians to become some of the strongest live performers of the past 30 years. Yet, his strongest musical collaborations would seek direction from female musicians such as Wendy Melvoin, Lisa Coleman, Sheila E and more, having recently recruited an all-female backing group, 3rd Eye Girl, (interesting name.)

Still, there is more to the 'love symbol' thematically than first appears. The male and female symbols are derived from astrological symbols for the planets Mars and Venus, which are associated with gods in the Roman pantheon, (and further back to the Greek and beyond).

The male/ Mars symbol has the circle forming a shield and the arrow forming the spear of the God of War. Indeed, war is often symbolised as the ultimate expression of male energy, in its most destructive and conquering form. The female symbol is the same as that of the planet Venus, and is said to represent the beauty of the goddess and aesthetic vanity – certainly something in which Prince has also had an interest.

But there are many other feminine qualities. She is, after all, the goddess of love as opposed to war. After 'Purple Rain' Prince set about questioning this conflict.

Paradox City

'Around The World In A Day,' Prince's critically underwhelming follow-up to 'Purple Rain,' is often said to have been inspired by psychedelia, most likely due to the striking cover artwork, best appreciated on the vinyl version. This opens into a two-page spread which communicates the themes that Prince would cover on the album, (criticism of foreign and social policy in America symbolised by a naked black toddler carrying an American flag,) and concerns about the next generation and Apocalypse:

> *"Jimmy Nothing never went 2 school,*
>
> *They made him pledge allegiance. He said it wasn't cool.*
>
> *Nothing made Jimmy proud, Now Jimmy lives on a mushroom cloud."*

The growing concern with temptation symbolised by the woman in the Raspberry Beret holding a picture of an apple, perhaps represents the Christian attitude that woman is the progenitor of original sin via Eve's yielding in the Garden of Eden. On the cover, the ladder sits in a pool and splits into two parts: on the left side, we see images of a black baby, the raspberry beret, a crying aged person, and a fighter plane flying overhead: on the right sit a group of musicians, some bearing similarities to members of his band.

There is also the suit that Prince would don in the video accompanying 'Raspberry Beret.' Prince's visage appears top-right, the middle of three robed figures evoking the Three Wise Men. There is also a Biblical nod to rebirth, with the Noah-inspired doves flying about clear blue skies. Finally, on the left, the waves are turbulent; on the right, the water is still.

The significance of the ladder in the middle, separating the turbulent world of temptation from Prince's concept of peace, is made clear in the song of the same name, which tells us that: "Everybody's looking for the ladder, everybody wants salvation of the soul." Prince evangelises, yet states that the road to salvation will be hard. But 'The Ladder' is followed by a song called 'Temptation,' which, despite its carnival feel, is profound in its expressed guilt over a descent into the dark side symbolised by sex, temptation and lust:

> *"Everybody on this earth has got a vice, and mine, little darlin', mine is the opposite of ice.*
>
> *Mine is the running hot water of the daughter of morality,*
>
> *In other words, this little Prince thinks a lot about U, see?*
>
> *Baby, baby, baby, I'm guilty in the first degree."*

Sexual guilt and subsequent punishment would inspire his next project. Musically speaking, if 'Around The World In A Day' marked a departure in style from 'Purple Rain,' then 'Parade' went even further. Indeed, to release what is essentially a European-inspired baroque jazz-funk album, is a risk for any mainstream American artist. Thematically, the album seems at first to lack any major theme. But when Prince's second film project, (of which 'Parade' formed the basis of the soundtrack,) is considered, guilt and punishment for sexual sin becomes evident.

'Under the Cherry Moon,' despite its lighthearted campy feel, tells the story of Christopher Tracy, a gigolo servicing the South of France's monied widows. In an attempt to make it big, he and his accomplice decide to seduce, and hopefully wed, the heiress of a huge financial dynasty. While the seduction is successful, Prince's character falls in love with the heiress and risks it all to rescue her from the clutches of an overbearing father, who orders, in a rather severe reaction, the execution of the gigolo. He dies under the moonlight.

If the plotline sounds glib and corny, it's because it is. However, it underlines a certain development in Prince's thinking at the time. His character is the ultimate representation of sexual avarice, coupled with a desire for the almighty dollar. In Prince's mind, despite being redeemed by his romantic realisation, he is still sinning. According to Prince biographer Matt Thorne, there was an alternative ending in which the character survived, which was more popular with the crew and the studio. But Prince – with full creative control – insisted on the character's death, which only reinforces that theme's importance to him.

There are two songs on the album with the theme of death: 'Sometimes It Snows in April' is the funeral lament to Prince's film character: "Tracy died soon after a long-fought civil war." There is also the title track to the film, 'Under the Cherry Moon': "If nobody thrills me or kills me soon, I'll die in your arms under the cherry moon."

This could be a reference to the Blood Moon, which has different meanings in ancient traditions. For the Pagans, it is often associated with the time of harvest, but in the Bible, (which Prince is much more likely to reference,) there is the Blood Moon prophesied by certain Christian ministers, involving four consecutive lunar eclipses, during which the moon will turn red. This is said to foreshadow the final Battle of Armageddon.

Given Prince's previous intimations of the end of the world, this is an interesting coincidence. He also appears in black-and-white on the album cover and in the film, which, again, could be symbolic of the theme of death. The artist is now beginning to seriously question his role as the pan-sexual violator in his early career and, with 'Parade,' it seems he is acknowledging his own guilt.

'Parade' would not only express the thematic death of one of Prince's alter-egos, but would also mark the death of his most important musical collaboration. At the end of 1986, while preparing material for the next project, he disbanded the Revolution, and in the process, cut ties with some of his oldest musical collaborators, including Wendy Melvoin and Lisa Coleman. Whether Prince anticipated it or not, the Dawn of a

New Age of music was nigh, with Hip-Hop bubbling under the surface and about to explode. His initial reaction to these changing times, was to return to a multi-instrumental solo approach on the double-album 'Sign O' The Times.'

Often lauded as his greatest work, and a regular amongst 100 Greatest Album polls, this LP marked the beginning of a new era. Michaelangelo Matos described it as: "The last classic R&B album prior to Hip-Hop's takeover of black music, and the final four-sided blockbuster of the vinyl era."

Certainly, 'Sign O' The Times' marks Prince's return to the popular black music styles he had often put to the side in his quest for superstardom. The James Brown groove of 'Housequake,' the Parliament-style party funk of 'It's Gonna Be a Beautiful Night,' echoes of Stevie Wonder in 'Strange Relationship,' classic soul ballads like 'Adore' and 'Slow Love,' all embrace the styles of his musical forebears in the R&B genre.

Thematically, the songs cover much ground. But the title track is as explicit an embodiment of Prince's social and political commentary as you will find in any of his songs. The AIDS epidemic, young gang warfare, poverty versus plenty, and the drugs war all feature in the commentary. The most striking verse and chorus echo a familiar theme in his work, however, augmented by the Campaign for Nuclear Disarmament's 'Ban the Bomb' symbol as a replacement for the 'O' in the album title.

"Baby make a speech, Star Wars fly, Neighbours just shine it on,

But if a night falls and a bomb falls, will anybody see the dawn?"

The Apocalypse and the dawn feature here. But Prince seems pessimistic. Whereas in earlier songs, the Apocalypse was the inevitable turbulence before the start of the New Age, here, there doesn't seem much hope for anyone.

Later in the album, though, Prince would analyse the world again from a religious perspective in 'The Cross': "He is coming" presages a New Age with the second coming of Christ. Indeed, on the sleeve notes, we are left with the final message that, "soon the boat will sail and take us all away."

Prince has not yet abandoned the sexual indulgences he has been battling for the last two albums. The straight-to-the-point 'It,' simply describes how he still likes "to do it all the time," while 'Hot Thing' charts the seduction of a 21-year-old girl, cynically recommending, "you should give your folks a call and tell them you're coming home late... if you are coming home at all." This is still 1987, and a long time before Britney Spears would sell the schoolgirl as a sex object. So while seducing a 21-year-old seems tame by contemporary standards, the implied sexual predation and the explicit threat to parents, could be seen as unsettling to a mid-1980s audience.

As he did with previous albums, Prince would then close off his voyage into temptation with one of his most overt songs regarding lasting commitment in a relationship. He seems to be evoking a change in direction and feeling – not just in his relationships, but in his music as well, in the song 'Forever in My Life.':

> *"There comes a time in every man's life, when he gets tired of fooling around,*
>
> *Juggling hearts in a three-ring circus, some day will drive your body down to the ground."*

So, at the end of 'Sign O' The Times,' it seems Prince is ready to settle down. In many ways, he has grown from a youthful lothario tearing down sexual and gender barriers and screaming for revolution, to a politically-aware, introspective man. He is on his way to some sort of personal redemption.

However, things would become darker before they would get any lighter.

Into the abyss

Despite his growing maturity, Prince would again lunge into the darkness on his next project. Whether it was the break-up of the Revolution, the end of his relationship with Susannah Melvoin, (Wendy's twin sister, and Prince's muse for much of his mid-80s relationship songs,) or the rise of Hip-Hop as a serious threat to his position, his darker feelings during this period are conveyed via 'The Black Album,' intended to be released with a plain black cover and no title.

The story behind 'The Black Album' has entered into legend. With it pressed and ready to ship, Prince recalled it at the last minute and refused to release it. Thus, it would become one of the biggest bootleg albums of all time, even making some polls for that year's greatest albums. (It would later be released by Warner Brothers as part of his contractual commitments in 1994).

The album starts with 'Le Grind.' His voice is slowed to a demonic groan, rendering it almost incomprehensible – a variation on a trick with which Prince would experiment throughout his career. It intimates that the listener has found their way into a secret group or club:

"So U found me. Good, I'm glad.

This is Prince, the cool of cools.

Some of U may not know this, but some of U may know.

Some of U may not want 2 know, We R here 2 do service.

Welcome to the Funk Bible. The New Testament."

'Le Grind' then welcomes the listener to a '*nouveau dance*,' which calls for all to have no fear on the dancefloor, and to indulge their carnal desires "like a pony would"; to "put it where it feels good" all night long. The album repeats the familiar themes of sexual temptation, with some of the darker aspects seemingly hinting at experiences that Prince had either witnessed, or taken part in during his years in the entertainment industry.

Next on the album is 'Cindy C,' on the face of it, a vulgar desire piece based on Prince's affection for supermodel Cindy Crawford. However, when we consider some of the darker aspects of the entertainment industry, and its possible ties to occult rituals, mind-control, and the high-class sex industry, some of the lyrics become more provocative:

> *"Cindy C, play with me, I will pay the usual fee,*
>
> *I'll give you seven sips of elderberry wine; maybe we'll unlock the secrets of your mind."*

Firstly, Prince indicates that he can have the 'high-class model' simply by paying the usual fee, and that he will need to use some sort of alcoholic encouragement to elicit her secrets. This suggests that the secrets are those of her high-class clients . . . or possibly, that the model herself could be a trauma-based mind-control slave. Either way, Prince continues to emphasise that Cindy C is nothing more than a sexual plaything to him: "I'm sure you're quite intelligent, a wizz at math and all that shit. But I'm a tad more interested in flying your kite tonight."

There are both stylistic and overt references to Hip-Hop in the album, very much indicating Prince's negativity toward the genre at this stage of his career. His position at the cutting-edge of black music was being dissolved not just by the emergence of a new musical genre, but by a cultural one, too. It's easy to see why Prince, the multi-instrumentalist workaholic who spent a lifetime crafting his tunes, was now being outsold and made to look out-of-date by musicians who were – as Alan Leeds put it – "making hit records in their bedrooms." '2 Nigs United for West Compton' would illustrate Prince's scorn, and in 'Dead On It,' he would mockingly rap:

> *"Riding in my Thunderbird on the freeway, I turned on my radio 2 hear some music play.*
>
> *"I got a silly rapper talking silly shit instead, and the only good rapper is one that's dead . . . on it."*

Another song on 'The Black Album' with a stylistic connection to Hip-Hop, is 'Bob George.' Having played with prostitution in 'Cindy C,' here, Prince – with his voice altered – assumes the role of a pimp berating his charge for playing around, and accepting a diamond ring from a decadent rock-and-roll manager, "Slick-Back Paddy with all the gold in his mouth."

He paints a none-too-pretty picture of the management system in music and – lest we think he is not speaking from experience – he makes it very clear in the pimp's conversation with the trick:

> *"Who bought you that diamond ring? Yeah, right.*
>
> *Since when did you have a job?*
>
> *You seeing that rich motherfucker again?*
>
> *What's his name? Bob? Bob, ain't that a bitch?*
>
> *What's he do for a living? Manage rock stars?*
>
> *Who? Prince? Ain't that a bitch? That skinny motherfucker with the high voice?"*

The pimp then threatens the trick with a gun, before making her wear the 'reddish-brown' wig that he bought her. She is then chased by the police, and has a phone conversation with a Mr. George, (speculated to be Nelson George, a music critic with whom Prince was said to have been upset,) asking him, "why don't you leave motherfuckers alone?"

After Prince has vented his frustration at Hip-Hop, his management and the critics, 'Superfunkycalifragysexy' sees him back at the party in "the 'house of ill-repute," for a disturbing trip involving blood, drugs, and sadomasochism.

Many theories have circulated, based on reports from band members, bodyguards, and sound engineers, that Prince had a bad experience on ecstasy, and had determined that 'The Black Album' was the devil working through him. This may have been the reason he shelved the album. That theory seems to be supported by 'Superfunkycalifragysexy.' But, as we have been delving deeper into the lyrics for any possible occult connections, then perhaps there might be something more to the following:

"If your body needs water, keep on dancing 'cause you oughta

Keep the blood flowing down to your feet,

Brother Maurice should be around in a minute with a bucket filled with squirrelled meat.

The blood is real good if you drink it real fast, but the aftertaste just lasts and lasts,

If you kiss somebody, you want to party all night, All right!

"If you do too much, your skin will be sensitive to touch,

The first person that touches you, you want to fuck.

You take them to your crib and you tie them to a chair,

Then you make funny faces 'til they get really scared.

Then you turn on the neon, then you play with yourself,

Til you turn them on."

Here, Prince is talking about drinking the blood of what appears to be an animal. In occult rituals, the drinking of blood signifies absorption of the power of that blood, (some might say this is analogous to the drug ecstasy.)

It seems that this blood makes him desire sex with the first person he touches. But then he goes further into sado-masochistic realms with a hint of torture, as he ties the victim to a chair before masturbating in front of them. Later, Prince mentions "seven measures to make you scream." Measure is another term for an alcoholic beverage, evoking the seven sips of elderberry wine that unlocked the secrets of Cindy C's mind earlier on.

Prince had gone to a dark place. It's interesting to consider how much he might have seen during his time at the very top of the music business. He would have dealt with executives, other musicians, and the criminals that are said to associate with the industry, (drug dealers, pimps, etc). It could be argued that some of this is reflected in the dark imagery of 'The Black Album.' Speaking through his alter-egos in the programme for the 1988 'Lovesexy' tour, he reflected:

> *"Camille set out to silence his critics. No longer daring, his enemies laughed. No longer glam, his funk is half-assed.*
>
> *"Tuesday came. Blue Tuesday. His canvas full and lying on the table, Camille mustered all the hate that he was able. Hate 4 the ones who ever doubted his game. Hate 4 the ones who ever doubted his name. 'Tis nobody funkier. Let 'The Black Album' fly.*
>
> *"Spooky Electric was talking, Camille started 2 cry. Tricked. A fool he had been. In the lowest utmostest. He had allowed the dark side of him 2 create something evil. '2 Nigs United 4 West Compton.' Camille and his ego. 'Bob George.' Why? Spooky Electric must die."*

The above excerpt provides the only testament from Prince personally about why he made 'The Black Album' the way he did.

When two worlds collide

The next album was 'Lovesexy', whose cover would again feature a painted portrait of Prince nude against a white background filled with flowers. But this time – in contrast to earlier albums – the scene arguably indicates purity and a spiritual rebirth.

The two symbols that appear consistently throughout the album sleeves are the Eye of Horus, and a stylised heart featuring the word 'yes.' This symbolic duet sums up this album's dichotomy. We have seen Prince use the Eye before, and he has always been fond of using numerical shorthand, ('2' for 'two', '4' for 'four,', etc,) so it's little surprise that he would embrace the Eye in place of the letter 'I.'

There is, however, a possible alternative reason for its use from the album's first song, 'No.' It starts with a spoken verse by poet Ingrid Chavez, which then fades into Prince's voice stating: "Welcome to the

New Power Generation, the reason why my voice is so clear is there is no smack in my brain."

This is not the first time Prince has sermonised against drugs, (he is critical of his fellow rock stars' fondness for cocaine in 1985's 'Pop Life.') But given his sexual licentiousness explored on 'The Black Album' – or indeed, if rumours of that bad ecstasy trip are true – he is directly announcing that his message on this album is free of that influence. This song is all about the title in many ways.

"I know there is a Heaven, I know there is a Hell,

Listen to me people, I got a story to tell,

I know there was confusion, lightnin' all around me,

That's when I called his name. Don't you know he found me.

No, is what Spooky Electric say, it's not okay.

But I know love is the only way, 'til my dying day.

No, 'til my dying day I'll be okay, cuz Lovesexy is the one,'til my day is done."

If we take the Eye of Horus as representative of the controlling occult societies, then Prince is possibly conveying two messages here. First, with the spelling of the title 'I No,' his rejection of the negative forces around him which he associates with the devil, as personified by Spooky Electric.

But there is a double meaning here; it's clear from the context that he also means 'know' as in awareness and understanding. That, too, makes sense, as 'I know' becomes 'I know about the eye.' The symbols, therefore, of the Eye meaning 'no' and the heart meaning 'yes,' are a simple reflection of the polarity between positive and negative forces.

This theme is continued in 'Anna Stesia.' Some have argued that this title is a play on the word anaesthesia, a means of inducing sleep. Indeed, the song tells the story of his awakening to positive forces, (personified here in a Christian sense as God,) as he seemingly inhabits the "houses of ill repute," seeking someone to "play with" to cure a desperate loneliness. After being ravished and then liberated by Anna Stesia, he begins to review his previous work, with a possible direct reference to 'The Black Album':

> *"Between white and black, night and day, black night seemed the only way."*

Prince then muses: "Maybe I could learn to love, I mean the right way," and later in the song undergoes a personal epiphany:

> *"Save me, Lord, I've been a fool. How could I forget you are the rule?*
>
> *I am your child, oh yes I am your child. From now on, I shall be wild.*
>
> *I shall be quick, I shall be strong.*
>
> *I'll tell your story no matter how long."*

As Prince personified the negative as Spooky Electric, so he would give the name 'Lovesexy' to the positive energy, describing it as, "the feeling you get when you fall in love, not with a boy or a girl, but with the Heavens above." The song of the same name proves that – despite his awakening – sex is never far from his mind, as he seeks to infuse his sense of spirituality with his sense of sexuality. The power of Lovesexy, he suggests, is as powerful as sex itself. There are some heavily sexualised lyrics in the mix, but he does stress at the end that, "we make love with only words."

The album's last message is offered in 'Positivity,' a slow groove with a melancholic feel. In contrast to the "no" of the first song, the first words here are "yes, yes, yes." Prince delivers this track as one final warning to society about the dangers of Spooky Electric, and of the temptation which has permeated his work:

> *"In every man's life there will be a hang-up. A whirlwind designed to slow you down,*

It cuts like a knife and tries to get in you, this Spooky Electric sound.

Give up if you want to and all is lost, Spooky Electric will be your boss,

Call 'People' magazine, 'Rolling Stone,' call your next of kin, 'cause your ass is gone.

He's got a 57 Mag with the price-tag still on the side, cuzzin,' when Spooky say dead, you better say died.

Or you can fly high right by Spooky, and all that he crawls for, Spooky and all that he crawls for."

This could arguably be directed at his industry colleagues selling their souls for success – a rite of passage long mythologised when it comes to musicians. Prince, however, seems to escape the fate of having Spooky Electric be his 'boss,' and leaves the listener – and perhaps any initiates in the music industry – with the following warning:

"You gotta hold on, to your soul, we've got a long way to go,

Don't kiss the Beast."

If there were ever any doubt that this was the story Prince wanted to tell and that, indeed, his internal conflict went beyond an adverse reaction to 'The Black Album,' the accompanying Lovesexy live tour would assuage it.

A recording was aired on the UK's Channel 4 in the late 80s, and remains one of the most interesting pieces of live footage of any popular musician. A concept concert in two parts, it tells the story of the battle of dark against light as, in the first half, he rips through some of his most salacious material. 'Erotic City,' 'Head,' 'Jack U Off,' 'Sister,' 'Dirty Mind,' 'Controversy' and Superfunkycalifragisexy, see Prince cavort around a circular stage, complete with a basketball hoop, park swing and bed, while depicting sex acts, sadomasochism, and a gun battle with members of the band.

Interestingly, he places 'Bob George,' the story of the pimp, at the end of the first set. As in the song, the police chase him on-stage, but the live concert shows them catching him up. As he realises his fate he reads the Lord's Prayer aloud, and is finally shot dead in an echo of Prince's message from 'Under The Cherry Moon' that, even in redemption, the guilty will be slain.

The second part of the concert opens up with 'I No.' He then plays most of the uplifting music from 'Lovesexy,' with a smattering of greatest hits and upbeat tunes. Even at concert level, Prince is telling the same story: the dark vs. the light, the joys and pitfalls of temptation, and the inevitable punishment, followed by revelation and rebirth. As the lights go down, Prince is heard addressing the audience:

"Cross the line, cross the line, God will take care of you."

The great beyond

The end of the 'Lovesexy' album is not the end of the story, and by no means is it the end of Prince's internal battles. He would go on, in the 1990s, to record some of his most sexually-explicit and aggressive tracks. He would also continue to be as politically, socially and spiritually aware as ever.

It could, however, be argued that 'Lovesexy' marks a definite turning point, from which he begins to look at the trappings of superstardom in a negative light, and possibly becomes aware of the occult influences upon it. From this perspective, it's possible to see the origin of the antipathy towards the music industry that would lead to his name-change, and his determination to find new, independent distribution models.

Also evident is a rejection of himself as a tool of the industry to foment the further sexualisation of society; though he doesn't completely reject it for some years, after 'Lovesexy,' he is playing by his own rules.

It is clear from what has been discussed, that Prince has used his art to highlight the dualistic nature of our reality, and that his major topic – other than the act of sex itself – has been the battle between the dark and light forces, and his own personal journey therein. All the themes of his albums – albeit maturing as time passed – concern its nature.

He conveys a lasting interest in the Apocalypse as the precursor to a New Age. His conversion to the Jehovah's Witness faith at the turn of the millennium is of little surprise, given that denomination's focus on the end times and the second coming. The research undertaken shows that, while Prince is no serious occult adept, he is aware of the meaning of symbols, and how to use both them and language to deliver coded messages which are best hidden in plain sight, and always open to interpretation.

This writer will confess that this work represents just that – an interpretation of music searching for an elusive, yet fascinating theme. Prince's reluctance to go on-record in any substantial way, leaves us only his output by which to figure it all out.

Epilogue

Most of this article was written in 2015, and was finished just prior to the artist's death the following year. His passing is therefore not mentioned, and it makes little difference to the content. It was written as a research piece to accompany the work of this book's author, and will be best appreciated within that context.

As one might gather from a work this in-depth, I have a long-standing admiration and respect for Prince's work, and grieve the loss of talent his death represents. As some of the topics were conspiratorial and occult in nature, it bears mentioning that – as with other early deaths of major artists – there are a number a conspiracy theories regarding his demise. I would direct your attention to the author's earlier chapter for an excellent summary of the major points.

Whether there is any truth to the rumours, or it was – as portrayed in the press – an unfortunate and untimely event, the battle for music's soul goes on, as corporate artists continue to sell an agenda of baser instincts for ever-larger profits. In the background – or even in the foreground – artists will perhaps be trying to convey something deeper and more spiritual through their work.

Sadly, there will be nothing new on the horizon from the artist formerly known as Prince.

Dan Monroe, 2017.

Dan Monroe can be e-mailed directly at secretfirefilms@gmail.com

APPENDIX 2

FURTHER DUBIOUS CONNECTIONS

In the spirit of many other parts of this book, here's another dizzying array of curious links and connections which readers might not have expected to have found before reading this tome, but which will surely come as no surprise to those who now have. We're darting around a bit, as always, and this is multi-music genre, but bear with me...

Let's start by going back to the aforementioned Wilde family. The real name of Marty's dad was Reginald Smith, and he was a military man, trained at the 'prestigious' Sandhurst Military Institute. Marty, like his dad, also went by the original name of Reginald Smith, and became the father of Kim. Marty, in his heyday as a performer and artist mentor, knew the celebrated record producer Joe Meek, and would take other musicians to recording sessions with him. Joe Meek had a dubious private life, having connections to the world of organised crime, and having been prosecuted in 1963 for 'importuning for immoral purposes,' homosexual acts still being illegal at the time. Meek had reportedly been one of several homosexual paedophiles to share a rent boy named Bernard Oliver, whose body was found cut into eight pieces and put into two suitcases in Suffolk in January 1967. Meek, by this point having suffered a mental breakdown, was reportedly terrified of being questioned by police over the murder, and in February 1967, used a shotgun that he'd taken from former Tornadoes bassist Heinz Burt to blast the landlady of his London home to death before turning the gun on himself.

Just before we leave the family, another of Marty's early industry associates, (and Joe Meek's,) was the celebrated producer Mickie Most, (real name Michael Hayes,) another key player whose father was a career military officer. A couple of decades later, Kim Wilde got signed to Mickie Most's RAK Records in her first label deal. The label later hosted the 1980s pop act Johnny Hates Jazz, of which Mickie's son Calvin was a member. Calvin and Kim were romantically linked for a time, with rumours of impending marriage, but the relationship fizzled out.

Back to Joe Meek now, and one of the most high-profile acts on his roster was The Tornadoes, best known for their UK number one hit 'Telstar.' One of the band members was a Robb Huxley. In his on-line autobiography, Robb notes that some digging into his genealogy revealed that he's a fourth cousin of the aforementioned 'Brave New World' author, eugenicist and co-architect of the CIA's MK-Ultra programme, Aldous Huxley. What were the chances?! There is a current-day DJ and producer named Huxley who has enjoyed great success, but disappointingly he turns out to have adopted the moniker, having been born Michael Dodman. It was Aldous' brother Julian, meanwhile, who created the idea of 'conspiracy theorists' wearing tin-foil hats to shield themselves from having their minds read in his 1927 science-fiction short story 'The Tissue-Culture King.' Now, of course, this notion is used to mock and deride those who challenge official government narratives and seek truth.

In a 2012 interview with 'It's Psychedelic Baby' Magazine, Robb Huxley spoke of his time working with Joe Meek, commenting:

> *"He (Joe) also arranged for us to play at the Aberfan Disaster charity event which was held in Cardiff... At the charity function, we as the Tornadoes became acquainted with the infamous Kray twins, and Ronnie Kray first became interested in stealing us away from Joe. When Ronnie was told that we were under contract to Joe Meek he told us: 'Don't worry we'll take care of him'."*

Could this be a hint towards what really happened to Joe?

This is far from the only link between the British music industry and the world of gangland crime, meanwhile. The criminal antics of Don Arden, the father of Sharon Osbourne and manager of several bands including Small Faces and Black Sabbath, were documented earlier. And readers of 'Musical Truth 1' may recall a link to an article originally penned by the former British intelligence operative known as T. Stokes and later expanded upon by the writer Chris Spivey on his website. It details many such links in a mind-blowing interconnected web. Here's the link again for anyone wanting to recap:

http://chrisspivey.org/sutch-as-it-is-based-on-the-unpublished-t-stokes-article-who-murdered-screaming-lord-sutch/#comment-172748

In 2010, a collection of personal items that had belonged to the Krays was sold for £20,000 at an auction in East Sussex. Among them was a handwritten letter from Ronnie Kray to the Krays biographer John Pearson, written during his time in Brixton prison, telling him that Cliff Richard had written to him to cheer him up. Isn't heart-warming to hear of Cliff doing his Christian duty?

In their criminal heyday, the Krays were associates of the Labour MP Tom Driberg and the Tory peer Lord Boothby, both of whom were homosexuals and alleged paedophiles. (Boothby is portrayed, none too flatteringly, in the 2015 Krays biopic 'Legend' starring Tom Hardy.) Cliff Richard was also a close associate of Boothby in his younger days, and according to some, a whole lot more. The Krays are believed by many researchers to have been involved in the procurement of children for 'elite' paedophile rings, and by some to have been subjects of mind-control experimentation themselves. Twins were favoured in the 'work' of Nazi 'doctors' such as Josef Mengele, and psychopathy and extreme violence are characteristics resulting from 'experiments.' The Krays also had working links to many other movers and shakers of the 1960s music scene, including the omnipresent Jimmy Savile, fellow BBC DJ Alan 'Fluff' Freeman, (the subject of male child-rape allegations in 2013,) and the Beatles' manager Brian Epstein who died very suddenly in 1967.

Staying with the Krays, an affiliate of theirs in the 1960s was a criminal by the name of James 'Jimmy The Dip' Kensit, who also worked on frauds for the notorious Charlie Richardson Gang. Jimmy The Dip went on to become the father of Patsy Kensit, born in 1968, whose first taste of fame was as a child star when she appeared in TV commercials for Birds Eye Peas. Ronnie Kray became godfather to Patsy's brother Jamie. Patsy went on to become a singer, and was another to rock the familiar 'blonde bombshell' image, fronting the group Eighth Wonder in the 1980s. She is better known for being a rock star wife, however, having married (and divorced) Dan Donovan of Big Audio Dynamite,

Jim Kerr of Simple Minds, Liam Gallagher of Oasis and Jeremy Healy of Haysi Fantaysi in rapid succession. In 2003, Patsy took part in the BBC ancestry programme 'Who Do You Think You Are,' where she was revealed to have been shocked by the criminal past of both her father and grandfather.

Military-intelligence, social-engineering think-tanks, organised crime, mind-control, paedophilia . . . . did we leave anything out? No, no . . . I think we've covered it all.

Resources:

Marty Wilde music industry links:

- https://www.sundaypost.com/fp/marty-wilde-on-touring-admirers-and-appalling-films/

Kim Wilde's relationship with Mickie Most's son, Calvin Hayes:

- https://www.wilde-life.com/encyclopedia/h/hayes-calvin

Tornadoes musician Robb Huxley related to Aldous Huxley:

- http://www.silvertabbies.co.uk/huxley/background.html

Obituary: Mickie Most:

- http://www.independent.co.uk/news/obituaries/mickie-most-36586.html

Chris Spivey's re-working of T. Stokes' article on dubious music industry links:

- http://chrisspivey.org/sutch-as-it-is-based-on-the-unpublished-t-stokes-article-who-murdered-screaming-lord-sutch/#comment-172748

Ronnie Kray's letter of praise for Cliff Richard:

- http://www.standard.co.uk/news/ronnie-kray-s-letter-of-praise-for-cliff-richard-6527292.html

Patsy Kensit discovers her family's criminal past:

- http://www.bbc.co.uk/whodoyouthinkyouare/past-stories/patsy-kensit.shtml
- http://www.dailyrecord.co.uk/news/uk-world-news/patsy-kensit-left-tears-bbc-985977

APPENDIX 3

FURTHER ORIGINS OF HAND SIGNS

The suggestion that there may be more to know about hand gestures of the type frequently flashed by celebrities than most of us have realised, was reinforced in a fascinating on-line article by the Canadian writer Henry Makow in 2016. In it, he draws attention to the breathtaking amount of aristocrats, dignitaries, royals and political and religious leaders who, over several centuries, have been painted or photographed displaying a Masonic-style 'clawed hand' gesture. This has been further identified as a Triad Hand Sign, and a motif of the Marranos, of which, more on this link – http://www.thebabylonmatrix.com/index.phptitle=911:Occult_symbolism_XVI#Triad_sign

The sign is shown in a portrait of the English philosopher and friar Roger Bacon, dating as far back as the 13th century. It goes on to appear in portraits of the likes of Christopher Columbus, Martin Luther, several 'British' (so German) monarchs, Sir Isaac Newton, Winston Churchill, Josef Stalin and Adolf Hitler, coming all the way forward to present-day with Michelle (Michael) Obama, Pope Benedict XVI and Canadian Prime Minister Justin Trudeau.

The gesture involves the two middle fingers being bunched together to leave the remaining two free, and has been interpreted as signalling the letters M and W. These together render three Vs. The letter V is "waw" in Hebrew and "vav" in Gematria and is the 6th letter in both, meaning the numerical value of the hand sign would be 666. (Is it just me, or have we come across that number somewhere else in this story?) These three Hebrew letters also form the 'claw' emblem of the popular 'Monster' energy drink brand.

Makow points out that the hands being so prominently shown in such a large number of portraits, and over such a vast period of time, goes beyond the realms of 'coincidence,' and that there has to have been a good reason for wanting them on display. He speculates that the sign may indicate genealogical links to a particular bloodline deemed to be of great importance in 'elite' circles, or membership to a particular order or fraternity. According to the alternative historian David Livingstone, the Triad sign is the calling card of an ongoing bloodline of Khazar crypto-Jews which has its roots in Jewish mysticism and the Kabbalah. The Vulcan hand sign frequently displayed by Mr. Spock in 'Star Trek' also becomes very interesting in this regard. Once again, the truth appears to be getting placed in plain sight, in the knowledge that only a few will be able to discern any real meaning from it.

As a commenter on Makow's on-line posting stated:

> *"... It is hard to believe that these people did not do this sign without intention. Firstly, the sign does take an effort to make, and secondly it has been performed over many centuries. As to the painters, I think they were most likely initiated as well, meaning they knew the meaning of that sign. It was purposely drawn this way.*
>
> *"You could equate the paintings from back then to our modern magazines, where you constantly see photographers taking one-eye, pyramid and other symbolic pictures."*

Resources:

Henry Makow: Hand sign indicates massive Satanic conspiracy:

- https://www.henrymakow.com/2016/10/Hand-Sign-Indicates-Massive-Satanic-Conspiracy%20%20.html

Hand signs of Freemasonry explained:

- https://veritas-vincit-international.org/2015/01/18/hand-signals-of-freemasonry-explained/

THE SOUND OF FREEDOM

TSOF is a free, regular showcase of conscious music old and new, compiled by Mark Devlin. It stands as the inspiring antithesis to the corporate agenda, offering meaningful music by switched-on, awakened artists.

The full archive so far is available at:

- https://www.spreaker.com/show/the-sound-of-freedom

TSOF can also be found on the following iTunes RSS feed:

- https://itunes.apple.com/gb/podcast/the-sound-of-freedom/id1272836020

GOOD VIBRATIONS

A free, ongoing series of conversation-based podcasts, covering a huge array of topics within the truth/ conspiracy/ consciousness/ spirituality fields.

The entire archive so far is available at:

- https://www.spreaker.com/show/good-vibrations-podcast

Good Vibrations can also be found on the following iTunes RSS feed:

- https://itunes.apple.com/gb/podcast/good-vibrations-podcast/id1272835109

CONTACTING THE AUTHOR

The author welcomes all feedback and communication, (as long as it's polite,) to the following e-mail address, and guarantees a personal reply to all messages received:

- markdevlinuk@gmail.com

INDEX

C

D

E

F

G

H

I

J

K

L

M

N

O

P

Q

R

S

T

U

V

W

Y

Made in the USA
Middletown, DE
17 March 2024

51048622R00235